Hellenists and Hebrews
Reappraising Division within the Earliest Church

Craig C. Hill

Fortress Press   Minneapolis

HELLENISTS AND HEBREWS
Reappraising Division within the Earliest Church

Copyright © 1992 Augsburg Fortress. All rights reserved. Except for brief quotations in critical articles or reviews, no part of this book may be reproduced in any manner without prior written permission from the publisher. Write to: Permissions, Augsburg Fortress, 426 S. Fifth St., Box 1209, Minneapolis, MN 55440.

Scripture quotations, unless otherwise noted, are from the New Revised Standard Version of the Bible, copyright © 1989 by the Division of Christian Education of the National Council of the Churches of Christ in the United States of America.

Cover Design: Patricia Boman
Cover Art: Reproduced by Courtesy of the Trustees of the British Museum.
Interior Design: Karen Buck

Library of Congress Cataloging-in-Publication Data

Hill, Craig C., 1957–
    Hellenists and Hebrews : reappraising division within the earliest church / Craig C. Hill.
        p. cm.
    Based on the author's thesis (doctoral)—University of Oxford.
    Includes bibliographical references and index.
    ISBN: 0-8006-2505-6 (alk. paper) : $24.95
    1. Church history—Primitive and early church, ca. 30-600.
2. Bible. N.T. Acts—Criticism, interpretation, etc. 3. Bible. N.T. Epistles of Paul—Criticism, interpretation, etc. I. Title.
BR195.J8H52 1992
270.1—dc20   92-4085
                                                                             CIP

The paper used in this publication meets the minimum requirements of American National Standard for Information Sciences—Permanence of Paper for Printed Library Materials, ANSI Z329.48-1984.

Manufactured in the U.S.A.   1-1205

96   95   94   93   92   1   2   3   4   5   6   7   8   9   10

For Walter and Virginia Hill, my parents

Contents

Preface · vii

Abbreviations · ix

Introduction: The Eclipse of a Dichotomy · 1

1. Background · 5

2. Acts 8:1-4: The Persecution of the Hellenists · 19
   "Hellenists" or "Hellenizers"? 22
   The Appointment of the Seven 24
   The Opponents of Stephen 28
   The "Severe Persecution" of Acts 8:1b 32
   Conclusion 40

3. Stephen and the Hellenists · 41
   Assumptions 43
   Was Stephen a Hellenist? 44
   Were Stephen's Beliefs Typically "Hellenist"? 49
   Do We Have Accurate Information about the Beliefs of Stephen? 50
   Speeches in Ancient Historiography 51
   The Relationship between Acts 6 and 7 53

The Accusations as the Locus of Tradition 54
The Speech as the Locus of Tradition 67

A Review of Source Theories 92

Conclusion 101

4. Galatians 2 and Acts 15: The Relationship between the
Churches of Jerusalem and Antioch   103

   The Hellenists and the Church of Antioch 105

   The Jerusalem Council 107

   Chronology of Events 115

   The Conversion of Cornelius 122

   The Incident at Antioch 126

   The Apostolic Decree 143

   Conclusion 146

5. Further Evidence   149

   Paul and the Church of Jerusalem 150

      The Opponents of Paul 152

      The Collection 173

      Acts 21: Paul in Jerusalem 179

   James, the Brother of Jesus 183

   Conclusion 191

Conclusion: Of People and Pigeonholes   193

Bibliography   199

Topical Bibliography   223

Index of Ancient Texts   224

Index of Modern Authors   231

Index of Subjects   234

Preface

In the spring of 1985 I submitted a proposal to the faculty of theology at the University of Oxford for a doctoral dissertation on the subject of Jewish Christian self-definition, to be titled "The Jerusalem Church and the Election of Israel." In the subsequent exploration of this topic, I came to realize how a particular reconstruction of the history of the Jerusalem church, one that challenged some of the conclusions I had been forming about the nature of that community, had come to enjoy a dominant position in New Testament scholarship. According to this view, the earliest Jerusalem church was divided into Hellenist and Hebrew Christian parties: Stephen, the leader of the Hellenist faction, was put to death for his radical criticism of the law and/or temple; the Hellenists — but not the Hebrews — were persecuted; and these same Hellenists, having fled Jerusalem, founded the church at Antioch, which remained in tension with (or even opposition to) its counterpart in Palestine.

Such a division of the Jerusalem church would have important implications for my study of early Jewish Christianity. Clearly, I could not ignore this interpretation. On reflection, I concluded also that I could not accept it. Thus, I set about composing a chapter for my dissertation that would outline what I thought were the interpretation's significant flaws. Unexpectedly, that chapter became two chapters, and then a dissertation in its own right. This dissertation underlies the present book. It is my hope that this work will reopen for many the question of the interpretation of Acts 6:1 — 8:4 and will clear the ground for some to undertake new studies of early Jewish Christianity, such as the one I proposed upon my arrival at Oxford.

Confronting this issue has meant that I have had to challenge the views of a number of scholars for whose work I have great admiration. In this, I have returned in my own mind repeatedly to the image of the person who may see a little farther than the giant, but only by standing atop the giant's shoulders.

In citing works in the footnotes below, I routinely omit details of publication, all of which appear in full in the Bibliography. For works originally published in a language other than English, I cite the page number first from the English translation (when available) and then, in brackets, the corresponding page number from the original. A reference, for example, to Baur, *Paul* 1:41 [48], thus refers to volume 1, page 41 of the English translation of this work, with the same information appearing on page 48 (of the first volume) of the original-language edition. Where an English translation is not available, I have prepared all translations made from foreign-language texts. Biblical citations follow the New Revised Standard Version of the Bible except where, for the purpose of conveying the literal sense of the text, I have favored my own translation.

I am grateful to those who have read the manuscript and offered their suggestions and insights: E. P. Sanders (my Oxford supervisor), Victoria Hobson, Susan Gillingham, Caroline Dobson, N. Thomas Wright, John Ziesler, and Richard Hays. Its faults are many fewer, thanks to the perception of these scholars. I am grateful also to the trustees of the Foundation for Theological Education, whose John Wesley Fellowship provided substantial financial support during my years of doctoral study; to the United Methodist Church, which provided support through Brandenburg and Dempster Graduate awards; to Oxford University, for a Hall-Houghton Award; and to the Committee of Vice-Chancellors and Principals of the Universities of the United Kingdom, for an Overseas Research Student Award.

My gratitude goes above all to Robin, my beloved wife, who, like the neglected widows of Acts 6, has had reason to murmur—and yet has not.

12 October 1990
New Haven, Connecticut

Abbreviations

AJT	*American Journal of Theology*
ANCL	Ante-Nicene Christian Library: Translations of the Writings of the Fathers Down to A.D. 325
ATR	*Anglican Theological Review*
AusBR	*Australian Biblical Review*
AusJBA	*Australian Journal of Biblical Archaeology*
BA	*Biblical Archaeologist*
Beginnings	*Beginnings of Christianity* [Lake and Foakes Jackson]
BETL	Bibliotheca Ephemeridum Theologicarum Lovaniensium
BGBE	Beiträge zur Geschichte der biblischen Exegese
Bib	*Biblica*
BJRL	*Bulletin of the John Rylands Library*
BTB	*Biblical Theology Bulletin*
BZ	*Biblische Zeitschrift*
BZNW	Beihefte zur Zeitschrift für die neutestamentliche Wissenschaft und die Kunde der ältern Kirche
CBQ	*Catholic Biblical Quarterly*
Conc	*Concilium*
EKKNT	Evangelisch-Katholischer Kommentar zum Neuen Testament
EvQ	*Evangelical Quarterly*
EvT	*Evangelische Theologie*
Exp	*Expositor*
ExpTim	*Expository Times*
FRLANT	Forschungen zur Religion und Literatur des Alten und Neuen Testaments
HTR	*Harvard Theological Review*
HTS	*Harvard Theological Studies*
ICC	*International Critical Commentary*
IDB	*Interpreter's Dictionary of the Bible*
Int	*Interpreter*
Interp	*Interpretation*

JBL	*Journal of Biblical Literature*
JEH	*Journal of Ecclesiastical History*
JETS	*Journal of the Evangelical Theological Society*
JJS	*Journal of Jewish Studies*
JSJ	*Journal for the Study of Judaism in the Persian, Hellenistic, and Roman Period*
JSNT	*Journal for the Study of the New Testament*
JSOT	*Journal for the Study of the Old Testament*
JTS	*Journal of Theological Studies*
KEKNT	*Kritisch-exegetischer Kommentar über das Neue Testament*
LCL	*Loeb Classical Library*
LNPNF	*Select Library of the Nicene and Post-Nicene Fathers of the Christian Church*
MTS	*Marburger Theologische Studien*
NovT	*Novum Testamentum*
NRSV	*New Revised Standard Version*
NTS	*New Testament Studies*
NTTS	*New Testament Tools and Studies*
RB	*Revue Biblique*
RelS	*Religious Studies*
RestQ	*Restoration Quarterly*
RevExp	*Review and Expositor*
RSR	*Recherches de science religieuse*
SBL	*Society of Biblical Literature*
SHR	*Studies in the History of Religions (Supplements to Numen)*
SJT	*Scottish Journal of Theology*
SNTS	*Society for New Testament Studies*
SNTSMS	*Society for New Testament Studies Monograph Series*
ST	*Studia theologica*
TDNT	*Theological Dictionary of the New Testament* [Kittel]
Th	*Theology*
THKNT	*Theologischer Handkommentar zum Neuen Testament*
TJ	*Theologische Jahrbücher*
TSK	*Theologische Studien und Kritiken*
TU	*Texte und Untersuchungen zur Geschichte der altchristlichen Literatur*
TZ	*Theologische Zeitschrift*
TZT	*Tübinger Zeitschrift für Theologie*
WMANT	*Wissenschaftliche Monographien zum Alten und Neuen Testament*
WTJ	*Westminster Theological Journal*
WUNT	*Wissenschaftliche Untersuchungen zum Neuen Testament*
ZDPV	*Zeitschrift des Deutschen Palästinavereins*
ZKT	*Zeitschrift für katholische Theologie*
ZLTK	*Zeitschrift für lutherische Theologie und Kirche*
ZNW	*Zeitschrift für die Neutestamentliche Wissenschaft*
ZTK	*Zeitschrift für Theologie und Kirche*

Introduction: The Eclipse of a Dichotomy

One genuine advance of contemporary biblical scholarship is that which W. D. Davies has termed "the eclipse of the dichotomy" between Judaism and Hellenism.[1] It is no longer possible to separate neatly "pure" first-century Judaism from "foreign" Hellenistic contaminants.[2] Moreover, modern archaeology has dramatically confirmed this view for Palestinian as well as Diaspora Judaism.[3] As Martin Hengel has written, "It is certain that ancient

---

[1] W. D. Davies, *Paul and Rabbinic Judaism* (4th ed.), p. xxiii. George Nickelsburg has termed the dichotomy between Judaism and Hellenism "one of the most damaging oversimplifications of earlier scholarship" ("Introduction: The Modern Study of Early Judaism," p. 11). On the term "Hellenism" (including a brief description of the work of J. G. Droyson, who coined the term in his 1831 doctoral dissertation in reference to the "Hellenists" of Acts 6:1), see Martin Hengel, *Judaism and Hellenism: Studies in Their Encounter in Palestine during the Early Hellenistic Period* 1:2–3 and 2:1 [1:2–3].

[2] "Jewish Palestine was no hermetically sealed island in the sea of Hellenistic oriental syncretism" (Hengel, *Judaism and Hellenism* 1:312 [2:567]). On the influence of Hellenism and the diversity of first-century Judaism, see also Martin Hengel, *Jews, Greeks, and Barbarians: Aspects of the Hellenization of Judaism in the Pre-Christian Period;* Shaye J. D. Cohen, "The Political and Social History of the Jews in Greco-Roman Antiquity: The State of the Question," pp. 41–51; John Ferguson, "Athens and Jerusalem"; A. T. Kraabel, "The Roman Diaspora: Six Questionable Assumptions"; Robert A. Kraft, "The Multiform Jewish Heritage of Early Christianity"; Gary G. Porton, "Diversity in Postbiblical Judaism"; W. D. Davies, *Jewish and Pauline Studies* (e.g., pp. 97–98); Nickelsburg, "Modern Study," pp. 11–12, 20–21, 25–26; Elias J. Bickerman, *The Jews in the Greek Age* (e.g., pp. 75–80, 101–16, 257–87, and, especially, 298–305); Paul D. Hanson, "Prolegomena to the Study of Jewish Apocalyptic"; and Morton Smith, "Palestinian Judaism in the First Century."

Also instructive is the contemporary debate concerning first-century Jewish orthodoxy; see Neil J. McEleney, "Orthodoxy in Judaism of the First Christian Century"; David E. Aune, "Orthodoxy in First Century Judaism? A Response to N. J. McEleney"; Lester L. Grabbe, "Orthodoxy in First Century Judaism: What Are the Issues?" McEleney, "Orthodoxy in Judaism of the First Christian Century: Replies to David E. Aune and Lester L. Grabbe."

[3] See, for example, Eric M. Meyers, "Ancient Synagogues in Galilee: Their Religious and Cultural Setting" (especially pp. 105–7); Dieter Georgi, *The Opponents of Paul in Second*

1

Judaism before 70 was extremely pluralistic—even in Palestine itself—and in turn was influenced in many ways by its 'Hellenistic' environment."[4] The Jews of the period, both in the Diaspora and in Palestine, were more "Hellenized" than previously had been supposed.

Even if the line (if not the dichotomy) between Judaism and Hellenism remains, it is no longer possible to maintain any clear-cut distinction between the theologies of Diaspora and Palestinian Judaism.[5] One cannot claim on the basis of language or nationality that any given individual Jew or group of Jews thought in a specific way. Hence, first-century Judaism has proved itself an entity far more variegated and eclectic—and, consequently, elusive—than had been imagined.

The eclipse of the dichotomy between Judaism and Hellenism has had significant effects, not only upon the study of Judaism per se, but also upon the vexed question of Christian origins. In particular, it has necessitated a reevaluation of received opinion about Jewish and Hellenistic backgrounds to the New Testament. Much that had been assumed to be Hellenistic—and therefore to have come to Christianity via the mystery cults, Greek philosophy, and so forth—is thought now by many to have entered the church via the agency of Judaism.[6] At the very least, it is recognized that the New Testament must be seen to stand against a rich and diverse background of overlapping influences.

In other words, scholarship has moved from division to diversity as its model for conceptualizing the distinctions within first-century Judaism and, by extension, Christianity. Simple polarities, such as the division between Hellenistic and Palestinian religion, have given way to more complicated and more nuanced understandings that allow for a range—rather than a dichotomy—of perspectives.

Corinthians, pp. 370–77 (Georgi supplies a copious bibliography on pp. 377–81 [English ed. only]); and Morton Smith, "Palestinian Judaism," pp. 68–71.

[4] Martin Hengel, *Between Jesus and Paul: Studies in the Earliest History of Christianity*, p. xiv [English ed. only]. See also Hengel, *Judaism and Hellenism* 1:310–12 [2:565–67], and *Jews, Greeks, and Barbarians*, pp. 110–26, 170–74 [152–75] (chap. 12, "The Influence of Hellenistic Civilization in Jewish Palestine down to the Maccabean Period"). See also Morton Smith: "Greek thought, in one way or another, had affected the court and the commons, the Temple and the tavern, the school and the synagogue" ("Palestinian Judaism," p. 81). On the relationship between the Jews of Palestine and the Diaspora, see S. Safrai and M. Stern, eds., *The Jewish People in the First Century: Historical Geography, Political History, Social, Cultural, and Religious Life and Institutions*, chap. 4, "Relations between the Diaspora and the Land of Israel" (1:184–215).

[5] Davies, *Paul and Rabbinic Judaism*, pp. xxiii–xxv. Samuel Sandmel notes that it is now impossible to "delineate what is native Palestinian Jewish and what is unmistakably hellenistic." He asks, "Is it not conceivable that a Jew could be thoroughly Palestinian in outlook yet reside in the Dispersion and find it possible to write in Greek, while the extent of Greek influences in Palestine make it also a possible area for a hellenistic essay to have been written there?" ("Palestinian and Hellenistic Judaism and Christianity: The Question of the Comfortable Theory," p. 140). Cf. Hengel, *Judaism and Hellenism* 1:311–12 [2:567]).

[6] This in essence is the thesis that Davies (in *Paul and Rabbinic Judaism*) attempts to prove with respect to the theology of the apostle Paul. Cf. James Barr, *The Semantics of Biblical Language*, pp. 9–10.

One of the most interesting (and surprisingly neglected) implications for New Testament studies of the eclipse of the dichotomy between Hellenism and Judaism concerns the dominant understanding of the "Hellenists" and "Hebrews" of Acts.[7] The prevailing interpretation of Acts 6:1–8:4 holds that the Hellenists and Hebrews were separate, ideologically based parties within the earliest Jerusalem church. The Hellenists, being universalistic in outlook and liberal in temperament, came after a short time to realize (in a way in which their narrow, conservative Hebrew fellow believers could not) the true ramifications of the gospel of Jesus Christ. The emergent picture of the Hellenists is highly attractive: these were not so unimaginative and legalistic as James and yet appear to have avoided the excesses of Paul. For those seeking a champion of the middle way, the Hellenists have appeared a sound bet.

The Hebrews, in contrast, are portrayed most unflatteringly in much of the relevant secondary literature. While Hellenist theology flowered into Christian universalism, Hebrew thinking sank into a retrenched Jewish legalism.

In light of the diversity of first-century Judaism, it must be asked whether this depiction of the Hellenists and Hebrews is founded upon anything but stereotype. Why should our acceptance of the cultural pluralism of first-century Judaism (both Diaspora and Palestinian) stop at the door of Jewish *Christianity?* Surely the historically credible picture here, as in the case of Judaism itself, is the complex one. We should expect to find Jewish Christians of various opinions, irrespective of their particular nationalities. We ought not to be surprised, for example, to learn of liberal Hebrews and conservative Hellenists.

This is not to say that, had we conducted a poll of the early church on various matters at issue, there would have been no discernible trends. Generalizations may be possible at a certain level; however, the usefulness of any historical generalization is inversely proportional to its breadth, and generalizations about Palestinian and Diaspora Judaism are very broad indeed.

The diversity of first-century Judaism challenges the notion that the earliest church was divided into ideological groups called Hellenists and Hebrews. Ultimately, however, the legitimacy of such an interpretation can be tested only within the framework of a thoroughgoing study of the texts upon which it is based.

Such, therefore, is the task before us. Specifically, we shall examine the claims of those who have found in Acts 6:1–8:4 evidence of the theological distinctiveness of Hebrew and Hellenist Christian parties. We shall also

---

[7] It is commonly accepted that the essential distinction between the terms "Hellenist" and "Hebrew" is linguistic; the first refers to Jews who spoke Greek, and the second to those who spoke Aramaic (see chap. 2 below).

consider those alleged effects for which such a division of the earliest church is thought to have been the cause. These include the animosity between the churches of Jerusalem and Antioch, the opposition of the Jerusalem Christians to Paul, and the legalism of James.

The primary thesis of this book is that the complex or pluralistic perspective is as true to early Jewish Christianity as it is to first-century Judaism generally. This is the positive counterpoint to the negative argument made concerning the inadequacy of the Hellenist-Hebrew dichotomy. We shall see that the earliest church was untidily diverse, not neatly divided. Differences of opinion existed within and not simply across cultural lines; disagreements were as often internal as external in nature. Put simply, the situation was complicated[8] — much more so than previous scholarly constructions would lead us to believe.

Before we consider the interpretation of specific texts, however, we shall take a brief look at the history and present state of scholarship on the question of the Hellenists and Hebrews. This will provide a logical as well as a historical context within which the argument of subsequent chapters can be fixed. This short survey will also highlight the extent to which a certain perspective has come to dominate contemporary interpretation of Acts 6:1–8:4. Thus I hope to provide in the next chapter both a structure and a reason for pursuing this study of the Hellenists and Hebrews of Acts.

---

[8] For example, the so-called Jerusalem Conference and Antioch Incident provide evidence of pluralism within the churches of Jerusalem and Antioch and, at the same time, demonstrate a substantial measure of conciliation and compromise between them (see chap. 4 below).

Chapter One

Background

That the early church, almost from its inception, was divided into two distinct ideological groups corresponding to the terms Ἑλληνισταί (Hellenists) and Ἑβραῖοι (Hebrews) is not a new idea. The notion is associated perhaps most closely with the Tübingen scholar Ferdinand Christian Baur, who, a century and a half ago, set forth his grand conception of the early church.[1] In "Die Christuspartei in der korinthischen Gemeinde, der Gegensatz des petrinischen und paulinischen Christenthums in der ältesten Kirche, der Apostel Petrus in Rom" ("The Christ party in the Corinthian community, the opposition of Petrine and Pauline Christianity in the early church, the Apostle Peter in Rome") (1831), Baur argued that primitive Christianity was divided into two opposing factions. "Thus already in those first days—in which Christianity had hardly begun to move beyond the narrow boundaries of Judaism and to open up to a more propitious circle of influence in the Gentile world—there were two opposing parties, each having distinct views. The party that opposed the apostle Paul originated in Jerusalem,

---

[1] The history of the research of Acts 6:1–8:4 is catalogued with considerable thoroughness by Heinz-Werner Neudorfer in his *Stephanuskreis in der Forschungsgeschichte seit F. C. Baur* (1983), originally prepared as a doctoral dissertation under the supervision of Martin Hengel at Tübingen University. Neudorfer's book is a most welcome tool. Its title is deceptively modest; in fact, substantial space is devoted to works that predate Baur. A highly condensed version of the history of the question is provided by Ernst Haenchen in *The Acts of the Apostles: A Commentary*, pp. 264-69 [218-22]. Relevant bibliographies are supplied on pp. 259-60, 270, 277-78 and 291 [213 and 242 only]. For additional bibliography, see Earl Richard, *Acts 6:1–8:4: The Author's Method of Composition*, pp. 361-79; Martin H. Scharlemann, *Stephen: A Singular Saint*, pp. 189-201; Gerhard Schneider, *Die Apostelgeschichte* 1:417-19, 431, 441-42, and 469-70; Martin Hengel, *Between*, pp. 129-32 [204-6]; and A. J. Mattill and Mary Bedford Mattill, *A Classified Bibliography of Literature on the Acts of the Apostles*, pp. 367-77.

where the younger James, the Lord's brother, stood in highest regard as head of the Christian community."²

"Jewish Christianity," led by Peter and James, was narrow and legalistic; "Gentile Christianity," for whom the apostle Paul was the champion, was universalistic and free, proclaiming the abolition of the law and, hence, the superseding of Judaism.

In 1845 Baur developed further the idea of the bipolarization of the early church in his important two-volume work on Paul.³ Baur asserted that beneath the murmuring of the Hellenist widows against the Hebrews over the "daily distribution" (Acts 6:1) lay some deeper ground of "dislike [*Verstimmung*] between the two parties."⁴ Specifically, the Hebrews, who "adhered as nearly as possible to the Jewish religion," could not accept the "liberal turn of thought" of the Hellenists. This led to an ever-widening "division between the two elements of the Church formerly allied together."⁵

The decisive moment came when Stephen, the first to attain "a clear consciousness" of the "antagonism of Christianity to Judaism," through his teaching aroused opposition among the "Hellenist communities in Jerusalem."⁶ Although it is not likely that Stephen was tried before the Sanhedrin as Acts records,⁷ the sentiments expressed in the speech of Acts 7 are Stephen's own.⁸ Primary among these is a denunciation of the "perversity" of the religion of the Jews, which consisted of "a formalism composed of outward rites and ceremonies."⁹ Attention was focused especially on the "external, sensuous, ceremonial worship" associated with the temple.¹⁰ The "massive, stationary temple, with its stern fixed worship" is compared with the "tabernacle of witness," which was "free, moveable, wandering from place to place . . . and therefore keeping the worship connected with it in

---

² Baur, "Christuspartei," p. 114.
³ Baur, *Paul, the Apostle of Jesus Christ, His Life and Works, His Epistles and Teachings: A Contribution to a Critical History of Primitive Christianity*. Baur's *History of the Church in the First Three Centuries*, published in 1853, contains a restatement of his position on Stephen and the Hellenists (1:44–46 [42–43]).
⁴ Ibid., p. 41 [48].
⁵ Ibid., pp. 41–43 [48–49] (see p. 60 [67]).
⁶ Ibid., p. 43 [49]. Baur felt that Stephen "had doubtless turned with especial confidence" to his fellow Hellenists, since "they, as *Hellenists*, would have understood the views and principles which he considered as the essence of his Christian faith" (p. 43 [49–50], emphasis added).
⁷ Ibid., pp. 54–57 [61–64]. Baur cites the inability of the Sanhedrin to pass a capital sentence and the surprising forbearance of the crowd in listening to the speech of Stephen as evidence for this view.
⁸ Ibid., p. 61 [68].
⁹ Ibid., p. 48 [54].
¹⁰ Ibid., p. 49 [55]. Unfortunately, Baur's scathing assessment of Jewish religion was by no means exceptional. See also Augustus Neander (himself one of Baur's harshest critics), who wrote of the Jews' "narrow-hearted sensuous tendency to confine the essence of religion to temple-worship" (*History of the Planting and Training of the Christian Church by the Apostles* 1:62 [74]).

constant motion." According to Stephen, "David also keeps nearer and more faithfully to this ideal in the σκηνὴ τοῦ μαρτυρίου [tent of testimony], inasmuch as with him the question is of a σκήνωμα [dwelling place] that he wishes to put in the place of the σκηνή [tent], and it was Solomon, whose reign was marked by so different a tendency, who really 'built a house' for God."[11]

In summary, Baur claimed that "there had already taken place in Stephen a breach between his religious consciousness and the Mosaic Law." "This inevitable rending asunder of Christianity from Judaism, whereby Judaism would be rendered negative as an absolute religion, and by which its final extinction was threatened, had been realized by Stephen; the high, liberal standpoint which he assumed, fostered in him the energetic zeal with which he laboured in the cause of Jesus — and in proportion to this was the opposition more earnest, which he drew down on himself."[12]

Stephen was "seized and stoned in a tumultuous insurrection."[13] There followed a "severe persecution" of the church in Jerusalem, as a result of which all were scattered, "except the apostles" (Acts 8:1b). Baur commented, "This may justly surprise us"; what persecution is directed at followers but not leaders? "However, it cannot be doubted that they [the apostles] remained behind in Jerusalem. . . . But if they remained we cannot believe that they were the only ones who did so, but rather that the persecution first directed against the Hellenist Stephen was in fact carried on *against the Hellenistic part* of the Church."[14]

This selective persecution of the Hellenists produced results of enormous consequence for the early church. "The two elements composing it, the Hellenistic and Hebraistic . . . now became outwardly separated from each other. At that time the Church at Jerusalem was purely Hebraistic; as such it adhered closely to its strictly Judaizing character, and a strenuous opposition to the liberal Hellenistic Christianity was consequently developed."[15]

For their part, the Hellenists, having been driven from Jerusalem, progressed naturally to "a universal system in which Jew and Gentile stood equal side by side."[16] In equal and opposite reaction, the church of Jerusalem, now wholly rigid (i.e., Jewish),[17] came to oppose the rapidly developing Gentile mission of the Hellenists.[18] This antagonism is evidenced most

---

[11] Baur, *Paul* 1:49, 50 [56]. This characterization of the Stephen speech is discussed in chap. 3 below.
[12] Ibid., pp. 61, 59 [69, 66–67].
[13] Ibid., p. 56 [63].
[14] Ibid., p. 39 [46], (emphasis added).
[15] Ibid., p. 40 [47].
[16] Ibid., pp. 60–61 [68].
[17] See Baur's description of the Jews in ibid., p. 51 [57].
[18] Ibid., p. 40 [47].

clearly in the confrontation between Paul and his Jerusalem-sponsored Judaizing opponents.[19]

Hence, we see that the opposition between Jewish Petrine and universalist Pauline perspectives, which dominated Baur's conception of the early church, was traced by him to its original manifestation in the tension between the Hebrews and Hellenists of Acts 6. Accordingly, Stephen, the exemplary Hellenist, was termed by Baur "the most direct forerunner of the Apostle Paul."[20]

Baur's reconstruction of the early church (of which I have outlined only the first part) elicited an extraordinary response; indeed, it may be said that through it Baur succeeded in setting the agenda for much of subsequent New Testament scholarship. Opponents tended to focus their attack upon Baur's treatment of sources (in particular, his skepticism toward Acts and his reliance upon the pseudo-Clementine literature) and his portrayal of the relationship between Paul and the Jerusalem church.[21] To a surprising extent, Baur's views on the Hellenists and Hebrews were ignored or else accepted without compunction. An example of this phenomenon is the essay

---

[19] Baur walked a tightrope with respect to the Jerusalem sponsorship of Paul's Judaizing opponents. He was obliged, because of Gal. 2:1-10, to admit that Jerusalem's "pillar" apostles accepted Paul's law-free mission to the Gentiles. But, he added, they did not do so willingly, since they were, in reality, the very ones who had been opposing him (*Paul* 1:117, 126 [128, 138]; *History* 1:52-53 [49-51]). Nevertheless, they felt constrained by the force of the apostle's arguments and his manifest success as a missionary to extend to him the right hand of fellowship (p. 130 [142]). Theirs was, however (and, I think, in contradiction to the previous statement), only an agreement to disagree: Paul's "Gentile Christianity" was not endorsed but merely granted the right of coexistence (p. 130 [142]). "They could do no otherwise, for they were not in a condition to resist the strength of circumstances and the overpowering personal influence of the Apostle. But they only consented not to oppose the Pauline Christianity, which with regard to their principles they were bound to oppose" (p. 131 [144]).

Baur then asserted that "there grew up within Jewish Christianity itself a strict and a liberal party." The stricter faction comprised "the declared opponents of the Apostle Paul," who "introduced themselves into all the churches founded by him." The "Jewish Apostles," however, were not numbered among these, having "renounced the . . . carrying out of their principles" (pp. 132, 133 [145, 146]). The distinction between the parties breaks down in practice, however, because the Judaizers from Palestine, engaged in a "systematic opposition to the apostle Paul" (*History* 1:56 [53]), claimed the authority of the Jerusalem apostles for themselves. Indeed, they were able to produce "letters of recommendation" (2 Cor. 3:1) from the apostles (James in particular), authorizing them to teach (pp. 292-93 [313-14]). Why James should not have restricted his teachers to the Jewish churches (assuming the separation of Jewish and Gentile churches; see *History* 1:53 [51]) as he had agreed, or why Paul did not simply defend himself to the Corinthians on the basis of the fact that there are two different gospels with two sets of teachers (ibid.), as he had agreed, is not explained. These and other quandaries could have been avoided if Baur had admitted that the Jerusalem apostles did in fact accept the legitimacy of the law-free mission to the Gentiles and that Judaizers who claimed their authority did so wrongly. (These matters are taken up at greater length in chaps. 4 and 5 below.)

[20] Baur, *Paul* 1:62 [69].

[21] On the work, impact, and criticism of F. C. Baur and the so-called Tübingen School, see W. Ward Gasque, *A History of the Criticism of the Acts of the Apostles*, pp. 21-95; and Werner Georg Kümmel, *The New Testament: The History of the Investigation of Its Problems*, pp. 127-84 [156-230].

"St. Paul and the Three" by J. B. Lightfoot,[22] the British scholar called by Gasque "the greatest of the early critics" of the Tübingen school.[23] Within the context of a sustained attack on Baur's reconstruction of early church history, Lightfoot mentioned (without reference to Baur) that the Hellenists would naturally "accept and interpret the new revelation in a less rigorous spirit than the Hebrew [Christian] zealot of Jerusalem." Perhaps for this reason, the Hebrews "regarded their Hellenist brethren with suspicion and distrust." Lightfoot continued, "At length a breach [with Judaism] was made, and the assailants as might be expected were Hellenists." It was Stephen, the "martyr of liberty" and "the acknowledged forerunner" of the apostle Paul, who "was the first . . . to sound the death-knell of the Mosaic ordinances and the temple worship, and to claim for the Gospel unfettered liberty and universal rights."[24] Following its flight from Jerusalem, the Christianity of the Hellenists went from strength to strength, while "the star of Jewish Christendom," by contrast, "was already on the wane."[25]

This is not to say that Baur's view of the Hellenists and Hebrews met with immediate and universal acceptance. Already in 1847 an article appeared by L. Wolff entitled "Der Bericht der Apostelgeschichte über Stephanus vertheidigt gegen die Angriffe Baur's" ("Act's Account of Stephen Defended Against Baur's Attacks"). Like other critics of Baur, Wolff rejected the notion that "Pauline Christianity" had nothing to do with "apostolic Christianity" (i.e., the Jerusalem church).[26] In addition, he repudiated the proposal that the persecution of Acts 8:1b was limited to the Hellenists. Hebrews also fled Jerusalem, but the author of Acts did not think it necessary to report their reappearance in the city, especially since they did not return en masse.[27] Pressing further, Wolff attacked Baur's interpretation of the Stephen speech of Acts 7:

> The idea that Baur attributes to Stephen—that the building of the temple itself was an evil thing, a misunderstanding of the divine promise, while the mobile tabernacle was much more appropriate to it—cannot be attributed to Stephen because the prophet he introduces in vv. 48-50 said nothing different from the builder of the temple himself in 1 Kings 8:37, and no such attack on what is based on the divine promise in the Old Testament is to be found in his speech.

---

[22] See also Lightfoot's criticisms of Baur in *Essays on the Work Entitled Supernatural Religion* (1889).

[23] Gasque, *History*, p. 108.

[24] Lightfoot, "St. Paul and the Three" (originally published in 1892 in *Dissertations on the Apostolic Age* and reprinted [in the second and subsequent editions] of the author's *Saint Paul's Epistle to the Galatians*, from which I quote), pp. 296-98.

[25] Lightfoot, *Galatians*, p. 303. Lightfoot does not assert that the Hellenists alone were persecuted in Jerusalem, although such a view would coincide with his understanding of their distinctive theology.

[26] Wolff, "Der Bericht," pp. 91-92.

[27] Ibid., pp. 92-93.

Stephen's criticism is directed against the opinion that temple worship was in itself the complete fulfillment of the worship of God.[28]

Similar doubts were expressed by Michael Baumgarten in his three-volume work on Acts, published in 1852.[29] Baumgarten considered Baur's Stephen to be "an imaginary character."[30] Like Wolff, he resisted the view that Stephen was a critic of the temple. "If Baur is disposed to see in these words a deprecation of the Temple, and an expression of a preference for the Tabernacle . . . this is a mere arbitrary conceit, which is opposed by the whole tenor of the discourse."[31] Baumgarten also attacked the notion of a selective persecution of the Hellenists. In its place he offered the improbable suggestion that a Christian "assembly was sitting at the very time that Stephen was stoned." It was "against those [alone] who were gathered together" that "a raging persecution now broke loose."[32]

For every nineteenth-century scholar critical of Baur on these points, however, one can uncover another (usually more influential) scholar who supported or at least made use of Baur's ideas. Baur's most enthusiastic partisan was undoubtedly his son-in-law, Eduard Zeller. His *Contents and Origin of the Acts of the Apostles Critically Investigated,* published in 1854, has been called "the only thorough study of Acts ever produced by the Tübingen School."[33] In it, Zeller, like Baur before him, gave special place to Stephen and the Hellenists. In fact, it is with the story of Stephen, wrote Zeller, that "we find ourselves for the first time on undeniably historical ground."[34] Zeller agreed with Baur in contending that Stephen attacked the building of the temple (the Jews "prefer the house of God built by human hands . . . to the true worship of God, just as their fathers in the wilderness preferred the golden calf to the living God") and questioned the "continued validity of the law."[35] Zeller also took the view that "the persecutions probably fell only on the Hellenistic believers connected with Stephen."[36]

Following in the same tradition, Franz Overbeck claimed that only "a detached . . . portion of the primitive church" was driven out of Jerusalem;[37]

---

[28] Ibid., pp. 96–97.
[29] Michael Baumgarten, *The Acts of the Apostles; or, The History of the Church in the Apostolic Age.*
[30] Ibid., *Acts* 1:138 [123].
[31] Ibid., p. 158 [141].
[32] Ibid., p. 177 [158]. Wolff and Baumgarten's criticisms are paralleled by, among others, Gotthard Victor Lechler in *The Apostolic and Post-Apostolic Times: Their Diversity and Unity in Life and Doctrine* (1851) 1:285–88 [241–44]; and (with K. Gerok) *Theological and Homiletical Commentary on the Acts of the Apostles, Specially Designed and Adapted for the Use of Ministers and Students* (1860) 1:261, 279 [77, 93].
[33] Gasque, *History,* p. 44.
[34] Zeller, *Acts* 1:237 [146]. See Baur, *History* 1:44 [42].
[35] Zeller, *Acts* 1:240, 238 [149, 146].
[36] Ibid., pp. 245–46 [153–54].
[37] Franz Overbeck, "Introduction to the Acts," p. 25.

Woldemar Gottlob Schmidt wrote that "with Stephen came the first full break with the Mosaic law. His polemic . . . caused the outbreak of a mighty animosity";[38] and H. J. Holtzmann asserted that "Stephen actually taught that in the messianic kingdom there would be an abrogation of "Mosaism" and, in particular, *a removal of this . . . holy place* (that is, the temple, as in 21:28)."[39]

Turning to the early twentieth century, we discover much the same situation. Against Baur, one may cite Wilhelm Soltau, who considered that Stephen's speech "was not directed 'against Moses and against God' (Acts 6:11); rather, it is precisely the opposite: a powerful document for God and for Moses."[40] Likewise, Wilhelm Mundle, who reckoned the speech to be a Lukan composition,[41] could discern neither law criticism nor temple criticism in its contents. Such criticisms were "not at issue."[42]

In contrast, Karl Pahncke saw in Stephen the antithesis of a normative Jewish perspective.[43] Stephen attacked "post-Mosaic Judaism," since it was not an accurate reflection of the true Jewish religion: "This pseudo-Mosaic, present-day Judaism is the object of Stephen's attack."[44] "The idea of unspirituality in their religion and religiosity is the defect and end of the Jewish people to this day, said Stephen. Judaism, with its τόπος ἅγιος [holy place] and its Solomon-inspired temple cult, is unprophetic and anti-Mosaic, an abandonment and surrender of the foundation given by the λόγια ζῶντα [living oracles]."[45]

Two years later, Julius Wellhausen wrote concerning Acts 8:1b: "Interestingly enough, the Jews make a distinction between the two parts of the Jerusalem church, whose attempted extinction in verse 1 fails. The persecution following the death of Stephen is directed only against the Hellenists and only they are scattered. Not just the twelve remain in Jerusalem; rather, the Hebrew Christians generally are not molested."[46]

Over the course of the past seventy-five years, there has occurred a decided and largely unheralded fixing of opinion in favor of at least the broad outlines of Baur's interpretation of Acts 6:1–8:4. It is now widely assumed that the Hellenists and Hebrews were distinctive ideological groups, that Stephen, the Hellenist leader, spoke against the temple (and

---

[38] Woldemar Gottlob Schmidt, *Der Bericht der Apostelgeschichte über Stephanus* (1882), p. 23.
[39] H. J. Holtzmann, *Die Apostelgeschichte* (1899; citing the 3d ed., 1901), p. 54.
[40] Wilhelm Soltau, "Die Herkunft der Reden in der Apostelgeschichte" (1903), p. 149.
[41] Wilhelm Mundle, "Die Stephanusrede Apg. 7: Eine Märtyrerapologie" (1921), p. 135.
[42] Ibid., p. 146.
[43] Karl H. Pahncke, "Der Stephanismus der Apostelgeschichte" (1912), p. 1.
[44] Ibid., p. 8.
[45] Ibid., p. 10. Eduard Meyer also believed that the temple represented, from the perspective of Stephen, a fall from true worship (*Ursprung und Anfänge des Christentums*, vol. 3, *Die Apostelgeschichte und die Anfänge des Christentums* [1923], p. 159).
[46] Julius Wellhausen, "Kritische Analyse der Apostelgeschichte" (1914), p. 14.

quite possibly the law), that he was put to death for his liberal (or radical) views, and that the Hellenists and not the Hebrews were persecuted by the Jews.

The triumph of this perspective is readily apparent. One measure is its now customary presence in popular or introductory works on the New Testament (a particularly good barometer of received opinion) as well as its place in more specialist writings. I cite a few of many examples.

In *The New Oxford Annotated Bible* we are told that the Hellenists were "Greek-speaking Jews or Jews who have adopted Greek customs." The Hebrews, by contrast, "probably spoke Aramaic and were more conservative." Furthermore, it is said that "Stephen saw more clearly than others that Jesus' teaching would *change the customs*," and that "it was wrong for *Solomon* to build *a house* for him [God]."[47]

The NIV Study Bible says the following about Acts 6:1: "At this stage of its development, the church was entirely Jewish in its composition. However, there were two groups of Jews within the fellowship: (1) *Grecian Jews*. Hellenists—those born in lands other than Palestine who spoke the Greek language and were more Grecian in their attitudes and outlook. (2) *Hebraic Jews*. Those who spoke the Aramaic and/or Hebrew language(s) of Palestine and preserved Jewish culture and customs."[48]

Originating from the same evangelical Christian perspective as *The NIV Study Bible* is *Eerdmans' Handbook to the History of Christianity*. It states that "among the Jerusalem Christians there were a few who were more forward looking.... One disciple, named Stephen, saw more clearly than others that the faith was for all people, and that a break with Judaism was inevitable. He belonged to a group of Jews called 'Hellenists' who spoke Greek and adopted a freer life-style than the more conservative Jews." Stephen's "bold preaching" resulted in a persecution directed especially against the Hellenists.[49]

In Christopher Rowland's introduction to Christian origins, it is said that the Hellenists' "outlook included much more radical ideas than was probably the case elsewhere in the Jerusalem church." Stephen's "hostility against the Temple" seems in particular to have distinguished him. Later, the focus of radical thought was to be found in the church of Antioch.[50]

In his *New Testament History*, F. F. Bruce affirmed that "the Hellenists ... were Jews ... whose way of life, in the eyes of stricter Palestinians, smacked too much of Greek customs." Likewise, the Seven, chosen from

---

[47] *The New Oxford Annotated Bible with the Apocryphal/Deuterocanonical Books: New Revised Standard Version*, pp. 168, 169, 171 (NT).
[48] *The NIV Study Bible: New International Version with Study Notes and References, Concordance and Maps*, p. 1620.
[49] *Eerdmans'* [= *The Lion*] *Handbook to the History of Christianity*, p. 60.
[50] Christopher Rowland, *Christian Origins: An Account of the Setting and Character of the Most Important Messianic Sect of Judaism*, pp. 200–201.

among the Hellenists, "maintained a more liberal outlook than the 'Hebrews,' including the apostles." One of their number, Stephen, made "a vigorous attack on the Temple cultus." Concerning the persecution following Stephen's death, Bruce wrote, "Luke does not say explicitly that the Hellenists . . . were the principal targets of this campaign, but it emerges fairly clearly from his narrative that this was so."[51]

Helmut Koester, in the collection of essays *Trajectories through Early Christianity,* stated that "only the group of the 'Hellenists' . . . was persecuted and forced to leave Jerusalem. . . . the circle around Peter and James remained within the realm of law observance and temple cult, whereas the Hellenists did not. Stephen was martyred, not because he was a Christian, but because as a Christian he rejected the law and ritual of his Jewish past."[52] More recently, Gerd Lüdemann has made these same points in his *Early Christianity according to the Traditions in Acts*[53] and in his *Opposition to Paul in Jewish Christianity.*[54]

Rudolf Bultmann was one of many to add another element to this reconstruction: the Seven were not deacons, as Acts 6:2-3 would have us believe, but leaders of the "Hellenistic party"; as such "their office was by no means serving table, but . . . they were proclaimers of the word."[55] This same observation is made by, among others, Luke T. Johnson in his New Testament introduction.[56]

J. Christiaan Beker's study of Paul included a reference to "the Stephen group that founded the Antioch church" and "'liberalized' the Torah with

---

[51] Bruce, *New Testament History,* pp. 206, 208, 210, 214-15. These same opinions are to be found in the work of Bruce's student J. Julius Scott ("The Church of Jerusalem, A.D. 30-100: An Investigation of the Growth of Internal Factions and the Extension of Its Influence in the Larger Church" [Ph.D diss., University of Manchester]; and derivative articles [see bibliography]). Bo Reicke's New Testament history gives the material much the same treatment (*The New Testament Era: The World of the Bible from 500 B.C. to A.D. 100;* see especially pp. 192, 212-17 [142-43, 158-61]).

[52] James M. Robinson and Helmut Koester, *Trajectories through Early Christianity,* p. 120 (in the essay "GNOMAI DIAPHOROI: The Origin and Nature of Diversification in the History of Early Christianity").

[53] Lüdemann, *Early Christianity,* pp. 73-93 [79-99].

[54] Lüdemann, *Opposition,* pp. 41-42 [69-70].

[55] Bultmann, *New Testament Theology* 1:55-56 [57]. According to Loisy: "The motive ascribed by the editor to the establishment of the Seven may not be the correct one because the general meaning that he is forced to give to this institution is certainly false. . . . It is all the more false to say that the Seven were the treasurers for the entire community, for in what follows they appear as ministers of the word, and they even spread the word so much that they provoke the expulsion of all the Hellenistic believers, after the most enterprising of them has been put to death" (*Les Actes des Apôtres* [1920], pp. 295-96). It is worth noting that E. Jacquier, Loisy's contemporary, condemned this interpretation as pure conjecture. Jacquier could see no basis for supposing that the early church was divided into groups of Hellenists and Hebrews (*Les Actes des Apôtres* [2d ed., 1926)], p. 183).

[56] Luke T. Johnson, *The Writings of the New Testament: An Interpretation,* p. 227.

respect to the validity of the temple and the cultic law."⁵⁷ Likewise, Günther Bornkamm, in his *Paul,* contended that behind the report of Acts 6 is concealed "a much more serious cleavage" within the early church. Specifically, the Hellenists advocated "an understanding of the gospel altogether revolutionary in the eyes of the rest of the church." Concerning Acts 8:1b he commented, "Obviously, the non-Hellenistic part of the mother church was left unmolested."⁵⁸

The majority of contemporary critical commentaries on Acts embrace at least part of what we may now call the traditional view of the Hellenists and Hebrews. C. S. C. Williams, for example, accepted that "Hellenists . . . may denote Greek-speaking Jews whose sympathies and interests were opposed to those of the Hebraioi." In his discussion of the Stephen speech, he wrote, "The tabernacle appropriate to a pilgrim people was replaced by a standing Temple. . . . The argument is that if the Jews had observed the Law they would have seen that Jesus had been sent to do away with the Temple and the customs of Moses." Finally, "Luke implies that the stricter Jewish-Christian apostles were not affected, as were the Hellenists, by persecution."⁵⁹

Hans Conzelmann's recent Hermeneia commentary contains the well-known combination of liberal Hellenists plus criticism of law and temple plus selective persecution,⁶⁰ as do the commentaries of Gerhard Krodel,⁶¹ Gerhard Schneider,⁶² Jacques Dupont,⁶³ and, representing more conservative scholarship, Richard Longenecker.⁶⁴ More important, each element has found a place in what is surely the preeminent commentary on Acts of the present day: Ernst Haenchen's *The Acts of the Apostles.* Interestingly, in

---

⁵⁷ J. Christiaan Beker, *Paul the Apostle: The Triumph of God in Life and Thought,* pp. 341-42.

⁵⁸ Günther Bornkamm, *Paul,* p. 14 [37]. According to Wayne A. Meeks and Robert L. Wilken, "the 'scattering' of the Jerusalem disciples" was actually, "in the consensus of most modern scholarship," a scattering "of the Jewish-Christian 'Hellenists'" (*Jews and Christians in Antioch in the First Four Centuries of the Common Era,* p. 13).

⁵⁹ C. S. C. Williams, *A Commentary on the Acts of the Apostles,* pp. 95, 110-11, 114. A close parallel to Williams's commentary is that of William Neil (*The Acts of the Apostles,* pp. 101-19).

⁶⁰ Hans Conzelmann, *Acts of the Apostles,* pp. 47-61 [49-60].

⁶¹ Gerhard A. Krodel, *Acts,* pp. 136-37.

⁶² Gerhard Schneider, *Die Apostelgeschichte* 1:406-80. Schneider is the most cautious of the four. Somewhat unusually, he asserts that "the law-criticism of Stephen is better attested historically than is his opposition to the temple" (p. 416).

⁶³ Jacques Dupont, *Les Actes des Apôtres,* pp. 70-83.

⁶⁴ Richard N. Longenecker, "The Acts of the Apostles" (in *John-Acts,* The Expositor's Bible Commentary 9), pp. 327-54. See also the well-known Acts commentaries of F. F. Bruce (*Commentary on the Book of Acts: The English Text with Introduction, Exposition, and Notes,* pp. 127-75) and I. Howard Marshall (*The Acts of the Apostles: An Introduction and Commentary,* pp. 124-51). Marshall has demonstrated an awareness of the problems surrounding this interpretation (see below); for this reason, his *Acts* offers a particularly vivid example of the pervasiveness of Baur's opinions.

reference to the account of the Hellenists and Hebrews in Acts 6, Haenchen wrote that "criticism has only gradually mastered this passage."[65] The result yielded by the efforts of criticism is strikingly familiar. "Stephen and his group" exercised "great freedom in relation to the law" and were selectively persecuted for it.[66]

Without question, the most influential contemporary advocate of a view of the Hellenists consistent with that of F. C. Baur is Martin Hengel. The place occupied by the Hellenists is vital to Hengel's understanding of the early church. His best-known and most impressive work, *Judaism and Hellenism*, concludes with a paragraph and a half devoted to these members of the Jerusalem church, who recognized above all that "the protective attitude of Judaism over against its environment . . . most strongly expressed by the absolutizing place of the Torah" was "shattered in pieces" by the message of Jesus.[67]

Hengel's essay "Between Jesus and Paul" presents the most articulate and learned formulation and defense to date of the theory of the theological distinctiveness of the Hellenists.[68] In addition to the components we have come to expect, Hengel added to the discussion his concept of "the eschatological 'enthusiasm' of the Hellenists, inspired by the spirit." It is to this dynamic that we must turn for an account of the Hellenists' surprising theological creativity.[69] Another important factor in the (rapid) development of their theological understanding was the translation of Christian tradition into "the new medium of the Greek language."[70]

---

[65] Haenchen, *Acts*, p. 264 [218].
[66] Ibid., pp. 264–68 [218–22].
[67] Martin Hengel, *Judaism and Hellenism* 1:313–14 [2:569–70].
[68] Martin Hengel, "Between Jesus and Paul," in the collection *Between Jesus and Paul* (pp. 1–29, 133–56). Hengel's position is restated in his subsequent essay "Acts and the History of Earliest Christianity" (see especially pp. 71–80 [63–70]). Hengel is willing in this second publication to allow for the fact that the *Hebrews* "did not form a 'monolithic block.'" This relative pluralism was maintained, however, only in the "early period" (p. 101 [86]). As time went on, "an increasing regression towards legalism . . . came about in Jerusalem," to the extent that "when James took over the leadership of the Christian community in the holy city, Peter was forced to do mission work outside Palestine" (pp. 122, 124 [102, 104]). The balance in Hengel's position is prompted perhaps by his criticisms of F. C. Baur. On p. 122 [102] Hengel derides Baur for having produced "a cliché-ridden approach to earliest Christianity." "Historical developments were much more varied and much more complicated than Baur supposed."

Despite these statements, it is clear that Hengel himself does little to moderate Baur's views. Elsewhere, for example, he writes that the Hellenists "called for the eschatological abolition of Temple worship and the revision of the law of Moses in light of the true will of God" (pp. 72–73 [64]). In fact, from the time the Hellenists (alone) were "driven out of Jerusalem," "the observance of the Torah was of virtually no significance at all" (pp. 99–100 [85]). "The Aramaic-speaking Jewish Christians," in contrast, "had a more restrained—one might almost say more conservative—attitude towards the Law" (p. 73 [64]; see Hengel's positive assessment of Baur's interpretation of Acts 6:1–8:4 on p. 71 [63]).

[69] Hengel, *Between*, pp. 22–24 [193–96].
[70] Ibid., pp. 24–29 [196–204]. For a critique of Hengel, see the review of E. P. Sanders (*JTS* 37 [1986]: 167–72).

In Bible notes, in New Testament introductions and theologies, in New Testament and church histories, in studies of Paul, and in Acts commentaries alike, at both popular and specialist levels and in works representing a variety of theological perspectives, we thus find the same basic idea repeated: the earliest church was divided into two groups, Hellenists and Hebrews, who, as such, thought differently theologically. That this conception is in tension with the eclipse of the dichotomy between Judaism and Hellenism seems to me prima facie to be true. Among contemporary scholars, I. Howard Marshall is one of the few to have noted this conflict. In his penetrating article "Palestinian and Hellenistic Christianity: Some Critical Comments," he wrote, "If no hard and fast distinction can be made between Palestinian and Hellenistic Judaism, it is unlikely that one can press the distinction between Palestinian and Hellenistic Jewish Christianity."[71] Therefore, "We must conclude that the hypothesis of a theological distinction between Aramaic- and Greek-speaking sections of the Jewish church rests on inadequate grounds."[72]

More recently, C. K. Barrett offered a similar analysis in his article "Acts and Christian Consensus."

> We have no evidence that there was ever a Christian group that gave itself, or was given by others, or was recognized under, the title, The Hellenists. . . . That there were Jews who had absorbed a measure of Hellenism is true; indeed, this was true of all Jews, in varying degrees. . . . There were Greek-speaking Jews who became Christians and exercised a specific influence in the development of Christian thought and institutions, but we should not think of them as a single party presenting a united "Hellenistic" front. This observation has an important bearing on the understanding of the history of early Christianity.[73]

---

[71] Marshall, "Palestinian and Hellenistic Christianity" (1972–73), p. 274.

[72] Ibid. Marshall did not, however, follow this insight to its logical conclusion. His interest was limited primarily to the supposition that Christology developed along expressly Hellenistic and Hebrew (or Palestinian) lines. Accordingly, he wrote that the "distinctive theology . . . associated with Stephen and his followers, who went further than the primitive church in their attitude to the law and the Gentile mission," did not affect "such basic matters as christology" (p. 280).

[73] Barrett, "Acts and Christian Consensus" (1987), p. 21. Barrett did, however, assert that there was a party called the Hebrews, for whom James was the probable leader. He based this opinion upon the occurrence of the title "Hebrew" (meaning, according to Barrett, one who "took the law . . . seriously"; p. 27) in Paul's self-descriptions of Phil. 3:5 and 2 Cor. 11:22. I do not find this convincing because (1) it necessitates a Jerusalem origin for Paul's Corinthian opponents, (2) it assumes an unjustified degree of antipathy between Paul and the Jerusalem church, (3) it makes the law (and opposition to Paul) the focus of the group's self-conception, (4) the term "Hebrews" in Acts 6:1 is used more generally than Barrett's interpretation allows, and (5) it ignores the much simpler explanation, which is that the opponents used the word "Hebrew" either as an impressive synonym for "Jew" (the opponents are also known as "Israelites" and "descendants of Abraham" in 2 Cor. 11:22) or as an indication of the fact that they were Aramaic-speaking Jews and/or Jews of Palestinian extraction (such as those of the "synagogue of the Hebrews" at Corinth itself). Each of these points is taken up in the chapters that follow.

Disputations concerning the theoretical foundation underlying the traditional understanding of the Hellenists and Hebrews since F. C. Baur can take us only so far. They raise but do not answer the question of the legitimacy of this interpretation. A thorough investigation of the relevant New Testament passages is required before an informed judgment can be rendered.

The need for such an investigation has not been ignored entirely. In particular, Edvin Larsson, in his 1987 article "Die Hellenisten und die Urgemeinde" (The Hellenists and the Early Christian Community),[74] reopened a number of intriguing questions concerning the interpretation of Acts 6:1 – 8:4 and, in so doing, formed conclusions reminiscent of those of Wolff and Baumgarten, writing more than a century before. Larsson's particular strength is his awareness of the implications of his results. About Acts 7 he wrote:

> There is no fundamental criticism of the temple in the Stephen speech. With this, one of the traditional arguments for a particularly Hellenistic theology comes under attack. The same result is to be obtained if the conception of the law is considered. According to 7:53, Stephen accuses the Jews of not having kept the law, although it had been given to them by angels. Statements of this kind prove no essential distancing from the law. With this, another argument in favor of a special Hellenist theology falls away.[75]

Similarly, the notion of the selective persecution of the Hellenists, offered by Hengel (among others) as proof of the theological distinctiveness of that group, is rejected by Larsson. Too much has been made of the simple account of Acts 8:1b.[76] In conclusion, "It is natural that these Hellenists, after they had been converted to Christianity, would have had a great significance for the life of the church. One cannot attribute to them a special theology, however, nor a separate life-style."[77]

The weakness of Larsson's presentation is one shared by a great many journal articles: the author is forced to consider in only a few pages a complicated subject requiring much fuller treatment. The persecution of Acts 8:1-4, for example, is covered in just two paragraphs. Despite its brevity, however, Larsson's article deserves an influential place in the secondary literature on Acts.

We have seen that there are good theoretical grounds for questioning the now-customary understanding of the Hellenists and Hebrews of Acts 6:1. We have also seen that, despite a long history of criticism, no thorough attempt has yet been made to examine and, perhaps, to challenge this interpretation. The study that follows represents such an attempt.

---

[74] The article was based on a paper read (in Swedish) at the "Nordischen Patristikerkonferenz" in August 1984.
[75] Larsson, "Die Hellenisten," p. 220.
[76] Ibid., p. 222.
[77] Ibid., p. 223.

Chapter Two

Acts 8:1-4: The Persecution of the Hellenists

As we have seen, F. C. Baur, in 1845 in *Paul, the Apostle of Jesus Christ*, "provided the basic stimulus for the critical interpretation of Acts 6 and 7."[1] It was his suggestion that the γογγυσμός (complaining) of the Hellenists against the Hebrews, as Acts 6:1 reports it, reflects some deeper ground of "dislike between the two parties."[2] Luke's[3] mention of a controversy surrounding ἡ διακονία ἡ καθημερινή ("daily distribution"), then, only serves to disguise, somewhat trivially, a much deeper ideological split within the early church.[4]

---

[1] Hengel, *Between,* p. 1 [152].

[2] Baur, *Paul* 1:41 [48].

[3] I follow scholarly convention in referring to the author of Acts as "Luke." In general, the question of authorship does not impinge on the present study. With the great majority of scholars, I assume that this same Luke wrote the Gospel bearing his name. Like the question of authorship, this is a matter of secondary importance to the present argument.

Linked to the problem of authorship but of greater significance is the question of the date of Acts. This bears most on my understanding of the place of the temple in Luke-Acts. I take the position that both Luke and Acts were written after the events of A.D. 70. One reason for this judgment is the apparent lateness of Luke 19:41-44 and 21:20-24. With Werner Kümmel, I agree that "Lk 13:34f must be regarded as historical, but in Lk 21:20, 24 there appears an apocalyptic prediction which has been reworked from the "abomination of desolation" (Mk 13:14ff) into a prediction of doom on Jerusalem that has been formed *ex eventu*. . . . The same is true of the portrayal in 19:43f" (*Introduction to the New Testament,* p. 150 [119]). On the authorship and date of Acts, see Kümmel, *Introduction,* pp. 147-51, 156-59 [116-20, 124-27], and especially Haenchen's introductory articles in *Acts,* pp. 3-132 [1-103]. For a defense of the traditional identification of the author of Acts with Luke, the colleague of Paul (referred to in Col. 4:14, 2 Tim. 4:11, and Philem. 24), see I. Howard Marshall, *Acts,* pp. 44-46. Marshall also favors a pre-70 date of composition (pp. 46-48).

[4] Support for this view may come from the manner in which Luke reports the split between Barnabas and Paul. In Acts, the two separate over the question of travel with Barnabas's nephew, John Mark (15:36-40). This reason looks suspicious, because Luke nowhere reports the more likely occasion for the division, the so called incident at Antioch (see Baur, *Paul* 1:134-35 [147]). But this is a matter worthy of reconsideration. It may be that the split between Barnabas and Paul has been overplayed (e.g., "the break between Paul and . . .

19

Furthermore, the description of the duties of the Seven raises questions. Although their reputation seems to have been made by preaching (see 6:8-11, and 8:5-40), the work to which they are assigned by Luke is "to wait on tables" (6:2). The conclusion here, as above, is that Luke has rendered innocuous what would otherwise have been an offense: the fact that the Seven were a group of outstanding leaders of the earliest Jerusalem church who may even have rivaled the Twelve in popular recognition and authority. If this is regarded as something of an overstatement, it is in any case supposed by a majority of contemporary scholars that they were the leaders of a separate party that differed from the Hebrews (or "Hebraists") in ideological/theological terms;[5] being Hellenists, they quickly came to realize (in a way that the Hebrews could not) that the law and the temple had become superfluous in light of the sacrifice of Christ. Such, it is claimed, is the view expressed in the speech of their representative, Stephen, and the reason why they, and not the Hebrews, were persecuted by the Jewish authorities.

This latter assertion is based upon Acts 8:1b: Ἐγένετο δὲ ἐν ἐκείνῃ τῇ ἡμέρᾳ διωγμὸς μέγας ἐπὶ τὴν ἐκκλησίαν τὴν ἐν Ἱεροσολύμοις, πάντες δὲ διεσπάρησαν κατὰ τὰς χώρας τῆς Ἰουδαίας καὶ Σαμαρείας πλὴν τῶν ἀποστόλων. (That day a severe persecution began against the church in Jerusalem; and all except the apostles were scattered throughout the countryside of Judea and Samaria.) The phrase πλὴν τῶν ἀποστόλων (except the apostles) is thought to mean, in reality, "except the *party* of the apostles, the Hebrews." Therefore a distinction was made by the Jewish leaders: the radical, offensive Hellenists were persecuted, but the more compliant, conservative Hebrews were left alone.

In summary, we may quote Hengel's own rehearsal of the now traditional solution to the difficulties of the passage, a statement that he rightly claims reflects a "relatively widespread unanimity" of scholarly support.

> The "Seven" are in reality not men who care for the poor, subordinate to the "Twelve," but the leading group of an independent community, the "Hellenists." . . . The persecution after the death of Stephen evidently affected only the Hellenists; the Hebrews were hardly touched by it. Like the Twelve (cf. 8:1), they remained in Jerusalem. The Hellenists who were expelled thus became the real founders of the mission to the Gentiles, in which circumcision and observance of the ritual law were no longer required.[6]

This reconstruction relies essentially upon three types of evidence to support its view that the Hellenists were distinguished from the Hebrews on the basis of their theology. The first is the belief that Hellenists as *Hellenists*

Barnabas . . . was irreparable" [Hans Dieter Betz, *Galatians: A Commentary on Paul's Letter to the Churches in Galatia*, p. 104]). The way in which Paul refers to Barnabas in 1 Cor. 9:6 seems to imply that at some point the two returned to their former relationship.

[5] See, for example, Robin Scroggs, "The Earliest Hellenistic Christianity," p. 180.
[6] Hengel, *Between*, p. 13 [175, 176].

would differ in predictable ways from their Hebrew coreligionists. The second is that the Hellenists alone were persecuted in Jerusalem. The third is that the theology of the Hellenists was demonstrably different: Stephen spoke out against the law and the temple, and his followers accepted uncircumcised Gentiles into the church, no longer requiring "observance of the ritual law."

The first of these claims may be dismissed in principle. As the Introduction makes clear, it is no longer possible to differentiate blithely between Hellenistic and Palestinian perspectives. We cannot assume a priori that a group composed of Diaspora Jews would differ as *a block* from Palestinian Jews. It is far more reasonable to suppose that there were broad differences of opinion within both groups, as in fact we shall see the evidence attests.

The last argument is without doubt the most complicated of the three. Potentially the most important source of information about the theology of the Hellenists is Stephen's lengthy speech in Acts 7; this will be addressed in the following chapter. Second in importance is the evidence of Galatians 2:1-10 and 11-14 concerning the two known meetings of representatives of the churches of Jerusalem and Antioch.[7] The significance of these passages will be reviewed in chapter 4. In chapter 5 other possible sources of evidence will be considered, particularly as found within the Pauline corpus.

The second piece of evidence—the selective persecution of the Hellenists—occupies our attention in the present chapter. Although one may enter the debate about the Hellenists at any one of a number of points, the significance of Acts 8:1b can hardly be overstated. Time and time again scholars have appealed to the selective persecution of the Hellenists as the controlling datum in their interpretation of the rest of Acts 6:1—8:4.[8] Haenchen, for one, explicitly espouses this method in his interpretation of Acts 6:1-7. "But the tangle may not be so easily unravelled. One must begin at the other end, and this means looking beyond the passage under discussion. We are told in 8:1 that the whole primitive community, apart from the Apostles, was persecuted and dispersed.... This inference [i.e., that the Hellenists were selectively persecuted], once admitted, sets off a chain reaction."[9]

Fundamental problems undermine this approach that have not been adequately considered, however, problems that may call into question the whole of the traditional interpretation of the Hellenists. Therefore it seems

---

[7] That the account of Acts 15 refers to the same meeting described by Paul in Gal. 2:1-10 is defended in chap. 4 below.

[8] Even Heikki Räisänen, one of the most sensible interpreters of the Stephen story, who himself realizes that "the whole idea of a persecution in Jerusalem" is dubious, grounds his speculations about the theology of the Hellenists on the question of sufficient reason for their selective persecution. "In any case there must have been a reason for his [i.e., Stephen's] death concrete enough to cause harm to the Hellenists but not to the Hebrews" (*The Torah and Christ*, pp. 249, 267).

[9] Haenchen, *Acts*, p. 266 [219].

proper to initiate our discussion of the distinctiveness of the Hellenists at its most critical point, the "severe persecution" of Acts 8:1b.

Before proceeding to the larger issue, however, we consider some preliminary matters. Specifically, we examine the difficulties associated with Luke's choice of terminology (the opposition of the unusual Ἑλληνισταί [Hellenists] with Ἑβραῖοι [Hebrews]) and his somewhat peculiar narrative on the appointment of the Seven, in Acts 6:1-7. We also consider the question of responsibility for the death of Stephen, since it is presumed that those accountable are also implicated in the persecution of Stephen's fellows, the Hellenists. The first pair of concerns in particular, while of interest in themselves and certainly of relevance to the meaning of Acts 8:1b, are in practice so thoroughly influenced by prior interpretation of that passage that we need only discuss them briefly. Obviously, the position one takes on the term "Hellenist" and one's notion of the author's redactional activity in the passage are inextricably linked with one's prior understanding of the distinctiveness of the Hellenists, the best evidence for which is their persecution by the Jews.[10] So the question of persecution—and of what we can claim to know from it—rightly occupies the central place in our discussion.

"HELLENISTS" OR "HELLENIZERS"?

It has often been claimed that Luke's choice of the term Ἑλληνιστής (Hellenist) in Acts 6:1 supports the view that these Hellenists were a distinct ideological group within the early church.[11] Accordingly, what is taken to be Hellenistic about them is their particularly Greek perspective, which, when applied by them to the interpretation of Jesus, led to the development of two disparate parties within the Jerusalem church. Laying aside for the moment the larger question of what we may know of the Hellenists from other sources, is there anything in the designation Ἑλληνιστής itself that would lead us to such a conclusion?

Much to his credit, Martin Hengel has provided us with the answer: No; there is not. In a careful analysis of the debate[12] (one, I might add, that

---

[10] Note the observation of Lake and Cadbury on attempts to interpret the terms Ἑλληνισταί and Ἑβραῖοι: "This is one of the places where the context must determine meaning rather than the meaning illuminate the context" (*The Beginnings of Christianity*, part 1, *The Acts of the Apostles* 4:64). Similarly, Johannes Bihler concluded, "If, however, the lifestyle or the philosophy of life should be thought to have been the distinguishing mark between Hebrews and Hellenists, that would probably also have to be made explicit in the context, and this is not the case" (*Die Stephanusgeschichte im Zusammenhang der Apostelgeschichte*, p. 218).

[11] See, for example, Oscar Cullmann, "The Significance of the Qumran Texts for Research into the Beginnings of Christianity," pp. 220-21.

[12] Hengel, *Between*, pp. 4-11 [157-72]. See also Haenchen's conclusion and useful bibliography (*Acts*, pp. 259-61 [213-15]; see especially n. 3). Three articles on the identity of the Hellenists deserve particular mention. The first is Henry J. Cadbury's "The Hellenists" (in

does nothing to benefit his larger thesis),[13] Hengel demonstrates that the term Ἑλληνιστής (Hellenist) was used by Luke in contradistinction to Ἑβραῖος (Hebrew) only as a way of indicating those Jews in Jerusalem, presumably from the Diaspora, who spoke Greek as their native language.[14] Indeed, Luke used this contrast only when speaking of Jews and then only in the context of Jerusalem (where his other, more customary distinction between Ἕλλην [Greek] and Ἰουδαῖος [Jew] obviously would not have applied). This makes perfect sense and is true both to the linguistic and to the textual evidence.

Although Hengel's presentation is convincing, the case can be strengthened. First, it might be noted that the Hellenists often are treated as though they were an identifiably *Christian* group. But Luke uses the term only twice,[15] and in the second instance it refers unquestionably to anti-Christian Greek-speaking Jews (9:29). Now if, as has been claimed, the offense of the "Stephen group"[16] was their liberal interpretation of the law or temple,[17] one would suppose that the group that persecuted them did so out of a conservative interest in those very issues. And who might these intolerant conservatives have been? According to Acts, they were none other than fellow

---

Beginnings 5), in which it is proposed that the Hellenists were Gentile converts to Christianity. This view has won few adherents because of the unlikelihood (especially in light of the controversies of Acts 10–11 and 15) that Gentiles were admitted into the Jerusalem church at such an early date.

One of the most comprehensive treatments of the subject was provided by Everett Ferguson in his "Hellenists in the Book of Acts." After considering the various options, Ferguson argued for the view that the Hellenists were "Graecizers" (p. 176)—whether Jewish or Gentile. I do not find his presentation convincing because, among other things, it does not account adequately for the fact that the supposedly Graecized Hellenists were the most adamant opponents of the "liberal" views of both Stephen and Paul (note the attempt to surmount this objection on p. 179).

Perhaps the most influential article on the subject is C. F. D. Moule's "Once More, Who Were the Hellenists?" Moule suggested that the Hellenists were "Jews who spoke *only* Greek," while the Hebrews were those "who, while able to speak Greek, knew a Semitic language *also*" (p. 100). While Moule's precise definitions may or may not be accurate (the second is particularly speculative), the fundamental point he argued remains: the distinction between Hellenists and Hebrews was a matter of language and not ideology.

[13] See below the discussion of Hengel's position on the role of the Pharisees in the death of Stephen.

[14] This interpretation goes back at least to John Chrysostom, who proposed it in Homilies 14 and 21 on the Acts of the Apostles, in reference to Acts 6:1 and 9:29 (*Saint Chrysostom: Homilies on the Acts of the Apostles and the Epistle to the Romans*, pp. 88 and 135). See Hengel, *Between*, p. 137 [160], n. 37. It is impossible to say on the basis of Acts 6 whether the Christian Hellenists were permanent residents of Jerusalem. The safest assumption is that some were and others were not.

[15] For a discussion of Acts 11:20, see Hengel, *Between*, p. 8 [164–65].

[16] On the characterization of Stephen as leader of the Hellenists, see chap. 3 below.

[17] James D. G. Dunn, for example, reflecting on the attitude of the Hebrews and the Hellenists to the law and the temple, says, "In effect we have uncovered in part at least the first division between two types of Christian—conservative and liberal" (*Unity and Diversity in the New Testament: An Inquiry into the Character of Earliest Christianity*, p. 275; see also pp. 273–75).

Hellenists (6:9 as in 9:29, a fact to which we shall return below). So much for the notion of a monolithic Hellenist perspective. We can only agree fully with Hengel's surprising statement: "'Hellenistic' Judaism was even less a clearly definable, unitary entity than Palestinian Judaism. . . . The only link was the Greek language, the Greek Bible and Greek synagogue worship."[18]

Luke's wider use of the term "Hellenist" leads to a second difficulty for the traditional interpretation. While one might be willing to accept on the basis of one verse in Acts the existence of a small, otherwise unattested Christian party, Luke has not so limited its membership. It must also be an identifiable, ideologically based party within Judaism itself. How willing would most scholars be to accept, without corroboration, the claim that such a party existed?

This leads to a final observation. Luke, as we have seen, uses the term Ἑλληνιστής (Hellenist) within the context of Jerusalem. How does he identify the Hellenists outside of Jerusalem, when they are no longer being distinguished from the Hebrews? The answer is that he invariably brings up their nationality. For instance, the next time we meet a specific group of Hellenists after the events in Jerusalem is in 11:19-20, where they are known to us as men of Cyprus and Cyrene.

Beyond this, Luke seems to employ the term in his descriptions of Jerusalem to avoid confusion and repetition, having ever and always to say "Jews of such and such a place." The Christian Ἑλληνιστής (Hellenist) Stephen is opposed by some of those who belonged to the synagogue of the Freedmen (as it was called), Cyrenians, Alexandrians, and others of those from Cilicia and Asia—in other words, by fellow Hellenists. Similarly, Paul's life is threatened in 9:29, although this time it is the antagonists themselves who are called Ἑλληνισταί. The next time Paul is confronted by Jews in Jerusalem is in 21:27, where his opponents are identified as the Jews from Asia. In fact, in every case in which Greek-speaking Jews, Christian or otherwise, are met in Jerusalem in Acts, they are either identified as Hellenists or else distinguished by their homeland.[19] By far the simplest explanation is that Luke has used Ἑλληνιστής interchangeably with "Greek-speaking Jew from the Diaspora." That, and that alone, is the significance of the term.

THE APPOINTMENT OF THE SEVEN

The account of Acts 6:1-7 has been assailed on the grounds that its portrayal of the Seven is out of keeping with their actual duties and prominence

---

[18] Hengel, *Between*, p. 12 [173].
[19] The introduction of Paul (who, according to Luke, was a bilingual resident of Jerusalem; Acts 22:2-3) in 8:1 being the exception. Cf. Luke's presentation of Barnabas in 4:36 and the description of the crowd on the Day of Pentecost in 2:5, 9-11.

within the early church. Before considering the matter, it is worth discussing a more fundamental (and much more widely neglected) historical problem: what to make of the fact that Luke's narrative appears to have been modeled on the story of the appointment of Moses' assistants in Exodus 18:13-27 (= Deut. 1:9-18).

David Daube has outlined the parallels between the two accounts in his article "A Reform in Acts and Its Models."[20] These include the multiplication of the people (Deut. 1:9-10 / Acts 6:1), the neglect of the leader's true work and the recognition that such neglect "is not good" (Exod. 18:17-23 / Acts 6:2), the suggestion that wise and reputed men be chosen to settle the dispute(s) (Deut. 1:13 / Acts 6:3), the positive reception of the idea (Deut. 1:14 / Acts 6:5), and its subsequent success (Exod. 18:26-27, Deut. 1:11 / Acts 6:7).

Daube also highlighted similarities between the appointment of the seventy elders in Numbers 11 and the appointment of the Seven in Acts. The most intriguing of these is the story of Eldad and Medad (vv. 26-30), who received the Spirit and prophesied in the camp. This brings to mind the Spirit-endowed ministries of Stephen and Philip. We might even imagine that the emphasis on the Spirit in Acts 6 and 7 is a deliberate response to Moses' statement in Numbers 11:29, "Would . . . that the LORD . . . put his spirit on them [all]!"[21] Furthermore, it is striking that Numbers 11 opens with an account of the "murmuring" (γογγύζων) of the people, which, in verses 4-6, is then focused explicitly on the issue of food (i.e., the daily distribution of manna).

It is extraordinarily difficult to judge how such literary modeling as is apparent in Acts 6:1-7 impinges on the question of historicity.[22] Daube merely observes that "this particular mode of composition is no ground for treating them [i.e., the events in question] as invented."[23] Doubtless it is legitimate to say that one cannot *assume* the fabrication of such events. Nevertheless, it must be said also that the modeling of one account on another *necessarily* raises the question of the extent to which events have been altered or added to suit the narrative paradigm.

A variety of tests may be employed in judging the historical credibility of such an account. These include (1) the presence of corroborating or conflicting evidence, (2) the historical probability of the event(s), (3) one's impression of the author's veracity and/or historical accuracy, (4) the specificity

---

[20] Supplementing Daube's work is the (somewhat more speculative) article of J. D. McCaughey, "The Intention of the Author: Some Questions about the Exegesis of Acts 6:1-6."
[21] One is reminded as well of Peter's sermon on the Day of Pentecost (Acts 2:17).
[22] Earl Richard observes: "One is never quite sure whether Luke has chosen carefully his OT texts to reinforce his ideas and his view of history, or whether the composition results, in large part, from a serious reading of the Jewish scriptures and meditation upon their meaning for the spread of Christianity" ("The Creative Use of Amos by the Author of Acts," p. 52).
[23] Daube, "Reform," p. 159.

of the agreements between the accounts, (5) the extent of the agreements, and (6) the extent to which the accounts differ or to which the later account supplies information not available in its model.

Despite a lack of relevant supplementary evidence (and dismissing for now the larger question of Lukan veracity or accuracy, which would require considerably more space than is available here), it seems to me that, on balance, Acts 6:1-7 stands up to these tests. The event it records is (as I shall argue below) historically probable. Moreover, the account supplies us with sufficient independent information[24] to be considered credible—or, at least, to deserve the benefit of the doubt. One must, nevertheless, remain open to the possibility that major features of the account have their source not in early Christian tradition but in the Old Testament.

As we have noted, much has been made of the reputed inconsistencies in the description of Stephen and Philip in Acts 6–8. But the degree to which Luke's account *is* inconsistent is a moot point; it depends finally upon how one wishes to color it. If one takes the apostles' statement in 6:2 to mean that the leaders of the Hellenists were henceforth meant to spend their time waiting on tables and, furthermore, were proscribed from preaching the word, then there is indeed significant difficulty in reconciling these verses with the report of the activity of Stephen and Philip in chapters 6–8. But surely this is to take the most extreme reading possible.[25] It is wholly natural to assume that the Greek-speaking Christians of Jerusalem would have had leaders. (Did the Twelve preach in Greek?) Luke's description in 6:3 does not debase them but presupposes their recognition and authority ("seven men of good standing, full of the spirit and of wisdom"). It was, after all, a Jewish practice to set up boards of seven men to administer some task.[26] It is also entirely reasonable to suppose that the "daily distribution," whatever that consisted of, would in a short time have become a considerable burden of responsibility. We are told repeatedly in Acts that individual believers sold their possessions and gave the money to the apostles to be distributed (2:44-45; 4:34-35, 36-37; 5:1-10). That the Jerusalem church had many poor in its care is confirmed by mention of the collection in Galatians 2:10 and elsewhere (e.g., 2 Cor. 8:1-15; see v. 14 τὸ ἐκείνων ὑστέρημα "their need"). The creation of a board of leaders to deal with so difficult a problem strikes me as eminently realistic, not fantastic. There is no reason to take the

---

[24] I refer in particular to the names of the Seven. The question of the presence of traditional elements in Acts 6:1–8:4 will be taken up in some detail in chap. 3 below.

[25] As we just saw, Luke quite possibly had in mind the model of Num. 11, in which persons appointed as assistants exercised a form of Spirit-inspired ministry.

[26] David Daube, *The New Testament and Rabbinic Judaism*, p. 237; and I. Howard Marshall, *Acts*, p. 126. See Haenchen: "There is possibly some connection here with a Jewish institution, for in Jewish communities the local council usually consisted of seven men known as the 'Seven of the Town' or the 'Seven Best of the Town'" (*Acts*, p. 263 [216]). See also Josephus, *Ant.* 4.287; *J.W.* 2.568-71.

understandably hyperbolic statement of verse 2 so literally as to suppose that the Seven were meant to spend their time as busboys and waiters.[27] And the fact that the apostles were set apart to devote themselves "to prayer and to serving the word" cannot be assumed to preclude prayer and ministry on the part of others. It is not an either/or; it is simply the recognition of their unique status as the disciples of Jesus. The ministry of the Twelve *was* special, and so was it considered by those of the early church.[28]

It has been argued that the account of the distribution cannot be accurate, since such charity would already have been available to the widows of Acts 6:1 through the synagogue.[29] Any specifically Christian relief would therefore have been necessary, according to Haenchen, only "if they [the widows] were no longer supported by the relief arrangements of the Jewish community. In other words, it presupposes a lengthy evolution and an estrangement from the synagogue."[30]

In contrast to this, however, one may cite Martin Goodman's assertion that private charity was common in Jerusalem in this period and, moreover, that it played a significant role in the shaping of Jewish society. "The result in Jerusalem was that the rich kept in their midst a host of shiftless poor sustained just above the breadline by private charity."[31] It should be noted how well suited to this context are passages such as Acts 2:45 and 4:37, as well as 6:1.

In any case, we must account for the fact that, by the time of the so-called Apostolic Conference, such assistance plainly was necessary (Gal. 2:10). If the practice began only then—that is, after the period described in Acts 6—then it becomes (by Haenchen's reckoning) evidence of "estrangement from the Jewish community" on the part of the *Hebrews*. This is, of course, the opposite of the point that Haenchen would wish to make elsewhere concerning the distinctiveness of the Hellenist and the Hebrew parties.

Finally, it should be noted that numerous other possibilities exist as to the exact details of the story.[32] The Seven, for example, might have concerned

---

[27] See Jacquier, *Les Actes*, pp. 184, 186.

[28] Consider, for example, the way in which the authority of the Jerusalem apostles plays a role in events in Antioch and Galatia.

[29] On the presence of Greek-speaking synagogue communities in Jerusalem in the first century, see Morton Smith, "Palestinian Judaism," p. 73 ("Palestine was not devoid of Jews from the Diaspora and these, too, formed separate communities"). It is not necessary here to settle the debate as to the number of synagogue communities (if that indeed is what they are) indicated by Acts 6:9.

[30] Haenchen, *Acts*, p. 262 [215].

[31] Martin Goodman, *The Ruling Class of Judaea*, pp. 65–66. For a more detailed critique of Haenchen's position, see David Seccombe, "Was There Organized Charity in Jerusalem before the Christians?"

[32] Assuming, of course, that the story does reflect historical fact. The parallel with Moses mentioned above may make one suspicious of the details of the account (see the discussion of

themselves only with the distribution among the Hellenists. In that case, the ἐξ ὑμῶν ("from among yourselves") of verse 3 would have been addressed solely to the body of Hellenists. It is also possible that the disciples had already delegated this responsibility to a group of Hebrews who had done an inadequate job serving the needs of the Hellenist community. The exasperated statement of the apostles would then be not unlike the statement of Jesus in Luke 12:14, "Friend, who set me to be a judge or arbitrator over you?"

Even if this view is wrong, and Luke is portraying Stephen and Philip in a way that obscures their respective ministries, we would still need to explain why. Luke indeed downplays conflict within his account of the early church. But he is even more interested in tying all new movements to the Jerusalem leadership. He is concerned with unity of *authority* as much as he is with unity of *doctrine*. The Seven are recognized by Jerusalem, as is Philip independently (8:14),[33] Peter's ministry to the Gentiles (11:1-18), Paul's ministry (15:22-29), and the ministry of the Hellenists at Antioch (11:22-26). Whatever the motive for Luke's interest in the centrality of Jerusalem, it is a theme common to Acts as a whole. In any case, we cannot say that, *if* Luke elevates the Twelve at the expense of the Seven, his motive is necessarily embarrassment at the theological distinctiveness and divisiveness of the Seven. At the least, such a distinction would have first to be proved on other, firmer grounds.

THE OPPONENTS OF STEPHEN

Who was responsible for the death of Stephen? The question is more puzzling than it may at first appear. Martin Hengel, among others, has pointed out the difficulties, but has not, I think, fully realized their implications.[34] The immediate antagonists, those who foment the uproar at which Stephen is seized, are apparently a group of fellow Hellenists, "some of those who belonged to the synagogue of the Freedman (as it was called),[35] Cyrenians, Alexandrians, and others of those from Cilicia and Asia" (6:9). This is as we would anticipate: if Stephen, preaching in Greek, met with opposition, we would expect the disturbance to have arisen from within the

---

7:37 in chap. 3 below), though the occasion for the appointment of the Seven as Luke records it seems plausible.

[33] Note that the story of the conversion of the Ethiopian (Acts 8:26-40) contains no reference to the Jerusalem church.

[34] Hengel, *Between*, pp. 19-24 [186-96]. Hengel also offers a helpful bibliography on the question (p. 150 [180], n. 130). See also Haenchen, *Acts*, p. 295 [246]; and Earl Richard, *Author's Method*, pp. 19-22.

[35] Freedmen or "Libertines" were probably "Roman prisoners (or the descendants of such prisoners) who had later been granted their freedom" (Marshall, *Acts*, p. 129).

Greek-speaking Jewish community.³⁶ But Luke does not leave the account there. In verse 12 τὸν λαὸν καὶ τοὺς πρεσβυτέρους καὶ τοὺς γραμματεῖς (the people as well as the elders and the scribes) are brought into the story. These take Stephen to the Sanhedrin, where he offers his defense before the high priest. The proceedings are most peculiar, for in the end (7:54-60; 58b being the exception) the council disappears and a "mob action" again ensues, this time resulting in Stephen's death. As Hengel puts it, the scene "fluctuates between an orderly trial before the Sanhedrin and a stormy example of lynch-law."³⁷

This peculiarity has led scholars to regard either the trial or the lynching features of the narrative as secondary. Hengel is among the majority who conclude that the reported meeting of the Sanhedrin is artificial; Luke uses it only "to give an effective framework for the speech." The incident occurs in the open air, and "all the discussions will have taken place in Greek."³⁸ Hence, the martyrdom of Stephen was not an act of Jewish officialdom but the violent result of tension within the Greek-speaking community. Haenchen echoes these sentiments:

> Now the pack is unleashed to hunt Stephen out of the city and stone him. Probably here a part of the older Martyrdom emerges, and it threatens to destroy the framework which Luke has so ingeniously, painstakingly constructed: that of ostensibly legal proceedings before the High Council. . . . He had no idea how judicial stonings were carried out — we know the details from the Mishnah tractate *Sanhedrin:* the condemned man . . . is pushed by the first witness off the brink of a steep drop; if this does not finish him the second witness lets fall a boulder on his chest. . . . Luke has in mind quite a different kind of stoning . . . the kind of thing which happened in the East when a man was stoned by a riotous mob, and this is probably how the story was told in the original Martyrdom (though we no longer have any means of restoring its text).³⁹

Haenchen also makes a number of other points in favor of this proposal. The mention of witnesses and the (inaccurate)⁴⁰ reference to the removal of their garments in 7:58b provide Luke with the mechanism he needs for the introduction of Paul to the story, a historically dubious association.⁴¹ Accepting that Stephen died as a result of mob action also frees us

---

³⁶ Those who, as in the case of Paul, would be responsible for disciplining their own.
³⁷ Hengel, *Between,* p. 20 [188].
³⁸ Ibid., p. 20 [189]. See Baur: "That Stephen was seized and stoned in a tumultuous insurrection is indisputably the best-established fact with which we have to deal" (*Paul* 1:56 [63]).
³⁹ Haenchen, *Acts,* pp. 295–96 [247].
⁴⁰ "In the official procedure it was the condemned man who was stripped; but Luke assumes that the witnesses would have to remove their outer garments" (ibid., p. 296 [247]).
⁴¹ I am inclined to agree with those who see in Gal. 1:22 an insurmountable obstacle to the belief that Paul persecuted the church in Jerusalem. See n. 62 below.

from the need to reconcile his death with the inaction of the Roman cohorts[42] and with the possibility that the Sanhedrin exceeded its authority in executing Stephen.[43] Additionally, we may cite other references in Acts to the state of relations between Christian and non-Christian Hellenists, such as the stories concerning Paul's conflicts with fellow Greek-speaking Jews in 9:28-30 and 21:27-32. We should also remember that Paul, the one persecutor of the church about whom we have primary source material, was himself a Greek-speaking Jew. We therefore know independently from Acts that such tensions existed within at least some of the Diaspora communities at a very early date.[44]

But the trial narrative does have its defenders.[45] In particular, it is argued that only the circumstances of a trial could make sense of Stephen's speech.[46] Clearly, no mob would be expected to stand back dispassionately while Stephen offered his lengthy recitation of the history of Israel.[47]

This argument leads to an interesting observation: there is a close correspondence between one's perspective on the authenticity of the Stephen speech and one's willingness to accept the genuineness of the trial narrative. For example, it is no accident that Haenchen and Hengel both believe the

---

[42] "The pursuit began somewhere in the warren of alleys which Roman military police were powerless to penetrate (cf. 23.21)" (Haenchen, *Acts*, pp. 296-97 [248]).

[43] Some scholars date the incident to the year 37 (i.e., following Pilate's recall) for this reason (ibid., p. 297 [248]). Others, such as F. F. Bruce (citing Josephus, *J.W.* 6.124-26), are not convinced: in the case of "offenses against the sanctity of the temple . . . the Sanhedrin was allowed to pronounce and execute the death sentence" (*Peter, Stephen, James, and John*, p. 53). The Josephus reference, however, is the exception that proves the rule. The Jews had the right to put offenders to death only in this one specific case (that is, Gentiles ["even . . . a Roman"] who pass the barrier into the temple). This is confirmed by the deposition of Ananus following the death of James (*Ant.* 20.200-203) and by the necessity of drawing Pilate into the trial of Jesus (Matt. 27; Mark 15; Luke 23; John 18-19).

Note, however, Origen's response to a question of Africanus ("How could they who were in captivity pass the sentence of death?"): "Private trials are held according to their [i.e., the Jews'] law, and some are condemned to death. And though there is not full licence for this, still it is not done without the knowledge of the ruler, as we learned and were convinced of when we spent much time in the country of that people" ("Letter to Africanus," chap. 14, in *The Writings of Origen* 1:385). On the question of *die Blutgerichtsbarkeit* of a sanhedrin, see Hengel, *Between*, p. 150 [188], n. 131.

[44] In the case of the Hellenists at Jerusalem, one wonders if the fact that they had chosen to come to the holy city tells us anything about their propensity for intolerance. It may be that their emotions were heightened to a degree that those of native Judaeans, who may have seen things with a bit more detachment, were not (see F. J. Foakes Jackson, *The Acts of the Apostles*, p. 57).

[45] See, for example, F. F. Bruce (*Peter, Stephen, James, and John*, pp. 52-53) and I. Howard Marshall (*Acts*, p. 148).

[46] It is equally possible to argue on the basis of this observation for the artificiality of the speech itself (see, for example, L. Wolff's 1847 article "Der Bericht der Apostelgeschichte über Stephanus vertheidigt gegen die Angriffe Baur's," pp. 88-89).

[47] Johannes Weiss considered this aspect of the Stephen story to demonstrate narrative *Geschmacklosigkeit* ("Das Judenchristentum in der Apostelgeschichte und das sogenannte Apostelkonzil," p. 498).

speech to be an intrusive Lukan addition to the traditional narrative.⁴⁸ If one takes the speech to be a more or less accurate historical record,⁴⁹ then one does feel compelled to account for its occasion, and an orderly trial (albeit one ending in a degree of chaos) seems the more likely alternative.

In light of the criticisms mentioned above and of my estimation of the Stephen speech,⁵⁰ I consider it more probable that Stephen was put to death as a direct result of unrest within the Greek-speaking Jewish community. Whether or not this is granted, however, one additional consideration remains that makes the choice of either of the available conclusions more tenuous still. This is the possibility that the combination of trial and lynching elements is attributable to Luke's own stylistic tendency. According to Earl Richard: "Their concomitant appearance does not, however, surprise the careful reader of Acts. Indeed, in 16:19f. and 19:24f. individuals incite the crowds, who in turn drag Paul (and others) before a magistrate where they voice their accusations. Furthermore, the mixture to some degree of mob rule and law-and-order is commonplace in Acts (see 17:5f., 18:12f., 21:18f.). In some cases Jewish officials form part of an unruly crowd (4:1f., 5:17f., 6:12f.)."⁵¹

A further and particularly interesting example is the presence of mob elements in the account of Paul's trial before the Sanhedrin in 22:30 – 23:10. "As a result of the great στάσεως [dissension] between the Sadducees and Pharisees (23:10), it is necessary to send in the troops to take Paul by force ... lest he be torn to pieces, διασπάω. Clearly one is dealing with literary technique rather than awkward compilation or editing of sources."⁵²

I prefer as more reasonable the belief that the death of Stephen was caused by non-Christian Hellenists and not by Jewish authorities. If so, it must be admitted that Stephen's death tells us nothing about how the theology of the Hebrews may have differed from that of the Hellenists. Richard's criticism, however, does caution us to leave the door open to the alternative possibility that Luke's account is accurate in portraying the death of Stephen as, at least in part, an official act. We shall soon see, however, that either possibility leads us to the same conclusion: the persecution of Stephen and the Hellenists does *not* demonstrate their theological independence.

---

⁴⁸ Hengel, *Between*, p. 19 [186–87]; Haenchen, *Acts*, pp. 286–90 [238–41]. See also Étienne Trocmé, *Le "Livre des Actes" et l'histoire*, pp. 185–86. See the discussion of the Stephen speech in chap. 3 below.
⁴⁹ As do Bruce (*Peter, Stephen, James, and John*, p. 53) and, to a lesser extent, Marshall (*Acts*, pp. 132–34).
⁵⁰ I.e., that it is a Lukan composition. See chap. 3 below.
⁵¹ Richard, *Author's Method*, pp. 280–81.
⁵² Ibid., p. 281.

THE "SEVERE PERSECUTION" OF ACTS 8:1b

A variety of reconstructions of the events recorded in Acts 8:1b and following is possible. Although these are not all equally plausible, we shall consider each of them in turn in order to demonstrate that none supports what is by now a traditional view of the Hellenists.

Figure 1. Questions about the "Severe Persecution"

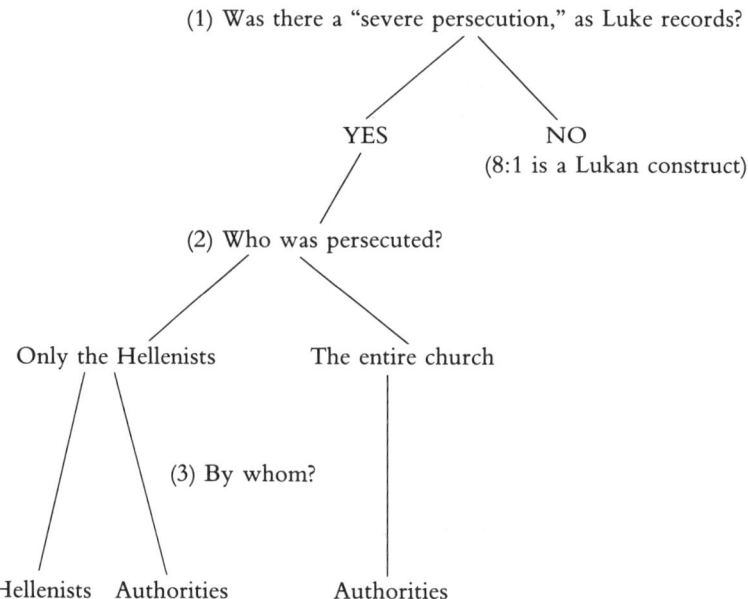

The alternatives are outlined as follows in figure 1. We begin by assuming an answer of yes to question (1). Acts 8:1b is, therefore, taken to be historically accurate; some type of large-scale persecution of the church did occur at this time. But—question (2)—who, specifically, was persecuted? The first and most popular option would be to conclude that opposition was aroused only against the Hellenists. If so—question (3)—who were their persecutors? One alternative is to imagine that the Hellenists were opposed by fellow Hellenists (that is, Greek-speaking Jews). As we have already seen, there is reason to suppose that this was indeed the case, especially if we regard the trial scene in 6:12—7:1 as secondary.

One notable advantage of this approach is the ease with which it accounts for a selective persecution of the Hellenist Christians: the non-Christian Hellenists attacked those disturbing their community, acting spontaneously (as in the mob action of Acts 6:8-12 and 7:54-60) or acting perhaps in recognition of their responsibility to discipline their own.[53]

However reasonable this may seem, it must be noted that such an "intra-Hellenist conflict"[54] would not have constituted a διωγμὸς μέγας ("severe persecution") in Lukan terms. As Luke has it, the persecution is directed from the top: the high priest himself sits in judgment of Stephen (7:1) and authorizes Paul's persecution of the church (9:1-2).

There are obvious and practical reasons why a persecution by the Hellenists should have been limited to the Hellenists. Is there, still further, an *ideological* reason for its limitation? In other words, did the Hellenist Jews fail to persecute the Hebrew Christians because they were considered to be less radical than the Hellenist Christians? Apart from the fact that such a motive is unverifiable (since it is based upon an argument from silence),[55] it does seem inherently unlikely. To imagine otherwise is, again, to assume the conditions of the "severe persecution" of Acts 8:1-3,[56] in which authority is exercised systematically (since acceptable and unacceptable Jewish Christians must be distinguished) to punish offenders throughout Jerusalem and beyond. But if one feels compelled to move in this direction, is it not more reasonable simply to accept the facts as Luke presents them: that opposition begun within the Greek-speaking community of Jerusalem was subsequently taken up by the Jewish authorities? After all, unless the antagonists of Acts 8:1-3 were in a position to attempt a general persecution of the church, their failure to do so proves nothing.

It should also be noted that any theory of a persecution undertaken by Hellenists that distinguished between Christian Jews on ideological grounds would necessitate two entirely separate causes for the persecution of the church in Jerusalem, since the non-Christian Hellenists ignored the Hebrews in their attacks, whereas the chief priests did not. In fact, the further one pushes the theory of a general yet selective persecution by Hellenists, the more complicated and unbelievable the result becomes. One is left to imagine a state of affairs in which Hellenist synagogue officials or Hellenist mobs could continue (that is, beyond the death of Stephen) to do as they pleased across Jerusalem; in which the high priests and elders themselves took no interest in the resultant commotion, although it was reputed to

---

[53] According to Hengel, "Ethnic synagogue associations in Jerusalem certainly had the possibility of exercising discipline within the community. . . . It seems to me that the martyrdom of Stephen was connected with a synagogue assembly of this kind. No wonder that the Roman authorities did not intervene" (*Between*, p. 20 [189]). Note the synagogue punishment of Paul in 2 Cor. 11:24 and the warning in Mark 13:9. See also Sanders, *Paul, the Law, and the Jewish People*, pp. 190-92 ("Conflict with His Own People").

[54] As Dunn terms it (*Unity and Diversity*, p. 274).

[55] That is, that the Hellenists would not have persecuted (or punished, depending upon one's perspective) the Hebrews, even if they could have.

[56] In that case, the persecution of Christians was sponsored by a sanhedrin (6:12; 22:5) and the high priest himself (7:1; 9:1-2; 22:5; 26:10 [chief priests]).

concern both temple and law; and further, in which no appeal to higher authority was ever made, either by Hellenist or by Hebrew Christians (the Hebrews, for their part, being ready to sacrifice their Hellenist brethren to keep the peace).[57] If the Hellenists were selectively persecuted and if their persecutors were fellow Greek-speaking Jews, we are therefore left to admit that the persecution itself tells us nothing about the relationship between the Hellenist and the Hebrew Christians.

It is fascinating to see how close Hengel comes to drawing this very conclusion. He shows that the term "Hellenist" means "Greek-speaking." He determines that Stephen was lynched by a mob of fellow Hellenists and that the report of collusion on the part of the Jewish authorities is artificial and inaccurate. We would then naturally expect him to maintain that the involvement of Jewish officials in Luke's even sketchier "severe persecution" is equally contrived. But he does not. Instead, he has to find a way to turn the persecution over to some Jewish body with enough authority to make it "severe." Thus, it is not the chief priests who take up persecuting the Hellenists but the Pharisees.[58] This gets Hengel out of a second very serious bind that we shall have cause to return to again: if the Hellenists and the Hebrews were persecuted by the same persons (i.e., the high priest[s] and associates), then the appeal to persecution as evidence of ideological distinctiveness is invalidated. Therefore Hengel supposes that the Hellenists were persecuted by the Pharisees, while the Hebrews (before and after) were persecuted by the high priest.[59] This also allows Hengel to give the place he wishes to Paul's role in the death of Stephen and the persecution of Hellenist Christians in Jerusalem.

Hengel bases his conclusion on four assertions: (1) the trial scene before the high priest is an inauthentic Lukan addition; (2) the elders and scribes mentioned in 6:12 were members of the Greek-speaking "synagogue communities" (and, by Hengel's reading, must have included Pharisees in their number); (3) the term "Sanhedrin" can simply mean "assembly"; and (4) Paul (and so, by implication, his fellow Pharisees) was involved in the stoning of Stephen.[60] Even if we accept for the moment that Stephen was put to death by members of the Greek-speaking synagogue (that is, assuming point [1]

---

[57] Dunn speculates that "the Hebrew Christians had virtually *abandoned* Stephen, so antagonized were they by his views on the temple.... Perhaps they believed that Stephen had brought his fate upon his own head." Subsequently, "the Hellenist Christians who shared Stephen's views would have few friends to shelter them; whereas local Hebrew Christians still loyal to temple and law would be relatively secure" (*Unity and Diversity*, pp. 273, 274). Division (and even animosity) of such an extent between the groups seems to me to be quite incredible, particularly as it is not supported by any tradition or by the facts as we know them concerning the subsequent relationship between the churches of Antioch and Jerusalem (see chap. 4 below).

[58] Hengel is not the first to single out the Pharisees as the opponents of Stephen. See, for example, Zeller, *Acts* 1:238 [146]; and Schmidt, *Der Bericht*, p. 10.

[59] Hengel, *Between*, p. 21 [190].

[60] Ibid., p. 20 [189].

above), the connection Hengel proposes to make between the Pharisees and the death of Stephen is dubious.[61] If we read "Pharisees" into the "elders" and "scribes" of Acts 6:12, then what are we to make of 4:5, the only other occasion in Acts where οἱ πρεσβύτεροι καὶ οἱ γραμματεῖς are mentioned, and where these are without question members of *the* Sanhedrin (the "assembly" that, it might be added, flogged the disciples Peter and John)? Clearly, the only link between the death of Stephen and the opposition of the Pharisees is that suggested by the presence of Paul, a detail of the Acts account that is itself made doubtful by Paul's own statement in Galatians 1:22.[62]

It should also be noted that Hengel's proposal rests upon an older view of the Pharisees that credits them with more authority than they were likely to have had.[63] Would a mob of Hellenists, even if made up, in part, of Greek-speaking Pharisees, have made a "severe persecution"? I doubt it. Who would have had the power to authorize or to encourage persecution on such a scale? Luke knows the answer, for in Acts 9:1-2 we see Paul the Pharisee going to the high priest for permission to persecute the Christians.

Let us say then that Luke's account is accurate, that the Jewish authorities themselves were responsible for the persecution of Acts 8:1b. Moreover, let us assume that only the Hellenists were affected by this persecution.[64] This is the view most commonly held, and as we have just seen, it has a certain amount to commend it. It also leads us straight into the dilemma that Hengel tried with such astuteness to avoid. Stated more fully, the problem is this: the argument that uses the selective persecution of the Hellenists as evidence for their theological distinctiveness relies upon the

---

[61] See J. A. Ziesler, "Luke and the Pharisees," p. 147. Ziesler argues persuasively that "throughout Acts the Pharisees are shown in a favourable light as the 'political,' if not always theological, friends of the Church" (p. 148). The Pharisees do not figure in the trial of Jesus, and when they do appear at trials in Acts, they speak in support of the Christians (5:34-39; 23:6-10).

[62] That is, ἤμην δὲ ἀγνοούμενος τῷ προσώπῳ ταῖς ἐκκλησίαις τῆς Ἰουδαίας ταῖς ἐν Χριστῷ. That Paul could not have been in Jerusalem at the time of Stephen's death is challenged by Hengel on the grounds that the Hebrew and Hellenist Christian communities existed separately to such an extent that Paul would not have been known "by face" to the Hebrews (*Between*, pp. 153, n. 145, and p. 172, n. 39 ["Die Ursprünge der Christlichen Mission," p. 24, n. 35]). Such complete segregation of Hellenist and Hebrew Christians seems most unlikely. It is more reasonable to suppose that the reference to Paul in Acts 8 has been inserted erroneously by Luke into the Stephen story. See E. P. Sanders's criticism of Hengel in his review of *Between Jesus and Paul*, pp. 169-71.

[63] See Martin Goodman, *State and Society in Roman Galilee, A.D. 132-212*, chap. 7, "Rabbinic Authority in Galilee," pp. 93-118, and *The Ruling Class of Judaea: The Origins of the Jewish Revolt against Rome, A.D. 66-70*, p. 234; E. P. Sanders, *Jesus and Judaism*, pp. 188, 193-98, 312-17, and *Jewish Law from Jesus to the Mishnah: Five Studies*, pp. 255-308, 359-368; Jacob Neusner, *From Politics to Piety: The Emergence of Pharisaic Judaism*, pp. 143-54; Morton Smith, "Palestinian Judaism," pp. 73-81; and Robert A. Wild, "The Encounter between Pharisaic and Christian Judaism: Some Early Gospel Evidence," pp. 105-12, 123-24.

[64] That is, in reference to fig. 1 above, (1) there was a "severe persecution," (2) it affected only the Hellenists, and (3) it was authorized or promoted by the Jewish authorities.

straightforward assumption that persecution reveals opposition—aversion to what another is or says or does. One is persecuted, in other words, for a reason. The death of Stephen was not accidental homicide. Although Stephen had committed no criminal act deserving of death, something he represented or said or did was felt by his persecutors to be equally offensive. As for the Hellenists, this line of argument continues, they were persecuted (in this case, by the Jewish authorities) because of the offensiveness of their teaching. If it was not in response to their teaching, then there is simply no ground for supposing that their teaching differed substantially from that of the Hebrews.

But the reasoning that demonstrates the offensiveness of the Hellenists' teaching is one of the most powerful evidences for their *solidarity with* – and not their distinctiveness from—the Hebrews, for the Hebrews are, if anything, the more persecuted by these same Jewish leaders.[65] In 4:1-22, John and Peter are arrested by "the priests, the captain of the temple, and the Sadducees," taken before "rulers, elders and scribes . . . and Annas the high priest, Caiaphas, John, and Alexander, and all who were of the high-priestly family," and threatened.[66] In 5:17-41, the apostles are arrested by "the high priest . . . and all who were with him (that is, the sect of the Sadducees)" and, after having been miraculously freed, are sought and then summoned to appear "before the council [sanhedrin]," where they are beaten. In 12:1-11, we are told that Herod "laid violent hands upon some who belonged to the church." He killed James with the sword and then, "after he saw that it pleased the Jews,"[67] had Peter arrested as well. Again, Peter is miraculously delivered "from the hands of Herod and from all that the Jewish people were expecting" (v. 11) and, it seems likely, forced to flee Jerusalem (v. 17). If these do not suffice, we have the example of James, the brother of Jesus, by all accounts the leader of the Hebrews, put to death at the instigation of the high priest.[68] We also have the testimony of Paul in 1 Thessalonians 2:14-16 concerning the persecution of the churches "in Judea."[69] Finally, passages in

---

[65] Significantly, a large part of the first chapter of Baur's *Paul* (vol. 1, "The Church at Jerusalem before the Apostle's Conversion") is taken up with an attempt to deny the historicity of the persecutions of the apostles recorded in the first chapters of Acts (see especially p. 34 [40]). Baur claimed that Luke's "idealizing" (p. 16 [20]) of the apostles provides a sufficient account for the stories of their opposition: "The glorification of the Apostles is the aim to which everything tends. . . . [this] requires the enemies of the cause of Jesus to be represented as taking fresh steps . . . directed anew . . . [at] the Apostles" (p. 28 [33–34]). Baur failed, however, to apply the same skepticism to the persecution of Acts 8:1 (which, if anything, is the most idealized account of opposition in Acts), since, of course, he is able to claim that this persecution did not affect the apostles.

[66] Cf. also 4:23: οἱ ἀρχιερεῖς καὶ οἱ πρεσβύτεροι.

[67] Which Jews would Agrippa I have cared about pleasing? The natural assumption is that it was those of the ruling class.

[68] The death of James is treated more fully in chap. 5 below.

[69] The authenticity of 1 Thess. 2:14-16 is much disputed, largely because of its harshness toward the Jews (especially in comparison with Rom. 11:25-32) and because v. 16c, ἔφθασεν

the Synoptic Gospels appear to presuppose a state of persecution (Matt. 10:23, locating this in Israel specifically).⁷⁰ Therefore, if persecution may be taken to mean something in the case of the Hellenists (as it is by most scholars),⁷¹ then recurrent persecution of the Hebrews by these same Jewish leaders means something equally significant.

So the difficulty is unavoidable: either the Hellenists were opposed by the same persons who opposed the Hebrews, or the opposition they met was from fellow Hellenists and therefore was something less than the "severe persecution" of Acts 8:1b. In either case, the most basic of the arguments marshaled in support of the theological distinctiveness of the Hellenists is disallowed.

Up to this point we have assumed that the phrase "except the apostles" in Acts 8:1b precludes the possibility that the Hebrews were persecuted along with the Hellenists. Just to exhaust all possibilities, let us assume for the moment that there *was* a large-scale persecution and that it was not limited to the Hellenists (after all, Luke does say that it was against τὴν ἐκκλησίαν ("*the* church") and that πάντες ("all") except the apostles, were

---

δὲ ἐπ' αὐτοὺς ἡ ὀργὴ εἰς τέλος, has been taken to refer to the destruction of Jerusalem in 70 (see Baur, *Paul* 2:88 [97]). The genuineness of the passage is, however, defended by a number of scholars, in part on the basis of its textual attestation (which is univocal) and the presence of other passages, such as Phil. 3:2, in which the severity of Paul's polemic toward the Jews is paralleled. A helpful discussion along with a thorough review of the history of the question is provided by Raymond F. Collins in his *Studies on the First Letter to the Thessalonians*, chap. 3, "Apropos the Integrity of 1 Thess." (pp. 96–135).

Even assuming the authenticity of the passage, questions concerning its meaning remain. It is probably safe to say that we shall never know what, if any, particular event is the actual referent of v. 16c (the expulsion of the Jews from Rome is a popular candidate). Uncertainty also surrounds Paul's cryptic phrase καὶ ἡμᾶς ἐκδιωξάντων in v. 15, although I think it can be explained if one imagines that the setting has shifted at this point away from the activity of the Jews in Jerusalem to the Jewish opposition experienced by the apostle Paul, quite possibly in Thessalonica itself (Acts 17:5; see I. Howard Marshall, *1 and 2 Thessalonians*, p. 78). In any case, it is evident from the passage as a whole that the Jewish Christians of Judea had suffered some type of persecution at the hands of their συμφυλέται.

⁷⁰ E.g., Matt. 5:11-12, 44 (= Luke 6:27); 10:23; 23:34-36 (= Luke 11:49-51). See, for example, Francis Wright Beare, *The Gospel according to Matthew: A Commentary*, pp. 135–36, 162, 245, 458–59; and Robert H. Gundry, *Matthew: A Commentary on His Literary and Theological Art*, pp. 73–74, 97, 194–95, 470–73. Because of the difficulty (if not impossibility) of fixing individual elements of gospel tradition in time and space, I defer discussion of these potentially significant passages. I hope to take up the matter in detail in some future work.

⁷¹ Jacob Jervell's essay "The Acts of the Apostles and the History of Early Christianity" provides us with an interesting example. Jervell states that the "persecution of the Hellenists [was] caused by their attitude to the temple and the law and so to the Gentiles." He goes on to say that "a persecution of a strict law-pious church in Jerusalem is inexplicable" (p. 28). There is much to be said for at least this second assertion. What is curious, however, is Jervell's belief that such a "strict law-pious church in Jerusalem" actually existed (pp. 26–27). According to Jervell's presuppositions, only the Hellenists could have been persecuted. But this was not the case. Therefore, it follows that we should question the extent to which the church of Jerusalem was "strict" and "law-pious."

scattered). As we have seen, it is simpler to assume that such a persecution would have been carried out by the Jewish authorities and not by the anti-Christian Hellenists. Such a detail is hardly worth discussing, however, if we realize that any general persecution of the church that did not distinguish between Hellenist and Hebrew would only serve to underscore our conclusion: the Hellenists and Hebrews were not distinctive ideological groups.

It should be obvious that selective persecution would not necessarily mean that the group that was persecuted differed (here, theologically) from the group that was not. Other reasons might be adduced for the particularity of their misfortune (such as the enforcement of discipline within the Greek-speaking synagogues). In any case, I do not believe that the Hellenists were especially subject to *systematic* persecution, since I do not accept that the severe persecution of Acts 8 and 9 is literal historical fact.[72] Consider its function in Acts. The persecution comes at the beginning of chapter 8, one of the key transitions in Luke's story. From this verse onward the gospel goes forth from Jerusalem. It is also at this juncture that Luke introduces Paul, the one on whom most of the rest of the book will focus. Thus the brief mention of a persecution in 8:1b serves the author's purposes admirably: it takes us smoothly from the first martyrdom in Jerusalem to the introduction of the persecutor extraordinary, Paul, to the preaching of the gospel "throughout the countryside of Judea and Samaria" (8:1b; see also vv. 4-5), to the conversion of Paul (9:3-22), to the conversion of the first Gentile (chap. 10), to the Gentile mission (11:19-21), to the ministry of Paul (11:25-26). Luke is, as it were, setting up his pieces for the next game. It is in his design both to get the gospel out—"in all Judea and Samaria and to the end of the earth" (1:8)—and to keep the *apostles* (not the Hebrews) in, centered on Jerusalem where they belong. It is no coincidence that if we were left with Acts as our only source, we would know nothing of the wider travels of Cephas, "the other apostles and the brothers of the Lord" (1 Cor. 9:5). For whatever reason, Luke's Twelve need to keep their authoritative feet planted firmly in the holy city.[73]

Reflecting on Acts 8:1, I find it astonishing that scholars have rested so much weight on a single verse of such precariousness. The entire sequence

---

[72] Already a century and a half ago W. M. L. de Wette had characterized the account in 8:1 as *hyperbolisch* (*Kurze Erklärung der Apostelgeschichte*, p. 67).

[73] Johannes Weiss saw Acts 8:1b as "only a redactional expedient to explain how it came about that the church continued peacefully on its way in spite of everything. The same thing occurs here as in so many later descriptions in which the author can never say too much in picturing the horrors of persecution; one can hardly understand how any one could ever have been left alive" (*Earliest Christianity: A History of the Period A.D. 30–150* 1:170 [123]). While I accept the second half of this statement, I think that there is more significance to the verse than Weiss describes.

of events it initiates is bereft of historical realism.[74] Paul, the young man who stood by as junior partner at the stoning of Stephen, emerged immediately (8:3) as the church's chief adversary, "ravaging" it, "entering house after house," and "dragging off" men and women to prison. *All* are scattered, except the apostles, and enough others to bury Stephen and to be dragged out of their homes by Paul. Everyone else flees — into Judea and Samaria? Why would Greek-speaking Jews escape to the surrounding region of Judea and nearby Samaria? When Paul was likewise threatened in Jerusalem, we are told that he was whisked away by the church to Caesarea and then home to Tarsus (9:30), an eminently more sensible plan. Why scatter "throughout the region of Judea and Samaria"? The answer is simple; it is because of Acts 1:8b: "you will be my witnesses in Jerusalem, and in all Judea and Samaria." The Hellenists leave Palestine only after the completion of the next stage of Luke's program. Philip must first preach to the Samaritans under the aegis of the Jerusalem church, a proselyte must then be won, and Peter must in turn convert the first full-blooded Gentile. Then and only then are the Hellenists allowed to move on, which they do in chapter 11 (v. 19). Furthermore, the persecution begins with the introduction of Paul in Jerusalem (a fact that alone ought to cast doubt on the whole enterprise) and ends with his conversion and subsequent departure from that same city (9:30).

In summary, it is difficult to believe that scholars would ever have interpreted a verse like 8:1 with such minute literalism, except for the fact that an entire superstructure is built upon it. This is not to say that Luke's account is fabricated. It is possible that it reflects what was a genuine heightening of tensions between the infant church and Judaism, tensions that may have broken out in violence particularly within the Greek-speaking Jewish community. Those who were not resident in Jerusalem (i.e., predominantly Hellenist pilgrims) might well have thought it best to leave the city at this time, as Luke records it in Acts 8:4-5 and 11:19-20. Luke would have known in any case that Paul was at one time a persecutor of Christians. His introduction within the context of the first general persecution of the church is therefore entirely understandable. It could even be argued that Luke located the persecution itself, along with Paul, in Jerusalem. Obviously, in such a case there would be no point in considering the (imaginary) persecution of the Hellenists. But this is only speculation, as any proposal must be that goes beyond the confines of the modest account of Acts 8:1-4.[75]

---

[74] Foakes Jackson writes: "This brief description of the persecution of the church in Jerusalem abounds in contradictory statements" (*Acts,* p. 69).

[75] Foakes Jackson makes a similar point: "It would appear that there was a *severe persecution in Jerusalem,* and that others besides Stephen lost their lives; but no definite record of it has survived. Thus the problems raised by what little we learn from Acts are practically insoluble" (ibid., p. 70).

CONCLUSION

We have seen that all interpretive roads lead finally to the same destination: there is nothing in the account of the persecution of Acts 8:1-4 that would cause us to believe that the church of Jerusalem was divided into ideological camps corresponding to the labels "Hellenists" and "Hebrews. " If, on the one hand, the persecution *was* selective and the Hellenist Christians were persecuted by their fellow Hellenists, we are able to infer nothing concerning their relationship with the Hebrews. If, on the other hand, the Hellenists were persecuted by the chief priests, we know only that they were opposed by those persons who on other occasions also opposed the Hebrews. If the persecution *was not* selective, then it would serve to unite, rather than to distinguish between, the Hellenists and the Hebrews. If, however, there was no severe persecution such as Luke describes, then the matter is laid to rest entirely.

The notion of the selective persecution of the Hellenists is perhaps the most vital, though not the only, argument made in favor of their ideological distinctiveness. Of next importance is the theology of Stephen, the figure considered by most to have been the leader of the Hellenists — and so the one to whom our attention must now be turned.

Chapter Three

Stephen and the Hellenists

At the center of the Hellenist debate stands the figure of Stephen. His importance to the author of Acts is manifest: the speech credited to him is the longest in a book of speeches;[1] his death precipitates the outward movement of the gospel from Jerusalem (a leitmotiv of Acts); and he is ennobled as the church's first martyr, one whose death is patterned after the passion of Jesus himself.[2]

Stephen is no less important to modern expositors wishing to uncover the theology of Luke's "Hellenists."[3] Martin Hengel sides with the majority when he calls Stephen the spokesman of the Hellenist community.[4] It is commonly assumed that Stephen not only spoke for the Hellenist party but was in fact the progenitor of their supposedly distinctive theology.[5] For this reason, we frequently encounter the Hellenists of Acts appearing under the

---

[1] Martin Dibelius counts a total of twenty-four speeches in Acts (*Studies in the Acts of the Apostles*, p. 150 [129–30]). Haenchen reckons that "in round figures, 300 of the book's 1,000 verses" are devoted to speeches (*Acts*, p. 104 [93], n. 1).

[2] Despite his importance to Luke, Stephen appears nowhere in the New Testament outside of Acts (in the story of his appointment and martyrdom, 6:1 – 8:2; in reference to the persecution that followed his death, 11:19; and in Paul's speech to the crowd in Jerusalem, 22:20) and is never mentioned in the Apostolic Fathers. "The first specific reference to Stephen in later church literature seems to be Irenaeus' remark that he was both the first deacon and the first martyr (*Contr. Haer.*, III, 12,10 and IV, 15,1)" (Martin H. Scharlemann, *Stephen: A Singular Saint*, p. 21, n. 36; this extensive footnote, covering much of pp. 21 and 22, contains a good summary of the treatment of Stephen in subsequent church tradition).

[3] For a summary of the history of relevant research, see Heinz-Werner Neudorfer, *Stephanuskreis;* Scharlemann, *Stephen*, pp. 1–7, 22–31; and Haenchen, *Acts*, pp. 82–90, 264–69, 286–90 [74–80, 218–22, 238–41].

[4] Hengel, *Between*, p. 19 [186; "ihres Wortführers Stephanus"].

[5] See Schmidt, *Der Bericht*, p. 23. For the characterization of the Hellenists' theology as distinctive, see, for example, Maddox, *The Purpose of Luke-Acts*, p. 52.

name "the Stephen circle" in much of the relevant literature.[6] Marcel Simon even refers to the Hellenists as the "disciples of Stephen."[7] Although we may not care to assume prima facie Stephen's status as the leader of the Hellenists, we must admit that he is in any case the only Hellenist who actually says anything in Luke's account.[8] Whatever else we may know about the opinions of the Hellenists we know only by inference. (Luke does not even explicitly say that the Hellenists at Antioch initially abandoned the requirement of circumcision for their Gentile converts.) Therefore Stephen's words must be, and indeed usually have been, a centerpiece of any reconstruction of the views of the Hellenists.

Most exegetes writing on the subject of Stephen begin with an observation about the impressive quantity of literature and diversity of opinion occasioned by Acts 6 and 7.[9] The amount of scholarly activity engendered plainly evidences the significance of these chapters. It also demonstrates the complexity of the issues they raise, as well as the lack of any general agreement as to their solution. There remains a host of competing hypotheses concerning the identity and theology of Stephen. This may not be surprising, given the tenuousness of the evidence and the resourcefulness of modern scholarship. But here as elsewhere, all hypotheses have not been created equal; some conclusions about Stephen are certainly more plausible than others. One of the tasks of the current chapter, therefore, is to sort the evidence to see what is the most reasonable interpretation of the materials presented to us in Acts 6:8–7:60.[10]

It should be admitted from the first, however, that the evidence concerning Stephen is not conclusive. It is highly unlikely for that reason that any one estimate of the "Stephen of history" will ever win the field. In light of this, it is all the more important not to lose sight of the larger issue — that is, what the story of Stephen's martyrdom tells us about the *Hellenists*. With this purpose in mind we see that it is not necessary to establish one single hypothesis against all others. It is not required, in other words, that we solve the unsolvable. The point is much the same as that made concerning the persecution of the Hellenists: although a certain historical reconstruction is preferred, it can be shown that *none* of the probable alternatives succeeds

---

[6] Note the title chosen by Neudorfer for his study of research concerning the Hellenists of Acts: *Der Stephanuskreis in der Forschungsgeschichte seit F. C. Baur.*

[7] Marcel Simon, *St. Stephen and the Hellenists*, p. 14. Similarly, Trocmé gives the Hellenists the name *"stéphaniens"* (*Le "Livre des Actes,"* p. 191).

[8] That is, apart from Philip's "Do you understand what you are reading?" in 8:30.

[9] "The account . . . simply bristles with difficulties" (Foakes Jackson, *Acts*, p. 57); "there is an amazing diversity of conflicting opinions." "These wide divergences . . . extend to almost every detail, every verse of both narrative and speech" (Simon, *Stephen*, pp. 1, 2); "one of the most complex problems in New Testament research" (Scharlemann, *Stephen*, p. 1).

[10] The scholar with whom I am perhaps most in agreement on these issues is Graham Stanton, whose 1978 article "Stephen in Lucan Perspective" includes many of the points set forth in this chapter.

in demonstrating what is truly at issue—in this case, the notion that Stephen was a leader of the Hellenist faction who died for his (and their) distinctively radical theology.

Before proceeding, let us pause a moment to consider the parallelism and interrelationship between the Stephen argument and the argument commonly set forth concerning the Hellenists. In both cases the persecution that has been stirred up is assumed to have been selective. Stephen—and not one of the Twelve—was put to death because of his peculiarly offensive theology. Stephen's fellow Hellenists—and not the Hebrews—were persecuted in turn for their share in the radicalism of Stephen. But earlier caveats concerning such reasoning still apply: selective persecution, even if it can be proved,[11] does not necessarily demonstrate uniqueness of ideology. Second, the danger of circular reasoning within any historical reconstruction needs to be re-emphasized. We might wish to interpret Acts 8:1b ("except the apostles") to mean that the Hellenist party was selectively persecuted. Such an interpretation may be justified on the grounds that the Hellenists would have been likely to share Stephen's radical theology.[12] If, however, the speech of Acts 7 does not demonstrate such a theology, how do we know that Stephen himself really was a "radical"? Because his followers were selectively persecuted.

It can therefore be seen just how important Stephen is to the whole question of Hellenist theology. The distinctiveness of the movement is in large part the distinctiveness of its martyr. So what do we know about the theology of Stephen?

ASSUMPTIONS

Interpreting Acts 6:8—7:60 involves first of all coming to terms with what may seem a tangled web of exegetical issues. Clarity about these questions, what they are and how they interrelate, is a prerequisite to evaluating the various interpretive strategies that have been employed in answering them.

We have already identified as our principal interest the question of what the Stephen materials tell us about the theology of the Hellenists. One way of proceeding is to consider the three assumptions that underlie any substantive response to that question. It must be assumed that (1) Stephen

---

[11] It cannot be proved in this case—others besides Stephen and the Hellenists were persecuted in Jerusalem, even to death, e.g., James, the brother of John (Acts 12:2), and James, the brother of Jesus (*Ant.* 20.200–203). See chap. 2 above.

[12] Scholars who characterize Stephen's theology as radical include Charles H. H. Scobie, "The Use of Source Material in the Speeches of Acts III and VII," p. 421; Wilfred L. Knox, *St. Paul and the Church of Jerusalem*, p. 51, n. 10; Haenchen, *Acts*, p. 286 [237]; and J. C. O'Neill, *The Theology of Acts in Its Historical Setting*, p. 88.

[13] Or how do we know to interpret the speech's many ambiguities in "radical" terms?

himself was a Hellenist, (2) his beliefs were typical of those of the Hellenists in general, and (3) these beliefs can reliably be ascertained on the basis of the text of Acts.[14] Each of these points is vital if the central place of Stephen in the study of the Hellenists is to be maintained, and yet none of them is entirely secure. It will be worthwhile to consider the problems and complexities associated with each. We shall then be in a position both to appreciate and to evaluate the variety of interpretations regarding the significance of Stephen.

WAS STEPHEN A HELLENIST?

The most consistent challenge to Stephen's Hellenist credentials comes from those who advocate a Samaritan source for the speech of Acts 7. These are pushed in the direction of arguing either that Stephen was not a Hellenist[15] or that his perspective was highly individualistic[16] or that the speech as it stands tells us little or nothing about the views of the historical Stephen[17] (thus undermining at least one of the three assumptions just mentioned). Those arguing for a Samaritan source but wishing to retain the place of Acts 6:8–7:60 in a study of the Hellenists contend that Stephen was indeed a representative Hellenist but that the Hellenists as a group were significantly influenced by Samaritan theology.[18] The Samaritan source will be discussed in more detail below; for now all that needs to be said is that the more one presses the theory of Samaritan influence, the harder it becomes to substantiate the claim that the Stephen speech is a piece of representative Hellenist theology. The alternative is to redefine completely the boundaries of the Hellenist group, in effect making it something entirely different from the group with which we have been dealing, namely, the Greek-speaking Jewish Christians who fled Jerusalem and founded the mixed church at Antioch.

It is instructive in this regard to consider the hypothesis of Charles Scobie that the "highly distinctive theological position" of Stephen finds its

---

[14] It is not necessary to maintain that Acts 7 reproduces the ipsissima verba of the martyr, either in whole or in part. It could be required of Luke only that the speech accurately recalls Stephen's theological perspective, or at least that of the Hellenists in general.

[15] This is the position of Abram Spiro. A summary of Spiro's influential proposal, first delivered in a paper to the 1965 Chicago meeting of the American Oriental Society, was compiled by W. F. Albright and C. S. Mann and printed in an appendix entitled "Stephen's Samaritan Background" to J. Munck's *The Acts of the Apostles* (pp. 285–300).

[16] Like the "Singular Saint" of Martin Scharlemann.

[17] So Scroggs, "Hellenistic Christianity," pp. 200–201. Scroggs believed that Stephen's speech, "which it seems clear he did not himself create . . . had been created in the missionary activity of . . . [the] Hellenistic church" (p. 200). Scroggs did assert, however, that Stephen rejected the temple, a view he credited also to the speech of Acts 7.

[18] This view has been furthered especially by the work of Charles H. H. Scobie ("Source Material" and "The Origins and Development of Samaritan Christianity").

closest parallel in Johannine theology. Scobie conjectures, in fact, that "the Johannine community was founded originally as an offshoot of the Stephen-Philip movement."[19] Speculations of this type share a common weakness: the influence they trace is invariably late and historically tenuous. I suspect that scholars turn to offshoot groups writing a generation or more later only when they cannot demonstrate influence where it ought to be found — in this case, among the larger Greek-speaking Jewish Christian community of the mid-first century, particularly as it was represented in Antioch.

Indeed, the more one assumes any kind of radically distinctive theology (Samaritan or otherwise) for Stephen *and* the Hellenists, the more one comes up against an embarrassing lack of evidence of any subsequent Hellenist influence in the very places one would ordinarily look to find it. The work of Marcel Simon can be cited as a case in point.[20] Simon characterizes Stephen's thought (and, by extension, the thought of the Hellenists) as "very personal and . . . almost completely aberrant."[21] He is then forced by this conclusion to minimize the subsequent effects of Hellenist theology.

> We learn from Acts . . . that the Hellenists were scattered abroad throughout the regions of Judaea and Samaria and, later on, that they travelled as far as Phoenicia and Cyprus and Antioch. There is, unfortunately, little help to be expected from this information, since all these cities and countries were, at a very early date, touched by other Christian preachers. . . . And as the newcomers were more numerous, and at any rate had a more continuous and protracted activity than their predecessors, it is most likely that the Hellenist message . . . was so to speak covered over by some other form of Christianity, or, at the very least, became mingled with it and consequently was deprived of its originality.[22]

It is not impossible that Stephen and the Hellenists did have a highly distinctive theology but that it was either lost or shunted off to the periphery of the Christian church. In either case, the popular conception of the Hellenists as the originators of a law-free (that is, law-*critical*)[23] gospel would

---

[19] Scobie, "Source Material," p. 421.

[20] Simon, while joining those who have seen in Stephen's speech certain parallels to Samaritan theology, postulated a reversal of influence: it was the Samaritans who borrowed the ideas from the Hellenists (*Stephen,* p. 38).

[21] Ibid., p. 98. Maurice Jones, writing in 1917, stated: "So on the whole St. Stephen appears as a lonely and isolated figure among the great personalities of the primitive Church" ("The Significance of St. Stephen in the History of the Primitive Christian Church," p. 178).

[22] Simon, *Stephen,* pp. 110–11. See J. Julius Scott: "These Jewish Christian Hellenists were scattered by the persecution which followed Stephen's martyrdom. Soon afterward they were probably swallowed up by the Larger Church and their distinctive theology became almost indistinguishable" ("Parties in the Church of Jerusalem As Seen in the Book of Acts," p. 221).

[23] That the gospel was law-free for the Gentiles was acknowledged, at least in principle, by the leaders of the church in Jerusalem at the time of Apostolic Conference. (It might also have received tacit acceptance by some members of the Jerusalem church before this time.) The

become indefensible for all practical purposes. Either the distinctive theology of the Hellenists is recognizable elsewhere, or it leads us nowhere. But solutions of the type proposed by Simon are highly improbable and are not supported by our findings. Among other things, I would ask how it is, if Stephen's (and perhaps the Hellenists') views had so little influence, that Luke, writing forty to fifty years later, could have enjoyed such ready access to them? Scharlemann, for example, states that "Stephen's point of view perished with him. His theology occurs nowhere else in the literature of the ancient church."[24] And yet Scharlemann zealously contends for the speech's historical authenticity on the basis of the likelihood of a source.[25] Indeed, it is a maxim in Stephen research that the more esoteric the view, the better the source standing behind it.[26] This difficulty is further compounded if we consider that it is Stephen's radical but uninfluential theology that is supposedly the cause of the persecution of one entire sector of the church.

The majority of scholars, however, do consider Stephen to have been a Hellenist, whatever that designation may imply. The chain of reasoning leading to this conclusion is fairly direct. In Acts 6:1, we find the first mention of the Hellenists. According to that account, seven men, all of whom had Greek names, were chosen to oversee the distribution to the widows. They are therefore presumed to have been Hellenists themselves. The fact that they were chosen and the fact that two of them, Stephen and Philip,[27] are subsequently found preaching, make us think that they were already Hellenist leaders. Stephen, being a leader, can be assumed to have spoken for the Hellenists generally.

This reasoning has been attacked by some on the grounds that the Greek names of the Seven prove nothing, since their use was not uncommon

---

question is whether or not we may attribute to the Hellenists a fundamental criticism of the law itself.

[24] Scharlemann, *Stephen*, p. 56.

[25] See, for example, ibid., pp. 22–30.

[26] "The speech of Ac 7 would surely not have presented materials for a distinctive theology if it had come into existence as the historian's own construction" (T. Francis Glasson, "The Speeches of Acts and Thucydides," p. 165). "No doubt the strangest feature of this speech is the idea that the building of the Temple was an act of rebellion.... It must have come to Luke from tradition, for there is nothing like it in the other passages of Luke-Acts in which the Temple is mentioned" (Maddox, *The Purpose of Luke-Acts*, p. 53).

[27] As a rule, scholars' perceptions of Philip's theology are based upon prior conclusions about the theology of Stephen. The only significant datum we possess concerning Philip is that he preached to those at the margins of Judaism, apparently some Samaritans and an Ethiopian eunuch. This might commend Philip to us as one in the vanguard of the church's mission—even its mission to Gentiles—but it does not provide us with evidence of law criticism or temple criticism on his part (a matter taken up below with reference to Stephen). Furthermore, there is no subsequent "Philip community" on the basis of whose theology we might test notions concerning the content of Philip's preaching. The only hard evidence of this sort we possess concerns the church at Antioch, founded, according to Acts 11:19-21, by believers (in particular, "some men of Cyprus and Cyrene") who had been scattered because of the persecution in Jerusalem (see chap. 4 below).

in Palestine in the first century.²⁸ In fact, two of Jesus' disciples, Andrew and Philip, had Greek names. Earl Richard argues that it would have been especially likely that those chosen by the church would have come from a higher social class in which the use of Greek names would have been common. If Galilean fishermen could have been named Andrew and Philip, we ought not to be amazed at a group of seven similarly named Hebrew and Hellenist leaders. In addition, "the rare occurrence of double names in Acts, almost limited to Simon/Peter and Saul/Paul, shows that tradition was very selective in its choice."²⁹

The notion that the church would have appointed a board composed exclusively of Hellenists to settle the problem of distribution to the widows is also problematic. "An arrangement based on the appointment of fellow Hellenists might have created a serious imbalance, aggravating rather than alleviating the situation which the Twelve moved to rectify."³⁰

Finally it is argued that no conclusions can be drawn from the fact that Stephen debated with the non-Christian Hellenists (Acts 6:9), since the apostle Paul, who was himself a "Hebrew born of Hebrews" (Phil. 3:5; see also 2 Cor. 11:22), encountered similar Hellenist antagonism while in Jerusalem (Acts 9:29; 21:27-28).³¹

These objections are not insurmountable. In the first place, the most that can be said is that the names of the Seven do not succeed in *proving* that they were Hellenists. Most scholars would still consider that conclusion more likely than the alternative, that a group of Jews chosen for their leadership or administrative abilities should all happen to have Greek names. The fact that one of their number, Nicolaus the proselyte, is specifically said to have been "of Antioch" works in this same direction as does (contra Scharlemann) the fact that those said to oppose Stephen were Greek-speaking Jews (6:5, 9). In the latter case, it should be made clear that citation of Pauline usage as an exegetical key to Lukan terminology is an altogether unacceptable methodology. It is evident that the term "Hebrew" has a different function in Philippians and 2 Corinthians from its use in Acts. According to I. Howard Marshall: "In Philippians iii.5 the term refers to strict Jewish descent and the maintenance of a rigid Jewish way of life; nothing in the context suggests that language is the main point at issue. The stress is on Jewish descent. Similarly, in II Corinthians xi.22 the term appears in parallel with others which indicate Jewish nationality, and refers to possession of a religious privilege.... [therefore] it is possible that Paul's 'Hebrews' included both Luke's 'Hebrews' and 'Hellenists.'"³²

---

²⁸ Richard, *Author's Method*, p. 341; Scharlemann, *Stephen*, p. 17.
²⁹ Richard, *Author's Method*, p. 342.
³⁰ Scharlemann, *Stephen*, p. 18.
³¹ Ibid., pp. 17, 18.
³² Marshall, "Palestinian and Hellenistic Christianity," p. 278. See also Trocmé, *Le "Livre des Actes,"* p. 190. Paul's use of Ἑβραῖος is discussed in chap. 5 below.

Furthermore, Acts is the only place in which the word is contrasted with the (Lukan) term "Hellenist." Paul, in Luke's nomenclature, would have been a Hellenist, and thus it is fitting that, according to Acts 9:29 (see also 21:27), we find him disputing with Hellenists while in Jerusalem.[33] It makes perfect sense as well to suppose that the trouble concerning Stephen arose within his own community, that is, the community of Greek-speaking Jews or, as Luke designates them, the Hellenists.

With regard to the supposedly incredible choice of a board of seven Hellenists, I have already proposed an alternative solution, that the Seven were chosen to oversee the distribution to their own widows, hitherto neglected by the Hebrews. But any reconstruction based upon the Book of Acts ought not to stand or fall upon such minutiae. For one thing, we cannot possibly know on the basis of such scant data which interpretation is the correct one — if indeed either is. We can only say that both are possible. Furthermore, to claim that an action taken by the leaders of the early church as it is recorded in Acts seems overly magnanimous (and therefore must be reinterpreted) begs the question. One first has to ask if Luke himself might not have held such a view. I would not rule out the possibility.

To press the matter further, the real issue is not whether Stephen was a Hellenist but whether Luke *thought* that Stephen was a Hellenist. If Luke believed that Stephen had been an early Hellenist leader, and if Luke had access to Hellenist materials of some sort, it would have been natural for him to put the two together in what is the only speech by a Hellenist in Acts. Even if the character of Stephen were fictional, we would still have to ask if the beliefs attributed to him are not themselves a genuine reflection of Hellenist theology.

Still, doubt remains. The link between Stephen and the Hellenists is less substantial than is usually acknowledged, especially if we concede that in raising the issue at all, we are asking Luke to answer questions that he never intended to address. It is very unlikely that Luke continued to think in terms of *groups* when describing the Jerusalem church after the resolution of the dispute in chapter 6; the division between Hebrew and Hellenist Christians vanishes as quickly as it appears.[34] Scholars interested in the Hellenists must commit themselves to reading between the lines the moment they step past the limits of Acts 6:1.

Obviously, if Stephen was not a Hellenist or at least was not considered one by Luke, there would be little point in proceeding. His martyrdom would then tell us nothing about the Hellenists. Of course, if this should be true, then a selective persecution of the Hellenists is rendered

---

[33] This is true if we assume, as many scholars do on the basis of Gal. 1:22, that Paul was not raised in Jerusalem.

[34] This is Earl Richard's fundamental criticism of speculation concerning Stephen and the Hellenists (*Author's Method,* pp. 342–46).

nonsensical. This is a real possibility, but unfortunately there are not enough data to settle the question either way. However one weighs the probabilities, the question of Stephen's identity will remain an open one.

WERE STEPHEN'S BELIEFS TYPICALLY "HELLENIST"?

Among those believing him to have been a Hellenist, Stephen's representative status is almost universally acknowledged. This is not unreasonable, given the community's choice of Stephen in 6:5 (first in the list of seven) and the subsequent role he appears to have exercised in proclaiming "the word of God" (6:7; cf. v. 2) to the Greek-speaking community. Yet even here caution is to be advised. First of all, the extent to which Stephen can be assumed to represent the *theological* concerns of the Hellenists is dependent upon prior assumptions about the theological distinctiveness and homogeneity of the group. In the usual understanding, Stephen's theology is taken to be both representative and theologically distinctive. This means that the Hellenists must be considered first of all to have been an ideologically defined party. But this is just the point at issue. The Hellenists were apparently a heterogeneous group of Greek-speaking Jewish Christians. Without proving the case either way, the question should be raised as to what extent any individual Hellenist may without question be taken to represent all other Hellenists. Stephen's exemplary status is itself an issue only if there is something that we can ascertain about his perspective that would differ notably from that of the Hebrews (if there was some unitary "Hebrew" perspective).

Second, we again must admit the difficulty of a distinctive theology, typical of the Hellenists in Jerusalem, that is hardly traceable elsewhere. Among those who write themselves into this corner is Wilfred Knox. On the one hand, Knox wishes to maintain that Stephen, whose views he characterizes as radical,[35] can correctly be viewed as a representative Hellenist: "It is quite reasonable to suppose that the persons chosen by the Hellenists were those who were naturally qualified to be their leaders and spokesmen, and that the subsequent career of S[t]. Stephen as a teacher should be due to the fact that as a recognized officer of the Church he was regarded in the Hellenist synagogue as its authorized representative."[36] In their capacity as officers, according to Knox's theory, Stephen and the six led "a doctrinal revolt" that infused the moribund Jerusalem church with "a new lease of energy."[37] But on the other hand, Knox elsewhere admits that "the attitude of S[t]. Stephen in primitive Christian literature can only be paralleled in the

---

[35] For example, Knox, *St. Paul and the Church of Jerusalem*, p. 51, n. 10.
[36] Ibid., p. 49.
[37] Ibid., pp. 49, 40.

Epistle of Barnabas."[38] So we are again left to ponder this dilemma: if Stephen was radical, then he was not representative; or, if he was representative, little became of those whom he is said to have represented.

DO WE HAVE ACCURATE INFORMATION ABOUT THE BELIEFS OF STEPHEN?

This is the most basic and, not surprisingly, by far the most contentious of the questions I have raised. It leads us directly to the fundamental issue in any interpretation of the Book of Acts—the question of sources.[39] Did the author of Acts have at his disposal traditional information, in either written or oral form,[40] upon which to base his account? Or, to paraphrase the famous question of Howard Baker, 'What did the author know, and from what or whom did he know it?"

The history of the source criticism of Acts is long and circuitous, but it would be fair to bring the question up to date by saying that scholarship as a whole has moved increasingly away from source theories in favor of some notion of Lukan composition. Single-source theories thus gave way to theories of parallel sources, which gave way in turn to theories of numerous

---

[38] Ibid., p. 54, n. 24.

[39] Cf. the remark of Johannes Munck concerning belief in a source behind Acts 6-7: "Clearly it is only thanks to this assumption that we can learn anything at all about the Hellenists" (*Paul and the Salvation of Mankind*, p. 221 [215-16]). For bibliography on the question of the sources of Acts, see Mattill and Mattill, *Bibliography*, pp. 157-65; Haenchen, *Acts*, pp. 81-90 (especially p. 90) [72-80]; and Jacques Dupont, *The Sources of Acts: The Present Position* (index of authors, pp. 171-73 [163-65]).

Contemporary literary studies of Luke-Acts tend to disregard the question of pre-Lukan sources and focus instead on the presence of thematic-compositional elements within the narrative. To the extent that such approaches demonstrate the presence of characteristic Lukan themes and expressions within Acts 6:1 – 8:4, they support indirectly my insistence on modesty with respect to historical claims. (Cf. Robert C. Tannehill's statement of purpose on p. 6 of *The Narrative Unity of Luke-Acts*. For the way in which Tannehill fits the Stephen story into the narrative whole, see, for example, 1:22, 73; 2:81-101).

[40] For the moment, a sharp distinction will not be maintained between the two. Those with a primary interest in the historicity of the narrative and/or speech are the most fervent advocates of a written source. This would include very conservative scholars as well as those who see the speech as a unique witness to some very early and highly unusual theology. A second and often complementary advocacy comes from those who find in the speech certain elements not readily explicable on the basis of oral tradition or Lukan composition (Semitisms, textual correspondences with the Samaritan Pentateuch, etc.). It is possible to argue the case for historical authenticity on the basis of the quality of oral tradition, but this is seldom done in modern scholarship. One reason is that such an argument has generally rested upon the problematic assumption that the author of Acts knew Paul, who himself was a witness to the martyrdom of Stephen. As a general rule, therefore, we could say that the further one gets from a written source, the further one stands from an uncritical acceptance of Luke's account in Acts 6 and 7.

complementary sources.⁴¹ At each step the work of the author's hand has grown progressively larger, whereas the breadth and clarity of the sources he employed has continued to diminish. Jacques Dupont, after an extensive study of source theories, comes to this conclusion: "The predominant impression is certainly very negative. Despite the most careful and detailed research, it has not been possible to define any of the sources used by the author of Acts in a way which will meet with widespread agreement among the critics." Dupont does believe that Luke utilized sources but that these have been so fully reworked as to be unrecoverable. "There are so many indications which set us on the track of pre-existing sources. We seize a link, which is very clear; we try to follow the source from which it comes and, almost immediately, it becomes lost and disappears, whereas other links present themselves, just as clear and just as disappointing."⁴²

Speeches in Ancient Historiography

Interest in sources has been evident particularly in the study of the speeches of Acts.⁴³ Here too the results have been largely negative. As Eduard Schweizer writes, "It has been more and more widely recognized that the speeches are basically *compositions of the author of Acts* who, to be sure, utilized different kinds of material for particular passages." Such material is, however, "probably present only in the traditional themes... the choice of scriptural passages and in the pattern of the proof from Scripture."⁴⁴

More than anything else, the study of the role of speeches in ancient historiography hastened the movement away from comprehensive source

---

⁴¹ Each of these types of source theory is reviewed in successive chapters (1-3) of Dupont, *Sources,* pp. 17-61 [17-60].

⁴² Ibid., p. 166 [159].

⁴³ The relationship between the speeches of Acts and the practice of speech writing in ancient historiography (including a examination of the oft-quoted words of Thucydides in *History of the Peloponnesian War* 1.22.1) is discussed at greater length in my 1989 Oxford D.Phil. thesis "Hellenists and Hebrews: A Reappraisal," pp. 84-92. For bibliography and further details of the debate, see Cadbury, *Beginnings* 5:402-427 ("The Speeches in Acts"; see especially pp. 404-5, n. 2, for bibliography), and *Making of Luke-Acts,* pp. 184-93 (chap. 14, "Speeches, Letters and Canticles"); Gasque, *History,* pp. 209-35; F. F. Bruce, *The Speeches in the Acts of the Apostles* and "The Speeches in Acts—Thirty Years After"; Ulrich Wilckens, *Die Missionsreden der Apostelgeschichte: Form- und traditionsgeschichtliche Untersuchungen;* Dibelius, *Studies,* pp. 138-85 [120-58] (chap. 9, "The Speeches in Acts and Ancient Historiography"); Max Wilcox, "A Foreword to the Study of the Speeches in Acts"; Merle Bland Dudley, "The Speeches in Acts"; and Eduard Schweizer, "Concerning the Speeches in Acts." Additional bibliography on the speeches of Acts is be found on pp. 165-73 of Mattill and Mattill, *Bibliography.*

⁴⁴ Eduard Schweizer, "Speeches," pp. 208, 214. Cf. Wilckens: "In that he [Luke] clothed his fundamental theological principles in the literary robe of apostolic preaching, he lent his theology the legitimacy and dignity of apostolic testimony, which—according to his conviction—was fundamentally valid for the Church; therefore, in this way he conferred upon his theology the legitimacy and dignity of the Word of God itself, which governs the story as a whole" (*Die Missionsreden,* p. 193).

theories for the speeches of Acts. The names of Martin Dibelius and Henry J. Cadbury are especially prominent in this connection.[45] Both argued that it was the common practice of ancient historians to compose speeches that would fill out and lend variety to their narrative.[46] More important, these speeches served as the means by which the author might interpret for the reader the significance of the events described. Although the careful writer attempted to compose speeches that would be in character, in practice these may have had little if anything to do with the historical occasion or even the speaker with whom they are associated. "It is evident that the ancient writers and their readers considered the speeches more as editorial and dramatic comment than as historical tradition."[47] Speeches were creations of authors included to serve their purposes and so must be viewed as inherently tendentious. Even where published speeches were known, as for example in the cases of Caesar, Claudius, and Cicero, they were not followed by the historians.[48] Josephus as well can be seen to exercise a very considerable degree of freedom in the composition of speeches. For example, in the first two books of *Antiquities*, he created speeches that set forth views differing from those of the purported speakers in Genesis, and he "twice reproduces the same speech—by Herod in the war against the Arabs (*Bellum Jud.*, I, 19.4, par. 373ff., *Ant.*, XV, 5.3, par. 127ff)—but in such a way as not to correspond with one another at all."[49]

This does not mean that we can say outright that Luke freely composed the speeches of Acts. It does mean, however, that this is at least a reasonable possibility. Additional considerations concerning Lukan vocabulary, structure, and themes, discussed below, may take us further in determining whether or not Luke employed a source in composing the Stephen speech. In any case, it is certainly true that the challenge of isolating a source multiplies considerably, once we grant the author's literary interest in creating speeches to suit their context.[50] Variety of style may be the sign of talent, not tradition.

---

[45] The essay that perhaps best introduces the question is Cadbury's "The Speeches in Acts." A good example of a contemporary approach to the speeches of Acts is Fred Veltman's "The Defense Speeches of Paul in Acts."

[46] "The ordinary reader scarcely realizes what a difference they make to the book as a whole, relieving its somewhat monotonously narrative character. . . . Even as a purely literary artifice they still accomplish what was no doubt an original purpose of this cherished tradition—an effective dramatic result" (Cadbury, *Beginnings* 5:402).

[47] Cadbury, *Making of Luke-Acts*, p. 185.

[48] Dibelius, *Studies*, pp. 138-39 [120-21]; Cadbury, *Making of Luke-Acts*, pp. 186-87.

[49] Dibelius, *Studies*, p. 139 [121].

[50] On Luke's considerable ability to do this very thing, see Eduard Schweizer, "Speeches," pp. 208-16; and Haenchen, *Acts*, pp. 77-80 [69-72] ("He varies his style according to the tone required and the situation he is depicting," p. 80 [72]).

The Relationship between Acts 6 and 7

Surprisingly, doubts surrounding the historicity of the speeches of Acts have done little to deter speculation about Stephen. In fact, it might be said that skepticism about the Stephen speech has been a considerable asset to many. The reason for this is the complex relationship that exists between the accusations in 6:11-14[51] and the speech in 7:2-53.

The chief difficulty in relating these two elements has long been recognized: Stephen's speech seems to have little if anything to do with the charges leveled against him. "If the speech in Acts vii. was his defence, it is strange that he makes no mention of the accusations, but gives a recapitulation of the facts of the ancient history of Israel, concerning which all his hearers were perfectly familiar as well as being in agreement."[52] It is instructive in this respect to compare Stephen's defense with, for example, Paul's explicit rebuttal of the accusations of the Jewish leaders in chapters 24 and 25 (24:11-13; 25:7-8). Stephen, by comparison, never mentions the accusations of 6:11-14, much less answers them.

This problem has been confronted in various ways. One solution seeks to maintain the integrity of the account by admitting that the accusations and the speech do not correspond but concluding nevertheless that this presents no problem, since Stephen would not have answered the charges anyway. According to this view, the martyr, despising death, seized this last opportunity for a plea, not of innocence, but of *veritas*. "All observation shows that religious or political pioneers when brought into court never attempt to rebut the accusations brought against them, but use the opportunity for making a partisan address."[53] Or, to quote Baur, "Stephen did not belong to that class of men who think more of their own personal interests than of the universal cause of truth."[54]

The student of the New Testament would be hard pressed to unearth a better instance where virtue has been made of scholarly necessity. It is

---

[51] Since Loisy's *Les Actes des Apôtres* it generally has been recognized that there are two accusations corresponding to (1) Moses, law, and customs and (2) God, holy place, and this place (p. 309; see Brodie, "The Accusing and Stoning of Naboth," p. 421; Richard, *Author's Method*, pp. 222, 287). John Kilgallen represents those who consider the accusations in vv. 13 and 14 to be successive clarifications and intensifications of the charge in v. 11 (*The Stephen Speech: A Literary and Redactional Study of Acts 7,2-53*, pp. 31-32; see Brodie, "Accusing," p. 424). For a critique of the view that two different sets of accusers signal two separate sources for the accusations, see Haenchen, *Acts*, p. 272-74 [225-27]. On the use of repetition as a Lukan rhetorical device, see Dibelius, *Studies*, p. 165 [142]; Henry J. Cadbury, *The Style and Literary Method of Luke*, vol. 2, *The Treatment of Sources in the Gospel*, p. 111; and Richard, *Author's Method*, pp. 181-82 (see also 174-75; repetition is a feature of Luke's writing that is highlighted throughout Richard's analysis).

[52] Foakes Jackson, *Acts*, p. 65. See also Baur, *Paul* 1:44 [50].

[53] Lake and Cadbury, *Beginnings* 4:70. Simon writes: "The problem indeed is not whether the speech is relevant, but whether it is genuine" (*Stephen*, p. 39).

[54] Baur, *Paul* 1:54 [61].

simply not the case, as Acts 24 and 25 demonstrate, that religious pioneers "never attempt to rebut the accusations brought against them." In the one instance in the New Testament where someone does categorically refuse to answer charges, the method employed is that of silence, not peroration, and it is met with amazement (Mark 15:5; cf. Luke 23:9-10). Second, if Stephen wished to use his trial as an occasion for proclaiming the gospel, it is passing strange that he fails to do so. The speech is no more a Christian proclamation than it is a personal defense. It is instead a denunciation. Jesus is mentioned only as one who has been betrayed and murdered, the prophet like Moses who was denied[55] and thrust away by the Jews. Contrary to every missionary speech in Acts, there is no call to repentance and no offer of salvation. The only moderating element is verse 60, "Lord, do not hold this sin against them," a verse in the closing narrative modeled on the words of Jesus on the cross (Luke 23:34).[56]

The Accusations as the Locus of Tradition

A second and more common approach is to deny outright that the speech fits the context of the accusations. It is therefore secondary, unnecessary, or even intrusive. Martin Hengel, for one, is prepared to dismiss the speech as a Lukan redaction, believing that the account makes better sense without it.[57] He therefore says concerning Acts 7:1-54 that "it remains extremely dubious whether we should connect it directly with Stephen and the Hellenists."[58] Helmut Koester holds a similar view: "The speech of Stephen in Acts 7:2-53 is a Lukan composition and cannot be used for the reconstruction of Stephen's views or those of his Hellenist associates. But there is a chance that the tradition used by Luke gave the reason for the eruption of the persecution

---

[55] See Acts 3:14.

[56] The saying is missing from several early texts, including $\mathfrak{P}^{75}$ B D* W Θ it[a, d] syr[s] cop[sa, bo]. Metzger calls this omission "most impressive." He believes, nevertheless, that the logion "bears self-evident tokens of its dominical origin" and therefore "was retained, within double square brackets, in its traditional place where it had been incorporated by unknown copyists relatively early in the transmission of the Third Gospel" (*A Textual Commentary on the Greek New Testament*, p. 180). Cadbury and Lake are among those who cite doubt about the saying in Luke as possible evidence "that there was a tendency to supplement the story of the Passion by details taken from the story of Stephen" (*Beginnings* 4:85).

[57] Hengel believes that Luke inserted the speech (between 6:15 and 7:55) into an account already received from his Antiochene source. The blandness of the defense had the effect of toning down the (factually true) accusations (*Between*, p. 23 [195]). According to Dibelius: "It has obviously been inserted by Luke into the story of the martyrdom of Stephen, which he already had at his disposal.... The speech breaks the sequence between the transfiguration and the looking upward to heaven; obviously Luke contributed it himself when he took the story of the martyrdom into his narrative" (*Studies*, p. 168 [145]). See also F. J. Foakes Jackson, "Stephen's Speech in Acts," pp. 284-86.

[58] Hengel, *Between*, p. 19 [186].

which led to Stephen's martyrdom. Acts 6:11 has preserved this traditional information: Stephen is accused of criticism of Moses, that is, of the law, and of blasphemy."[59]

We glimpse here the importance of the accusations against Stephen. Even if Stephen's speech is ruled inadmissable evidence, it can still be claimed that we may know the substance of his views by reference to the claims of his accusers, claims that came to Luke via Christian tradition. It should be recognized that such a strategy offers one overwhelming advantage: it allows the exegete to attribute to Stephen attitudes that cannot be substantiated by his words. Thus one is spared by a single admission the impossible task of demonstrating the existence of temple criticism and law criticism[60] in the speech of chapter 7.[61] So we find Hengel claiming, on the one hand, "a historical foundation" for the belief that the Hellenists criticized both law and temple[62] and yet, on the other hand, stating that "the positive picture of Moses . . . seems to contradict 6.11" and that the criticism of Solomon's temple is in fact "relatively mild."[63]

This attitude of preferring the accusations to the speech is actually an adaptation of the theory of an Antiochene source,[64] a hypothesis tracing its origins back to the work of Harnack,[65] who sought to identify traditions that might have had a particular interest to and thus have been preserved by the church at Antioch.[66] Although scholars who accepted an Antiochene source seldom agreed as to its precise boundaries, it was usually assumed that the

---

[59] Helmut Koester, *Introduction to the New Testament: History, Culture, and Religion of the Hellenistic Age* 2:90 [523]. Cf. Walther Schmithals, who says that Luke moderated the accusations by placing them in the mouths of false witnesses and then countered them by deliberate interpolations into the speech (*Paul and James*, p. 20 [12–13]).

[60] By "temple criticism" and "law criticism" I mean statements that attack the foundations of temple worship and obedience to the law. An assertion that all temple worship is idolatrous (a view that some would attribute to Stephen) would be an example of temple criticism. Likewise, much of what Paul has to say about the law is critical. The answer he gives when considering the question, Why then the law? takes the form of a series of negative designations and justifications: the law was added as something of a latecomer to the purposes of God, being of temporary value only, given or mediated by angels, acting as a custodian to restrain or bind until the coming of Christ; it is an impotent ordinance that succeeds only in increasing transgression, inflaming desire, and giving power to sin; by it, the practitioner is enslaved, cursed, and killed (Gal. 3:19, 17, 19, 20, 24–26; Rom. 7:13–17, 7–11, 19–20; 1 Cor. 15:56; Gal. 4:1-5; 3:10; 2 Cor. 3:7).

[61] That this task is impossible is by no means universally acknowledged. The issue will be taken up again below. Some of the numerous attempts to elucidate Stephen's criticism of the temple or the law will be discussed in the next section of the chapter.

[62] Hengel, *Between*, p. 23 [195].

[63] Ibid., p. 22 [193].

[64] A good introduction to the history of the Antioch source is provided by Dupont, *Sources*, pp. 35–36, 62–72 [35–36, 61–70].

[65] Adolf Harnack, *The Acts of the Apostles*, chap. 5, "The Sources and Their Value," pp. 162–202 [131–158].

[66] Such a pursuit in turn goes back to earlier Hellenistic source theories. See Haenchen's summary, *Acts*, pp. 24–34 [22–32].

entire Stephen account of 6:1–8:4 was to be included. Criticism of the speeches of Acts gradually eroded this confidence, so that, for example, Rudolf Bultmann, writing in 1959, excluded the speech in his assessment of the limits of the Antiochene source.[67]

The extent of the Antiochene source was further limited by Bultmann in his rejection of Acts 6:12b-15 as a Lukan interpolation.[68] This is the view of Koester, quoted above, in which only the accusation of 6:11 is accepted as primary. Hengel's position is slightly more complicated. Although he tends to emphasize verse 11[69] and summarily rejects verses 12 and 15,[70] he is willing to accept the validity of the accusations in verses 13 and 14.[71]

The gradual diminution of the Antiochene source presents the exegete with an interesting trade-off: positively, it means that there is less to defend; negatively, it means that the case for Stephen's distinctive theology — and the Hellenists' with it — is made to hang by an ever thinner thread. In the case of Bultmann's proposal, we are left with only one strand — 6:11.

Because of the variety of approaches, it will be useful to consider the question of the authenticity of the accusations in three parts: (1) general considerations regarding the interpretation of the charges and their probability, (2) arguments specific to 6:13-14, and (3) arguments specific to 6:11.

The strongest argument in favor of the authenticity of the charges of law criticism and temple criticism arises from the need to find an adequate explanation for the fact of Stephen's death. When we consider the martyrdom, we are forced to admit the need for reasons not unlike those furnished us by Luke. Stephen did something considered by some of his contemporaries to be deserving of death, and words spoken against the temple and the law could well supply us with such a sufficient cause. After all, if we did not have Luke's own account of the accusations, we would be left to create one for ourselves. And if we accuse Luke, writing only a generation later, of historical inaccuracy, how is it that we believe that we can do better?

But this line of reasoning is weaker than it appears. First, it is said that Stephen vehemently criticized the law and the temple and that in these criticisms we discover both the core of his teaching and the reason for his death.[72] It is further maintained that, by these criticisms, Stephen showed himself to be a precursor of other notable Christian thinkers, the author of Hebrews (on the temple) and Paul (on the law), to mention only two. But what the witnesses actually said in the one verse in which their accusations

---

[67] Rudolf Bultmann, "Zur Frage nach den Quellen der Apostelgeschichte," p. 78.
[68] Ibid.
[69] Hengel, *Between,* p. 19 [187].
[70] Both verses contain references to the Sanhedrin, something Hengel takes to be artificial (ibid., p. 20 [188]).
[71] Ibid., pp. 22 [191] and 56 ["Die Ursprünge," p. 26].
[72] See Baur, *Paul* 1:43-53 [49-61].

are made explicit (v. 14) is that Stephen threatened a *future, eschatological* destruction of the temple and changing of customs. One has to wonder whether the question of probable cause is so well served by the actual charge.[73] And if this really was Stephen's attitude, he is much more distant than is commonly assumed from those later Christian authors with whom he is generally compared.

Second, according to Luke, the accusations against Stephen were set forth by *false* witnesses. Almost universally, commentators have assumed the opposite: that the supposedly false witnesses were in fact telling the truth. This interpretive reversal is accomplished by means of an intriguing sleight of hand. It is said that Luke knows and wants to report the reason for Stephen's death, and yet the witnesses he employs to do so *must* be "false" since they are witnessing against Stephen, who is "true." Wilfred Knox calls this "a genuine literary curiosity": "any witness who gives evidence against a martyr must be a 'false' witness since he is against the truth."[74] Or, as Martin Scharlemann has written, the charges were indeed false, "but not in the sense of being contrary to fact"![75]

But it would have been obvious to Luke and to his readers, living after A.D. 70, that the charges were precisely contrary to fact. The temple had in truth been destroyed—but not by Jesus. Heikki Räisänen is one of the few commentators to have recognized this: "The reader of Luke's Gospel will also know that Jesus, according to that book, never said that *he* will destroy the temple, but only that it will be destroyed."[76] It also needs to be said that it is fully in keeping with Luke's purposes in Acts that he both introduce and refute the charge of blasphemy against Moses. S. G. Wilson, in his thoughtful monograph *Luke and the Law,* concludes that in Luke's perspective, "there is no conflict in living according to the law, indeed doing so zealously, and being a Christian."[77] In fact, Luke "viewed living according to the law as a natural and appropriate way of life for Jews and Jewish-Christians."[78] Moreover, Luke goes to considerable lengths to demonstrate the piety of the Jewish Christians in general,[79] and of the apostle Paul in

---

[73] According to Schmithals, "Any Jew might announce the abolition of the Temple at the end of time" (*Paul and James,* p. 21 [13]). Cf. Zeller: "No context can be imagined in which the announcement of a kingdom of God without a Temple . . . could have appeared as anything but blasphemy to the Pharisees" (*Acts* 1:239 [148]).

[74] Knox, *The Acts of the Apostles,* p. 25.

[75] Scharlemann, *Stephen,* p. 102.

[76] Heikki Räisänen, *The Torah and Christ,* pp. 264–65 (see Luke 13:34-35, 20:9-19, 21:6). See also Stanton, "Stephen," pp. 348–49; and Krodel, *Acts,* pp. 135–36.

[77] Stephen G. Wilson, *Luke and the Law,* p. 102.

[78] Ibid., pp. 114–15.

[79] For example, Acts 2:46; 3:1; 5:12-13, 34ff.; 21:20; 22:12. See also Luke 1:6; 2:22-24, 29, 39; 10:25-26. Deprecating references to the law that do occur within the context of Jewish Christianity are of a particularly vague nature (e.g., 13:39). Real criticism of the law, where it can be found, exists invariably within the context of the question of Gentile admission and obedience (e.g., 10:15; 15:10).

particular.⁸⁰ There is no doubt that, to Luke, the witnesses are patently false.

It might be argued that there is still likely to be truth to the accusations. After all, the similarly false charges against Paul in Acts 21:21, 28 are clearly exaggerations of charges that could genuinely have been leveled against him. In Paul's case, however, we have the means for verifying the extent to which the accusations have been falsified by exaggeration. In Stephen's case no such verification is possible; we are left only to speculate about what historical kernel may lie hidden within the supposedly exaggerated charges of the false witnesses.⁸¹ A healthy dose of skepticism about such speculation is entirely in order. In studies of this sort one is usually able to find whatever kernel one is looking for.

It is also necessary to consider the possibility that it was the question of *Paul's* faithfulness to the law that was actually at issue in Acts,⁸² and that Luke reads the Pauline defense—that is, the one that he knows and the one that most concerns him—back into the story of Stephen. This would of course explain the otherwise coincidental parallelism between the charges against Paul in Acts 21:28 and those against Stephen in 6:13. Whether or not this is the case, it is clear that Luke is arguing a point with respect to the law; it is the Jews who have disobeyed, not the Christians (7:53). Given Luke's apologetic (or, I might say, polemical) agenda, it would be very hazardous to stake out our claim to the Stephen of history on the basis of this one, stereotyped accusation.⁸³

Finally, why is it necessary to suppose that the accusations of chapter 6 must be true in order to explain Stephen's death? James, the brother of John, was also put to death according to Luke (Acts 12:2), but it is seldom if ever imagined that James shared Stephen's supposedly radical views. Why did Stephen's death require different and greater causes than that of James?

I thus do not feel that the authenticity of the accusations can be defended on grounds of their inherent probability. On the contrary, such a defense rests upon an improper understanding of the accusations and also fails to appreciate the author's redactional motive for including them in the Stephen story.⁸⁴

The defense, however, has not rested its case. A second level of argumentation seeks to demonstrate the authenticity of the accusations by

---

⁸⁰ Wilson, *Luke and the Law*, p. 102. On Paul as the pious Jew and Pharisee, see Acts 21:24; 22:3, 17; 23:5, 6, 9; 24:14-16; 25:8, etc.

⁸¹ See Räisänen, *The Torah and Christ*, p. 265.

⁸² See, for example, Wilson, *Luke and the Law*, p. 102, and Robert L. Brawley, *Luke-Acts and the Jews: Conflict, Apology, and Conciliation*, pp. 68-83.

⁸³ See 18:13 and 21:24, 28, as well as Paul's defense against the same charge, *by this time already understood* by the reader, in 25:8.

⁸⁴ The way in which the Stephen story meshes with Luke's purposes in composing Acts will be taken up again below.

pointing to their non-Lukan vocabulary and ideas. It is assumed that these would have come to Luke from some earlier, and presumably accurate, source. As noted, the accusations are sometimes divided between verse 11 and verses 13-14, with preference usually being given to verse 11. We therefore consider the question of the source of the accusations in these two parts.

The possibility that Acts 6:13-14 might have been influenced by the charges made against Paul (especially those of Acts 21:28) has already been mentioned. Of even greater significance is the fact that Luke has fashioned his account of Stephen's martyrdom at least in part after the story of Jesus' passion. The parallels between the two narratives are as follows:[85]

1. Trial before high priest/Sanhedrin (Mark 14:53 and par. / Acts 6:12; 7:1)
2. False witnesses (Mark 14:56-57; Matt. 26:60-61; *not* in Luke / Acts 6:13)
3. Testimony concerning the destruction of the temple (Mark 14:58; Matt. 26:61; *not* in Luke / Acts 6:14)
4. Temple "made with hands" (Mark 14:58; *not* in Luke / Acts 7:48)
5. Son of man saying (Mark 14:62 and par. / Acts 7:56)[86]
6. Charge of blasphemy (Mark 14:64; Matt 26:65; *not* in Luke / Acts 6:11)
7. High priest's question (Mark 14:61; Matt. 26:63; *not* in Luke (cf. 22:67, "they") / Acts 7:1)
8. Committal of spirit (*only* in Luke, 23:46 / Acts 7:59)
9. Cry out with a loud voice (Mark 15:34 = Matt. 27:46; Mark 15:37 and par. / Acts 7:60)[87]
10. Intercession for enemies' forgiveness (*only* in Luke 23:34 / Acts 7:60)

Such a degree of correspondence is hardly accidental. It would be difficult enough to claim coincidence if each of these elements were simply paralleled by the synoptic tradition. But that is the case with only three of the items listed. Five of the ten were omitted in Luke's Gospel and included

---

[85] A similar listing is to be found in Richard, *Author's Method*, p. 281.

[86] Luke 22:69 and Acts 7:56 both omit reference to the Son of man's coming μετὰ τῶν νεφελῶν τοῦ οὐρανοῦ. The Acts version also differs in terms of the posture of Jesus; in the Synoptics he is seated, in Acts he is standing. Much has been made of this discrepancy, although there is no way of knowing what significance (if any) it might have had for Luke (welcoming? eschatological anticipation?).

On the interpretation and significance of Acts 7:55-56, see H. P. Owen, "Stephen's Vision in Acts VII. 55-6"; M. Sabbe, "The Son of Man Saying in Acts 7, 56"; C. K. Barrett, "Stephen and the Son of Man"; Eberhard Nestle, "Acts 7:55-56" and "The Vision of Stephen"; George D. Kilpatrick, "Acts vii.56: Son of Man?" and "Again Acts vii.56: Son of Man?" (arguing for the reading υἱὸν τοῦ θεοῦ of $\mathfrak{p}^{74}$); Eduard Schweizer, "The Son of Man"; and P. Doble, "The Son of Man Saying in Stephen's Witnessing."

[87] Mark's version differs slightly:

Mark 15:37   ἀφεὶς φωνὴν μεγάλην
Matt. 27:50   κράξας φωνῇ μεγάλῃ
Luke 23:46   φωνήσας φωνῇ μεγάλῃ
Acts 7:60   ἔκραξεν φωνῇ μεγάλῃ.

instead in the Stephen story. The remaining two elements are repeated only in Luke and in Acts.

This last observation has given rise to the theory that it was the Stephen story that influenced the passion narrative and not the reverse.[88] This conclusion would in a sense exonerate Luke (if only in Acts!); the Stephen story in its details comes from early Christian tradition. But it is hardly credible to imagine that Stephen, of whom we hear only in Acts, was so towering a figure that his death overshadowed and became the literary model for that of Jesus.

The scaled-down proposal that Luke has borrowed Jesus' words on the cross in 23:34 and 46 from the Stephen tradition is possible if not probable. Stephen's committal of his spirit to the "Lord Jesus" (i.e., as opposed to the "Father," Luke 23:46) is linked to the vision of Jesus in verse 55, which is in turn a reiteration of the Son of man saying found in verse 56 and in Luke 22:69.[89] Furthermore, it is possible that both Luke 23:24 and Acts 7:59b are "modelled on a short Jewish evening-prayer taken from Ps. 31.5."[90]

The link between the intercessions in Luke 23:34 and Acts 7:60 is much more difficult to establish. It might be argued that Stephen's prayer, "Lord, do not hold this sin against them," seems artificial next to the words of Jesus, "Father, forgive them for they do not know what they are doing." The gospel saying alone supplies a rationale for the request (his attackers' ignorance); the Acts version, in omitting this and in calling the deed of the Jews a sin, is more possibly polemical. Such an escalation of Jewish culpability is fully in keeping with the scheme of Luke-Acts, in which the Jews, who acted first in ignorance and according to the purposes of God in Scripture in putting Jesus to death,[91] persistently and knowingly rejected the church's witness to Jesus and so were found ultimately to be without excuse. The martyrdom of Stephen marks a critical turn in this unfolding drama, the point at which Jewish opposition is crystallized, at which Saul is introduced, and at which Jewish rejection leads to Gentile acceptance. Stephen's vision of the glory of God, his angelic face (6:15), and his dying words underline *his own* innocence, not that of the Jews. Given the degree to which the account of Acts 6–7 is stylized after the passion narrative (the "loud voice"

---

[88] "It is possible that there has been a tendency to supplement the story of the Passion by details taken from the story of Stephen" (Cadbury and Lake, *Beginnings* 4:85). See also Räisänen, *The Torah and Christ*, pp. 266–67. Note the trenchant remark of Wilfred Knox: "On these points there is a total absence of evidence, which leaves a pleasing field open for speculation" (*Acts*, p. 77).

[89] Sabbe made the very plausible suggestion that Acts 7:55-56 is linked to Luke 6:22: "Ac 7, 55-56 . . . is understandable as a perfect Lukan redaction presenting Stephen as an exemplary witness of Christ. They exclude him and revile him and cast him out of the city, on account of the Son of Man" ("Son of Man Saying," p. 279).

[90] Haenchen, *Acts*, p. 296 [247].

[91] Acts 2:23; 3:17-26.

with which Stephen made this prayer is, after all, another of the parallels mentioned above) and the fact that the differences that do exist between the accounts seem explicable on grounds of Lukan redaction, we might conclude that this detail as well has been borrowed from the passion story. Against this, however, is the relatively poor attestation for the saying of Jesus.[92] This uncertainty about the text leaves us with very little.

If the saying does rightfully belong to Luke's Gospel, it could be that both Jesus and Stephen prayed for their enemies,[93] or that both instances are Lukan compositions, or that Luke borrowed from one of the accounts in composing the other. As we have just seen, the case for borrowing from the passion narrative to the Stephen story seems strongest. If the saying was inserted only later into Luke's passion narrative, we might imagine either that Luke knew of the logion of Jesus but included it in modified form in the Stephen story (as he did with other details) or that some later copyist adapted the words of Stephen and included them at an appropriate place in Luke's passion narrative. In the first case, Luke is still seen to be borrowing from the passion story; in the second, someone else is borrowing in the opposite direction. In no case is it likely that the passion story itself was influenced by traditions concerning the death of Stephen. Therefore, the parallels listed above work only in one direction; they call into question the veracity of the account of Stephen.

Or do they? Defenders of the historicity of the accusations point out that, although the themes in Acts 6:11-14 are repeated elsewhere, differences nevertheless remain.[94] Revealing discrepancies of this kind are said to be found in both of the charges credited to false witnesses in verses 13-14.[95] In these, Stephen is accused of speaking incessantly against the temple (ὁ τόπος ὁ ἅγιος [the holy place]) and the law. The content of these charges is then filled out in verse 14: ὅτι Ἰησοῦς ὁ Ναζωραῖος οὗτος καταλύσει τὸν τόπον τοῦτον καὶ ἀλλάξει τὰ ἔθη ἃ παρέδωκεν ἡμῖν Μωϋσῆς (this Jesus of Nazareth will destroy this place and will change the customs that Moses delivered to us).

It is said that these accusations differ markedly from those made against Jesus in the Gospels. The first of these, the temple charge, is of course notorious. Each of the Evangelists handled it differently, Matthew and John

---

[92] On the manuscript evidence for Luke 23:34, see n. 56 above.

[93] It has been argued that Stephen knew of Jesus' conduct at the cross and so deliberately imitated him in his death (e.g., Scott, "The Church of Jerusalem," p. 101).

[94] "For if we find differences between what Luke says of the trial of Jesus and what he tells of the trial of Stephen, we are, I think, entitled to take them at their face value, as giving a true account of the events" (Simon, *Stephen*, p. 23).

[95] The authenticity of v. 13 is supported less often than that of v. 14. Earl Richard, who defends vv. 11 and 14, says, "In considering v. 13, however, the situation is entirely different" (*Author's Method*, pp. 288-89). The reason is that v. 13 seems to be dependent upon v. 11, the account of the false witnesses in Mark 14:55-56, and the charges against Paul in Acts 21:28. Where it does differ, its vocabulary is nonetheless Lukan. See Räisänen, *The Torah and Christ*, pp. 262-63.

with the most evident discomfort (Matt. 26:61: δύναμαι καταλῦσαι τὸν ναὸν τοῦ θεοῦ, "I am able to destroy the temple of God"; John 2:19, 21: λύσατε τὸν ναὸν τοῦτον . . . ἐκεῖνος δὲ ἔλεγεν περὶ τοῦ ναοῦ τοῦ σώματος αὐτοῦ, "Destroy this temple . . . but he was speaking of the temple of his body"). The version in Acts is closest to Mark's:[96] in both, Jesus is said to claim that he himself would destroy[97] the temple. The most significant difference[98] between the two is that in Acts, Luke has deleted the final two-thirds of Mark's verse, the part which mentions the rebuilding of a temple ἀχειροποίητος. (This observation assumes Markan priority.) Thus it is asserted that Stephen did not believe that the temple should be rebuilt; rather, he "claims that Christ will bring the end of the temple and its worship."[99] The reason is supposed to have been either that the legitimacy of the temple ceased with the sacrifice of Christ[100] or that its fundamental *illegitimacy* has been made manifest by the revelation of Christ.[101]

The text of Acts 6:14 cannot possibly support this heavy load of interpretation. All that matters is that Jesus was supposed to have threatened the temple. Luke is no more interested in expanding this charge than he is in telling us what Jesus was going to change about the customs of Moses. Luke's terse and dramatically effective threefold repetition of the charges would be broken by such an unnecessary addition. "Furthermore, it should be pointed out that the χειροποίητος / ἀχειροποίητος of Mark will have a decided effect upon the speech (see 7:41, 43, 44, 48, and 50)."[102] Our earlier discussion concerning the actual falsity of the "false witnesses" should apply also. Those who would claim that Stephen denounced the temple will have to look elsewhere for their evidence.[103]

At least three specific points are made with respect to the charge in verse 14b. Two of these concern Luke's phrase τὰ ἔθη ἃ παρέδωκεν ἡμῖν Μωϋσῆς (the customs that Moses delivered to us). This is considered traditional even by a careful scholar such as Earl Richard, because of the unusual equation of ἔθος (custom) with νόμος (law), and because of "the uniqueness

---

[96] Richard, *Author's Method,* pp. 289–90. Cadbury noted that "violent acts of Jesus whether actual, as at the cleansing of the temple, or threatened, as when he is said to have threatened to destroy the temple (Mark 14, 58) are omitted by Luke" (*Style and Literary Method* 2:91).

[97] In Mark 14:58, καταλύσω; in Acts 6:14, καταλύσει.

[98] Scharlemann and others who advocate a Samaritan source set great store by the fact that Luke has replaced "temple" with "place," the Samaritan's term for their temple. The same phenomenon can be found in 7:7, in which "place" has been substituted for "mountain" in the quotation from Exod. 3:12. But Luke uses the same terminology in the charge against Paul in 21:28, and the alteration of the reference from Exodus can readily be explained as an accommodation by Luke to the situation of Stephen in Acts.

[99] Hengel, *Between,* p. 22 [192].

[100] Ibid., pp. 22–24 [191–96].

[101] See "Is the Speech Temple-critical?" below.

[102] Richard, *Author's Method,* p. 290.

[103] As, of course, they do. See the discussion below concerning Acts 7:46–50 and 42–43.

of Moses 'handing on' (παραδίδωμι) these customs."¹⁰⁴ Various authors have found significance in this peculiar terminology. Hengel, for example, believes that the accusation against Stephen, unlike that made against Paul in 21:28, had to do with "individual, specific points of teaching." Stephen did not see Christ as "the end of the law" (Rom. 10:4) but as "a new legislator."¹⁰⁵

But these supposed anomalies are in fact neither unique nor unusual. As S. G. Wilson has shown,¹⁰⁶ on occasion Luke uses the terms "custom" and "law" interchangeably and moves "naturally from the one to the other in describing the same phenomenon. The occurrences are scattered in a way that does not suggest dependence on a source."¹⁰⁷ To Wilson, this terminology *is* significant, but not in the way that Hengel suggests. "Luke's language implies an attitude towards Jewish law that is both tolerant, in that it upholds the right of the Jews to follow the practices most natural to them, and yet also restrictive, in that it would view as unnatural the imposition of this law where it does not belong, i.e. on Gentiles."¹⁰⁸ In any case, use of ἔθος (custom) in reference to the Jewish law is commonplace, particularly where the context is an explanation of Jewish laws to Gentiles.¹⁰⁹

The verb παραδίδωμι is used some fourteen times in Acts and another seventeen times in the Gospel of Luke. It is used most often in the sense of being "delivered over" to one's enemies.¹¹⁰ Correspondingly, it is often used in the Gospel to mean "betray."¹¹¹ But the more technical use of παραδίδωμι in 6:14 to refer to the transmission of tradition is found perfectly mirrored in 16:4 where Paul is said to have "delivered" to the churches of Asia τά δόγματα (the decisions) of the council at Jerusalem.¹¹² Perhaps even more striking, in *Antiquities* 15.268 we find a parallel example of the conjunction of παραδίδωμι and ἔθος.¹¹³

The most difficult question raised by verse 14 concerns the expression ἀλλάξει (will change). The verb is never used in the Gospels and is a hapax legomenon in Acts. None of the other five occurrences in the New Testament¹¹⁴ has anything to do with the changing of law or customs. And

---

¹⁰⁴ Richard, *Author's Method,* p. 291.
¹⁰⁵ Hengel, *Between,* p. 22 [191].
¹⁰⁶ Wilson, *Luke and the Law,* pp. 1–11.
¹⁰⁷ Ibid., p. 4. See, for example, Luke 2:27; Acts 15:1, 5; 21:21.
¹⁰⁸ Ibid., p. 11.
¹⁰⁹ See, for example, Josephus, *Ant.* 14.213, 216, 223 and 15.268. See Hengel, *Between,* p. 151 [191–92], n. 137, for additional examples and bibliography.
¹¹⁰ E.g., Acts 3:13; 22:4; 27:1.
¹¹¹ E.g., Luke 22:4, 21, 48.
¹¹² The fact that it is *Paul* in Acts 16 who is said to have delivered the Apostolic Decree makes it almost certain that the passage is a Lukan composition (see the discussion in chap. 4 below).
¹¹³ I owe this reference to E. P. Sanders.
¹¹⁴ Rom. 1:23; 1 Cor. 15:51, 52; Gal. 4:20; Heb. 1:12.

'the idea of a *future* change of the law(s) does not appear elsewhere" in Luke-Acts.[115] Have we arrived at the core of the Stephen tradition?

It is unlikely. For one thing, the use of the verb ἀλλάσω (change) in connection with the law *is* fixed in the tradition concerning Antiochus Epiphanes found in Daniel 7:25 and 1 Maccabees 1:49.[116] It would therefore have been available to Luke and, by association, would have represented the most heinous offense possible. Such an association may also lie behind the coupling of this with the charge of speaking against the temple. Räisänen also conjectures that the choice of the verb may have been influenced by the word ἄλλος (another), which was before Luke in Mark 14:58.[117] In any case, I would consider a house built on a hapax unlikely to stand. "Destroying" the temple has to be paralleled by something, after all. Why would Luke not have chosen the term he used?

As we have seen earlier, verse 14 refers to a future changing of customs. Interestingly, for just this reason its authenticity has been challenged by some who believe Stephen to have been critical of the law "here and now." Schmithals, for example, stated that verse 14 "*concealed* the antinomianism of Stephen's theological position."[118] Furthermore, it should be observed that the uniqueness of the terminology within the New Testament tells *against* the notion that Stephen was the leader of a distinctive and influential theological movement within the early church.

A considerable number of scholars who do not accept as genuine verses 13-14 do, however, believe that verse 11 has come to Luke from a traditional source. Is the case that much stronger? Earl Richard presents a fairly guarded defense of verses 13-14 but says about verse 11, "A careful examination of the style of v. 11 has convincingly shown that the verse owes a considerable debt to tradition."[119] Despite this confidence, I do not feel that the arguments for verse 11 are any more assured than those set forth in defense of verses 13-14.

There are two anomalies to verse 11. The first of these is Luke's use of the verb ὑποβάλλω (suborn), a hapax in the New Testament. The other is the adjective βλάσφημος (blasphemous), used elsewhere in the New Testament in this grammatical construction only in 2 Peter 2:11, where it is not accompanied by the preposition εἰς (against).[120] It is difficult to see how either peculiarity necessitates a source. Let us consider the latter of these first.

---

[115] Räisänen, *The Torah and Christ*, p. 263.

[116] I owe this insight to Heikki Räisänen, who writes, "Stephen's Jesus is portrayed by his opponents in a way that draws up a parallelism between him and the archenemy Antiochus Epiphanes" (ibid., p. 264).

[117] Ibid., p. 265.

[118] Schmithals, *Paul and James*, p. 27 [19], emphasis added.

[119] Richard, *Author's Method*, p. 288.

[120] Richard considers this last point especially significant. "The combination of the elements found in 6:11 is unique, particularly the adjective βλάσφημος followed by εἰς" (ibid.).

While it is true that Luke does not use the adjectival form of βλασφημέω elsewhere, the noun βλασφημία is used in Luke 5:21, and the verb itself appears seven times in Luke-Acts, once in connection with εἰς ("blaspheming against the Holy Spirit," Luke 12:10; see Mark 3:29). The term modified by βλάσφημα—ῥήματα (words) — is a "good Lukan" word,[121] while "blasphemy" itself might almost be called a good Lukan theme. Just as it is the Jews who disobey the law,[122] it is the Jews who are guilty of blasphemy.[123] In Acts 26:11, Paul even describes his persecution of the church as an attempt to compel Christian Jews to blaspheme! So we are brought again to a now-familiar consideration, namely, the Lukan apologetic or polemic vis-à-vis Judaism. Stephen is falsely charged with the crime of which the Jews themselves are culpable.

Finally, there is the question of the suborned witnesses who uttered the charge of blasphemy. It might be claimed that Luke did not get these "secretly instigated" men from Mark 14:56-57, where, we remember, the false witnesses were completely unable to agree on their story. Does their appearance here signify the presence of some distinct tradition, a historical foundation upon which Luke chose to build his verses 14-15?

Once more the answer is no. There is an alternative explanation for the singularity of the verse that is more compelling than the assumption of a "Stephen source." The suborned men, as well as a number of other motifs in the account of Stephen's martyrdom, are attributable to the influence on Luke of the Old Testament story of Naboth.[124] The subject is treated perceptively in a 1983 article by Thomas Brodie,[125] whose conclusions I shall summarize briefly.

Brodie begins by discussing the widely recognized fact that the infancy narrative of Luke 1-2 is "heavily dependent on the OT."[126] In a similar way, the account of Stephen's martyrdom depends heavily on the Old Testament, in this case, on "the only one example of the stoning to death of a really good man — Naboth."[127] The Naboth story (see 1 Kings 21:1-16) provided the framework "to which Luke has grafted other elements, especially elements which have an affinity with the accusations levelled against Jesus and

---

[121] Räisänen, *The Torah and Christ*, p. 263.
[122] Acts 7:53.
[123] Luke 22:65; 23:39; Acts 13:45; 18:6; 26:11.
[124] In chap. 2 I proposed a number of tests that might be employed in assessing the historical credibility of a story thought to have been modeled on some earlier account. My appraisal of the charges against Stephen is, on the basis of these considerations, negative, unlike the positive judgment formed in relation to the appointment of the Seven. The reason is that there exists in this case a very considerable degree of detailed correspondence between Luke and his models, and nothing of substance appears that is obviously independent of them.
[125] Thomas Louis Brodie, "The Accusing and Stoning of Naboth (1 Kgs 21:8-13) as One Component of the Stephen Text (Acts 6:9-14; 7:58a)."
[126] Ibid., p. 417.
[127] Ibid., p. 420.

Paul."[128] The similarities between the two accounts are laid out by the author as follows:

> General theme:
>   The accusing and stoning to death of a just man
> General structure:
>   Basic twofold (doublet) arrangement
> Actions (plot):
>   Concerted hostility
>   The suborning of witnesses
>   The two-pronged accusation
>   The manipulation of people and leaders
>   Setting the victim before the (popular) court
>   The false witnesses
>   The two-pronged accusation(s)
>   The stoning
> Some details:
>   Repetition of "men/witnesses . . . saying"
>   Involvement of "the people"
>   Involvement of free(d)men[129]

It is easy to see how well the novelty of verse 11 is accounted for in Brodie's analysis. Although the language is slightly different, the structure is the same. The repetition and similarity of the double accusations of the suborned witnesses are especially remarkable. If Luke knew that the church's first martyr died by stoning, he could not have picked a more evocative and useful device for the presentation of his story.

Brodie is interested in the question of the historicity of the Stephen narrative, and it is instructive to see how he goes about considering it. Because he cannot accept verse 11, he turns hopefully toward verses 13-14. "However, the problem is not easy, for it is precisely within the later accusations (Acts 6:13-14), in other words, within some of the matter which has least resemblance to the OT and which might be used as a basis for building historicity, that we find the greatest affinity with the texts concerning Jesus and Paul. In other words, what has not been adapted from the figure of Naboth, has, to some degree at least, been borrowed from the figures of Jesus and Paul."[130]

Reviewing the findings of this section, we come to the following conclusion: the accusations in 6:11-14 do not come from an early "Stephen source"[131] and so cannot properly be used as the basis for determining the theology of Stephen. Many who doubt the historicity of the speech do in

---

[128] Ibid., p. 432.
[129] Reproduced from ibid., p. 420.
[130] Ibid., p. 431.
[131] E.g., the "Antiochene source" alluded to earlier.

fact choose this approach, avoiding the proverbial frying pan by opting instead for the fire. Their plight illustrates the difficulties that suffuse the whole of the Hellenist debate.

The Speech as the Locus of Tradition

Earlier the question was asked, Do we have accurate information about the beliefs of Stephen? This led us directly to the matter of sources. Did some authentic church tradition mediate the theology of Stephen, or did Luke devise it ad hoc? The speech of Stephen seems the most natural place to turn in looking for sources, but certain objections to this approach may be raised. Chief among these objections is the view that the speech is a Lukan composition based upon a comparative analysis of the place of speeches in ancient historiography. The apparent lack of correspondence between the accusations in chapter 6 and the speech in chapter 7 presented a further difficulty. An appreciation of these problems gave rise to the position just discussed, that the accusations and not the speech are the locus of the author's traditional information about the beliefs of Stephen.

Because of what has been said, it might seem that all of New Testament scholarship is agreed on this solution, but that is certainly not the case. A good many exegetes do contend that there is a recognizable source behind the speech of chapter 7, and a large percentage of these would argue as well that the speech fits the context of the accusations.

How likely is this alternative approach? It is difficult to offer a single answer, in view of the tremendous variety of source theories that exist. Because of the complexity and significance of the problem, and the enduring presence of competing and conflicting answers, it will be necessary to examine the matter in some detail. This I propose to do first by looking at problems germane to those theories that propose a source for the speech of Stephen. By means of this general analysis we shall avoid much unnecessary repetition and shall be in a better position to evaluate specific source theories. Such an evaluation will then be followed by a summary of conclusions concerning the relationship between Stephen and the study of the Hellenists of Acts.

Is the Speech Law-Critical?

The first objection to a majority of the source theories concerns their reliance upon the accusations in chapter 6. Most of those who defend the historicity of the speech also hold to the veracity of the accusations. The exceptions tend to be those who, such as Schmithals, cited above, recognize that these charges are not really radical enough to support their conclusions concerning the theology of Stephen. But these are not typical.[132] Source theorists believe overwhelmingly that the traditions underlying the speech extend as well to the accusations. It is at the very least presumed that the accusations are an accurate reflection of the content of the speech. In other words, the speech really does address the accusations. In what way? By demonstrating that Stephen was in fact critical of the temple and the law.

One has to wonder which is the interpretive horse and which is the cart. The great preponderance of scholars have chosen to interpret the speech in light of the (generally misinterpreted) accusations.[133] Even those who dismiss the veracity of the charges in 6:11-14 seem bound to them when it comes to understanding 7:2-53.[134] Ernst Haenchen, for example, who is very far from being a champion of source hypotheses,[135] believes that the speech contains "a radical denunciation of the temple worship."[136] He also accepts that "Stephen and his group" must have exercised "great freedom in relation to the law."[137]

Are the "true" accusations of the "false" witnesses substantiated by the speech? Martin Dibelius addressed this question perceptively when commenting on the supposed temple criticism of the speech. "The speech is extremely reticent and seems to be very loosely connected with the charge — indeed, we ourselves shall probably be reading into it any significance that we may find."[138] This observation should be extended to both of the charges against Stephen. It is extremely doubtful that the speech would ever have been interpreted as law-critical if it were not for the charge in chapter 6 that "this man never stops saying things against . . . the law" (v. 13). If anything, the speech is emphatically pro-law. This is most evident in the treatment of Moses, the one who received the "living oracles" (λόγια ζῶντα, 7:38) at Mount Sinai. Johannes Munck has remarked that Acts 7 "gives us the highest appreciation of Moses that we meet in the New Testament."[139] It is likely that Moses and the law have been elevated for the dramatic purpose of heightening the guilt of the Jews. The law itself was received εἰς διαταγὰς

---

[132] Even Schmithals uses the now toned down accusations as his point of departure (p. 27 [19]).

[133] On the misinterpretation of the accusations against Stephen, see the discussion above.

[134] Consider the attitude of Marcel Simon: "The problem indeed is not whether the speech is relevant, but whether it is genuine" (*Stephen*, p. 39). Simon thinks that the speech can stand on its own, but it is difficult to believe that his interpretation is guided by the evidence of the speech itself.

[135] "Thus in relating the trial of the first martyr, Luke had the trial of Jesus in mind and used material which might have been dangerous if applied to the earlier occasion" (Haenchen, *Acts*, p. 274 [227]).

[136] Ibid., p. 286 [237].

[137] Ibid., pp. 267-68 [221].

[138] Dibelius, *Studies*, p. 168 [144].

[139] Munck, *Paul*, p. 221, n. 1 [215, n. 15].

ἀγγέλων (as ordained by angels).¹⁴⁰ The fault lay with the Jews, who failed to keep it.¹⁴¹ Attempts to find criticism of the law in Stephen's speech are wholly unconvincing. W. Knox, for example, objected to Harnack's terming the attitude of Stephen as "quite obscure":¹⁴² "Exactly what more definite condemnation of the law was needed than to say that Israel in the desert rejected the 'living oracles' originally given and made a Golden Calf, and were in consequence left to serve the host of heaven does not appear."¹⁴³ Such criticism misses the point. It is not the law that is the subject of Luke's attention; it is the Jews. Luke *needs* the law in much the same way that Paul needs it in Romans 2:17-24; it is the bar at which the Jews may be arraigned.

Is the Speech Temple-Critical?

Scholars who consider the Hellenists to be a bridge to Paul on the question of law criticism are in a fascinating dilemma. They want to emphasize the law-critical side of Stephen, but there is no evidence. A somewhat better case can be made for criticism of the temple — at least here there is some ambiguity as to Stephen's position — but an attack on the temple seems something of an irrelevance. While questions about the law did concern the churches of Jerusalem and Antioch, no data suggest that the temple was also a point of controversy. In fact, the one type of temple "criticism" that can adequately be defended on the basis of the speech is not unique and fails to attack the institution of the temple itself.¹⁴⁴ Furthermore, the persecution of Stephen and the Hellenists over the temple might not distinguish them from but rather unite them with Jesus and the Hebrews, both of whom may have suffered for similar reasons.¹⁴⁵ Consequently, it must be shown that Stephen's criticism of the temple was of such a fundamental nature that it brought into question the validity of the law itself.¹⁴⁶

---

¹⁴⁰ V. 53; see also vv. 30, 35, and 38. Unlike Paul's deprecating reference to angelic agency in Gal. 3:19, Luke mentions the angels at Sinai in order to emphasize the sanctity and importance of the law (compare angelic agency in Luke 1:11-20, 26-38; 2:9-15, 21; and Acts 5:19-20; 8:26; 10:3-7, 22; 11:13; 12:7-11, 23; 23:9; 27:23-24). The mediation of angels in the giving of the law is also referred to in Heb. 2:2.

¹⁴¹ Acts 7:53; see vv. 38-39.

¹⁴² Harnack, *Acts*, p. 173 [138].

¹⁴³ Knox, *Acts*, pp. 23-24.

¹⁴⁴ That is, the idea that the destruction of the temple came as a result of Jewish unbelief. See Matt. 21:33-41, 42-44 and parallels. This does not, as I noted earlier, constitute *criticism* of the temple.

¹⁴⁵ On the temple and the death of Jesus, see Sanders, *Jesus and Judaism*, pp. 296-306. While it is not known why, for example, James, the brother of Jesus, was put to death, it is once again the high priest who was responsible for his death (in this case Ananus, brother-in-law of Caiaphas [John 18:13]; Josephus, *Ant.*, 20.197-203).

¹⁴⁶ Marcel Simon, for example, believed that when Stephen denounced the temple, it was really the law that was "at the very core of his thought." Specifically, Stephen is said to have assailed the "adulterated Law" "as symbolized and summed up by the Temple and the

It is for this reason, I believe, that Stephen's negative statements concerning the temple are portrayed as being so strong.¹⁴⁷ This is a necessity if he is to be made a critic of the law.

Acts 7:46-50. At two principal places in the speech, scholars claim to find radical criticism of the temple. The most significant of these is in verses 46-48a:

[Δαυιδ] εὗρεν χάριν ἐνώπιον τοῦ θεοῦ καὶ <u>ᾐτήσατο εὑρεῖν σκήνωμα</u> τῷ οἴκῳ Ἰακώβ.¹⁴⁸

---

sacrificial worship. As regards the authentic Law, those 'lively oracles' delivered unto Moses, Jesus' divinely assigned task is to bring it back to its original purity" (*Stephen*, p. 46).

¹⁴⁷ A small sample of opinion demonstrates the entrenched position of the interpretation within modern scholarship.

> Stephen . . . rejects it [the temple] a priori; he puts it in opposition to the legitimate cultic place of the tabernacle, and on the same level with the golden calf and shrine of Moloch. (Wellhausen, "Apostelgeschichte," p. 13)
>
> The tabernacle gave way to the temple, but it was not that God wanted it so. . . . God, creator and master of the universe, cannot be contained within a temple. (Loisy, *Les Actes*, p. 341)
>
> Stephen however rejects the temple entirely as a falling away from the true worship of God. (Eduard Meyer, *Die Apostelgeschichte und die Anfänge des Christentums*, p. 159)
>
> The building of the Temple was an act of rebellion. (Maddox, *Purpose*, p. 53)
>
> Sacrifice and the building of the temple are for the speaker signs of the falling away by the fathers from the saving will of God. (Bihler, *Stephanusgeschichte*, p. 135)
>
> The temple worship practiced by the Jews is . . . a service of idols. (Hahn, *The Titles of Jesus*, pp. 373-74 [383])
>
> He rejects not God's presence among his people via the tabernacle . . . but the temple/house/"this place." (Richard, *Author's Method*, p. 329)
>
> David . . . found favour with God and planned to make him a σκήνωμα, a word that is used occasionally for the tabernacle. At this point the decisive rot set in. Solomon built God a house, οἶκος. This was contrary to God's will. (C. K. Barrett, "Old Testament History according to Stephen and Paul," p. 67)

There have always been some scholars, however, who have recognized that the Stephen speech is not temple-critical. W. M. L. de Wette wrote in 1841, "Stephen does not speak with disapproval of the building of the temple but warns merely against its misinterpretation and overestimation" (*Kurze Erklärung der Apostelgeschichte*, p. 65). Similar sentiments are found, for example, in Gerhard Krodel's *Acts* (pp. 150-51) and in Dennis D. Sylva's recent article "The Meaning and Function of Acts 7:46-50." Sylva's work is a particularly valuable contribution to the debate, especially in its convincing defense of the "transcendence" interpretation of the temple passages. Sylva provides a useful bibliography on the question in n. 4, pp. 261-62.

¹⁴⁸ The form of this verse is the subject of some contention. Οἴκῳ has the better textual attestation (𝔓⁷⁴ ℵ* B D et al.) and for that reason is generally preferred. The difficulty of the reading is also cited as evidence for its originality, since assimilation to the LXX (θεῷ of Ps. 132:5) is assumed to have been the secondary impulse. (See Metzger, *Textual Commentary*, pp. 351-53, for a detailed presentation of this view.) Nevertheless, despite its weaker attestation (ℵᶜ A C E Ψ 𝔪 in Nestle-Aland 26th ed. et al.), the reading θεῷ is defended by a number of scholars on the grounds that it makes more sense of the passage (especially the αὐτῷ of v. 47; see F. F. Bruce, *The Acts of the Apostles: The Greek Text with Introduction and Commentary*, p. 175; Jack H. Wilson, "Luke's Role as a Theologian and Historian in Acts 6:1–8:3," p. 185; Johannes Bihler, *Die Stephanusgeschichte im Zusammenhang der Apostelgeschichte*, p. 74; and Conzelmann,

Σολομων δὲ <u>οἰκοδόμησεν</u> αὐτῷ <u>οἶκον</u>.
ἀλλ' οὐχ 'ο ὕψιστος ἐν <u>χειροποιήτοις</u> κατοικεῖ.

[(David) found favor with God and *asked that he might find a dwelling place* for the house of Jacob.
But it was Solomon *who built a house* for him.
Yet the Most High does not dwell in *houses made with human hands*.]

The primary debate concerns the supposed contrast between finding a dwelling place and building a house. If such a contrast exists, it is usually interpreted to mean that the simple, approved intentions of David were thwarted in the actual disposition of his son, Solomon. So, for example, Haenchen remarks that "the speaker understands σκήνωμα (dwelling place) in the sense that the pious David wanted to "find" God only a tented dwelling, i.e. the tabernacle, not build him a solid house."[149]

This seems highly doubtful. Verse 46b draws directly upon Psalm 132:5: <u>ἕως οὗ εὕρω</u> τόπον τῷ κυρίῳ, σκήνωμα τῷ θεῷ 'Ιακωβ (until I *find* a place for the Lord, *a dwelling place for the God of Jacob*).[150] This is, of course, quite enough to account for the peculiar phrase εὑρεῖν σκήνωμα (to find a dwelling place). Similarly, the vocabulary of verse 47 (οἰκοδομεῖν οἶκον [to build a house]) is to be found in a number of related verses in the Septuagint (2 Sam. 7:13; 1 Kings 5:3; 6:2; 8:16-17),[151] where it also refers to the building of the temple.[152] Therefore it seems most reasonable to take verses 46-47 at face value and not be diverted by them. The author indeed wishes

---

Acts, p. 56 [56]). The strength of the variant οἴκῳ could be attributed to a primitive corruption of the tradition (according to Haenchen, "οἴκῳ [was] probably inserted for an illegible θεῷ by an early copyist"; *Acts,* p. 285 [236]). Richard also argues in favour of θεῷ on structural grounds: v. 46a (the author's own construction) and 46b (a quotation), following the pattern of v. 5a and b, were placed together as parallel expressions (εὑρεν χάριν ἐνώπιον τοῦ θεοῦ / ἠτήσατο εὑρεῖν σκήνωμα τῷ θεῷ 'Ιακώβ), a parallelism that is lost with the alternative reading (*Author's Method,* pp. 131-32).

It is questionable whether much should be inferred on the basis of either reading. Θεῷ is sometimes favored by those interpreters who contrast v. 46 with 47, since, one imagines, any association of the favored David with an οἶκος is perforce to be avoided (see, for example, Simon, *St. Stephen,* p. 51). But the οἶκος 'Ιακώβ could just as well be interpreted to mean the people of Israel rather than the temple per se (as in *Beginnings* 5:81: "David wished to build a habitation [of God] for the house of Jacob"). In either case, then, the principal term is σκήνωμα, since a habitation of one form or another could have been sought either for "the God of Jacob" or for "(the God of) the house (i.e., people) of Jacob." The meaning of σκήνωμα will be discussed below.

[149] Haenchen, *Acts,* p. 285 [236]. The same interpretation is found in Baur, *Paul* 1:47-52 [54-59].

[150] Note that English Psalm 132 = LXX Ψαλμός 131. Subsequent references to the psalm are based on the English enumeration.

[151] Note that the English 1 and 2 Samuel = LXX Βασιλειῶν A and B; English 1 and 2 Kings = LXX Βασιλειῶν Γ and Δ.

[152] The use of αἰτέω, while not present in this connection in the LXX, is also entirely consistent with the sentiment of Ps. 132:1-5 and the account of 2 Samuel 7.

to make a point about the temple (among other things), but it is overly subtle to detect the sort of contrast that so many have found in these verses.

Nevertheless, Marcel Simon has pursued this idea further by contending that what lies behind Psalm 132/Acts 7:46b is not David's wish to build a temple (2 Sam. 7) but rather his desire to move the ark to Jerusalem (2 Sam. 6).[153] Accordingly, the σκήνωμα (dwelling place) of Psalm 132 is taken to be a reference to the σκηνή (tent) of the ark, and Acts 7:46-47 sets forth a "radical opposition . . . between two men and two types of habitation," between the tent of David and the temple of Solomon.[154]

In Simon's favor, one may cite 2 Samuel 6:17, in which we are told that the ark was set εἰς τόν τόπον αὐτῆς εἰς μέσον τῆς σκηνῆς ἧς ἔπηξεν αὐτῇ Δαυιδ (in its *place* in the midst of the *tent* that David pitched for it). The language is indeed reminiscent of Psalm 132:5 (εὕρω τόπον τῷ κυρίῳ σκήνωμα [I may find a *place* for the Lord, a *dwelling place*]), and in fact there is no doubt that the story of the relocation of the ark from Kiriath-jearim to Jerusalem, recorded in 2 Samuel 6 and 2 Chronicles 1:4, underlies Psalm 132. Verse 6 of the psalm refers to it explicitly, and the whole of verses 6-10 probably represents a ceremonial reenactment of the event.[155] But the psalm does not *only* refer to 2 Samuel 6. It is a commemoration of the Davidic line and of God's choice of Jerusalem and probably "represents part of the festal liturgy of *the feast of the dedication of the Jerusalem Temple.*"[156] For this purpose the psalm relies even more heavily upon 2 Samuel 7 than it does upon chapter 6. The desire of David to find a σκήνωμα τῷ θεῷ Ιακωβ (a dwelling place for the God of Jacob), which opens the Psalm in verses 1-5, is almost certainly a reference to 2 Samuel 7:2,[157] Simon notwithstanding. Significantly, this verse also contains both of the terms that are supposed to be in contrast in Acts 7:46-47 — σκηνή (tent) and οἶκος (house; see 2 Sam. 7:13). Moreover, this οἶκος κέδρινος, David's own home, is referred to in Psalm 132:3 as σκήνωμα οἴκου μου (literally, "dwelling place of my house"). So, despite its verbal similarity, the σκήνωμα τῷ θεῷ Ιακωβ almost certainly does *not* correspond to the σκηνή of Acts 7:44 but rather to the οἶκος of verse 47. Furthermore, verse 11 of Psalm 132, concerning the ascent of David's son to the throne, is also paralleled by 2 Samuel 7:12 (ἐκ τῆς κοιλίας σου (from your body [literally, "belly"]); followed in 2 Samuel by a reference to the building of the

---

[153] Simon, *Stephen*, p. 51.
[154] Ibid., p. 53.
[155] See Artur Weiser, *The Psalms: A Commentary*, p. 780 [2:539].
[156] Ibid., p. 779 [2: 538], emphasis added. "The connection of the psalm with the dedication of the Temple is also evident from II Chron. 6.41f., where Ps. 132.8-10 forms the conclusion of the prayer offered on the occasion of the dedication of the Temple and put back into the mouth of Solomon, a custom that probably dates back to early tradition" (ibid.).
[157] "The two fundamental ideas of the psalm, the promise made to the house of David and the problem of the election of Zion as God's dwelling-place, are linked together in II Sam. 7" (ibid., p. 780 [538]).

temple). Therefore Psalm 132 commemorates the establishing of the Davidic dynasty and the cult in Zion in toto, making use of both 2 Samuel 6 and 7. Finally, it should be added that Luke's choice of the verb αἰτέω (ask) in Acts 7:46 almost certainly indicates that he himself was thinking of 2 Samuel 7:1-2 as the background to Psalm 132:2-5. Therefore, Simon's appeal to the context of Psalm 132 backfires against him.[158]

The supposed contrast between the good tent and the bad house is further undermined by the fact that the categories are not used consistently by the author. Specifically, we are told of a bad σκηνή in Acts 7:43 (τὴν σκηνὴν τοῦ Μολοχ [the tent of Moloch]) and, if the reading is correct,[159] of an apparently good house in verse 46. If the author genuinely had intended to create a contrast between the terms, he could certainly have done a better job of it.

Two other arguments marshaled in support of radical criticism of the temple in Acts 7:46-48 ought to be mentioned. The first of these concerns the use of οἶκος (house) without an article in verse 47. Earl Richard believes either 1 Kings 6:2 or 6:14, both of which refer to ὁ οἶκος (*the* house) built by Solomon, to have been Luke's source. "By the omission of the article the writer lifts the line of argument to a philosophical level . . . as opposed to a historical one."[160] This is reaching too far, especially since 1 Kings 8:17-18, which reiterates the contents of 2 Samuel 7, has a far better claim to be a Lukan source. This twice refers to Solomon building an οἶκος (house) without a trace of a definite article.

Second, attention is sometimes drawn to the word order of verse 47. It is noted that the direct object οἶκον (house) is placed after the indirect object αὐτῷ (him), in contradistinction to the Septuagint in verses such as 1 Kings 5:3, 5, and 6:2, where the reverse order is employed. The assertion is then made that "by placing οἶκος in the final position the author draws particular attention upon the term and further stresses the contrast between v. 46b and 47, between σκήνωμα and οἶκος, between David and Solomon."[161]

In point of fact, Luke is quoting none of these verses. Instead, he is summarizing,[162] and the word order with which he chooses to do so is used on at least four other occasions in the speech.[163] Verse 8a, another of Luke's historical summaries, says, for example, that God "gave him [Abraham] *a* covenant of circumcision" (ἔδωκεν αὐτῷ [Abraham] διαθήκην περιτομῆς, note as well the lack of a definite article). There is simply no case for building an

---

[158] It is difficult, in any case, to know how to weigh arguments concerning the original meaning of the psalm, since these presuppose that Luke or Stephen was thinking in terms of context rather than (simply) words in making this quotation.
[159] See n. 148 above.
[160] Richard, *Author's Method,* p. 132.
[161] Ibid.
[162] Again, if anything, 1 Kings 8:17-18.
[163] Vv. 5, 8, 10, and 40.

argument based on either the omission of the definite article or the supposedly unusual word order in verse 47.

Finally, it is important to note a fact that is almost universally ignored in discussions of this passage: verse 48, which summarizes verses 46 and 47 (and almost certainly the author's own point of view), omits the words οἶκος and σκήνωμα entirely. Thus, the verse makes a simple point that has nothing to do with an opposition between temples and tents: God does not reside in things made by human hands (ἀλλ' οὐχ ὁ ὕψιστος ἐν χειροποιήτοις κατοικεῖ).[164] It is a point that any Jew might make in a polemic against paganism and about which no Jew would probably be able to disagree (see 1 Kings 8:27).[165] At most, it represents the perspective of one who would resist any tendency to localize worship exclusively in the temple. The assertion of verse 48 takes on additional significance, however, when it is made in the context of a Gentile church or mission, and that after the destruction of the temple in A.D. 70. We return to this theme shortly.

The real problem with verses 46-50 is their relationship to Stephen's accusations against the Jews in verses 51-53. These are so vehement in tone that it seems necessary to find justification for them in preceding verses. Thus scholars are led to overestimate the force of the polemic in verses 48-50 and to assume that a repudiation of the temple is at the heart of the Stephen speech. According to Haenchen, "The swift passage to the string of charges in verses 51-3 which goad the audience into fury can only be explained if the preceding verses form a radical denunciation of the Temple worship."[166] In point of fact the allegations of verses 51-53 have nothing to do with the temple. In these verses, "the author appears to have as his goal to list as many accusations as possible against the Judaism of NT times."[167] The Jews are "stiff-necked"[168] and "uncircumcised in heart"[169] "and ears."[170] They "are forever opposing the Holy Spirit,[171] having killed the prophets,[172] and are

---

[164] Cf. the more typical translation of Eduard Meyer: "Gott wohnt nicht in *Bauten* von Menschenhand" (God does not dwell in *buildings* made with human hands) (*Apostelgeschichte*, p. 160, emphasis added).

[165] Sylva writes: "According to Luke, the Christian message is not that Jesus will destroy the temple 'made with hands'... but rather that God transcends (*ho hypsistos*, Acts 7:48) anything made with human hands" ("Meaning and Function," p. 274). Note Sylva's masterly defense of this transcendence thesis on pp. 265-75.

[166] Haenchen, *Acts*, p. 286 [237]. Given Haenchen's views concerning the composition of the speech, it is curious that he makes an argument based on the probable response of a fictitious audience.

[167] Richard, *Author's Method*, p. 138

[168] As Richard says, the vocabulary of Stephen's "invective is thoroughly OT" (ibid.). For σκληροτράχηλος, see Exod. 33:3, 5; 34:9; Deut. 9:6, 13.

[169] See Lev. 26:41; Deut. 10:16; Jer. 4:4; 9:26; Ezek. 44:7.

[170] See Jer. 6:10.

[171] See Isa. 63:10 and, within the Stephen material itself, Acts 6:3, 5, 10; 7:55.

[172] On the notion that "being murdered [was]... the normal lot of a prophet," see

now becoming the betrayers[173] and murderers[174] of the righteous one.[175] For the crowning accusation he returns, not to the temple or even to the death of Jesus, but to that which has occupied the greatest part of his attention, the rejection of Moses and the law: "You are the ones that received the law as ordained by angels, and yet you have not kept it."[176]

It is worth considering this last statement more carefully. It is my understanding that the dominant (although by no means the only) question being addressed in the Acts of the Apostles is, Who are the people of God? According to Robert Maddox: "Luke's answer is that the Christians are the heirs of the promises made by God to the Hebrew patriarchs about a coming time of salvation.... Those promises were made by God [who] ... intended, through Israel, to open up salvation for those who accepted and judgement for those who rejected it. As things have turned out, it is largely Gentiles who have accepted the offered salvation and Judaism that has rejected it. Therefore, surprisingly, Judaism has been judged by God."[177]

Accordingly, it is not the institutions of Judaism, which are by definition good, but the unbelieving Jews themselves that are assailed. This is as true in the Stephen speech as it is in the rest of Acts.[178] Jewish disobedience, although to some extent a theme of the entire speech, is centered upon the rejection of Moses and his teaching.[179] The point is twofold: (1) it shows by

---

Haenchen, *Acts*, p. 286, n. 1 [237, n. 3]. The immediate source of the passage is surely the traditions underlying Luke 11:47-51/Matt. 23:30-35, Luke 13:34/Matt. 23:37, and Matt. 5:12.

[173] See also Luke 6:16. Προδότης is used elsewhere in the New Testament only in 2 Tim. 3:4.

[174] Matthew uses the term φονεύω twice in the accusations of chap. 23 (vv. 23:31, 35). Φονεύς itself appears in the Gospels only in Matt. 22:7, a passage that Richard asserts "is obviously related to the present text" (*Author's Method*, p. 139). It is found in Acts also in 3:14 (a verse closely paralleling 7:52) and 28:4.

[175] The presence of δίκαιος in Matt. 23:35 (πᾶν αἷμα δίκαιον) is significant. The parallel passage in Luke's Gospel refers instead to τὸ αἷμα πάντων τῶν προφητῶν (11:50). Interestingly, Matthew's use in 23:35 of ἔρχομαι ἐπί with an accusative object is also paralleled in the Stephen speech in 7:11, ἦλθεν δὲ λιμὸς ἐφ' ὅλην τὴν Αἴγυπτον (Richard, *Author's Method*, p. 139). Further, Matthew's verb φονεύω is matched by the φονεῖς of Acts 7:52; and both δίκαιος and φονεύς appear in the closely parallel passage of Acts 3:14. Therefore it seems most likely that the tradition associated with Jesus in Matt. 23:35/Luke 11:50 lies behind Acts 7:52 and, at least in part, 3:14 as well. One might in any case question the likelihood of a supposedly Hellenistic source that evidences a Christology of ὁ δίκαιος.

[176] Sylva noted that the Jews' resistance of the Holy Spirit (v. 51) was demonstrated by their resistance of Stephen, the archetypal bearer of the Spirit (6:3, 5, 10, 55; "Meaning and Function," pp. 273-74).

[177] Maddox, *Purpose*, p. 183. According to Brawley: "The evidence warrants a new reading of Luke-Acts as a product of a struggle for the legacy of Israel as the people of God" (*Luke-Acts and the Jews*, p. 159).

[178] See, for example, Jack T. Sanders, *The Jews in Luke-Acts*, "The Jewish People in Luke-Acts," and "The Salvation of the Jews in Luke-Acts"; Lloyd Gaston, "Anti-Judaism and the Passion Narrative in Luke and Acts"; Stephen G. Wilson, "The Jews and the Death of Jesus in Acts"; David L. Tiede, "'Glory to Thy People Israel!': Luke-Acts and the Jews"; and Robert C. Tannehill, "Rejection by Jews and Turning to Gentiles: The Pattern of Paul's Mission in Acts."

[179] The Moses section covers the entirety of vv. 17-43, by far the bulk of the speech.

their earlier example that the Jews are likely to be wrong in their present rejection of Jesus, and (2) it demonstrates the tragic consequences to which rejection of this "Second Moses" must lead.[180] This is the true heart of the Stephen speech.[181]

It is important to recognize that although the institutions of Judaism are not themselves attacked directly, their value is necessarily depreciated. The Christian church was not, after all, a back-to-Moses movement. The author is not contending that the Jews need simply become better (i.e., more law abiding) Jews.[182] He is not asking, in other words, that they accept their heritage but that they accept the thing to which he believes their heritage should lead. To Luke, Judaism is inherently good but also inherently *not good enough*.

This insight goes a long way toward explaining the strangely contradictory attitude of Acts toward the Jews, and it certainly helps to explain the inclusion of verses 48-50 within the Stephen speech. Luke's perspective encourages a spiritualizing tendency that also appears in verse 51 (uncircumcised in heart and ears) and perhaps in the story of Abraham as well (he [God] did not give him [Abraham] any of it as a heritage not even a foot's length, v. 5 [Deut. 2:5]; compare Heb. 11:39-40).[183] In a sense this allows him the luxury of denying what he at the same time must of necessity affirm. Christians accept the law and the temple—*rightly understood.* Johannes Weiss has commented, "The point of the speech is plainly directed against the overestimation of the temple in Jerusalem."[184] Although I cannot agree that this is the point of the speech, I do agree that this theme has been taken up by the author in verses 48-50.

The tendency to spiritualize is assumed by many to have been common within Diaspora Judaism,[185] and for this reason these verses are sometimes taken as evidence of an Antiochene cum Hellenistic source for the speech of

---

[180] This explains the peculiar finality of vv. 42-43, a part of the speech that does not work logically with the verses that follow but fits the author's purpose perfectly by emphasizing the seriousness of Jewish disobedience and unbelief. See the discussion below.

[181] This perspective is shared by Johannes Bihler in his study *Die Stephanusgeschichte im Zusammenhang der Apostelgeschichte.* Bihler writes, "With the stoning of Stephen, the Jewish people as a whole (although not each individual) have fundamentally pronounced their rejection of the call to repentance" (pp. 28-29; see also pp. 79-81, 183). See also Daniel Arichea, "A Critical Examination of the Stephen Speech in the Acts of the Apostles," pp. 254-65.

[182] The type of argument employed in Acts 7 also appears in Romans 2. In both places it is open to criticism, since it achieves its ends only by exaggerating the culpability of the Jews. Could, for example, the Jews fairly be *typified* as adulterers and plunderers of temples (Rom. 2:22)?

[183] C. F. D. Moule has made the interesting suggestion that Acts 7 witnesses to a spiritualizing "sanctuary and sacrifice apologia" that was "a part and parcel of early Christian catechesis" ("Sanctuary and Sacrifice in the Church of the New Testament," citing p. 40).

[184] Johannes Weiss, *Earliest Christianity* 1:169 [123].

[185] E.g., Räisänen, *The Torah and Christ,* p. 288.

Stephen.[186] But if this sort of spiritualizing was as typically Hellenistic as is often supposed, there is no reason to limit it to Antiochene Christianity, much less to the Stephen circle particularly. Indeed, the point made about the temple in Acts 7:48-50 is repeated (including use of χειροποίητος [made by human hands])[187] in Paul's speech on the Areopagus in Acts 17:24.[188] Räisänen's observation is pertinent: "This makes it probable that verses 48-50 represent *Luke's* own point of view."[189] This confirms an observation made by S. G. Wilson in a somewhat different context: "Luke seems to stand closer to hellenistic Judaism in his understanding of the law, [reflecting] . . . some of the major changes which took place in Judaism after 70 C.E."[190]

Even if the tendency to minimize the temple is understandable, we have not yet answered the question as to why the theme is brought into the speech. A number of plausible answers could be offered,[191] but I believe that one in particular makes more sense of the presence of the temple, and indeed of its dramatic location within the speech, than any other. The key may be found in the attitude toward the temple expressed in Luke 13:34-35a.

---

[186] Räisänen appears to lean in this direction (ibid., pp. 287-88).

[187] The form of the temple accusation in 6:14 most closely resembles that of Mark's Gospel (14:58). Mark's term χειροποίητος is not, however, taken up in Acts 6. Instead it appears *in the answer to the charge* in chap. 7 (v. 48).

[188] This theme is already present in the story of the dedication of the temple in 1 Kings 8.

[189] Räisänen, *The Torah and Christ*, p. 274.

[190] Wilson, *Luke and the Law*, p. 114.

[191] Among the possibilities: (1) a *rather bland* temple section was part of a so-called neutral source used by the author; (2) a *strongly critical* temple section was a part of genuine tradition preserved by the Hellenists and transmitted to Luke; (3) Luke knew that criticism of the temple was (at least part of) the reason for Stephen's death and so, not knowing specific details of the incident, chose to include the only materials available to him concerning controversy over the temple; (4) Luke knew that a dispute over the temple had contributed to Jesus' death and chose, for whatever reason, to include those materials here instead; (5) Luke knew of charges against Paul (in 21:28) and superimposed these onto the account of Stephen's trial; (6) Luke's story necessitated that *some* charge(s) be brought against Stephen, and the combination of law criticism and temple criticism seemed useful for this purpose (see above, for the possible association of the twin charges with the tradition concerning Antiochus Epiphanes). All but the second of these could be seen to complement the reasons mentioned above.

The fourth raises an intriguing question concerning the omission of the temple charge in Luke 22. Räisänen conjectures that Luke self-consciously omitted it from the trial narrative and placed it here instead because he knew this is where it "properly belongs," i.e., that it is with *Stephen* and not Jesus that the temple logion should be associated (*The Torah and Christ*, pp. 266-67). This is a creative, though questionable, supposition. In addition to what has already been said above concerning Luke's borrowing, I would add that it is not only the temple charge that has been omitted by Luke's Gospel and subsequently incorporated into the Stephen story; the false witnesses, the charge of blasphemy and the high priest's question are all similarly treated. Additionally, a prayer for the martyr's enemies and the committal of his spirit to God are elements found only in Luke's Gospel *and* the Stephen story. Also, the theme of the destruction of the temple, though omitted from the trial narrative, is in fact present in Luke's Gospel in 13:34-35. The very inclusion of the saying, considering its apparent difficulty for the evangelists, also tells in favor of its dominical origins. Therefore, some other dynamic in which the Stephen story was made to share elements of the passion narrative generally seems to have been at work.

Ἰερουσαλήμ Ἰερουσαλήμ, ἡ ἀποκτείνουσα τοὺς προφήτας καὶ λιθοβολοῦσα τοὺς ἀπεσταλμένους πρὸς αὐτήν, ποσάκις ἠθέλησα ἐπισυνάξαι τὰ τέκνα σου ὃν τρόπον ὄρνις τὴν ἑαυτῆς νοσσιὰν ὑπὸ τὰς πτέρυγας, καὶ οὐκ ἠθελήσατε. ἰδοὺ ἀφίεται ὑμῖν ὁ οἶκος ὑμῶν. [Jerusalem, Jerusalem, the city that kills the prophets and stones those who are sent to it! How often have I desired to gather your children together as a hen gathers her brood under her wings, and you were not willing! See, your house is left to you.][192]

It is highly likely that the sentiment expressed in this passage lies beneath the treatment of the temple in the Stephen speech. Indeed, a number of key words reappear in Acts 6–7: Ἰερουσαλήμ, ἀποκτείνω, οἱ προφῆται, λιθοβολέω, οὐκ ἠθελήσαι, ὁ οἶκος (Jerusalem, kill prophets, stone, you would not, house). Viewed in this light, the temple takes on enormous symbolic significance. The destruction of the temple is Luke's contemporary parallel to the incident in the wilderness, in which "God handed [the Jews] over" for their rejection of Moses (v. 42).[193] If Luke was writing in the years after A.D. 70, the relationship between these events could hardly have been missed by his readers. The Stephen speech is very much at the center of the program of Acts, and the inclusion of the temple is one critical element in its presentation.[194] Verses 46–50 do not fit logically within the speech if they are related only to the occasion of Stephen's martyrdom; but their logic is inescapable if one looks beyond to the underlying movement of the Book of Acts.

Heikki Räisänen has written that "Stephen's speech does not contain the vehement criticism of the temple and its sacrifices sometimes ascribed to it.... The temple section does not really lead anywhere."[195] We may now appreciate the perceptiveness of the first of these assertions while choosing to disagree with the second. Stephen does not vehemently criticize the temple, but the vehemence his remarks incite does portend the rejection of

---

[192] Luke 13:34-35a = Matt. 23:38; see also Luke 20:9-18/Matt. 21:33-41/Mark 12:1-12.

[193] It is worth noting that this renunciation was not absolute; despite their corporate unbelief, the support or faith of individual Jews is assumed and commended throughout Acts (e.g., Gamaliel, the Pharisee, in 5:34-40 and the "great many of the priests [who] became obedient to the faith" in 6:7). Also, it is possible in light of Luke 21:24b and 13:35 that Luke believed in a future, eschatological repentance of Israel similar to that envisioned by Paul (Rom. 11:25-27). On the ambiguous attitude toward Judaism in Acts, see the recently published work of Robert L. Brawley, *Luke-Acts and the Jews: Conflict, Apology, and Conciliation.*

[194] It may even be that Luke has shifted the saying of Mark 14:58 to its present context in Acts for this reason. One of the themes of Luke-Acts is the gradual hardening of the Jews (F. F. Bruce, *Acts* [English], p. 92). The stoning of Stephen is in this sense even more significant than the crucifixion of Jesus. Hitherto, the real possibility of Jewish national repentance seems to have been held forth (see Acts 3:17-19). As a consequence of the death of Stephen, however, the tide has turned, and the offer of the gospel is increasingly focused upon the Gentiles, who "will listen" (28:28). Thus Stephen's death may presage the destruction of the temple even more than did the death of Jesus, whom the Jews and their rulers crucified κατὰ ἄγνοιαν (3:17). An echo of this may perhaps be found in the contrast between the ὑγρὸν ξύλον and the ξηρὸν ξύλον of Luke 23:31.

[195] Räisänen, *The Torah and Christ,* p. 274.

Stephen and the Hellenists 79

the temple and of its people. The temple section does indeed lead somewhere.

Acts 7:39-43. It should be noted that the kind of temple criticism most often (and erroneously) attributed to this passage, that "God was happy with a tent but never wanted a house,"[196] does not actually present a fundamental challenge to the law. Some find that challenge instead in the account of Israel's idolatry in the wilderness in 7:39-40. The impetus for this interpretation comes from the citation of Amos 5:25-27 (v. 42): God was not the object of their sacrifices. Indeed, God never wished to be. Thus the cult and the adulterated law that enshrined it were merely an Israelite extension of the golden calf of Egypt.[197] Stephen "draws a distinction between the divinely ordered 'lively oracles,' i.e. the authentic law of Moses, and the ordinances concerning sacrifices and temple, which were invented by the Jews."[198] For this reason the people of Israel were finally removed by God "beyond Babylon" (v. 43).[199]

The obvious difficulty with this interpretation is the fact that it is not sustained in the verses that follow. In verse 44 the polemic suddenly disappears. The tabernacle was a "tent of testimony" whose construction was directed by God. It was brought by the people into the land that God gave to them. David himself is said to have found favor with God. There simply is no reasonable way to interpret the people as unrelenting idolaters given up by God after the incident with the golden calf.

Many who do not go to these lengths still believe that there is an essential link between the wilderness story and the building of the temple. This correspondence is based in part upon the account of the idolatrous Israelites, who rejoiced ἐν τοῖς ἔργοις τῶν χειρῶν αὐτῶν (in the work of their hands, v. 41); the temple is characterized in verse 48 as χειροποιήτοις (made by human hands). Hence it is concluded that "the superstitious attachment of the Jews to their temple is made to appear as a continuation of their idolatry in the desert."[201]

Again, the claim to temple criticism is dubious. For one thing, it ignores the fact that the tabernacle was also handmade. It may be objected that the construction of the tabernacle was, however, directed by God

---

[196] Cf. Bruce: "A movable shrine was more suitable for a pilgrim people" ("The Church of Jerusalem in the Acts of the Apostles," p. 64).

[197] Simon, *Stephen*, p. 46. See also Wilfred Knox, *St. Paul and the Church of Jerusalem*, p. 44; and Benjamin Bacon, "Stephen's Speech: Its Argument and Doctrinal Relationship," pp. 264, 269-76.

[198] Simon, *Stephen*, p. 48.

[199] "The substitution of Babylon for Damascus seems — and most commentators agree — best explained as a post-exilic correction" (Richard, *Author's Method*, p. 126; see also Richard's n. 233).

[200] Jacques Dupont, *The Salvation of the Gentiles: Essays on the Acts of the Apostles*, p. 134 [251].

(v. 44).²⁰¹ This is true, but it is also true that David, whose idea it was to construct the temple, is treated favorably and is not chastised for his wish. The treatment of Solomon is neutral or else an amazingly subdued criticism.²⁰² And verses 48-50, as we have seen, minimize the role of the temple (that is, of the notion that God dwells only [or perhaps is uniquely present] in any handmade structure), without attacking it directly.

The solution to the difficulties of verses 39-43 should by now be clear. The severity of these verses is directly attributable to the severity of the judgment awaiting the Jews (from the perspective of Stephen's—and realized by Luke's—day). If Israel's rejection of Moses led to God's rejection of Israel (v. 42), what other consequence might the reader expect of present Jewish rejection of the "prophet like Moses"?²⁰³ The corollary works only if the first judgment can be made to parallel and thus to justify the second. Thus the finality of God's judgment in verses 42-43, while making a logical nonsense of verses 44-45, makes its own admirable sense. To regard these verses as the tokens of some obscure theology of the two laws encompassing a rejection of the sacrificial system is to miss the point entirely.

Redactional Themes. In summary, then, we may conclude that there is no evidence from the speech that would lead us to believe that Stephen was a radical critic of either the law or the temple. This is true whether or not we believe that a source lies behind the charges of chapter 6 or the speech of chapter 7. It is possible that the historical Stephen was put to death because of something he said about the law or the temple and that this memory lies behind the composition of Acts 6 and 7. But there is nothing here that would substantiate the claim that Stephen died because of a peculiarly radical attack on the law and the temple. In the latter case, let us not forget that Jesus himself was probably put to death at least in part because of statements he made concerning the temple, and it is the temple authorities who almost certainly are implicated in the deaths of James, the brother of John (Acts 12:1-3),²⁰⁴ and of James, the brother of Jesus, the leader of the so-called Hebrews.

This conclusion raises some serious doubts about a number of source theories whose raison d'être appears to be to explain the radicalism of Stephen. The chief defense of an Essene source, for example, is the anti-temple perspective of Stephen (this although the Essenes were not themselves

---

²⁰¹ See Scobie, "Samaritan Christianity," pp. 394-95.

²⁰² Cf. vv. 51-53, where the author could scarcely be accused of subtlety.

²⁰³ David P. Moessner has argued that Luke's presentation of Stephen is itself modeled in Deuteronomic fashion after "the pattern of a prophet like Moses" ("Paul and the Pattern of the Prophet like Moses in Acts," pp. 203-9). See also B. Dehandschutter, who sees in Luke's portrayal of Stephen the archetypal presentation of a prophet's destiny of suffering ("La persécution des chrétiens dans les Actes des Apôtres," p. 544, n. 10).

²⁰⁴ See chap. 2 above.

antitemple). But there is no point in postulating a source for views that did not exist.

We were led to the present discussion by asking whether or not the Stephen speech may be reconciled with the accusations of chapter 6. Our negative conclusion concerning the radicalism of Stephen does not mean that such a reconciliation is impossible. It is indeed wholly possible—if we are willing to see that Stephen in Luke's account did just as we would have expected: he addressed and refuted the *false* allegations of his accusers. Stephen criticized neither temple nor law, for—again, from Luke's perspective—it is the *Jews* who were disobeying the law of Moses, the Jews who were guilty of turning from the true worship of God, and the Jews who, by their continued obduracy, brought upon themselves the destruction of their temple. Such was undoubtedly the attitude of many later Jewish Christians.[205] Luke accepted and expanded upon the idea that it was Jewish unbelief that occasioned the fall of Jerusalem.[206] For Luke, there was no Christian critique per se of Judaism; Paul remained a devout Pharisee, while the piety of Jewish Christianity in general was shown to be beyond reproach. Luke did not attempt to solve the problem of the relationship between Christianity and Judaism in terms that are familiar to us, that is, in terms taken from the writings of the Jewish Christians themselves, those most directly confronted by and most sensitive to the complexity of the issues involved. Therefore it is not surprising that Luke's agenda can sometimes be missed. In Acts 6 and 7 it is the Jews who are on trial and the Jews who unwittingly act as their own accusers. In rejecting Christ, they—and Judaism with them—have been rejected.[207]

Viewing the matter in this way, we can see that there *is* an underlying logic and consistency to the account, even if it is one that the author imposes. Accordingly, the accusations are not a summary of the theology of the historical Stephen; if anything, they are a programmatic summarization of Luke's own purpose for the introduction of Stephen and, in all likelihood, for the story that is to follow: that of the unbelief of the Jews and the consequent movement of the gospel out to the Gentiles. It is a story that culminates in the momentous verse of Acts 28:28: "Let it be known to you then that this salvation of God has been sent to the Gentiles. They will listen." One thus need look no further than the author of Acts to explain the theology of Stephen.[208]

---

[205] Compare Matt. 23:38/Luke 13:35; Matt. 21:33-41/Mark 12:1-12/Luke 20:9-19.

[206] Luke also developed the notion that it was a lack of Jewish response that opened the door to Gentile acceptance.

[207] As I mentioned in note 193 above in connection with Acts 7:42, the corporate unbelief and consequent rejection of the Jews did not, in Luke's view, disallow the possibility of Jewish faith in Christ. With respect to Judaism, Luke was both polemicist and apologist.

[208] Bihler, who, having considered in some detail the linguistic and theological points

Language and Style

Consideration of the question, Do we have accurate information about the beliefs of Stephen? has so far yielded decidedly (and perhaps surprisingly) negative results. The study of ancient historiography raised doubts that have been reinforced by a closer examination of both the accusations of Acts 6 and the speech of Acts 7. In particular, these do not contain any of the esoteric theologies repeatedly ascribed to them, the elements of which are better understood within the framework of Luke's own purposes in Acts.

This conclusion undermines what might be called the primary line of defense of source theories, namely, that the Stephen story retains a point of view unaccountable in terms of Lukan authorship. This we may call the *theological* defense of the authenticity of the Stephen story. A second and overlapping approach may be termed its *literary* defense. Accordingly, one looks to the language and style of a passage, in addition (or even in exception) to the ideas it contains, for signs of a non-Lukan source.

It is interesting to note that an increased emphasis in recent years upon strictly literary evidence has coincided with a weakening of the source theorists' position. Rather than pointing to a distinguishable, distinctive theology within the text, one is content to find traces or hints or remnants of it in peculiarities of vocabulary or syntax. This approach is typical of those who recognize the likelihood of Lukan redaction but at the same time wish to hold out for some underlying source. Max Wilcox, for one, concludes that while most of the narrative of Acts is indeed Lukan, there are numerous places, within the speeches especially, where "protruding Semitisms" reveal the presence of a source. Indeed, apart from these, "we might never have known that he did use any source." Furthermore, these alleged Semitisms are "a sign to us of the authenticity and antiquity of the material." So "the work is Luke's own creation, but he did not create it 'out of nothing.'"[209]

Looking for a source in the Stephen material thus becomes an exercise in finding exceptions to the rule. (This position thus presupposes the "rule" of Lukan authorship.) It should be recognized how much of a shift away from traditional source theories is signaled by this approach. To put the matter simply, let us imagine that someone noting our discussion of Acts 7 posed the relatively straightforward and sensible question, Is this what Stephen really said? The advocate of a rather far-reaching source theory may well answer Yes, without undue equivocation: Luke *received* the speech from his Antiochene/Samaritan/Alexandrian/Essene source and, with the most minor revision, has *recorded* it here for us in Acts. The exegete more conversant with current scholarship will answer the same question much more

---

of contact between the Stephen speech and the rest of Acts, wrote, "Thus only one conclusion can be drawn: the speech is a Lukan composition" (*Stephanusgeschichte,* p. 86).

[209] Wilcox, *Semitisms of Acts,* p. 184.

tentatively: Luke did *compose* the speech, but probably knew *something* about Stephen, some traditional *elements* that he *incorporated* into *his* speech or narrative. Such differences only highlight the extent to which source theories must be complicated by a rule of Lukan composition.

Certain reservations about even this more limited enterprise need to be voiced. First, it is much simpler to talk about what *is*, rather than what *is not*, Lukan. Luke's penchant for imitating the Septuagint makes this ordinarily precarious procedure even more hazardous.[210]

Second, it becomes necessary to ask at what point it is no longer profitable even to speak in terms of a source. Seeming exceptions to Lukan vocabulary and style are significant only if there is some discernible pattern that underlies them. It is always possible to hypothesize about a source with sufficient vagueness to ensure that its existence may never be falsified. So the question does not concern the mere theoretical possibility of a source, which must always remain open, but the meaningfulness with which any particular source can be spoken of. Furthermore, the harder one is forced to look for non-Lukan traces as evidence of that source, the more one may question the significance of any that one might find. A source that is almost wholly subsumed within the Lukan composition is an academic curiosity but of little practical help in determining the theology of Stephen.

How far, on the basis of literary criteria, Lukan authorship of the Stephen story may legitimately be assumed to be the rule is the subject of a number of studies. The most thorough and by far the finest of these is Earl Richard's *Acts 6:1 – 8:4: The Author's Method of Composition*. Richard's findings are important and so are worth considering in some detail.[211]

Richard's primary concern is the question of the literary unity of Acts 6:1 – 8:4. This is a matter of significance because, as we have seen, the majority of scholars have divided the passage into Lukan and non-Lukan sections. The most common division is that made between the narrative and the speech, in which it is believed that one or the other, in whole or in part, has come to Luke from a source, whether "traditional" or "neutral."[212]

Richard is critical of those who theorize about sources without first doing the kind of careful literary analysis undertaken in his book. "Without such a procedure, namely, a detailed stylistic and structural examination of

---

[210] Richard, for example, speaks of Luke's "constant tendency of taking from the LXX many of his favorite idioms and stylistic patterns" (*Author's Method*, pp. 79–80).

[211] The density of Richard's analysis is another reason the work has been summarized at some length below. It is unlikely that the nonspecialist reader will take the time required to come to terms with this exhaustive study.

[212] E.g., cf. Dibelius's remark about the speech ("It has obviously been inserted by Luke into the story of the martyrdom of Stephen, which he already had at this disposal" [*Studies*, p. 168 (145)]) with that of Wilcox ("it may well be the framework, rather than the speeches, that is secondary" ["Speeches," p. 219]).

the Stephen story, the investigation of the episode remains a very hypothetical selection of components to defend a particular theory."[213] Richard's work is encyclopedic in scope, and commentators cannot be faulted for having failed to pursue their study of the passage on an equal scale. Nevertheless, the criticism concerning methodology is a telling one. Rather than considering the Stephen story first in detail and as a whole, scholars have appeared to pick and choose those elements best suited to their particular source theory.[214] This approach leads, understandably, to a host of interpretive errors. Specifically, peculiarities that are in fact "special features of the author's method of composition are often enlisted in formulating [inappropriate] theological or historical conclusions."[215] One example among many is Ernst Haenchen's treatment of the authenticity of Acts 7:39-43: "Verses 39-43 accuse Israel of idol-worship, *citing a Septuagint text*. Nobody will maintain that Stephen sought to persuade the High Council with a Septuagint text which diverges widely from the Hebrew. In sum then, verses 35, 37, 39-43, and 48-53 appear to be Lucan additions."[216] But as Richard rightly protests, "the entire speech depends, in an amazingly detailed fashion at times, upon the Septuagint translation of the Old Testament. By Haenchen's own logic, it should then be concluded that the complete discourse owes [itself] to the author of Acts."[217] In other words, by focusing upon a single occurrence of what is in fact a common literary phenomenon, Haenchen has been led to a make a historical misjudgment.

Probably the most original and significant part of Richard's book is his second chapter, "The Speech and the Use of OT Quotations."[218] Stephen's lengthy address, nearly all of which is a recapitulation of the history of Israel, contains over a hundred biblical quotations and allusions.[219] Richard examines each of these in an effort to ascertain the method(s) by which the author (whether Luke, Stephen, or some unknown source) has constructed the speech.

Viewing Acts 7 in juxtaposition to the Old Testament, one soon becomes aware of distinct and *consistent* features that together might be called the author's style of quotation and composition. These include the use of parallelism[220] (sometimes imposed upon the Septuagint text by the changing of word order)[221] and doublets;[222] alteration between singular and plural

---

[213] Richard, *Author's Method*, p. 246.
[214] Ibid., p. 249.
[215] Ibid., p. 246.
[216] Haenchen, *Acts*, p. 289 [240].
[217] Richard, *Author's Method*, p. 252.
[218] Ibid., pp. 33–155.
[219] A list of those commonly accepted by scholars is to be found on ibid., p. 37.
[220] Note Richard's list (ibid., pp. 173–74).
[221] E.g., v. 5 (see ibid., p. 48).
[222] E.g., ἐπ' Αἴγυπτον καὶ [ἐφ'] ὅλον τὸν οἶκον αὐτοῦ (v. 10c, combining elements of Gen.

constructions;²²³ the conflation of Old Testament texts,²²⁴ including the imposition of the word order of one text upon another;²²⁵ the use of independent introductory phrases;²²⁶ alteration of the Septuagint text to the passive voice;²²⁷ the use of negative-positive contrast;²²⁸ the extensive use of cognate expressions;²²⁹ the imposition of contemporary usage²³⁰ and, apparently, personal preference²³¹ upon the vocabulary of the Septuagint; the reordering of Septuagint verses for structural reasons;²³² the repetition of key terms;²³³ the reformulation of Old Testament elements "into a series of independent clauses connected by καί (and)";²³⁴ the employment of lists;²³⁵ the quotation of the author's own revised text;²³⁶ the introduction of

---

41:40 and 41:43), λατρεύω and προσκυνέω, and ἡ στρατιά τοῦ οὐρανοῦ and τὸ ἄστρον τοῦ θεοῦ 'Ραιφάν (vv. 42-43, making use of Deut. 17:3 and Amos 5:26; on the addition of προσκυνέω to the text of Amos 5:26, see Richard, *Author's Method*, pp. 125-26; compare the treatment of 7:45 on p. 129).

²²³ See the long list of citations on ibid., pp. 159-61.

²²⁴ Conflation of Old Testament texts is axiomatic of the quotation process of the speech. See the summary charts on ibid., pp. 57, 75, 120, 136.

²²⁵ E.g., the combination of the word order of Exod. 3:7 with the vocabulary of Exod. 2:24 in 7:34 (ibid., p. 100), and the similar relationship that exists between Deut. 18:18 and 18:15 in 7:37 (p. 109), and Isa. 41:20 and 66:1-2 in 7:49-50 (p. 135). See also pp. 72-73 for a discussion of the influence of Gen. 12:10 upon Gen. 46:6 as cited in Acts 7:15, and the somewhat similar conflation of Exod. 7:3 and Deut. 34:11 in 7:36 (pp. 105-7).

²²⁶ A list of over twenty entries is provided (ibid., p. 175). Richard speaks of the author's "usual freedom . . . in composing such formulae" (p. 108).

²²⁷ The author demonstrates a "predilection for such constructions (see vv. 16, 17, 19, etc.)" (ibid., p. 70); "The transformation from an active construction to a passive one is a common feature of the writer (e.g., see vv. 13, 26, 29, etc.)" (p. 82; see also p. 84).

²²⁸ A list is included on ibid., pp. 163-64.

²²⁹ E.g., συνιέναι and συνῆκαν in 7:25 and ἀποστείλω and ἀπέσταλκεν in 7:34-35. A list comprising a few dozen comparable examples is found on ibid., pp. 165-69.

²³⁰ E.g., see the discussion of the substitution of contemporary idiom for the "archaic terminology" of 7:31 (ibid., p. 90; see also the discussion of 7:32, p. 96). Along similar lines, see the discussion of the substitution of Sinai for Horeb in 7:30 (p. 88, n. 145).

²³¹ E.g., καί for δέ (vv. 7, 10, 15, etc.), θεός for κύριος (vv. 2, 6, 9, 17, etc.; "elimination of ὁ κύριος or substitution of ὁ θεός is a constant feature of the speech" [ibid., p. 40; see also pp. 331-32]), and ἀνήρ for ἄνθρωπος (v. 46; 6:3; note the elimination of ἄνθρωπος in 7:40 and the repeated use [some fourteen times] of ἄνδρες ἀδελφοί [7:2, 26] in Acts—and only in Acts in the New Testament [p. 85, n. 137; pp. 117, 130, 272]).

²³² See especially the discussion of 7:31-33 (= Exod. 3:6, 7, 5) in ibid., pp. 91-98.

²³³ E.g., repetition of οὗτος in 7:35, 36, 37, 38, 40 (referring to Moses, see Exod. 6:26-27; 32:1), 6:13 (Stephen), 6:14 (Jesus), 7:4 (place [i.e., the temple; see also the variant reading of v. 13]), and 7:4, 7 (land/place [of Israel]). It is significant that repetition of terms occurs across all sections of the speech. Note, for example, the twofold use of κατάσχεσις in vv. 5 and 45, πάροικος in vv. 6 and 29, and ἐπαγγέλλομαι/ἐπαγγελία in vv. 5 and 17 (ibid., pp. 181-82; see the list on p. 241).

²³⁴ Ibid., p. 118, in reference to v. 41. See vv. 8, 9-10, 13, 15-16.

²³⁵ A "list of lists" may be found on ibid., pp. 176-77.

²³⁶ E.g., Richard's note on v. 44: "ἐν τῇ ἐρήμῳ[,] which doubtless could be related to a number of OT texts, is more properly viewed as a quotation from his own text, vv. 42, 38, 36, 30, but particularly the first" (ibid., p. 127); and note his discussion of the various phrases employed in v. 45: "In reality the author's own text is the primary source for several of these" (p. 129; see also p. 121 on 7:35-41).

compound verbs;[237] summary passages in which the terminology of the Septuagint but not its structure is retained;[238] and a stream-of-consciousness quotation process whereby a *Stichwort* in one Old Testament passage leads to the citation of another.[239] "Far from being a peculiarity of any specific section of the text, the characteristics referred to are persistently employed throughout the speech."[240] This leads to an inescapable and weighty conclusion: the speech is a unity that cannot be subdivided on the basis of literary criteria.

Richard next turns his attention to the narrative portion of the Stephen material. This he examines in three segments: 6:1-7 (the selection of the Seven),[241] 6:8—7:2a (Stephen's activity and arrest),[242] and 7:54—8:4 (the death of Stephen and its consequences).[243] In each case, he discovers an abundance of the same stylistic tendencies that were found to characterize the speech of Stephen.[244] "The distribution of these data throughout all sections of the Stephen story testifies to the homogeneity of the writer's creativity. All parts of 6:1—8:4 show a consistent use of the stylistic techniques, patterns, and categories listed in the corpus. From this the conclusion follows that the entire episode, *besides its biographic and thematic unity*, possesses coherence of structure and composition."[245] The various parts of the Stephen story have "too much in common to be the product of secondary editing."[246]

Although the question is somewhat outside the purview of Richard's study, one is led to ask whether the literary unity of Acts 6:1—8:4 extends beyond the bounds of the passage. In other words, is the author of the

---

[237] E.g., vv. 12, 24, 29, 39, etc. ("the author ... often adds or drops prepositional prefixes while using his source" [ibid., pp. 82-83, n. 129]).

[238] E.g., the use of key words from Exod. 1:9-22 in 7:19. Richard comments, "In effect the author has simply chosen four terms from the OT text and has used them in mosaic-like fashion to construct an entirely new narrative." This is representative of his "constant tendency of taking from the LXX many of his favorite idioms and stylistic patterns" (ibid., pp. 79-80; see also p. 81 on 7:20-21, p. 89 on 7:31, p. 100 on 7:34, and pp. 113-14 on 7:38).

[239] For the phrase, see ibid., pp. 121, 124, etc. One example is the way in which the ἐξάγω of Exod. 3:8, 10 (= Acts 7:34; cf. the ἐξάγω of Exod. 32:1, 23 = Acts 7:40) probably led the author to quote Exod. 6:26 in Acts 7:36 (pp. 104-5); see the similar analysis of 7:42-43 on pp. 123-24.

[240] Ibid., p. 181.

[241] Ibid., pp. 215-19.

[242] Ibid., pp. 219-24.

[243] Ibid., pp. 224-29.

[244] As a part of which he also includes a brief study of the author's distinctive vocabulary. This is presented in a series of lists (ibid., pp. 232-33, 233-38, and 239-40) that demonstrate the interrelation between the three narrative sections themselves (i.e., "The author has united these episodes and has not simply joined unrelated sources," p. 233) and between the narrative as a whole and the speech. The continuity of the links between the sections introducing and concluding the speech further underscore the continuity of the Stephen (e.g., ἀτενίσαντες εἰς . . . εἶδον of 6:15 and ἀτενίσας εἰς . . . εἶδεν of 7:55; see pp. 230-31).

[245] Ibid., p. 231, emphasis added.

[246] Ibid., p. 238.

Stephen story one and the same as the author of Acts?[247] Yes, according to Richard. The basis for this judgment is once more the striking literary correspondence between the materials.

Richard does not dwell long on the point, although in the course of his study he often pauses to highlight characteristically Lukan language and style (as well as theology) as it is found in the Stephen material. A few instances may be cited by way of example:

1. The attitude toward David in 7:46a is mirrored in a very similar context in Paul's speech at the synagogue at Pisidian Antioch in Acts 13 (v. 22).[248] Interestingly, "the writer also uses a psalm [Ps. 89:20[249] in Acts 13, 132:5 in Acts 7] to supplement his source [1 Sam. 13:14] and to illustrate his theme."[250]
2. The attitude toward Moses in 7:37 is also reflected in another of the speeches of Acts, that of Peter in chapter 3 (vv. 22-23). Additionally, "The word order is identical to that found in 7:37 and so would also indicate the influence of Dt 18:18."[251] Both texts employ a similar speech formula and demonstrate the author's "preference for the verb λέγω rather than λαλέω. The remainder of 3:22 and 23 betrays the type of editorial work encountered in the earlier part of the speech."[252] Some seventeen lexical parallels between the two passages are also catalogued.[253]
3. The resemblance of the charges against Stephen in Acts 6 and Paul in Acts 21 has already been noted, as has the presence of law-and-order and mob elements in both accounts. It is striking also that both defenses begin with the same phrase, "Men, brothers, and fathers, listen" (7:2; 22:1). Paul is mentioned in connection with the Stephen story (8:1), in an incident that is then recapitulated in Paul's speech (22:20). Both speakers are cut short in an almost identical way by the violent reaction of the crowd (ἀκούοντες δὲ ταῦτα [and when they heard these things], 7:54; ἤκουον δὲ αὐτοῦ ἄχρι τούτου τοῦ λόγου [literally, "and they heard him until this word"], 22:22), but in each case the author "has terminated the speech at the very point he wished to make."[254]
4. Richard notes that periphrastic constructions with γίνομαι (become), such as the ὑπήκοοι γενέσθαι (to obey) of 7:39, are "common within the speech

---

[247] That is to say, of the Acts of the Apostles generally. This is not intended to imply the absolute literary unity of the entire work, which is an issue of another order of magnitude.

[248] David is in fact mentioned eleven times in Acts. He is, for the author, "the personification of true Judaism, a descendant of the father Abraham, a man according to God's own heart" (Richard, *Author's Method*, p. 338).

[249] Ps. 89:20 = LXX Ψαλμός 88:21.

[250] Richard, *Author's Method*, p. 131.

[251] I.e., in addition to Deut. 18:15, the verse being quoted. See above on the conflation of these texts.

[252] Richard, *Author's Method*, p. 110.

[253] Ibid., p. 256.

[254] Ibid., p. 259.

(13, 29, 32, 39) and in Acts generally (9:42; 10:4, 10; 12:23; 16:27, 29; 19:17, etc.)."[255]

5. Concerning the relationship between 7:26 and Exodus 2:13, Richard observes, "The change of τῇ ἡμέρᾳ τῇ δευτέρᾳ [literally, "the second day"] to τῇ τε ἐπιούσῃ ἡμέρᾳ [the next day] is to be understood in light of the use of ἔπειμι [be next], which appears [in the New Testament] only in Acts . . . (7:26; 16:11; 20:15; 21:18; 23:11)."[256]

6. Five of the six appearances of the verb κακόω (7:6, 19) in the New Testament are to be found in Acts. Compare also τὴν κάκωσιν (the mistreatment) (7:34 = Exod 3:7).[257]

7. Ἄχρι οὗ (until) of 7:18 "is noteworthy and doubly so followed by the indicative past, since there are only two such examples in the NT: Acts 7:18 and 27:33."[258]

8. The combination in 7:17 "of αὐξάνω [increase, as an active, intransitive verb] and πληθύνω [multiply] [is] utilized only by the author of Acts (6:7; 7:17; and 12:24) in the NT [and] always bears the same peculiarities: both verbs are intransitive, the first being active, the second passive in form."[259]

As might be inferred on the basis of the first three of these points, the most striking clusters of literary and thematic parallels exist between the Stephen speech and the other speeches in Acts.[260] Max Wilcox, among others, has taken note of this, conjecturing that "one source has been made to do duty for a variety of speeches and occasions," "a common block or blocks of tradition" that do not come from "the mind of the author."[261] This might be a satisfactory deduction if the speeches of Acts contained only verbal parallels. But this is plainly not the case, as our other examples have illustrated. Much more satisfying is Richard's own conclusion. "The speech, written on the basis of the Septuagint account of Israel's history, has been composed *by the author of Acts* as a complementary text to his narrative and bears in relation to it numerous thematic and structural interconnections."[262] Besides, a speech tradition as flexible as Wilcox supposes is worthless as evidence for the content of any specific address, whether from Stephen, Peter, or Paul.[263]

The published work of John Kilgallen (among others) complements that of Earl Richard. In *The Stephen Speech: A Literary and Redactional Study*

---

[255] Ibid., p. 115.
[256] Ibid., p. 83.
[257] Ibid., p. 79, n. 127.
[258] Ibid., p. 79.
[259] Ibid., p. 78.
[260] Additional examples are listed by Richard on ibid., pp. 256-57.
[261] Wilcox, *Semitisms*, p. 159.
[262] Richard, *Author's Method*, p. 238, emphasis added.
[263] See Wilcox, *Semitisms*, pp. 158-59.

of Acts 7,2-53,[264] Kilgallen devotes some forty pages to examining the speech's vocabulary, "turns of phrase, use of articles, sentence composition, expressions, . . . adverbs," and interrogative particles. His conclusion represents that of a growing number of scholars: "The speech of Stephen is the product of one man, namely, the man who wrote the rest of the Acts of the Apostles and the Gospel of Luke."[265]

What may we say, then, in response to the question, Do we have accurate information about the beliefs of Stephen? Richard's ambivalence about the relationship between redaction and historicity is instructive in this regard. On the one hand, he repeatedly assails the historical skepticism of scholars such as Bihler, Haenchen, and Vielhauer. "I object to a method which on principle labels as redactional, and probably unreliable, expressions and verses which reveal the author's literary activity (vocabulary, theology, style)."[266] On the other hand, Richard employs just this method in his critique of those who cite Acts 6–7 while speculating about the Hellenists. "The Stephen story furnishes very little data for the construction of such theories, *since the speech in its present form owes not to Stephen but to the author of Acts.*"[267]

This is straightforward self-contradiction. These statements reveal, however, a subtle (and probably unconscious) sifting. On one level, there is little reason to doubt the historicity of the Stephen story. Saying that it is a Lukan composition does not mean that the author created the episode and its characters out of thin air.[268] There is no reasonable basis for doubting that there was such a person as Stephen, that he was an early leader of the Greek-speaking Christian community, and that he was the church's first martyr. Why should not the general outline of the story (including the names of the Seven and the occasion for their selection) reflect an authentic memory of the early church?[269]

So long as Stephen is spoken of in such general terms, there is little to conflict with the notion of Lukan composition. Luke had heard of Stephen and used his martyrdom effectively within the scheme of Acts. Within this context most skepticism does indeed appear to be extreme. But as soon as one moves from the general to the specific, as all theories about the radicalism

---

[264] The literary analysis is found on pp. 121–63.
[265] Kilgallen, *Stephen Speech,* p. 121.
[266] Richard, *Author's Method,* p. 306. The author's arguments in support of the historicity of 6:11 are cited above.
[267] Ibid., p. 341, emphasis added.
[268] According to Räisänen: "Luke must have had some traditional information at his disposal when composing the account of Stephen's martyrdom . . . [but he] would not have needed a *written* source" (*The Torah and Christ,* pp. 260–61).
[269] Note Lienhard's similar conclusions: "This kernel consists of the fact that a dispute arose within the early community, that the dispute was resolved by the appointment of seven men, whose names are preserved, to an office within the community" ("Acts 6:1-6: A Redactional View," p. 236). See also the discussion of the Antiochene source below.

of Stephen must do, the room for skepticism widens considerably. The occasion may have been given Luke by Christian tradition, but there is ample reason to believe that he has made of it what he wished.

I have said that the defense of source theories is an exercise in finding exceptions to the rule. Now that the rule of Lukan authorship is so firmly established, it should be seen how narrow a space exists for such exceptions. Time and time again the putative exceptions have been shown in the end to be illustrations of the rule. The radical or even heretical theology of the speech is a chimera; the speech's themes are in reality best explained in terms of Lukan authorship — as are its numerous peculiarities of language and style. But it has not been proved that there are *no* genuine exceptions and, in particular, no exceptions of a caliber that would lead us to accept a particular source theory.

My method has been to show the obstacles that stand in the way of all source theories. This should now make the evaluation of individual hypotheses a much simpler matter. Are there significant details for which the hypothetical source is a better account than Lukan composition? That is the question that will concern us in the final section of this chapter, and on the basis of our findings there, we shall draw our conclusions as to what we may or may not know about the Hellenists from the account about Stephen. Before proceeding, however, I add a few last remarks about the problem of sources in Acts.

Additional Considerations

We have already had some occasion to consider how the theory of a source relates to the question of historical veracity. Our concern at that time was essentially a negative one: is the apparent *absence* of a source evidence of a *lack* of historicity? I determined that it might be, depending upon the extent to which historical conclusions have been drawn that are based upon the details of the account. The other side of the issue is this: can the positive equation of source and historicity be justified?[270]

Use of a source may well indicate the presence of genuine tradition, but not necessarily. It is possible that Luke employed sources in two distinct ways (or that he employed two distinct types of sources). On the one hand, he may have had access to traditional information about the earliest church, on the basis of which, either by direct quotation or paraphrase, his own account was constructed. This is a typical understanding of the function of sources in Acts. On the other hand, it is also possible that Luke employed

---

[270] According to Simon: "Once this [i.e., employment of a source] is admitted, it becomes very likely that something at least of Stephen's own views has been preserved" (*Stephen*, p. 40).

helpful but historically irrelevant sources in composing his narrative. Hence the argument has been made that Luke incorporated into the speech of Acts 7 material that had been culled from some "neutral" source (e.g., a synagogue sermon).[271] So the question is not simply, Did Luke use a source? as if the demonstration of non-Lukan vocabulary or ideas would be enough in itself to authenticate a text like that of the Stephen speech. The issue has as much to do with the *kind* of source employed as it does with the bare fact of a source. Obviously, a Christian Hellenist cum Antiochene Stephen cycle is something altogether different from a Samaritan tract or a Diaspora synagogue sermon.

But this raises a further point. If one postulates a neutral source, one still must admit that Luke could have used it in one of two ways. If Luke had known at least a few essential facts about Stephen (e.g., that he was killed for criticizing the law of Moses) or perhaps about the beliefs of the Hellenists, Luke could have selected a source that would reflect accurately what he knew of Stephen or his followers. In this way a neutral source would lose a large measure of its neutrality. A second possibility is that Luke made use of the source without knowledge of or reference to Stephen's particular beliefs. Granting that possibility would again lead us to conclude that the story of Stephen cannot be used as a source for determining the theology of the Hellenists.

Finally, there is the question of the origin of the source(s). This is important in two ways. It is, first of all, the other side of the question of the origin of Stephen's theology. If the Stephen traditions were preserved by Christians who were former Essenes, it would be imagined that Stephen himself had been influenced by Essene ideas or at very least that his ideas were similar enough to win their sympathy.[272] Second, it provides the hermeneutic according to which the speech is then interpreted. As elsewhere, method is both inspired by and in control of the text. One does not believe in a Samaritan source for its own sake, but once it is believed, one is able to find numerous other, often subtler affinities with Samaritan theology than were at first perceived. We might say that the source hypothesis (including, it must be admitted, the hypothesis that Luke himself is the source of the speech) is the lens through which the text is viewed. And in the case of the Stephen speech, there is a very considerable range of lenses from which to choose.

With this number of variables, it is easy to understand why so many divergent opinions about Stephen have arisen: He is a shadowy figure about

---

[271] Haenchen considers several examples of this approach in his brief history of research (*Acts*, pp. 286–88 [238-39]). His own view is that Luke has taken over a neutral "history sermon" to which he has added vv. 35, 37, 39-43, and 48-53 (p. 289 [240]). Cf. Barrett, "Old Testament history," pp. 66-69.

[272] For Cullmann's "Qumran source," see the following section and n. 274 below.

whom we know almost nothing; he is the one solid figure of the earliest church about whom we have firm tradition. He was a Hellenist; he was not a Hellenist. He was a leader; he was a loner. He was from the Diaspora; he was from Palestine. As a Samaritan, he criticized the location of the temple; as an Alexandrian, he spiritualized the worship of the temple. The movement he began conquered the church; the movement he began perished with him. The variations seem endless. To what extent may they now be narrowed?

A Review of Source Theories

The Aramaic, Alexandrian, and Essene Sources

Among the many sources that have been proposed for the Stephen speech and/or narrative, three in particular stand out by virtue of their persistence and wide acceptance: the Antiochene source, the Samaritan source, and the so-called neutral source. Because of their importance, these will be reviewed individually below.

A second group of three source theories may also be mentioned. These have merited some attention but little adherence in contemporary scholarship: the Aramaic source,[273] the Alexandrian source,[274] and the Essene source.[275] Although they are of interest, they have all been adequately refuted and need not occupy our attention at any length. The essential difficulty with the Aramaic source is the thorough dependence of the speech upon the Septuagint.[276] The Alexandrian source may be discounted on the grounds that radical temple criticism for which it attempts to account is

---

[273] Set forth in Charles Cutler Torrey's *The Composition and Date of Acts*.

[274] The names of Benjamin Bacon and Wilhelm Soltau in particular are linked to the theory of an Alexandrian source. Bacon used Alexandrian typology as his key in interpreting the Stephen speech (in "Stephen's Speech: It's Argument and Doctrinal Relationship"). Soltau was more concerned than Bacon with the question of authorship and concluded that "This speech is therefore rather to be regarded as a free product of an Alexandrian [author] which Luke utilized because such words seem[ed] to him to correspond best to the ideas of the Hellenist Stephen" ("Die Herkunft der Reden in der Apostelgeschichte," pp. 149-50).

L. W. Barnard later suggested but did not insist upon this view in his article "Saint Stephen and Early Alexandrian Christianity." He believed, in any case, that Stephen's anti-temple, anti-Jewish polemic was influential in Alexandria and might possibly have been carried there by his followers (pp. 44-45). There it "prepared the soil for the later use of his theology by Barnabas" (p. 45). Maurice Jones, by contrast, held unambiguously to the view that Stephen himself was an Alexandrian ("The Significance of St. Stephen," p. 166).

[275] This theory was proposed by Oscar Cullmann in the article "The Significance of the Qumran Texts for Research into the Beginnings of Christianity" and was adopted by, among others, Martin Scharlemann (who refers to the Hellenists as "former Essenes"; *Stephen*, p. 18) and A. F. J. Klijn ("Stephen's Speech—Acts vii. 2-53").

[276] See Dupont, *Salvation of the Gentiles*, pp. 139, 153-54 [257, 272-74]; Wilcox, *Semitisms*, pp. 180-81; Haenchen, *Acts*, pp. 72-75 [64-67].

simply a misinterpretation of the Stephen speech. The spiritualizing tendencies of the speech are also best explained in terms of the Hellenism of Luke himself and not by reference to an obscure link with Alexandrian typology.[277] The suggested relationship between Stephen and Qumran on the basis of their common "rejection of Temple worship" is equally artificial.[278] Whatever temple criticism there may be in the Stephen speech is a far cry from that articulated by the Essenes.[279] Although these three proposals have gained little credibility, the criticisms they have evoked are quite telling with reference to other source theories, as we shall see.

The Antiochene Source

One of the most enduring theories concerns the existence of a written source containing the Stephen narrative and/or speech that would have come to Luke through contact with the church in Antioch, where it was presumed that traditions such as Acts 11:19-30, 12:25—15:35, and, by extension, 6:1—8:4 would most naturally have been preserved.[280] Although there has been little agreement as to the precise boundaries of the proposed source, it has in principle been widely adopted, most notably, in terms of our study, by Martin Hengel in his study of the Hellenists, *Between Jesus and Paul*.[281]

It must be admitted that this theory has in its favor a certain tidiness, especially if one agrees with Hengel as to the character of Stephen and the Hellenists. If we accept for the moment the link between the persecution of Acts 8:1 and the founding of the church in Antioch in Acts 11:19-21, we can see that the conceptual persuasiveness of the theory is enhanced in direct proportion to our willingness to see the Hellenists as an ideologically distinctive group. The more separate we believe Stephen and the Hellenists to have been from the rest of the church in Jerusalem, the more appealing it is to suppose that Luke must have turned to Antioch to obtain the (supposedly) detailed and sympathetic information he possessed about them.

The question of the conceptual persuasiveness of this approach will not be argued directly, since such an argument would be circular. In any event, the real strength of the Antiochene source is its claim to provide the best explanation for the detailed account of Acts 6–7.[282]

---

[277] For a critique of the Alexandrian source, see Scharlemann, *Stephen*, pp. 25-26.

[278] Cullmann, "Qumran Texts," p. 220.

[279] See, for example, the criticisms in Fitzmyer, *Studies in Luke-Acts,* p. 238; and Haenchen, *Acts,* pp. 260-61, n. 3 [214-15, n. 1].

[280] On the history of this proposal, see Dupont, *Sources,* chap. 4 (pp. 62-72 [61-70]). See also the bibliography provided by Hengel (*Between*, p. 135, n. 16). Proponents of the Antiochene source (in one form or another) have included A. Harnack, H. H. Wendt, J. Weiss, J. A. Findlay, R. Bultmann, J. Jeremias, and M. Hengel.

[281] Hengel, *Between,* p. 4 [156].

[282] The relevance of its sympathy toward Stephen depends again upon the extent to which the martyr was a divisive figure in the early church.

As I have already intimated, the Stephen story contains certain facts that have almost certainly come to Luke from tradition. These include the dispute over the distribution to the widows, the presence within the church of so-called Hellenists and Hebrews, the choice of the Seven along with the list of their names, and the death of Stephen. Among these, it is without question the list in 6:5 that has aroused the most interest, since "apart from the name list Luke's knowledge seems so vague that it is very difficult to assume an old written source."[283]

Even if the list of names, as Räisänen says, is "on any reading the hardest core of the story,"[284] its association with Antioch is only conjecture. None of the Seven is mentioned in the list of Antiochene leaders in 13:1, where we would expect to find them, or indeed in any other connection with that church. "Instead, Philip gets to Caesarea (8,40; 21,8) and Nicolaus, the Antiochene proselyte . . . is located in Christian lore in Asia minor as the founder of the sect of the Nicolaites."[285] There is nothing, in other words, in Acts 6:1-7 that would in itself lead us to imagine that the account is anything but a Lukan composition based on "a few bits of received information,"[286] information that may have come to Luke from any number of possible sources.

I mentioned above the link with the story of the founding of the church at Antioch in Acts 11:19-21. It is interesting to turn to that account because there above all we would anticipate finding solid evidence of an Antiochene source. But such evidence is entirely lacking. "There are no names and no concrete scenes. Luke's story instead moves on the most general level."[287] The few lines that do present themselves are self-evidently Lukan, "employing such favorite expressions as λαλοῦντες τὸν λόγον, πολὺς ἀριθμός, ἀνὴρ ἀγαθός κτλ., προσετέθη ὄχλος ἱκανός (spoke the word, a great number, a good man . . . , a great many people)."[288] Even the mention of the "men of Cyprus and Cyrene" (11:20) may be explained as a Lukan inference built upon the tradition found in 13:1 ("Barnabas," from Cyprus [4:36], and "Lucius of Cyrene").[289] Haenchen pronounces: "Thus fades Harnack's pipe dream of an Antiochian source ('the oldest missionary history of the Christian Church' — Jeremias, 220)."[290]

---

[283] Räisänen, *The Torah and Christ*, p. 245.
[284] Ibid., p. 246.
[285] Ibid.
[286] Ibid., p. 245. See also the discussion on the Lukan composition of 6:1-7 on pp. 244-45. Cf. Richard's more extensive argument about the narrative section 6:1—7:2a in *Author's Method*, pp. 214-24.
[287] Räisänen, *The Torah and Christ*, p. 247.
[288] Haenchen, *Acts*, p. 369 [313] (see pp. 368-71 [312-15]).
[289] Ibid., p. 370 [314-15]; Räisänen, *The Torah and Christ*, p. 247.
[290] Haenchen, *Acts*, p. 369 [314]. The reference is to Joachim Jeremias's influential 1937 article "Untersuchungen zum Quellenproblem der Apostelgeschichte," which supports the notion of an Antiochene source underlying the whole of Acts 6:1—8:4.

Räisänen adds one further argument that bears repeating. He writes ironically, "If there was one [a written source], then Luke must have confused it considerably. His account, it should be remembered, differs markedly from the story of the Hellenists as normally reconstructed by modern scholars."[291] By "modern scholars," we may feel free to read "Martin Hengel," for it is Hengel whom Räisänen takes to task for this inconsistency. What is the point of arguing for reliability based upon a source if the source itself has not been followed?

In short, then, we may conclude that there was no Antiochene source for the Stephen narrative and/or speech. Luke may have received some general information about Stephen from members of the church at Antioch, but then he may just as well have received it from persons elsewhere. In either case it did not come to him in a form like that of the proposed Antiochene source.

The Samaritan Source

By the "Samaritan source" I refer broadly to the idea that beneath the speech of Stephen lies the theology of the Samaritans.[292] In practice, the exact nature of the hypothesis varies. Perhaps Stephen himself was a Samaritan,[293] perhaps he was influenced by Samaritan ideas,[294] or perhaps it was his followers who took his independent ideas to a sympathetic Samaritan audience, where they received their form as we have it in Acts.[295]

On the face of it, the Samaritan source must seem the most unlikely of the three possibilities we are examining. It should, however, be said that, of all the source theories, it raises the most interesting questions. These concern alleged correspondences between the speech and Samaritan religion. Charles Scobie conveniently lists these according to three categories: (1) textual variants common to Acts and the Samaritan Pentateuch, (2) the use of

---

[291] Räisänen, *The Torah and Christ*, p. 246. Cf. Haenchen's similar point (*Acts*, p. 84 [75-76]).
[292] A brief history of the question is provided by Earl Richard in his article "Acts 7: An Investigation of the Samaritan Evidence" (pp. 190-93). A similar history (including additional bibliography) is provided by Charles H. H. Scobie, "Samaritan Christianity" (pp. 391-93). For further criticism of the Samaritan source theory, see W. Harold Mare, "Acts 7: Jewish or Samaritan in Character?" and R. J. Coggins, "The Samaritans and Acts." Interestingly, Coggins argued (here and elsewhere) that Stephen repudiated the temple but that there is no reason to link this attitude to Samaritanism: "It may be better to see in Stephen's speech and in Samaritanism variant forms of the same attitude of rejection of the claims of Jerusalem" (*Samaritans and Jews: The Origins of Samaritanism Reconsidered*, p. 141).
[293] So, for example, Spiro, "Samaritan Background"; and James D. Purvis, "The Fourth Gospel and the Samaritans" (p. 176).
[294] So, for example, Scharlemann, *Stephen*, pp. 34-51; and Scobie, "Source Material," p. 415.
[295] So Scroggs, "Hellenistic Christianity," pp. 200-201. This is Scobie's alternative suggestion ("Source Material," p. 415).

Samaritan traditions, and (3) non-Pentateuchal quotations that "reflect a Samaritan bias."[296] He also enumerates a number of the speech's features that he feels reflect a Samaritan outlook.

Among scholars impressed by affinities between the text of Acts 7 and the Samaritan Pentateuch is Robin Scroggs. In an article entitled "The Earliest Hellenistic Christianity," Scroggs notes four such "Samaritanisms" in the Stephen speeech (in 7:4, 5, 32, and 37). About these he writes, "The cumulative impression these passages make is striking. No *text* outside the Samaritan Pentateuch and Targum supports any of the deviations we have discussed, and only Philo and possibly Justin . . . [show] any knowledge of these traditions."[297]

This line of argument has been refuted, however, by contemporary advances in Septuagint studies, which demonstrate that the Samaritan Pentateuch is merely one example of a complex textual tradition.[298] Thus, Earl Richard, having taken account of a considerable array of parallel texts (the Syriac Old Testament, the Old Latin and Ethiopic versions, the Peshitta of Deut. 2:5, etc.), writes concerning the conclusions of Robin Scroggs: "The present study, I believe, reveals the inadequacy of Scroggs' statement in relation to the four passages surveyed above [7:4, 5, 32, and 37]: 'No *text* outside the Samaritan Pentateuch and Targum supports any of the deviations we have discussed. . . .' On the contrary the textual evidence is . . . plentiful as we have seen and it is the failure to recognize this fact which constitutes the principal weakness of Samaritan hypotheses."[299]

Even Charles Scobie, who earlier (1973) considered the textual variants common to Acts and the Samaritan Pentateuch to be one of three categories of evidence favoring a Samaritan source, by the time he wrote "The Use of Source Material in the Speeches of Acts III and VII" (1979) had recognized this criticism and admitted that "of the four alleged Samaritan readings in Stephen's speech, none reflects a specifically Samaritan variant; these readings simply show that at these four points Acts 7 is influenced by a form of Palestinian text."[300]

The points Scobie makes about Samaritan traditions and bias, included in categories (2) and (3) above, are also open to question. The vast majority of the references cited have to do with the speech's hostility toward the temple,[301] although animosity toward Jerusalem and the Jews themselves is

---

[296] Scobie, "Samaritan Christianity," pp. 393–96. A similar list of twelve individual entries is found in Spiro, "Samaritan Background" (pp. 285–88), and of fifteen entries in Scharlemann, *Stephen,* pp. 50–51.

[297] Scroggs, "Hellenistic Christianity," p. 193.

[298] See, for example, Reinhard Pummer, "The Samaritan Pentateuch and the New Testament."

[299] Richard, "Acts 7," p. 207.

[300] Scobie, "Source Material," p. 403.

[301] Cf. Scobie's treatment of 7:47-50 and 7:42 ("Samaritan Christianity," pp. 394, 395).

also mentioned.³⁰² A critique of the Jerusalem temple is part and parcel of Samaritan self-understanding,³⁰³ so it is little wonder that the supposed temple criticism of the Stephen speech would play such an important part in this debate. Charles Scobie, for instance, states that "according to Acts vii the climax of Israel's apostasy in Old Testament times comes with the building of the Jerusalem Temple."³⁰⁴ It should be clear from our earlier discussion that this is simply not the case. It is the Jews themselves who are the focus of the attack, not the temple. It is also difficult to imagine how 7:48-50 can constitute a scathing Samaritan denunciation of the Jerusalem temple. The sentiment expressed could, after all, apply just as well to a shrine built on Mount Gerizim as on Mount Zion.³⁰⁵

In a similar vein, much is made of the presence of the word τόπος (place), "which is a Samaritan way of referring to a sanctuary."³⁰⁶ The word occurs twice in the accusations against Stephen (6:13, 14) and three times in the speech (7:7, 33, 49). The most significant of these occurrences is usually reckoned to be in 7:7, where the author has apparently modified the text of Exodus 3:12 from ἐν τῷ ὄρει τούτῳ (on this mountain) to ἐν τῷ τόπῳ τούτῳ (in this place). The fact that in Exodus the words are addressed to Moses, whereas in Acts it is Abraham who is their object, is also assumed to be of consequence. To Scobie this recalls "the appearances of God to Abraham in Gen. xii. 6, 7 (at Shechem) and in Gen. xv. 1-21 (at an unnamed locality). . . . The net result of this blending of Old Testament passages is to make God assure Abraham that Shechem (i.e. Mt Gerizim) is the place where God is to be worshipped."³⁰⁷ Genesis 15:14 is, to be sure, quoted in verse 7a, but there is no blending of passages. That Luke quotes the Old Testament out of context is not unusual in the speech (note the same phenomenon in v. 5, in which elements from the discourse of Moses [Deut. 2:5] and Jacob [Gen. 48:4] are

---

³⁰² As are a number of lesser themes (e.g., the role of Joseph and Joshua in the speech and in Samaritan tradition). Scobie admits that these do "not in themselves constitute evidence" ("Samaritan Christianity," p. 395), and it seems best to leave the matter at that. We would do well to observe Richard's cautious words about the value of so-called cumulative arguments (see "Acts 7," p. 194).

³⁰³ John Macdonald, *The Theology of the Samaritans*, pp. 24-25, 52, 310-11; Scobie, "Source Material," pp. 408-10, and "Samaritan Christianity," pp. 394-95.

³⁰⁴ Scobie, "Samaritan Christianity," p. 394.

³⁰⁵ The claim that the Samaritans' temple, "because of its heavenly pattern . . . was *not* considered so built" (Spiro, "Samaritan Background") is overly subtle, especially considering that the audience in Acts 7 is Jewish. Spiro himself admits that "the Old Testament makes clear . . . that heaven *was* involved in the building of Solomon's temple (II Sam xxiv 18; I Kings xviii 24, 38; I Chron xxi 18-26, xxviii 19; II Chron iii 1, vii 1; Ps lxxviii 68-69)." But he adds, "the sanctity of a temple is a relative matter, depending on whose temple it is and who the witnesses are" (p. 288). But the witnesses in this case are Isaiah (66:1-2) and Stephen's Jewish hearers.

³⁰⁶ Scharlemann, *Stephen*, p. 50.

³⁰⁷ Scobie, "Samaritan Christianity," p. 394. Cf. Spiro, "Samaritan Background," p. 286; Scroggs, "Hellenistic Christianity," p. 190; Scharlemann, *Stephen*, p. 38.

made to apply instead to Abraham),[308] nor is the fact that Luke would modify the Septuagint to suit the speech's context.[309] Furthermore, repetition of τόπος in reference to the temple is also a feature of Acts 21:28. So once again the selective citation of peculiarities of language and style without reference to their larger literary context has led to an error of judgment.

What makes all of the imagined parallels with Samaritan theology seem more convincing than they really are is the fact that Luke *does* carry on an antitemple, anti-Jerusalem, anti-Judaism polemic that in some ways runs parallel to that of the Samaritans. He *does* believe that God has forsaken the temple (Luke 13:35), and this belief without question colors the account of Acts 7. In fact, the rejection of the temple, the city, and the people are all tied up together in Luke's interpretation of the events of A.D. 70.[310] Furthermore, the divinely sanctioned movement of the gospel out from the Jews to the Gentiles and thus out from Jerusalem to Rome is a primary theme of the entire work. In accord with this there should be a minimizing of the land (7:5) just as there is of the temple (7:48-50). For a community that is struggling with its concrete identity vis-à-vis Judaism, these are not trivial concerns. So, while certain themes in the speech and in Acts generally may have their counterparts in Samaritan theology, such theology is not necessary or even reasonable to explain them.

We turn finally to Scobie's second category, "the use of Samaritan traditions." The middle two of the four items he lists have already been mentioned above in connection with temple criticism.[311] The fourth is the well-known affinity between the figure of Acts 7:37 and the Samaritan *Taheb*, the restorer who will come in fulfillment of the promise of Deuteronomy 18:15. "This figure played relatively little part in Jewish messianic expectation, but is the key figure in Samaritan eschatology."[312] It is possible that verse 37 (and the whole Moses-centeredness of the speech with it) is in reality a "protruding Samaritanism," to paraphrase Wilcox, but there is good reason to doubt it. That reason is the presence of the Moses Christology elsewhere in Luke-Acts, notably in Acts 3:22-23 (a parallel passage) and Luke 9:31, where Moses and Elijah "were speaking of his (Jesus') departure (exodus), which he was about to accomplish in Jerusalem." Additionally, I note the discussion above concerning the way in which the figure of Moses functions within the Stephen story. Again, it seems unnecessary to resort to the theory of a Samaritan source to explain the contents of Acts.

Scobie's most impressive piece of evidence is the (twofold) mention of

---

[308] Cf. Richard, *Author's Method*, pp. 51-54.
[309] Luke's treatment of the LXX has been discussed in some detail above.
[310] See Luke 20:9-18.
[311] I.e., that Acts 7:7 is really about God's choice of Mount Gerizim and that Acts 7:47-50 is a denunciation of the building of the Jerusalem temple.
[312] Scobie, "Samaritan Christianity," p. 395.

Shechem in Acts 7:16. That Jacob and his sons with him should have been buried at Shechem (vs. Hebron; Gen. 50:13) does indeed *sound* like a Samaritan tradition. There is no actual substantiation for this surmise, however, since the details of Acts 7:16 correspond to no known tradition. The verse could reflect a Samaritan outlook, or it could simply be another example of the way in which Luke has conflated Old Testament texts, in this case the stories about the purchase of sites in Hebron and Shechem in Genesis 23:16 and 33:19 together with the stories concerning the burial of Jacob and Joseph in Genesis 50:13 and Joshua 24:32 (the final verse being primary in the author's mind). Luke's treatment of the calling of Abraham in 7:2-8 may provide us with something of a parallel to this process. In this case it is the two calls of Abraham in Genesis 12 and 15 that have been telescoped together.[313] Interestingly, the location of the event(s) has been altered in the process (in Mesopotamia). That the author seems capable of this kind of imprecision cum freedom earlier in the speech should make us aware of the possibility that it is present in verse 16 as well. At least that seems much more probable than the supposition of an otherwise unfamiliar Samaritan tradition.

Thus, the arguments in favor of a Samaritan source, while intriguing, do not carry conviction. If I have failed to discern the presence of Samaritan ideas, themes, or traditions, however, we should note that any such might have come into the text, not via a Samaritan source, which in view of the overwhelming evidence in favor of Lukan composition seems unlikely, but through the sympathy of Luke himself for the Samaritans (see Luke 10:33; 17:16).

Finally, I would refer the reader to our earlier discussion concerning the representative status of Stephen. If Stephen held the opinions ordinarily ascribed to him by the advocates of a Samaritan source, it is difficult to imagine him as anything other than the "Singular Saint" of Martin Scharlemann. The alternative is that the Hellenists with whom we are dealing are also singular, separate, and unknown. But the Samaritan source itself does not seem genuinely credible.

The "Neutral Source"

Each of the source theories we have considered attempts to explain a certain set of peculiarities about the speech of Stephen. The so-called neutral source is no exception. It aims to resolve the difficulty posed by the length and overwhelmingly prosaic style of the address. It also seeks to answer the question of the seeming unrelatedness of the accusations and the speech.

---

[313] Cadbury and Lake, *Beginnings* 4:74. Genesis 17 (vv. 8, 10-11) also figures prominently in the passage.

The proposed solution is that for the body of the speech in Acts 7 Luke has simply taken over a neutral history of Israel, possibly in the form of a Diaspora synagogue sermon.[314] The majority of the chapter is therefore "sacred history told for its own sake and with no other theme."[315] This explains its disjunction with the narrative of Acts, its length (it is, after all, a sermon!), and its style. But the speech is not altogether tedious. Verses 35, 37, 39-43, and 48-53 are openly polemical and therefore may be assumed to be Lukan interpolations.[316]

Although we do not possess a Diaspora synagogue sermon, it is obvious that numerous other didactic summaries of the history of Israel would have been readily available as models. Traugott Holtz has compiled the following list of those known to us:[317]

> Credal summaries
>   Deut. 6:20-24; 26:5-9; Josh. 24:2-13
> Texts presenting the stages of salvation history
>   Pss. 78, 105, 106, 135, 136[318]
> Historical synopses
>   Neh. 9:6-31[319]
> Histories from late Jewish writings:
>   Judith 5:6-18; 1 Mac. 2:52-60; 3 Mac. 2:2-20;
>   Josephus *Ant.* 3.86-87; 4.43-45; *J.W.* 5.379-419;
>   Heb. 11 (cf. 4 Esdras 3:4-36; 4:29-31);
>   Qumran CD 2.14–6.11

The Stephen speech does not appear to be dependent upon any of these passages. The parallels that do exist are attributable to a common source (the Old Testament narrative) and are not structural in nature. Indeed, it seems that the author of Acts exercised considerable independence "in his selection of quotations and episodes, editing process, and method of composition."[320] Therefore, while it cannot be said that Luke has copied any known history, the genre as it is represented by the histories we do know has no doubt influenced him considerably. Whether it influenced him to copy a document or to mimic a style is another matter.

The decisive factor is yet again the consistently Lukan character of the

---

[314] Haenchen, *Acts,* pp. 287-89 [239-40]. Foakes Jackson speculates that Acts 7 has its origins in "an earlier prophetic diatribe, popular amongst the earliest Christians, which Luke considered as a speech well suited to the first martyr" (*Acts,* p. 68).

[315] Haenchen, *Acts,* p. 288 [239].

[316] According to Haenchen (ibid., p. 289 [240]). As usual, the borders of the proposed source fluctuate from scholar to scholar.

[317] Traugott Holtz, *Untersuchungen über die alttestamentlichen Zitate bei Lukas,* pp. 100-101.

[318] In the LXX, these are Pss. 77, 104, 105, 134, 135.

[319] Neh. 9:6-31 = LXX Ἔσδρας Β 19:6-31.

[320] Richard, *Author's Method,* p. 143.

chapter *including* those sections of a less overtly polemical nature.[321] In framing the question as he has, Haenchen skips over basic considerations that would have given more balance to his judgments about the continuity of the speech. Nevertheless, the distinction between a source and a model is a relatively fine one, and in my opinion the neutral source theorists have come closer than the others whom we have discussed in their understanding of the nature of Acts 7.

CONCLUSION

What do we know about the Hellenists on the basis of the Stephen story of Acts 6:8 – 7:60? Probably very little. Although it seems reasonable to associate Stephen with the Hellenists, theories concerning the ideological distinctiveness of the group gain little, if anything, by that association. We have no genuine reason to suppose that Stephen was a radical critic of the law or the temple. Inasmuch as his views on these matters were the subject of controversy, we have instead good cause to believe that they were shared by other Christians, Hebrews and Hellenists alike, who suffered for the sake of their faith. Moreover, apart from the fact of his martyrdom, we can know almost nothing about Stephen; the account in Acts appears to have been composed of little more than a few pieces of traditional information. So, while Stephen may rightly be called a saint, he is not the patron of every cause that would claim him.

---

[321] Ibid., pp. 249–53. The repetition of οὗτος through vv. 35-40 (vv. 36 and 38 are a part of Haenchen's source) ought to tell us that there is something amiss with Haenchen's method.

Chapter Four

Galatians 2 and Acts 15: The Relationship between the Churches of Jerusalem and Antioch

The following lines taken from Martin Hengel's *Between Jesus and Paul* illustrate what has become a typical assessment of the relationship between the churches of Antioch and Jerusalem.

> *According to Gal. 2.1, relations between Jerusalem and Antioch were evidently not particularly lively.* Paul had not been there for fourteen years. Rather, according to Acts 9.31, the communities in Judea, Galilee and Samaria were living in deep peace and building themselves up.[1]
>
> The local Jewish Christians were only indirectly affected by the catastrophe which descended upon the sister community of the Hellenists. They saw that the storm had passed them by and only affected those whose spiritual freedom towards the temple and the ritual law they could not completely share. *The later difficulties in making contact with the community in Antioch up to the time of the apostolic council could have their basis here.*[2]

According to this view the Hellenists, following their expulsion from Jerusalem, came to settle in Antioch, where they founded the church that quickly became the second center of early Christianity. Perhaps because of lingering Hellenist resentment toward the Jerusalem Christians, perhaps because of ongoing "Hebrew" suspicion or opposition, it is supposed that the church of Antioch from its inception lived in tension with its Palestinian sister. The description of the severity of that tension varies from one author to the next. Chiefly it reflects prior conclusions about the level of conflict between the

---

[1] Hengel, *Between*, p. 13 [175], emphasis added.
[2] Ibid., p. 25 [197–98], emphasis added.

apostle Paul and the leaders of the Jerusalem church. In its extreme form, one can almost imagine the existence of a cold war between these two superpowers of the early church, Jerusalem and Antioch.

Such speculations are bolstered by (if not actually founded upon) two premises: (1) that the Hellenists were a second party in the church of Jerusalem who came to be selectively persecuted because of their distinctive and offensive theology, and (2) that Paul's relationship with Jerusalem can be regarded as representative of that of the other Antiochene Christians. As has already been shown, the first of these assumptions is faulty. The persecution of the Hellenists, if it occurred, does not provide us with evidence of their theological distinctiveness. And we certainly cannot use the persecution of Acts 8:1-3, as some have done, to show that the Hellenists were shunned or opposed by the *Hebrews*.[3] Likewise, the second supposition is found wanting. Paul may have been closely associated with the city at one time, but we should remember that he was a controversial figure long before his arrival in Antioch. We must therefore question the extent to which he owed his gospel to the Antiochene church.[4] Also, as we shall see, he broke with the Hellenists of Antioch over the very position that is said to have characterized them: freedom from the law. So we cannot assume by virtue of the prominent example of Paul that the church at Antioch could not get along with the church at Jerusalem. Better data are required if we are to speculate about relations between the two communities of believers.

Fortunately, such data exist. We have at our disposal information concerning two specific meetings of the churches, commonly referred to as the Jerusalem Council (or Conference) and the incident at Antioch. These events are of extraordinary value because in them we see the churches dealing directly with two of the issues most frequently cited as having distinguished (and separated) them: the stipulations surrounding Gentile admission and the question of Jewish legal observance. Galatians 2 is of particular importance, since it is the only undisputed primary source of direct relevance to these issues. In this chapter I show that both Galatians 2 and Acts 15 contain vital support for our hypothesis concerning the internal diversity of the churches of Antioch and Jerusalem and, by extension, the pluralism (and in their pluralism, similarity) of the groups associated with the terms Hellenist and Hebrew.

---

[3] According to Haenchen, "This element in the preaching of the Hellenists [i.e., their great freedom in relation to the law] must have estranged and repelled not only the Jews but also the 'Hebrews.' . . . If so, this would explain the shabby treatment of the Hellenistic widows. . . . the Hellenistic Christians had become suspect" (*Acts*, p. 268 [221]).

[4] It is often overlooked that Paul was in trouble already at Nabataea and Damascus (2 Cor. 11:32-33; Acts 9:23-25) and very probably during his first visit to Jerusalem as well (Gal. 1:19, 22 and Acts 15:29-31; was Paul hiding from the Jews?).

THE HELLENISTS AND THE CHURCH OF ANTIOCH

Whether we may justly associate the Hellenists of Acts 6:1 with the church of Antioch is a question too seldom asked. The link joining the two is less secure than is usually appreciated. It is based upon a particular reading of Acts 11:19-20, a passage whose details we have already had reason to question. Nevertheless, as Heikki Räisänen says, "Whoever founded the congregation in Antioch must have come from *somewhere*."[5] Why should not the Hellenists of Jerusalem be those "who were scattered . . . men of Cyprus and Cyrene" who founded, if not the church of Antioch, at least its Gentile mission?[6]

The probability that it was the Hellenists who founded the Antiochene church is directly related to the specificity with which one defines that group. As we have noted, none of the names of the Seven is associated with the church at Antioch (cf. 13:1). Barnabas, however, who was *not* one of the Seven and apparently had close ties with Jerusalem,[7] is from an early date reckoned as one of its leaders (Acts 11:22-26; 13:1 [first on Luke's list]; Gal. 2:1, 13). It may even be Barnabas whom Luke had in mind when writing of the "men of Cyprus" in 11:20.

Was Barnabas a Hellenist? If one defines the Hellenists in essentially ideological terms, as do the majority of scholars, then it is very difficult to imagine that he was.[8] If, however, one defines the Hellenists more generally as Greek-speaking Jews (it seems most likely that Barnabas himself was bilingual), probably from the Diaspora, then it is quite reasonable to call Barnabas a Hellenist and quite reasonable to assume that the church at Antioch was indeed founded by Hellenists like him from Jerusalem.[9] But the

---

[5] Räisänen, *The Torah and Christ*, p. 248.

[6] Although Acts 11:19-20 is unclear on this point, it seems logical that only a minority of the nascent church at Antioch first preached to Gentiles.

[7] See Acts 4:36-37, where Barnabas is said to have owned a field in Jerusalem; see also Acts 9:27; 11:22. His choice as representative of the church of Antioch to the Apostolic Conference (Acts 15:2; Gal. 2:1) may also say something about his standing in Jerusalem. Philip Esler considers Barnabas's connection with Jerusalem a Lukan contrivance, along with countless other details of the account of Acts; here as elsewhere, the author has knowingly falsified his chronicle of the early church for the sake of his argument (*Community and Gospel in Luke-Acts*, p. 107). Esler's extreme skepticism will be addressed later in the chapter. For now we need only say that there is no reason for supposing that the connection between Barnabas and Jerusalem was fabricated by Luke. On the contrary, the little knowledge we do have of Barnabas apart from Acts (such as his willingness to be persuaded by the "certain people" from James [Gal. 2:12-13] and thus to oppose Paul) tends to support his association with Jerusalem.

[8] Baur calls Barnabas a Hellenist but then claims that it is doubtful that "he had been in Jerusalem before he went to Antioch." In any case, "there is no trace of his being in any way dependent on the Church at Jerusalem" (*Paul* 1:41 [48]). These statements find support only in Baur's presuppositions and must be judged as being quite incredible.

[9] This is not to say that Barnabas himself founded the Antiochene church. But his close

more one narrows the field and sets up the Hellenists as a radically distinct group within the Jerusalem church, the harder it becomes to establish their connection with Antioch.[10] The leads we do have do not take us in that direction, nor would what we know of the theology of the Antiochene church (Hengel and others notwithstanding).[11]

That the mission to the Gentiles should have begun and found its focus in Antioch does not contradict the thesis of this book. After all, whom else would we expect to evangelize the Gentiles if not those who lived as their neighbors and spoke their language? That the mission to the Gentiles was a bold step cannot be denied. That it necessarily involved criticism of the law and the temple is another matter altogether. Its development in Antioch is therefore noteworthy, but so is its recognition on the part of the Jerusalem church.

Therefore, while I am willing to accept as a working hypothesis the association of the Hellenists with the church of Antioch, I am not in so doing accepting a priori all that this association is so often taken to signify.[12] Its significance instead must be determined on the basis of the evidence before us—in particular, the accounts of Galatians 2 and Acts 15.

It is not possible, however, to assess the implications of the events described in these chapters without first addressing the fundamental question, What actually happened? Plainly, we cannot talk about the interpretation of history without first finding some agreement regarding the facts of history, and the facts that concern us here are by no means agreed.

The difficulty of historical reconstruction is in this case compounded by the complexity of the interrelationship between the two events. The way we think about the one must necessarily affect our view of the other. For example, if we say with some that the events at Antioch predated and thus precipitated the Jerusalem Council, we would be inclined to think that Paul was not telling the whole truth to the Galatians in 2:1-10, since it is inconceivable that a council following Antioch would not have dealt with the question of food laws—as in fact Luke claims in Acts 15 it did. Similarly, it can be appreciated how one's understanding of a prior agreement between Peter and Paul in Jerusalem will influence one's interpretation of Paul's charge against Peter at Antioch. So we see that, although we are on promising ground, it is ground that will require much preparation to be of use to

---

association with it is striking (especially in Gal. 2:1), as is the lack of such an association on the part of the Seven, Philip in particular.

[10] See the discussion concerning this problem in relationship to the interpretation of the Stephen speech in chap. 3 above.

[11] The subject of the present chapter; see below.

[12] For the sake of argument, I shall also treat the Jerusalem church from the time of the persecution in Acts 8:1b-4 as if it consisted only of Hebrews. I can see no evidence to warrant such an assumption. (Are we to believe, for example, that the Hellenist widows also fled Jerusalem?) There is probably little to be gained, however, by pressing the point in this context.

us. The two examples just cited suggest the particular importance of the chronological question. Chronology is indeed significant because it allows us to make hypotheses about causation and influence, about which event interprets which. Clearly, in the case of the Jerusalem Conference and the Antioch Incident, this is of primary concern. Even more basic still is the question of the relationship between Galatians 2 and Acts 15. Until that is settled, we do not yet know if we are ordering two events or three (inasmuch as some have claimed that there were actually two councils—the first, much earlier meeting being that described by Paul and the second, occurring sometime soon after the Antioch Incident, recounted by Luke). So it is with this question that we shall begin. From there we may profitably discuss the sequence of events, the events themselves, and, finally, their implications for our larger study.

THE JERUSALEM COUNCIL

There is one unavoidable problem related to the Jerusalem Council: whom to believe, Luke or Paul—or both?[13] I do not wish to prejudice the case by saying that the last answer cannot be the proper one. Just as more conservative scholars are often guilty of harmonization by brute force, so those of a more liberal disposition may find conflict or disparity where it does not exist. In this question I believe that the arguments of those who see no contradiction between the accounts of Galatians and Acts are too forced to carry conviction.[14]

The essential difficulty is that, although the description of the calling of the council in Acts 15 seems to parallel Paul's own statement about the purpose of the council ("I laid before them . . . the gospel that I proclaim among the Gentiles, in order to make sure that I was not running or had not run in vain," Gal. 2:2),[15] the reported outcomes are very different. According to Paul, the council decided in favor of Gentile admission apart from circumcision, to which "those of repute added nothing" (2:6), "only . . . that we remember the poor" (2:10). The demand for circumcision is rejected as well

---

[13] This problem has received an immense amount of scholarly attention. About this Jacques Dupont commented, "Every solution, possible and impossible, has been proposed" ("Pierre et Paul," p. 43). Already in 1845, Baur wrote, "How this journey (Galatians ii. 1), stands related to the journeys to Jerusalem narrated in the Acts of the Apostles has been endlessly treated in modern times" (*Paul* 1:118 [129]). Baur's own analysis of the difficulties (pp. 118–25 [129–37]) has seldom been equaled.

[14] I believe that the majority of scholars would concur with this statement. Dissenters (of whom the most influential is perhaps F. F. Bruce) are sufficient in number, however, to require that I account at least briefly for my conclusion.

[15] According to Betz, "This way of putting it presupposes that Paul's gospel was the point of controversy because he did not prescribe circumcision while other Jewish Christians did demand it" (*Galatians*, p. 85).

in Luke's account, but additionally a decree is issued requiring observance by the Gentile believers of τούτων τῶν ἐπάναγκες (these essentials) (15:28b): "abstain from what has been sacrificed to idols and from blood and from what has been strangled and from fornication" (v. 29a; cf. v. 20).[16] Two attempts have been made at circumventing this obstacle. The first is to say that the two accounts are not really contradictory; Paul and Luke simply have differing concerns and so report matters from their own individual perspectives. The prohibitions of Acts 15 do not contradict Paul's "nothing added" because Paul really meant "nothing added like circumcision."[17] F. F. Bruce says of the Acts passage:

> No conditions were to be imposed on the Gentile Christians for salvation or admission to full Christian fellowship, save . . . faith in Christ. Once that principle had been established, it was easier to deal with the practical question of social intercourse. . . . *It is nonsense to say, as some have said, that Paul would never have accepted such conditions for his Gentile churches.* Where principles were at stake, Paul was uncompromising; where these were not compromised, he was the most conciliatory of men, and there are several places in his letters where he urges upon his converts and others this very duty of respecting the scruples and consciences of others (cf. 1 Cor. 8:1ff.; Rom. 14:1ff.).[18]

In spite of Bruce's scorn for the idea, I believe that Paul would *never* have accepted such *requirements* for his Gentile churches.

When at Antioch Paul opposed Peter "to his face" (Gal. 2:11), calling him a hypocrite, he did not do so because Peter now demanded circumcision, but because he was now in some way more strict in his observance of just these supposedly "trivial" rules that Paul, according to Bruce, is about to accept at Jerusalem. While Paul may be conciliatory about these matters in 1 Corinthians 8 and 10 and Romans 14, he is most certainly *not* repeating the attitude expressed in Acts 15:28-29. Nor does he mention the Jerusalem agreement in these chapters where its citation would seem obligatory—had he in fact joined in such an accord.[19] Instead, what according to Acts is a necessity is to Paul a pragmatic option, a gesture toward the weak.

---

[16] In support of the authenticity of the third prohibition (omitted by the Western text), see Kümmel, *Introduction to the New Testament*, pp. 180-81 [148].

[17] This is a very questionable distinction. Although circumcision *was* different inasmuch as it functioned as an outward sign of Jewish election and exclusiveness, even Paul is able in another context (the *same* context in which he is able to be conciliatory about other laws) to say, ἡ περιτομὴ οὐδέν ἐστιν, καὶ ἡ ἀκροβυστία οὐδέν ἐστιν, ἀλλὰ τήρησις ἐντολῶν θεοῦ (1 Cor. 7:19; see Gal. 5:6; 6:15). Paul's attitude toward food laws forms a close parallel: they are of no account so long as obedience to them is considered *optional*, a matter of personal preference (1 Cor. 8:8; 10:28-30; Rom. 14:1–15:2).

[18] F. F. Bruce, "The Acts of the Apostles," in *The New Bible Commentary: Revised*, p. 992, emphasis added. I. Howard Marshall writes: "Once the basic issue had been settled . . . it seems wholly likely that Paul could assent to some measures for the sake of peace with Jewish Christians which involved no real sacrifice of principle" (*Acts*, p. 247).

[19] See Baur, *Paul* 1:140 [153-54].

It does seem inconceivable that Paul would have agreed to the Jerusalem Decree in light of the events at Antioch,[20] especially considering the emphatic tone of Galatians 1 and 2 (ἰδοὺ ἐνώπιον τοῦ θεοῦ ὅτι οὐ ψεύδομαι [before God, I do not lie!], 1:20). In addition to this, there are other, less important discrepancies with Luke's account. In Acts 21:25, Paul appears not to have heard of the decree; in Galatians, the council is held privately (1:23), whereas in Acts the debate seems wider (15:6, 12, 22); in Galatians, Paul plays a major role in the decision, whereas in Acts he hardly speaks (though, admittedly, this difference in perspective would not be surprising in itself).[21]

There is still another problem with this approach. In Bruce's opinion, the Antioch Incident both preceded and precipitated the Jerusalem Conference. But the incident at Antioch did not have to do with Gentile admission; it had instead to do with the conditions surrounding mixed fellowship, which is to say, laws governing food or purity. In other words, the issue in Antioch, unlike that at the Jerusalem Conference, was not Gentile but *Jewish* obedience.[22] This is confirmed by the remedy applied by Peter, Barnabas, and others for the difficulty at Antioch: they withdrew from eating with the Gentile believers. There is no indication that, by this withdrawal, the Jewish church disavowed its Gentile members (as would be the case if circumcision had been the issue). It is significant that Paul did not say, "For before certain men came from James, he [Peter] did not require circumcision of the Gentiles." Instead, the point of contention was the allegiance to the law on the part of Jewish believers in the context of mixed table-fellowship with Gentiles. This in turn makes sense of other elements in Paul's narrative. First, it explains how Barnabas was led to side against Paul in the controversy. (Bruce overlooks the fact that his reconstruction contradicts the account of Acts 15:2, in which Paul and Barnabas contend together at Antioch [vs. Gal. 2:13] for the circumcision-free gospel to the Gentiles. Bruce's view also makes the participation of Barnabas with Paul at Jerusalem [Gal. 2:1; Acts 15:2] problematic.) Second, it gives a straightforward account of the order of events in Galatians 2 and of the failure on the part of Paul to offer a conclusion to the story in 2:11-14. It is hard to believe that Paul would not have reversed the two accounts (2:1-10 and 2:11-14), had this been their true chronological order, since doing so would have demonstrated his triumph at Antioch and so greatly enhanced the effectiveness of his argument in Galatians. Third, it makes understandable Paul's charge against Peter: "you . . .

---

[20] It is even less reasonable if one supposes that the incident at Antioch occurred *after* the Jerusalem Council. In that case, the terms for mixed fellowship would already have been agreed, and the whole controversy is rendered nonsensical.

[21] It would be possible to circumvent these final two difficulties if one supposed that there were two councils in Jerusalem corresponding to the accounts of Galatians 2 and Acts 15 respectively. On the problems raised by such a view, see below.

[22] See George S. Duncan, *The Epistle of Paul to the Galatians,* pp. 60–62; and Loisy, *L'Épître aux Galates,* pp. 122–23, 132–33, 136–37.

live like a Gentile" (ἐθνικῶς . . . ζῇς, v. 14); again, this suggests that it was the *behavior* of the Jewish believers that precipitated the controversy. Finally, we know from 1 Corinthians (8 and 10:14-33) and Romans (14) that Paul advocated a position on the subject of dietary restrictions of exactly the sort likely to have given rise to the problems at Antioch.[23]

Therefore, when Paul asked Peter πῶς τὰ ἔθνη ἀναγκάζεις Ἰουδαΐζειν (how can you compel the Gentiles to live like Jews?),[24] he was not assuming that Peter had become an advocate for the proselytism of Gentiles. Instead, it was because he knew the opposite to be true that he could accuse Peter (and even Barnabas) of hypocrisy (v. 13). They had not abandoned their convictions, but they had acted in a way inconsistent with them.[25] It was not a matter of betrayal, but of inconstancy: <u>οὐκ ὀρθοποδοῦσιν πρὸς τὴν ἀλήθειαν τοῦ εὐαγγελίου</u> (*not acting consistently* with the truth of the gospel, v. 14). Specifically, Paul knew that Peter did not believe that Gentiles should be required to Judaize; nevertheless, this is the end to which he believed Peter's behavior (i.e., no longer eating with Gentiles) must lead. By Peter's example, the Gentiles might infer that they really did need to become Jews, since the old distinction between Jew and Gentile was apparently still valid.

Clearly, faced with the problems of mixed table-fellowship, it was necessary that someone compromise. According to Burton,

> The practical decision that the Jewish Christians should continue to observe the law and the Gentiles be free from it left it undecided which of these principles should take precedence over the other when they should come into that conflict which was sooner or later inevitable. . . . The Jerusalem brethren practically took the position that . . . the Jewish Christian must keep the law whatever the effect in respect to the Gentile Christians. Paul, carrying to its logical issue the principle which underlay the position which he had taken at Jerusalem, maintained that the Gentile Christians must not be forced to keep the law, even if to avoid such forcing the Jews themselves had to abandon the law.[26]

The Jewish Christians compromised on the side of the "certain people . . . from James." Paul believed this compromise to be based on a false interpretation of the gospel and so confronted Peter.

---

[23] For example, Paul commended the bliss of ignorance to those ("weak" persons) concerned about the possibility of eating meat sacrificed to idols (1 Cor. 10:26-28).

[24] Bauer's lexicon translates ἰουδαΐζειν as "live as a Jew, acc[ording] to Jewish customs (so Plut., Cic. 7, 6; Esth 8:17; Jos., Bel. 2, 454 περιτομῆς ἱ.; s. also 463; Acta Pilati A 2, 1) Gal 2:14; IMg 10:3*" (*A Greek-English Lexicon of the New Testament and Other Early Christian Literature*, p. 379). The word "Judaizers" can refer either to those who have Judaized or, in more customary usage, to those who would compel others to live as Jews. It is in this second sense that the word is used below. Likewise, when I refer to Paul's Judaizing opponents, I have in mind Paul's opponents who would require that Gentiles Judaize.

[25] See Heinrich Schlier, *Der Brief an die Galater*, p. 85.

[26] Ernest deWitt Burton, *The Epistle to the Galatians*, p. 114.

It is worth bearing in mind that the context of Paul's polemic is no longer Antioch but Galatia, where the distinctions and choices are clearer.[27] Interpretation of Paul's accusation must take into account that it is really the Galatian believers and those troubling them who are being charged. Thus Paul is able to use the incident at Antioch to serve his purposes in Galatians. We should not be surprised that he recounts the Antioch Incident in such a way as to blur distinctions between it and the controversy at Galatia. However, the precise issues at Antioch and Galatia were not the same (i.e., Jewish vs. Gentile obedience), although from Paul's perspective both disputes were fought in defense of the same principle—the equal standing of Jewish and (law-free) Gentile believers.

The other effort to reconcile Galatians with Acts postulates that the accounts cannot record the same event. The consequent assumption is that we have before us reports of *two* councils. The first meeting is that recorded by Paul, at which only the matter of circumcision was discussed. Then came the incident at Antioch, at which time the omissions of the earlier agreement were recognized. A second, fuller, and more public meeting was held at which the larger issue of table-fellowship in the mixed congregations was considered.

Clearly, this is a step in the right direction, and an occasion *like* a second council is not improbable—except for the matter of Paul's attendance. It must be noted, however, that this supposition does not permit us to claim that the accounts of Acts and Galatians have been reconciled. For one thing, even though it attempts to be faithful to Luke's account, it unwittingly denies his version of the calling of the council, since, according to Acts 15:1-2, the crucial issue was that of circumcision, a matter supposedly already settled. Second, it requires that we move Paul to Jerusalem twice in a fairly short space of time, no mean feat considering the chronological obstacles posed by the Letter to the Galatians.[28] Yet, here as elsewhere, the ingenuity of the determined exegete does not disappoint us: we are told that it is actually Paul's famine relief visit of Acts 11:30 (and 12:25) that lies behind the account of Galatians 2.[29] The supposition does double duty in that it also attempts to reconcile the numbers of visits mentioned by Paul with those in Acts.[30] This reconstruction is dependent upon a South Galatia hypothesis and a consequent early dating of Galatians. Thus, the idea is advanced that the Jerusalem Conference occurred after the dispute in Galatia

---

[27] See Loisy, *L'Épître aux Galates*, pp. 137–38.

[28] See Robert Jewett, *A Chronology of Paul's Life*, pp. 63–92.

[29] For one of the most articulate statements of this position, see I. Howard Marshall, *Acts*, pp. 242–47. The idea is prominent in Colin J. Hemer's recent study of the historicity of Acts, *The Book of Acts in the Setting of Hellenistic History* (see especially chap. 7, "Galatia and the Galatians," pp. 277–307).

[30] In Galatians, Paul is adamant that this was only his second visit to Jerusalem. The visit of Paul to Jerusalem in Acts 15 is the third recorded by Luke.

and so could not have been discussed in Paul's epistle. In other words, there is no conflict between the narratives of Galatians 2 and Acts 15, since they recount two separate meetings in Jerusalem.

Debate concerning this proposal has been a prominent enterprise within New Testament scholarship, not least since the publication of Sir William Ramsay's defense of the South Galatia hypothesis in the last decade of the nineteenth century.[31] The defense of the Galatians 2 = Acts 11 theory (including its component interpretation of Galatians) is nearly a sine qua non of conservative scholarship, and immense effort has been expended on its behalf.[32] The significance the question has assumed for the study both of Acts and of the Pauline epistles (in particular, concerning matters of chronology) is reflected in the title of a recent discussion of the problem: "The Heart of the Historical Question."[33]

It is not necessary for us to settle matters concerning the date and recipients of Galatians. It is enough to note simply that the South Galatia proposal, whatever its merits, does not succeed in achieving its intended result: it cannot rescue from difficulty the account of Acts concerning the visits of Paul to Jerusalem, particularly in relationship to the Apostolic Conference of Acts 15.[34] Shifting dates does nothing to satisfy the objection raised above, that it is most doubtful whether, either before or after the events in Antioch, Paul would have agreed to the requirements specified in Acts 15. Nor does equating Galatians 2 with Acts 11 explain what must be an incredible disregard for the Jerusalem agreement in 1 Corinthians 8 and 10 and Romans 14 (where, in fact, Paul's advice goes directly against the mandate of Acts 15:20, 29).[35] Also, as we have seen, such a notion actually creates a new discrepancy between the accounts of Acts and Galatians, since the description of the calling of the conference in Acts 15:1-2 fits the situation mentioned in Galatians 2:1-5 but not that in Galatians 2:11-14 (which it was supposed to have followed). Finally, it is incredible that the supposed

---

[31] Set forth in Ramsey, *The Church in the Roman Empire before A.D. 170* (1883), *St. Paul the Traveller* (1895), and the *Historical Commentary on St. Paul's Epistle to the Galatians* (1899). Ramsay's work is discussed in Gasque, *History*, pp. 136-42, and in Neill and Wright, *The Interpretation of the New Testament, 1861-1986*, pp. 154-56.

[32] A good source for bibliography on the question is Mattill and Mattill, *Bibliography*, pp. 220-26, 229-32. See also Schneider, *Apostelgeschichte* 2:169-71.

[33] In Colin J. Hemer's *Acts* (1989), p. 247.

[34] It is worth noting that the point I am defending is not dependent upon this conclusion. (The question of Paul's relationship with Jerusalem, discussed in this and the next chapter, would, however, be modified somewhat by such an understanding.) If I am wrong and Paul did go to Jerusalem a second time and win a second (and perhaps more public) approval of his circumcision-free mission to the Gentiles, my point concerning the moderation of the Jerusalem church would be enhanced. I do not find the Gal. 2 = Acts 11 proposal convincing, however, and I shall assume for this reason the harder case: the incident at Antioch raised questions that were not answered by a subsequent meeting between Paul and the leaders of the church in Jerusalem.

[35] Cf., for example, the attitude reflected in Acts 15:28 with that of Paul in 1 Cor. 8:8.

earlier conference of Galatians 2 does not figure in the debate of Acts 15. As Zeller observed, "How could the whole question in dispute, concerning which so much had been said and done, and a formal compact effected between the leaders of the two parties . . . how could this be treated as an entirely new and untouched subject?"[36]

So, in answer to our question (Whose account to believe, Luke's or Paul's—or both?), we must conclude that the third, harmonizing option is only remotely possible. And if one must choose in principle between Paul and Luke, it seems prudent to follow the advice of John Knox and turn to Paul first, because in him we have our sole primary source, the reflections of one who actually participated in the events recorded.[37] Even laying methodological principle aside, we would still want to exercise caution in handling Luke's references to Paul in Jerusalem, owing to the substantial difficulties encountered in similar material elsewhere in Acts.[38]

The best solution seems to be that now widely recognized in scholarly circles: the Apostolic Decree of Acts 15:20, 29 originated "at a later date than that of the Council, as Paul does not seem to know about it when writing Galatians or I Corinthians."[39] This is not to say that Luke's account of the council is a prevarication; it is much more likely a conflation. Luke knew of the later decree and knew also that on one occasion Paul and others (including James) had met in Jerusalem to discuss somewhat similar issues. It would have been a simple matter to bring the two together in a unified account, especially here in chapter 15 of Acts: from this point on the Gentile mission, now fully approved, moves forth in earnest, and Jerusalem is in a sense left behind, only to be mentioned again as it figures in the story of Paul.

---

[36] Zeller, *Acts* 2:10 [218].

[37] "Thus of our two sources the letters of Paul are obviously and incomparably the more trustworthy" (John Knox, *Chapters in a Life of Paul,* p. 31). Note Baur's (characteristically) unequivocal statement: "It is self-evident that as the Apostle appears as an eye-witness and individual actor in his own affairs, his statement alone ought to be held as authentic" (*Paul* 1:109 [120]).

[38] E.g., Luke's accounts of Paul the Jerusalemite and the persecutor of the Jerusalem church (Acts 22:3; 8:1-3). These seem strange in light of Paul's own statement in Gal. 1:22, ἤμην δὲ ἀγνοούμενος τῷ προσώπῳ ταῖς ἐκκλησίαις τῆς Ἰουδαίας ταῖς ἐν Χριστῷ (cf. Acts 26:4: Τὴν μὲν οὖν βίωσίν μου ἐκ νεότητος τὴν ἀπ' ἀρχῆς γενομένην ἐν τῷ ἔθνει μου ἔν τε Ἱεροσολύμοις ἴσασι πάντες Ἰουδαῖοι). It seems likely that Luke knew Paul was an early and vigorous persecutor of the church and that some form of persecution had broken out in connection with Stephen in Jerusalem. He then conflated these facts in his account of the "severe persecution" of Acts 8 (see chap. 2 above).

[39] Bengt Holmberg, *Paul and Power: The Structure of Authority in the Primitive Church As Reflected in the Pauline Epistles,* p. 21. According to Hengel: "The two accounts cannot be reconciled in connection with the Apostolic Decree. Here Luke may have introduced a later, local agreement possibly connected with Gal. 2.11ff" (*Between,* p. 168, n. 18 ["Die Ursprünge der christlichen Mission," p. 18, n. 17]). The origin and purpose of the stipulations of Acts 15:20, 29 will be considered more fully below. Their relationship to the incident at Antioch is—not surprisingly, in view of what is at stake—one of the most contentious points in the whole debate.

So the description in Acts 15 of the calling of the conference seems likely to be accurate. A delegation of Jewish Christians from Judea came to Antioch and caused an uproar by claiming that Gentile converts must be circumcised. After much debate, the church sent Barnabas and Paul as representatives to seek out a ruling from the "pillars" in Jerusalem. These agreed that the Gentiles should not be required to be circumcised. This very considerable concession on the part of the leaders of the Jerusalem church would not have appeared to affect their own practice. Jewish obedience was taken for granted and was not at issue.

We have already noted above how closely this corresponds to Paul's own account of the purpose of the council. The greatest dissimilarity is that in Paul's account matters are personalized (e.g., "the gospel that I proclaim," 2:2; "the grace that has been given *to me*," 2:9), whereas Luke sees the concerned parties acting more in representational terms. This is an altogether understandable difference in perspective. Paul's narrative plays a critical role in the defense of his apostleship to the Galatians, and so of course it is his recognition that is underscored. But Holmberg is right in emphasizing that this was intended to be a meeting between two churches—although not between two equals; Jerusalem alone held power to settle questions of doctrine, to determine whether or not Paul's ministry had been "in vain." Furthermore, the issue of concern was circumcision, and so it was not "primarily the nature of Paul's or Barnabas' apostolate" that was under discussion.[40] But as James D. G. Dunn has recently observed, the latter perspective is true to Paul's slant in his Epistle to the Galatians and is very probably an accurate reflection of the way in which he himself perceived the occasion.[41]

Again, while the Acts narrative is probably accurate in its setting, it is almost certainly erroneous in its conclusion: "there was no discussion of any general, clearly defined freedom from the law for the Gentile Mission in its relations with Christians of Jewish descent."[42] And this conclusion is valid, no matter what the order of events.

Finally, it is worth underlining the fact that, at least until the time of the conference, the church of Jerusalem was divided on the question of the admittance of Gentiles apart from the law. In Acts 15:1, we are told that "certain individuals" whom the leaders in Jerusalem had not instructed (v. 24) came to Antioch from Judea and taught that Gentile converts must be circumcised. Likewise, in Galatians 2:3-5 we learn of "false believers" (literally, "false brothers") in the Jerusalem church (distinguished from the

---

[40] Holmberg, *Paul and Power*, p. 19.
[41] James D. G. Dunn, "The Relationship between Paul and Jerusalem according to Galatians 1 and 2," pp. 461-78. See also Alfred Loisy, *L'Épître aux Galates*, pp. 103-4.
[42] Holmberg, *Paul and Power*, p. 23.

"acknowledged leaders" [literally, "pillars"] of v. 6), who, it appears, pressed for the circumcision of Titus.[43]

This diversity of opinion is consistent with the complex view of the Jerusalem church I am here advancing. It is also, particularly at this early stage in the development of the church, understandable. It should be remembered that there was no obvious paradigm to which the church might turn in considering its position on the status of Gentile believers. From the point of view of Jewish theology, there were no rules about Gentiles and the law in the last days. Eschatologically, the church was caught in a classic tension between the "already" and the "not yet." Gentiles had received the Spirit and were taking part in some new entity that did not correspond directly to any known category. Was proselytism into Judaism the proper context by which to understand their experience? It may have been so for some, but the majority appeared to think otherwise. The participation of Gentiles in the church was not precisely coterminous with the participation of Gentiles in Israel, and most, including the leaders in Jerusalem, realized this.

What cannot be known is whether the ψευδάδελφοι (literally, "false brothers") in Jerusalem maintained their position after the decision of the conference. Nearly all scholars assume that they did, but I can see no real evidence, either positive or negative, by which such a view might be judged.[44] I would reject outright, however, the popular notion that these hardliners came in subsequent years to *control* the church in Jerusalem. As we shall see in the following chapter and conclusion, there is no evidence of a dominant conservatism in the Jerusalem church. For now, it is sufficient to say that the pluralism of the Jerusalem church might or might not have continued along the lines witnessed in Acts 15 and Galatians 2.[45]

CHRONOLOGY OF EVENTS

We have yet to answer the question of the order of events. As we saw earlier, the issue is an important one. Fundamentally, it will govern our understanding

---

[43] Adolf Schlatter argued that the "false believers" were non-Christian Jews who infiltrated and influenced the early church (*Die Briefe an die Galater, Epheser, Kolosser und Philemon*, p. 32). This seems most unlikely, particularly in light of the influence these "believers" appear to have possessed. On the question of the (non)circumcision of Titus, see Baur, *Paul* 1:127–28 [139–40] (n.); and Loisy, *L'Épître aux Galates*, pp. 109–12.

[44] For example, the possible threat toward Paul from the "many thousands" of Jews who believed (Acts 21:20) arises over the question of Jewish—not Gentile—obedience (v. 21). See chap. 5 below.

[45] As I shall note again, references in subsequent chapters to the so-called Jerusalem church will have in mind primarily that segment of the church about which we have information: James and his followers.

of the outcome of the crisis at Antioch, a view that in turn colors a whole range of other issues.⁴⁶

Those who argue that the conference occurred *after* the Antioch Incident cite the following reasons:

1. The incident at Antioch roughly fits the description of trouble found in Acts 15:1, 2.
2. If the conference occurred after the controversy in Antioch, Paul would then be telling us how the dispute ended.
3. If the conference came first, one must postulate two times of trouble with Judaizers in Antioch. "It is more economical to suppose that St. Paul has described the same disturbance twice."⁴⁷
4. One can see in Acts 15:29 a compromise remedy to the difficulties encountered by the Jewish Christians in Antioch.

The shortcomings of this scheme should by now be fairly obvious. We have seen that the incident at Antioch does *not* fit the description of Acts 15:1, 2. The latter had to do with Gentile entrance, while the former was concerned with Jewish obedience. These are often confused, but they are very different issues. Second, there is no reason to assume that Paul is telling us how the dispute ended; it would be useful if he did, but our readiness to believe that this is the case in Galatians 2:1-10 is for apologetic and not exegetical reasons. The third point suffers from the same lack of precision as the first. The problem at Antioch was not one of Judaizing; at least, it does not appear to have been seen as such by anyone but Paul. It would be closer to the truth to imagine that for the majority of participants the risk was that of "Gentilizing," because the basic issue was the behavior of Jewish, not Gentile, Christians. The fourth argument is actually the best, but then we must return to the idea of two councils, for the accounts of Galatians 2 and Acts 15 simply do not square.

I would join the majority of scholars in placing Jerusalem, as it were, before Antioch, not only because of the weaknesses of the alternative, but for the following additional reasons:

1. It is the most natural reading of Paul's narrative.⁴⁸
2. It fits in well with the split between Paul and Barnabas mentioned in Acts 15:36-41.
3. It is difficult to believe that the Epistle to the Galatians was written "to deal with a situation created by reports of the council, which turned out in

---

⁴⁶ E.g., the independence of the Gentile mission, Paul's later relationship with Jerusalem, Paul's understanding of the collection, and the interpretation of the Apostolic Decree of Acts 15:29.

⁴⁷ John Bligh, *Galatians: A Discussion of Saint Paul's Epistle,* p. 178.

⁴⁸ The ὅτε δέ of v. 11 is paralleled in v. 12, in which the sense of chronological succession is clear. See Dupont, "Pierre et Paul," p. 52.

Paul's favour."⁴⁹ The events in Antioch brought the issue of Paul's authority and doctrine into question again and did not resolve it, which would explain not only his defense of these throughout Galatians but also the tone of the letter vis-à-vis the Jerusalem apostles, Peter in particular.⁵⁰

Hence, I support Ridderbos's conclusion from "the whole bearing of the context" that "Peter came to Antioch *after* the apostolic conference."⁵¹

To reiterate then, these are the facts as we have understood them so far. The circumcision-free gospel of the church of Antioch was challenged by some unauthorized⁵² but influential visitors from Jerusalem. Barnabas and Paul traveled to Jerusalem to receive a ruling on the matter from the "pillar" apostles. These agreed that circumcision should not be required of the Gentiles. The question of Jewish obedience in the context of a mixed congregation was not discussed. That issue would arise soon thereafter as the focus of the further controversy in Antioch.

While this reconstruction, equating as it does the settings of Galatians 2:1-10 and Acts 15:1-29, seems the most sensible, its validity is not essential to the larger argument. Perhaps there is some previously unrecognized way for the accounts of Acts and Galatians to be reconciled. If so, we must then imagine that the Jerusalem church agreed *twice* to the mission to the Gentiles, being careful on the second occasion to propose rules that would make possible table-fellowship within a mixed congregation. There are a number of subtle differences between this and the reconstruction I am advancing, the most significant of which is the assent of Paul to the second Jerusalem accord (something that, for reasons already expressed, I consider implausible). In either case, however, the point is clear: the leadership of the Jerusalem church, on the only occasion(s) of which we have any knowledge, agreed to the admission of Gentiles apart from circumcision.

Finally, it should be asked what significance may be attached to the observation that the conditions surrounding mixed table-fellowship were not discussed at the Jerusalem Council. Logically, this would lead to one of two conclusions. Either the practice had not yet arisen, or else in its initial form it was not controversial. This is so because the dispute over the admission of Gentiles appears to have been initiated by persons "from Judea" (Acts 15:1, a probable parallel to Gal. 2:4). Since it seems unlikely that these would not have witnessed or at least known of the practice of mixed table-fellowship had it existed, we can infer that its omission at Jerusalem is significant.

Whether or not we believe that the practice had already begun will

---

⁴⁹ Bligh, *Galatians*, p. 179.
⁵⁰ Loisy provides a lively discussion of Paul's attitude toward the notable apostles (*L'Épître aux Galates*, pp. 112-14, 117-18).
⁵¹ Herman Nicholaas Ridderbos, *The Epistle of Paul to the Churches of Galatia*, p. 95.
⁵² There is no evidence that the Jerusalem apostles authorized this opposition to the mission to the Gentiles.

therefore depend upon how innately controversial we imagine it to have been. If mixed table-fellowship was indisputably abhorrent to Judaism, then we must surely conclude that the practice had not yet arisen at Antioch, since it only became an issue sometime later. If, however, we can imagine conditions under which table-fellowship would not have been inherently objectionable, we would be in a position to postulate its existence from a relatively early date.

Unfortunately, the scant evidence available to us on the subject is not conclusive. Philip Esler (whose thesis is fundamentally grounded on the point) is one of the most vigorous advocates for the view that any table-fellowship with Gentiles would have been repugnant to Jews, since it "involved a most serious dereliction from the fundamental objective of preserving the separate identity of the Jewish people. How could one keep the outside world at bay and yet sit down at table with its representatives, an action expressing the warmest intimacy and respect?"[53]

In a section entitled "Jewish Antipathy to Dining with Gentiles," Esler lays out the evidence he has garnered from seven classical authors and a handful of Jewish sources. In the first instance, he demonstrates what we might already have assumed for reasons other than the avoidance of table-fellowship: the Jews of antiquity were regarded by various pagan authors as antisocial. Three of Esler's references do, however, refer explicitly to "table separation" practiced by Jews.[54] These show that in certain times and places it was possible for Gentile writers to characterize Jews as dining separately. Given the fact that the Jews did separate themselves from pagan cum civic sacrifices and festivals, this is not an altogether unexpected characterization on the part of a pagan observer. The problem is one of knowing how literally and generally to take these descriptions. What do they actually prove? A closer examination of the sources leads one to conclude: very little indeed. In the case of Diodorus, Esler has invoked Gager's assessment that the author was not an anti-Semite.[55] This implies that we have before us the representation of a disinterested or even sympathetic Gentile. What Esler fails to mention is that the quotation he cites is actually spoken by "the anti-Semites in the camp"[56] who were advising Antiochus "to take the city by storm and to wipe out completely the race of Jews."[57] In fact, Menahem Stern, from whose work Esler is quoting, explicitly writes: "It is noteworthy that the

---

[53] Esler, *Community*, p. 76.

[54] The first of these, from Diodorus Siculus, dates from the first century B.C., and the other two, from Tacitus and Philostratus, date from the first decade and the last half of the second century respectively (ibid., pp. 79-80).

[55] Ibid., p. 79, citing Gager, *The Origins of Anti-Semitism*, p. 68. Gager is also appealed to in the case of Hecataeus of Abdera (Esler, *Community*, p. 78).

[56] Menahem Stern, *Greek and Latin Authors on Jews and Judaism* 1:184.

[57] Diodorus, *Bibliotheca Historica* 63.1; in Stern, *Greek and Latin Authors* 1:182-83 (cf. quotation in Esler, *Community*, p. 79).

ultimate source, as expressed not only in Josephus but also in Diodorus, does not agree with the arguments of the anti-Semites, but instead praises Antiochus Sidetes for not having been won over by them."[58]

Similarly, the quotation from Philostratus is attributed rather baldly to "one of the characters in his *Life of Apollonius of Tyana*."[59] According to Stern, however, "This view is put by Philostratus into the mouth of Euphrates, the opponent of Apollonius and one of the less attractive characters of the *Life*."[60]

Second, it should be noted that the observations of these writers are, if not openly polemical, unquestionably hyperbolic. One need only consider some of the other attributions occurring in the sections from which Esler quotes. Diodorus says, for example, that "Epiphanes was shocked" by the hatred of the Jews "directed against all mankind."[61] Tacitus wrote that "toward every other people they [the Jews] feel only hate and enmity," being "the worst rascals among other peoples."[62] And, from Philostratus, we hear that "the Jews have long been in revolt not only against the Romans but against humanity."[63] Therefore, when one of these authors writes, as for example Tacitus does, that the Jews "take their meals apart,"[64] we ought to be careful to take the description with more than a grain of salt—that is, unless we are willing also to accept unquestioningly Tacitus's conclusion to this same sentence: "yet among themselves nothing is unlawful."[65]

At most, such blanket statements by pagan authors may demonstrate the existence of some broadly held opinions concerning Jewish practice. They do not account for exceptions, and they do not explain the origin of such beliefs from the Jewish point of view. For the second of these, we must turn to the Jewish sources themselves.

Esler's Jewish references may be divided into three types.[66] The first are examples of heroes of the faith who are commended for their separation in matters of food (Daniel, Esther, Tobit, and Joseph).[67] The second are

---

[58] Stern, *Greek and Latin Authors* 1:84.
[59] Esler, *Community*, p. 80.
[60] Stern, *Greek and Latin Authors* 2:339.
[61] Diodorus, *Bibliotheca Historica* 63.3; in Stern, *Greek and Latin Authors* 1:183.
[62] Tacitus, *Historiae* 5.1; in Stern, *Greek and Latin Authors* 2:26.
[63] Stern, *Greek and Latin Authors* 2:339.
[64] Tacitus, *Historiae* 5.2; quoted by Esler, *Community*, p. 80.
[65] Tacitus, *Historiae* 5.2; in Stern, *Greek and Latin Authors* 2:26 (not quoted by Esler).
[66] Betz offers a similar though shorter list and mentions a few discussions of the subject in the secondary literature (*Galatians*, p. 108, n. 463). This part of Esler's argument is treated in detail in a recently published essay by E. P. Sanders, "Jewish Association with Gentiles and Gal. 2.11-14." Sanders assembles a quantity of evidence in support of the view that many Jews did have frequent social contacts (including dining) with Gentiles, and that "the only *real* problems with associating with Gentiles were idolatry and the biblical food laws (especially not to eat pork, blood and fat)," p. 185.
[67] Esler, *Community*, pp. 80, 81, 83 (referring to Dan. 1:3-17; the apocryphal book of Esther 14:17; Tob. 1:11; and *Joseph and Asenath* 7:1).

examples of famous Jews who ate with Gentiles but dined on separate food (Judith, the Jews at the banquet of Ptolemy).[68] Last, there is the explicit prohibition of *Jubilees* 22:16b, "Keep yourself separate from the nations, and do not eat with them; for their rites are unclean and all their practices polluted, an abomination and unclean."[69]

Of the first category, only Joseph is said explicitly to have made a point of dining separately, "because he would not eat with the Egyptians, for this was an abomination to him."[70] We can best explain *Joseph and Aseneth* 7:1, however, as an apologetic gloss on the story of Genesis 43:32, in which it is stated that it was an abomination *to the Egyptians* to dine with Hebrews.

The nearest parallel is the case of Esther, who prays, "Your servant has not eaten at Haman's table, and I have not honored the king's feast or drunk the wine of libations" (14:17, NRSV). Plainly, the dominant concern is loyalty to Jewish dietary laws. It is only by extension that it may be thought to apply to dining in the presence of Haman as well as eating the food provided at his table. The exemplary character of the other heroes consists of their obedience to food laws alone. (Note that in Tobit's case, such obedience is in contradistinction to "everyone of my kindred and my people [who] ate the food of the Gentiles," 1:11, NRSV.)

In the second category, it is straightforwardly the matter of dietary laws that is at issue, since the Jews in question were willing to eat with Gentiles. For example, we are told concerning Judith that "she took *what her maid had prepared* and ate and drank *before him* [Holofernes, commander of the Assyrian army]."[71] Esler's reference to the separatism of the Jews at the Egyptian court is simply wrong; the king and the Jewish translators together ate Jewish food.[72]

Finally, the prohibition in *Jubilees* may well be taken to be the exception that proves the rule. If an extreme document like *Jubilees* finds it necessary to inveigh against table-fellowship with Gentiles, what may we assume to have been the normal standard of behavior on such matters? Likewise, the notable association of obedience to food laws with the heroes of the faith ought to make one suspicious. The rectitude of the pious is not, after all, paraded without reason. What are we to make then of the broader audience for which these were raised as exemplars? The very stridency of a source, therefore, may in the end be the best evidence for the existence of the thing it opposes.

---

[68] Esler, *Community*, pp. 81, 82 (citing Jdt. 10:5; 12:2, 17-19; and the *Letter of Aristeas*). Note the parallel discussion of drinking wine with a Gentile (*m. 'Abod. Zar.* 5.5) on p. 84.

[69] Quoted from H. F. D. Sparks, *The Apocryphal Old Testament*, p. 72. The citation is discussed by Esler in *Community*, p. 83.

[70] *Joseph and Aseneth* 7:1 (Sparks, *Apocryphal OT*, p. 479).

[71] Jdt. 12:19 (NRSV).

[72] *Aristeas* 181; cf. Esler: "he [the king] ate his and they ate theirs" (*Community*, p. 82).

Hence, the case against mixed table-fellowship is not convincing. In particular, most of the attention that Esler believes to have been directed at table-fellowship was focused more narrowly on obedience to the dietary requirements of the law. Even these, of course, would have imposed very real social constraints upon the observant Jew—constraints which help to explain, from the Jewish side, pagan observations concerning Jewish separatism. However, obstacles presented by Jewish dietary laws would not necessarily have *precluded* dining with Gentiles, the obvious case being those instances in which Jews themselves were able to provide the meal.

That a Jewish Christian in a situation of mixed fellowship might have provided at least his or her own meal is supported by 1 Corinthians 11:21, in which we are told that individuals brought their own food to the Lord's Supper. Something like this might have been practiced at an early date in Antioch. Even if not, we may still wonder why it did not occur to the Jerusalem apostles—who had agreed in principle to the admission of Gentiles (and thus had in some sense already transcended their separate identity as Jews, the very thing that we are told necessitated the avoidance of mixed table-fellowship)[73]—that Jewish and Gentile disciples in Antioch might sometimes eat together. What, after all, of the Lord's Supper?[74]

Although the text moves us beyond the present discussion, it is worth closing with a reference to Esler's reflections on the Apostolic Decree of Acts 15:20, 29. "Now it is quite clear that these four prohibitions are singularly appropriate in a context where a Christian community has been established in which Jews and Gentiles engage in table-fellowship.... On this view, the difficult verse 15.21 may be interpreted as a recognition that the fourfold prohibition goes a long way to satisfying Jewish or Jewish Christian criticism of Christian fellowship."[75] In other words, the point at issue in the controversy over table-fellowship was *Jewish obedience to food laws*, after all. Hence the statement that the Jewish Christians of Jerusalem "were never reconciled to Jews eating with Gentiles in the Christian communities"[76] is unconvincing. The supposedly common Jewish understanding upon which it is based (i.e., that Jews must not eat with Gentiles) is, in the final analysis, attributed among Christian Jews only to those in Jerusalem. In other words,

---

[73] "Circumcision was not something pressed upon Gentile Christians [by Peter and James] for some abstract theological reason; it was seen as a remedy for a situation involving grievous risk to the continued existence of the Jewish people" (ibid., p. 98).

[74] Esler, for one, takes it for granted that the Lord's Supper was celebrated at Antioch (ibid.). Would not Peter and James have made the same assumption? According to my reconstruction, eucharistic fellowship could have continued between Gentile and Jewish believers at Antioch so long as Jewish legal obedience was not compromised. For the view that mixed table-fellowship at Antioch was *restricted* to the Lord's Supper, see Ernst Haenchen, "Petrus-Probleme," p. 196.

[75] Esler, *Community*, p. 99.

[76] Ibid., p. 106.

when Esler's larger thesis concerning the Jerusalem church is not in view, he is willing to accept that obstacles to mixed table-fellowship could have been overcome without great difficulty. Clearly, we are in the same old circle: the staunch legalism/conservatism of the Jerusalem apostles is supported by evidence that requires a prior belief in their legalism/conservatism.

THE CONVERSION OF CORNELIUS

One problem yet to be discussed concerns the relationship between the Apostolic Council and the story of the conversion of Cornelius in Acts 10 and 11.[77] The essential difficulty is this: how is it possible that the Jerusalem church, having already recognized that "God has given even to the Gentiles the repentance that leads to life" (11:18), found it necessary to settle the issue a second time? There can be little doubt that in Luke's account, the conversion of Cornelius—a providential act complete with angel (10:3-7), vision (vv. 10-16), and gifts of the Holy Spirit (vv. 44-46)—was meant to provide the fundamental justification for the subsequent mission to the Gentiles. The point is not even, as Haenchen believes, that it was "no 'freelance' who began the mission to the Gentiles, but the legitimate, apostolic Church."[78] No, it is God who initiated the mission.[79] So, how is it that a second, more mundane "justification story" has been included? Are not the two in contradiction?

As the record stands, with the Cornelius account culminating in the categorical recognition of the Gentiles (11:18), it is difficult to maintain that they are not.[80] Recognizing this problem then leads to one of two possible answers. Either the account of Acts 10-11 is only partly right, or else it is entirely wrong. Dibelius is one of many who opt for the first possibility. While recognizing that there are other problems with details of the account as it stands (Haenchen emphasizes the difficulties raised by the imagined presence of Roman troops in Caesarea during the years of Agrippa I's jurisdiction and the presence of the Italian cohort at such an early date),[81] Dibelius nevertheless proposes that at the core of the story stands reliable tradition concerning the evangelization of a Gentile named Cornelius by the apostle Peter. Luke, in appropriating the event, has embellished and "elevated the story of Cornelius in order to make it represent a principle. . . . Here, as

---

[77] Haenchen provides a history of the question in *Acts,* pp. 355-57 [301-2].
[78] Ibid., p. 360 [305].
[79] The fundamental debate is with Judaism, not Jewish Christianity.
[80] Loisy believed that "the story of Cornelius has been specially invented to contradict and annul what Paul tells of the conflict that took place between Peter and himself after the Jerusalem meeting" (*L'Épître aux Galates,* p. 124).
[81] Haenchen, *Acts,* p. 360 [305].

elsewhere, Luke has abandoned an exact reproduction of history for the sake of a higher historical truth."[82]

Haenchen is among those who feel compelled to follow the second route: the account is simply unhistorical. He considers it intrinsically unlikely that the Jerusalem church could have accepted Gentiles at such an early date. "It was precisely in the earliest days that the admission of Gentiles must have been most unthinkable to the community. By such a step it would have forfeited all toleration in Jerusalem."[83] The force of this argument is difficult to judge, since Cornelius and his family were not, according to Acts, actually joined to the Christian community in Jerusalem, and since we do not know how much toleration the church enjoyed in Jerusalem at the time. Haenchen also criticizes Dibelius on the grounds that the early church, in the intensity of its eschatological expectation, would not have had the inclination to preserve stories like that of Acts 10-11. "People who believe that the end of the world is near, and who confidently expect to be transfigured into angelic beings, have no interest in retailing the conversion story of a centurion."[84] This is not an altogether satisfying argument, given the significance of the conversion of *this particular* centurion. The real issue in the end concerns the probable importance of the event. If it must automatically have led to an open conflict that would have necessitated a resolution such as that found in 11:18, then contradiction with the story of the Apostolic Council is unavoidable. If, however, the conversion was a unique occurrence that did not preempt but perhaps set the stage for the later controversy, then it may indeed echo a genuine historical incident. In favor of this understanding one might cite Peter's initial willingness to participate in the mixed table-fellowship at Antioch as well as his apparent difficulties with the Jewish authorities in Jerusalem (Acts 4:1-22; 5:17-40; 12:3-5, 17).[85]

---

[82] Dibelius, *Studies*, p. 122 [106-7].
[83] Haenchen, *Acts*, p. 361 [306].
[84] Ibid., p. 360 [305-6].
[85] The movements of the apostle Peter would constitute a worthy study in themselves. One wonders, for example, what Peter was doing in Antioch (Gal. 2:11). Betz suggests that this could have been an occasional visit or a "stopover on the way to some other place." Or, he says, "it could have been a final move from Jerusalem because of unfavorable circumstances in Jerusalem." The occasion for this move may have been that mentioned in Acts 12:17 (*Galatians*, pp. 105-6; see Loisy, *L'Épître aux Galates*, pp. 126-27). A few other factors deserve consideration. Betz mentions earlier in his commentary (p. 76) that in Gal. 1:19 "Peter appears ... to have been the leading man among the apostles ... [but] at the so-called Apostolic Conference (2:1-10) Cephas appears behind James and before John." In the Acts 15 account, James is very clearly the leader in Jerusalem (see also Acts 21:18). Meanwhile, we know from 1 Cor. 1:12 and elsewhere that Peter traveled well outside of Judea in the exercise of his office (cf. 1 Cor. 9:5). Peter's apparently diminishing role in Jerusalem appears to be in conflict with his commission as the apostle to the circumcised in Gal. 2. Holmberg, for example, takes this appointment to be territorial: Peter would lead the mission to the "Jews of the Holy Land" from its center in Jerusalem (*Paul and Power*, p. 30). If so, Peter does not appear to have had the opportunity to fulfill this commission.

So broad an interpretation is no less difficult in the case of Paul. For all his success, it

The historicity of Cornelius's conversion will simply have to remain an open question. If it *is* true, then it is notable that we find the first Gentile being converted at the preaching of a *Hebrew*. But the point cannot be pressed. Even or especially if the story is a Lukan creation ex nihilo, we are left to theorize about the meaning of its inclusion. It must above all else have been included to justify the mission to the Gentiles in a way that the Apostolic Council, according to Luke's way of thinking, could not. The Gentiles were not received in the first instance by the action or decision of mere human beings, but manifestly by the power and will of God. Peter asks, "Who was I that I could hinder God?" (11:17). It is a question that recalls Peter and John's earlier declaration, "whether it is right in God's sight to listen to you rather than to God you must judge" (4:19), and the logic of Gamaliel's statement to the Sanhedrin, "If this plan or this undertaking is of human origin, it will fail; but if it is of God you will not be able to overthrow them—in that case you may even be found to be fighting against God!" (5:38b-39, an extraordinarily good summary of the Lukan perspective on both the legitimation of the gospel and its relationship to the Jews). One may also cite the verse that is the turning point in Paul's defense before Agrippa in chapter 26, "I was not disobedient to the heavenly vision" (v. 19). The point is obvious. God has acted and must not be resisted. In this sense, the apostles have not led, they have followed. This is the Lukan apologetic, and it is all that is necessary to account for the inclusion of the story in Acts.

I therefore consider as misplaced any attempt to find some other, more polemical reason for the story's incorporation. According to one commonly held theory, Luke created the story to domesticate the Hellenistic Gentile mission by bringing it under the wing of the Jerusalem church. As has already been said, there can be no doubt that Luke had an interest in promoting the centrality of Jerusalem. Admitting this concern does not, however, supply us with his motive. More likely than embarrassment over the premature success of the Hellenists, it seems probable that Luke was motivated by a conception of the central place of Jerusalem in the scheme of salvation history. Luke's apologetic vis-à-vis Judaism is strengthened if the Gentile mission, like the inception of the church itself, can be associated with the holy city.[86] For this purpose Peter, still the figurehead of the

---

is certainly not clear that Paul was regarded as the *leader* of the Gentile church. Indeed, Holmberg is careful to put Paul in his place as the junior partner to Barnabas (p. 18). Is there something more to Gal. 2:7-8 than self-aggrandizement? Perhaps so. Taken together, these factors lead me to tender what is admittedly a very speculative hypothesis: Peter, partly as a result of pressure from outside of the Christian community, was commissioned (or recognized) at the Jerusalem Conference as the missionary counterpart of Paul, being sent to preach to a primarily Jewish audience. He then came to Antioch as a stopover point on his way into the larger missionary field of the Mediterranean world.

[86] Note the place of Jerusalem (vs. Galilee) in the resurrection appearances of Luke 24 as well as its role as the place of assembly for the believers at Pentecost in Acts 2.

Jerusalem church, is the ideal instrument. To argue about Luke's mistaken chronology is to miss the point entirely.[87]

---

[87] Esler's conclusion that the Cornelius story has fundamentally to do with table-fellowship is another case in which the forest has been missed for the trees. Esler decrees, "Commentators ... who find it curious that Peter is called to account by the church in Jerusalem not for baptizing Gentiles, but for eating with them, have missed the entire point of the narrative" (*Community*, p. 96). The story, we are told, does indeed have to do with Gentile admission, but much more than that is concerned with the issue that embroiled Luke's own mixed community, that of obedience to Jewish food laws (pp. 96, 97).

Esler's thesis depends, in the first instance, upon his belief that Luke wrote to serve the needs of a mixed congregation. I find this assumption very dubious. He concludes his chapter on the law, for example, with the assertion that Luke's "conservative attitude to the law ... really only makes sense if there were a significant number of Jews in his community whose grip on the gospel was under threat on account of criticism from Jews, or from Jewish Christians.... Luke's legitimatory strategy consists of assuring them that Christianity and Judaism are not incompatible and that the very Jews who are worrying them are themselves unfaithful to Moses" (p. 129). But surely Luke's "conservative attitude to the law" leads us in the opposite direction: it shows that he was *not* writing to an audience for whom legal obedience was a burning issue. Otherwise, the whole tendency of Acts would work *against* mixed table-fellowship. As we have already had occasion to mention above, Luke writes as one once removed from the debate of the early church over the question of legal obedience. (For this reason it is overly subtle to read significance, as Esler does, into accounts like that "of the table-fellowship in the house of the gaoler at Philippi" [16:34; p. 101]. It is very hard to believe that we find Luke here mulling over the question of whether Paul has broken the law by eating with his captor.) The law is good insofar as it is the law of the Jews — *and only the Jews*. Luke is able to be so positive about the law precisely because obedience to it is not for him a live issue.

The presence of the theme of clean and unclean animals in Peter's vision (10:11-16; 11:5-10) and the criticism he encounters concerning eating with uncircumcised men (11:3) is best explained, I believe, as an integral part of Luke's introduction to the theme of the Gentile mission. Behind the account is the basic question, What barrier needs to be overcome if Gentiles are to be admitted into the church? The answer, according to Luke, is their impurity. Although the sentiment may have existed in Judaism (cf. Esler, *Community*, pp. 85-86; the argument is, however, considerably weakened by the confusion of "purity" and "ritual purity"), there are no laws stating that Gentiles qua Gentiles are unclean. The things that are unclean *by nature* are, of course, various animals (Lev. 11:1-38, 41-47). Luke uses these as a metaphor for the Gentiles, a symbol whose meaning is explicitly stated in 10:28 (κἀμοὶ ὁ θεὸς ἔδειξεν μηδένα κοινὸν ἢ ἀκάθαρτον λέγειν ἄνθρωπον). This is not to deny that in this passage Luke is also doing away with the regulations of Lev. 11. But this is not the point of their mention in this context. (On the question of Gentile uncleanness, see E. Sanders, "Jewish Association with Gentiles and Gal. 2:11-14," which includes a critique of Gedalyahu Alon's influential essays [themselves, it should be noted, of primary importance to Esler's own thesis] on the impurity of Gentiles.)

The reference to eating with the uncircumcised in 11:3 is, therefore, also understandable. The accusation essentially reiterates the issue of purity raised by Peter himself in 10:28. This includes, in Luke's mind, going to the Gentiles (10:28a/11:3a) as well as eating with them (11:3b). Thus Haenchen is absolutely right in claiming that the point of the whole passage is the sentiment expressed in 10:28 and rephrased in 10:34-35: 'Ἐπ' ἀληθείας καταλαμβάνομαι ὅτι οὐκ ἔστιν προσωπολήμπτης ὁ θεός, ἀλλ' ἐν παντὶ ἔθνει ὁ φοβούμενος αὐτὸν καὶ ἐργαζόμενος δικαιοσύνην δεκτὸς αὐτῷ ἐστιν. Acts 11 "clearly has this sense, too ... where the men of Jerusalem similarly do not infer 'So now we can eat unclean food as well,' but 'So God has given repentance unto life to the Gentiles also'" (*Acts*, p. 362 [307]).

THE INCIDENT AT ANTIOCH

At some time Peter came to the church at Antioch. Initially he joined in the practice of table-fellowship with Gentiles. After the arrival of unspecified persons "from James," Peter and the body of Jewish Christians with him separated and began to eat apart from the Gentiles. Paul, rather than follow his example, found it necessary to confront Peter publicly concerning his conduct.

Despite the banality of this description, there is probably no event that is of greater importance to one's understanding of the character of the early church than this so-called incident at Antioch. Its fuller reconstruction is a notoriously thorny problem, one that has led scholars to diametrically opposing views concerning the relationship between Jewish and Gentile Christianity in the critical period of the mid-first century. To some, the events of Galatians 2:11-14 signal the triumph of Paulinism, the full recognition of Gentile equality, and the acknowledgement, for Jews as well as for Gentiles, that the law had been superseded by the work of Christ. To others, the passage records the moment at which the great and irreversible split between Jewish and Gentile, conservative and liberal wings of the Christian church was made final.

One reason for this broad disparity of opinion is the surprising fact that Paul fails to inform us of the outcome of the incident. Did Peter (and, with him, the other Jewish Christians) repent at Paul's rebuke? The answer is silence. Then how is this silence to be read? Some have argued that Paul passed over the conclusion of the story because it was so obvious. Yes, the Jewish Christians did relent, and that is precisely the reason why Paul is able to introduce them in his argument in Galatians.[88] It could be supposed, however, that the narrative ends where it does because Paul did not prevail and therefore had no interest in reporting the story's unhappy conclusion.[89]

The notion that Paul won the day at Antioch is seldom defended in contemporary scholarship.[90] In its favor, some commentators have noted the high regard for Paul in the later church, most especially on the part of Ignatius, the bishop of Antioch. There is some merit to this point, especially if one supposes that the only alternative is a loss for Paul of the magnitude outlined above. Nevertheless, numerous other data seem better accommodated by the alternative proposal. These include Paul's breakup with Barnabas in Acts 15 (better explained by the graver controversy of Gal. 2),[91] the independence of his mission subsequent to the controversy (Rom. 15:20), the issuing of the Apostolic Decree (unnecessary if Paul prevailed), Paul's

---

[88] See Pierre Bonnard, *L'Épître de Saint Paul aux Galates,* pp. 48-49.
[89] See Loisy, *L'Épître aux Galates,* p. 125.
[90] But see, for example, Ragner Bring, *Commentary on Galatians,* p. 82 [91].
[91] The relative value of this argument is noted in chap. 2 above.

troubles with the church in Galatia (less likely if Paul received an unambiguous recognition of his authority at Antioch), and the unfavorable light in which the apostles, Peter in particular, are cast in the Book of Galatians. The final three considerations are, in my opinion, particularly persuasive. The Antioch Incident appears to have left dangling a number of loose ends, in particular, the conditions surrounding mixed table-fellowship and the nature and legitimacy of Paul's apostolate. A victory for Paul at Antioch would have solved these problems in advance, as it were, and so seems improbable.

To say that Paul lost is certainly *not* to consider the second viewpoint mentioned above to be the only or even the correct option: that the failure of Paul at Antioch meant the rejection of the Gentile (i.e., circumcision-free) mission and the consequent division of the church. It does, however, mean that the resultant picture must be complicated, since we find Paul in Galatians presenting an argument in favor of his authority and gospel based at least in part upon a confrontation he *lost*. Little wonder, then, that so many able minds have been exercised by this short passage. There is a riddle here that we must do our best to solve.

Perhaps the best way of proceeding is to ask what was at stake at Antioch. To Paul, writing to the Galatians, the issue was straightforwardly one of Judaizing. Peter and the other Jewish Christians were compelling the Gentiles 'Ιουδαΐζειν (2:14). But did the other parties view matters in this same way? What, in particular, was at stake as far as the other Jewish Christians were concerned, and what viewpoint does their change of mind represent?

It cannot be assumed a priori that the Jewish Christians withdrew from mixed table-fellowship for ideological reasons. We must first consider the possibility that they were motivated, at least in part, by more pragmatic considerations.

A number of commentators have attempted to examine the Antioch Incident in light of its larger historical context. James D. G. Dunn adopts this approach in the first section of his 1983 article "The Incident at Antioch (Gal. 2.11-18)." His discussion focuses upon the increase in "pressures towards conformity" within "the mainstream of nationalistic Judaism,"[92] in Antioch as well as in Jerusalem, in the mid-first century. He concludes that "wherever this new Jewish sect's belief or practice was perceived to be a threat to Jewish institutions and traditions its members would almost certainly come under pressure from their fellow Jews to remain loyal to their unique Jewish heritage."[93] This follows the lines laid down by Robert Jewett in his discussion of the motivation of the Galatian agitators[94] and is a fairly typical

---

[92] James D. G. Dunn, "The Incident at Antioch (Gal. 2:11-18)," p. 9.
[93] Ibid., p. 10.
[94] Robert Jewett, "The Agitators and the Galatian Congregation," pp. 204-6.

assessment of the sociopolitical conditions under which the incident occurred.

How much the events at Antioch may have been the result of rising Jewish intolerance is clearly one of the questions that must concern us. It is not inconceivable that, under such circumstances, the churches of Jerusalem and Antioch might have adopted a more rigorous posture as a useful (and temporary?) expedient and not as a true change of policy.[95] In that case the "certain people from James"[96] might have said something like, "Yes, we agree that there is nothing *wrong* with what you're doing, but don't you see the position it's putting us in?"

Certain considerations weigh in favor of this conclusion. For one thing, this perspective helps to make sense of Paul's charge that Peter's reversal was (at least in part) motivated by fear (Gal. 2:12b).[97] It also helps to explain the reversal on the part of the Jewish Christians of Antioch, in particular, that of Barnabas.

Of whom or what was Peter afraid? Bligh's conclusion is that Peter was afraid of ridicule: "He feared that the Judaizers might answer back with theological arguments which he could not refute—in which case he would be made to look foolish before the church in Antioch."[98]

Peter's fear of "those of the circumcision" (τοὺς ἐκ περιτομῆς) may or may not refer to the "certain persons from James." Considering the tone of Galatians, it is reasonable to suppose that Paul had in mind both those representing James, on one level, and the Jews more broadly (including non-Christian Jews), on another. Ragner Bring comes to a similar conclusion: "It is . . . likely that it refers to all who *think* according to Jewish patterns."[99] For Paul in Galatians, this description would have included the "men from James" (whom he does not accuse of hypocrisy) as well as the Jews in general. This does not mean, however, that their views were necessarily identical.

---

[95] But even this rather generous interpretation assumes that a policy had existed that needed amending. I have argued instead that the question had not previously been deliberated, and so it is in that sense wrong to claim that Jerusalem's intervention represents a change of heart—for pragmatic or for more ideological reasons. And yet it is reasonable to suppose that the climate of the times made Jerusalem's request both more urgent (from the side of the Hebrews) and more compelling (from the side of the Hellenists).

[96] The trend among scholars is to accept that the delegation from James did in fact represent James, the brother of Jesus. The only contrary evidence is in Acts 15:24, which may be apologetic (Betz, *Galatians*, p. 109). George S. Duncan suggests that these even bore letters of commendation from James (*The Epistle of Paul to the Galatians*, p. 57). What is particularly striking is the ability of this group to persuade Peter, who was himself presumably knowledgeable of the situation in Jerusalem. I do not therefore see any reason to take Paul's words here at anything but face value.

[97] The NRSV translates τοὺς ἐκ περιτομῆς as "the circumcision faction." This is more interpretation than translation.

[98] Bligh, *Galatians*, p. 186.

[99] Bring, *Galatians*, p. 83 [92].

John Chrysostom felt that reference was being made to Jewish-Christians who might hear of Peter's action. Peter's "cause of fear was not his own danger ... but their defection."[100] Similarly, others have believed that Peter was afraid of rendering ineffective the mission to the Jews of Israel. This would have been a fear of scandalizing those *outside* the church. Aquinas calls this a "fear inspired by charity."[101] According to Duncan, "If Jews who become Christians were to degrade themselves to the level of Gentile sinners, what hope would there be of winning Israel to an early acceptance of the gospel?"[102]

Peter Richardson offers a very helpful analysis at this point by reminding us of each of the apostles' respective spheres of activity. "Paul's concern for the Gentiles puts one pressure on Paul, but Peter's concern for the Jew weighs things differently for him." So long as Peter is in "Paul's sphere of activity," he is willing to "adopt Paul's practice. However, when some men from James arrive ... the situation changes. It then becomes a matter affecting not just the Pauline mission to the Gentiles ... but includes also a consideration of the nature and basis of Peter's mission to the Jews."[103] Seen in this light, Peter's fear does indeed appear highly legitimate.

One additional concern has been brought forward by Ragnar Bring, among others. He sees the threat to be not so much that of the failure of the Jewish mission (although such a failure is implied in his position) as that of possible Jewish persecution. "Such an action would separate them from the Jews and make them the object of their hatred and persecution." "The men from James may have pointed this out."[104] This interpretation may be supported by Galatians 6:12, in which Paul accuses the Galatian Judaizers themselves of acting out of fear of persecution.

If there is anything to these speculations, then we would be led to believe that the incident at Antioch arose at least in part for pragmatic as opposed to strictly ideological reasons. In such a situation, everyone concerned (including Peter and Barnabas, excluding Paul) might have felt that a low profile was to be advised at that time. Peter would not then be changing his mind at all about his, let alone the Gentiles', freedom from the law (whatever that consisted of) but would be bowing to the more pressing expedient. This would help to explain the willingness of the Jewish Christians to be persuaded by the representatives of James and would also form an interesting argumentative link between Peter and the Judaizers troubling

---

[100] Chrysostom, Homily 2 on Galatians (*Saint Chrysostom: Homilies on Galatians ...*, p. 19).

[101] St. Thomas Aquinas, *Commentary on St. Paul's Epistle to the Galatians*, p. 47.

[102] Duncan, *Galatians*, p. 59.

[103] Peter Richardson, "Pauline Inconsistency: I Corinthians 9:19-23 and Galatians 2:11-14," p. 360; *Paul's Ethic of Freedom*, p. 93.

[104] Bring, *Galatians*, pp. 84, 83 [93, 92].

the Galatians: although their means were strictly different (Jewish separation vs. Gentile circumcision), their motivation (fear), goal (to quiet opposition through the recognition of Jewish legal scruples), and the final outcome of their practice (the elimination of the gospel of grace) were the same. Thus, although they represent differing perspectives, Paul is able to draw a line of correspondence through the "false believers," the representatives of James, Peter, and the Galatian Judaizers.

A number of commentators have linked the Antioch Incident specifically to an increased tension between the Jews of Palestine and the pagan occupiers of their land in the years leading up to the Jewish Revolt of 66. From this we might reasonably expect that a closing of the ranks occurred within Judaism, which might in turn have placed new pressures for conformity on the church, in Jerusalem particularly.[105]

The problem with this approach is that it relies upon a historical model that is probably inappropriately applied to the events of A.D. 66. Revolt is generally considered to be the end consequence of a long, cumulative process of ever-increasing social and political tension. With respect to the Jewish Revolt, however, this does not seem to have been the case.[106] Instead, the process by which certain events (in particular, the suspension of the daily sacrifice offered on behalf of the emperor) led to revolt seems to have occurred very quickly. Martin Goodman writes, "The slide into war was rapid and dramatic."[107] Furthermore, even if tensions did increase in the years prior to the war, it is unlikely that the Antioch Incident occurred near enough to the time to benefit from this form of explanation.[108]

Heightened fears of persecution might thus have played a role in the

---

[105] E.g., Jewett, "Agitators," pp. 204–6; Dunn, "Incident," pp. 7–11; and Bruce, *The Epistle of Paul to the Galatians: A Commentary on the Greek Text*, p. 130.

[106] See Goodman, *Ruling Class*, pp. 7–19. Robert Jewett's "Zealot hypothesis," while not concerned primarily with events in Jerusalem itself, is subject to the same criticism. Jewett bases his speculations to a large extent on Martin Hengel's now-discredited thesis concerning an early and widespread Zealot movement (in *The Zealots: Investigations into the Jewish Freedom Movement in The Period from Herod I until 70 A.D.*). For critique of Hengel's position, see, for example, Morton Smith, "Zealots and Sicarii, Their Origins and Relation," pp. 10–15; Solomon Zeitlin, "Zealots and Sicarii," pp. 397–98; David Rhoads, *Israel in Revolution: 6-74 C.E. A Political History Based on the Writings of Josephus*, pp. 53–59; John S. Hanson and Richard A. Horsley, *Bandits, Prophets, and Messiahs: Popular Movements in the Time of Jesus*, pp. xiii–xv, 190–243 (chap. 5, "Fourth Philosophy, Sicarii, Zealots"); and *Jesus and the Spiral of Violence: Popular Jewish Resistance in Roman Palestine*, pp. x–xi, 61–62, 77–78. See also Kirsopp Lake's earlier discussion of the Zealots in *Beginnings* 1:421–25.

[107] Goodman, *Ruling Class*, p. 152. Hanson and Horsley write: "It is clear that the Jewish revolt was not the result of any long-standing resistance movement agitating for decades until finally touching off a more widespread national insurrection against the Romans" (*Bandits*, p. 254; cf. p. xv); see also *Jesus and the Spiral of Violence*, p. 54.

[108] By Jewett's chronology, the Antioch Incident occurred in the winter of 51–52 (*Chronology*, chart). Niels Hyldahl places it a year later (*Die Paulinische Chronologie*, p. 122). Other chronologies vary, but the date of the conference is never, to my knowledge, fixed as late as the 60s.

affair, but it is just as possible that they did not. We simply cannot know the degree to which, or even if, such a solution is true. The same can be said concerning the extent to which fear of offending the Jews (and thus spoiling the Jewish mission) figured in the event. Was it the non-Christian Jews *alone* who were offended by the Antiochene practice? It is a supposition, but it cannot be demonstrated. If the body of Jewish Christians in Jerusalem had themselves been scandalized, we would then be forced to search for some other basis for the conflict.

I do not find the pragmatic solution to be wholly convincing. The reason is the existence of the prohibitions of Acts 15:20, 29 and the tension between Paul and the Jerusalem apostles that appears to have continued well beyond Antioch.[109] This judgment is of course necessarily subjective. I am assuming, for example, that the proscriptions of Acts 15:20, 29 were motivated by a genuine interest in the Jewish food laws and not simply by the desire to put on a good face for the sake of the Jews (cf. Gal. 2:13). This latter opinion would have involved the Jewish Christians in a level of circumspection bordering on cowardice—something I am not inclined to accept, particularly in light of the death of James, the brother of Jesus. Furthermore, Paul's ambiguous attitude toward Jerusalem seems to require the existence of a conflict that was neither total nor trivial. It is difficult to believe that this occasion of Jewish Christian pragmatism (hypocrisy), as serious as it may have seemed to Paul when he was in Antioch, provides us with that sufficient conflict.

So, if there was a clash of ideas at Antioch, what was it? The answer is by no means obvious and yet is of undoubted importance. Some commentators have taken sides with Paul, seeing the issue as one of circumcision, pure and simple. As we have already seen, this is the position that Philip Esler comes to, on the basis of his understanding of table-fellowship. The "certain people" from James were unwilling to accept the practice of mixed dining. Therefore "the behavior of Peter in Antioch (Gal 2.11-14) probably amounted to a repudiation of the agreement by the leadership in Jerusalem."[110] Henceforth the Jerusalem apostles may fairly be considered Judaizers, since they demanded the proselytism of Gentiles,[111] and the

---

[109] The Apostolic Decree will be discussed in more detail below. Paul's relationship with Jerusalem is one of subjects to be considered in chap. 5, "Further Evidence."

[110] Esler, *Community*, p. 144.

[111] This position, according to Esler, was "the only way to rehabilitate" the practice of mixed fellowship: "the Gentiles [must] become Jews through circumcision" (ibid., p. 88). Francis Watson, in *Paul, Judaism and the Gentiles: A Sociological Approach* (p. 55), makes much the same point concerning the Judaizing stance of the Jerusalem church. Unlike Esler, however, he thinks that the position taken by the "pillars" was consonant with the Jerusalem agreement alluded to in Gal. 2:6-10.

church may rightly be described as divided, since it was now separated into two camps, those with and those against the Gentiles.

This position is not without appeal. It is clear and forceful. It accounts for the vehemence of Paul's language in Galatians (Paul is not using the term Ἰουδαΐζειν [to judaize], 2:14, in vain),[112] and it helps to explain the subsequent Judaizing opposition Paul experienced in his mission field (inspired, or perhaps even actively promoted, by the church in Jerusalem).[113]

But the either-or perspective on the early church promoted by this view is unsustainable in light of the more complicated witness of the New Testament. Despite its undoubted appeal, the proposal must in the end be judged to be incredible. The reasons for this are as follows:

1. It dismisses or ignores the only real evidence we have on the attitude of the Jerusalem apostles toward the Gentiles, that of Acts 15 and Galatians 2.[114]
2. No adequate account is offered for the dramatic volte-face of the Jerusalem Christians (whom Paul does *not* accuse of hypocrisy — a startling fact if they were now demanding the circumcision of Gentiles).[115]
3. Nor is there any explanation for the sudden and extraordinary change of mind on the part of Barnabas, the very one who with Paul had won from the "pillars" in Jerusalem (James included) the recognition of this freedom for the Gentiles. And even if Barnabas is somehow suspect, what of the entire body of Jewish Christians (*Hellenists*) who separated with him?
4. It is not explained how Paul's argument in Galatians can be saved from the morass of contradictions introduced by this reconstruction. In particular, *why would Paul recognize the authority of the "pillars" to falsify his gospel (2:2) if they had in fact done this very thing?*

On this fourth point, I am willing with most to allow for a generous degree of exaggeration and one-sidedness on the part of the apostle, but it requires nothing short of cynicism to accept that Galatians could have been written by one who knew that the Jerusalem apostles were now directly opposed to his circumcision-free gospel to the Gentiles. The same can be said

---

[112] "2:13f should therefore be taken absolutely literally: in response to instructions from James, Peter, Barnabas and the Antiochene Christians other than Paul withdrew from fellowship with the Gentile Christians, demanding that they adopt the Jewish way of life" (Francis Watson, *Paul,* p. 54). See also Esler, *Community,* p. 88.

[113] See, for example, Watson, *Paul,* p. 58; and Esler, *Community,* p. 87.

[114] This is one of the most telling criticisms of Esler's thesis. He rejects the historicity of the Acts 15 account (*Community,* pp. 97-98) and seems to imagine that the problems the passage raises have disappeared with it. The prohibitions of vv. 20 and 29, while genuine, *must* have come from some other source (p. 98; see above). Gal. 2:1-10 might just as well have never been written; of Esler's seven references to it, only two mention the agreement it records (pp. 87, 97), and in both of these cases the matter is reported and then dropped without comment. (See also Watson's dismissive treatment of Gal. 2 in *Paul,* pp. 51-54.)

[115] Why would Paul feel free to attack Peter but not James? The answer is that the issue in Antioch was *Jewish,* and not Gentile, obedience. On this matter Peter had reversed himself, but on the issue of Gentile obedience James had not.

for the rest of the Pauline corpus, since it assumes and asserts an underlying unity to the message preached both to Jew and to Gentile (Gal. 2:9; Rom. 1:16; 1 Cor. 1:12-13; 15:11; 1 Thess. 2:13-14) that would be made a mockery of by a split of this severity;[116] for, while Paul acknowledged the legitimacy of the Jerusalem apostles (Gal. 2:2, 7-9;[117] 1 Cor. 3:22; 9:5; 15:7, 9; Rom. 15:31), he openly renounced those who preached circumcision (Gal. 1:8-9 [where they are cursed]; 5:4, 12[!]; Phil. 3:2).[118] While there does seem to have been a real tension between Paul and Jerusalem, the proposal of an open break with the leaders of that church over the circumcision of Gentiles generates very many more problems than it solves.

But what other conflict would explain Paul's differences with the Jewish Christians of Jerusalem and Antioch? One of the few and certainly most original alternatives is that offered by James Dunn. The core of Dunn's essay on the Antioch Incident is his section "The Limits of Table-Fellowship in the Judaism of the Late Second Temple Period."[119] These limits, he says, "would be determined partly by the explicit laws in the Torah, particularly concerning unclean foods (Lev. 11:1-23; Deut. 14:3-21), and in differing degrees by the multiplying *halakhoth* of the oral tradition concerning tithes and ritual purity."[120] It is to these final two items, tithing and ritual purity, that Dunn turns for his key to the events at Antioch. He summarizes his thesis as follows:

> The table-fellowship at Antioch had not totally disregarded the law but probably had paid due heed to the basic dietary laws of the Torah. Peter, having already become less tied to the more elaborate scruples of the brothers in Judea (Acts 10-11), found no difficulty in joining in such table-fellowship, as Barnabas, more used to Diaspora ways, was already doing. The men from James however were shocked at what seemed to them a minimal level of Torah observance and a far too casual and unacceptable attitude to the Torah. They would no doubt point out that the earlier agreement made in Jerusalem had in no way changed the obligations to Torah obedience on the part of the Jewish believer.... Peter, persuaded by this charge of disloyalty and out of concern for the future of the Jewish Christian assemblies and the "mission to the circumcised" withdrew into a more disciplined ritual and "the rest of the Jews" followed suit... hoping, we may presume, that the Gentile believers would adapt their own life style to this more rigorous code of conduct.[121]

Thus the incident did not concern Jewish obedience versus disobedience

---

[116] It must not be forgotten how serious this breach would have appeared to Paul.

[117] Note the assumption behind Rom. 11:13, that there was a legitimate apostolate to the Jews.

[118] Another consideration is the ongoing collection for the saints in Jerusalem, a matter taken up in the next chapter.

[119] Dunn, "Incident," pp. 12-25.

[120] Ibid., p. 12.

[121] Ibid., p. 36.

but *degrees* of Jewish obedience. For evidence Dunn turns to the example of the Pharisees, who were concerned with ritual purity and thus, by extension, with the question of proper table-fellowship. One of the "most striking features about the Pharisees in Palestine ... was their preoccupation with defining the limits of table-fellowship." "As to *ritual purity,* the Pharisees quite simply sought to apply the purity laws governing the temple ritual to their everyday lives. Others might properly conclude that these laws referred only to the priests as they performed their temple service and to themselves only when they went to the temple."[122] "Tithing was important according to the same logic, since only food which had properly been tithed was ritually acceptable."[123]

It would be wrong, we are told, to conclude that these matters were a concern only to the Pharisees and then only locally. They were debated widely both in and outside of Palestine. The Essenes' views on ritual purity were even stricter than those of the Pharisees, while the Sadducees' were much laxer. "And we know that within the ranks of the Pharisees there were many debates between the schools of Shammai and Hillel about particular details, where concern was to define the precise limits of table-fellowship. We also know that the Pharisees of our period already distinguished several degrees of purity."[124] We may therefore conclude that "in the Palestine of our period there was a wide spectrum of teaching and practice on this precise issue," but "insofar as the new sect of followers of Jesus was to any extent influenced by Pharisaic views, its members were bound to be caught up in these debates and cross-currents about the acceptable limits of table-fellowship."[125]

It is a fascinating proposal, but one that is almost certainly wrong. Dunn is mistaken in believing that the laws of tithing and ritual purity would have been of relevance in Antioch because, in the first instance, it was not required that Diaspora Jews tithe,[126] and, second, it was unnecessary[127] and, in point of fact, *impossible*[128] that they should be ritually pure. It is even questionable whether the Pharisees of Palestine were themselves as

---

[122] Ibid., p. 14.
[123] Ibid., p. 15.
[124] Ibid., p. 16.
[125] Ibid., p. 17. Dunn notes that this issue stands behind the well-known discrepancy between Mark 7:19 and Matt. 15:17, 20.
[126] Only those living in "the land" (Lev. 27:30) were expected to tithe.
[127] That is, unless they journeyed to Jerusalem to worship at the temple, in which case it would be required that they purify themselves.
[128] Sacrifices were required for cleansing from, for example, bodily discharges (Lev. 15:13-15), menstrual bleeding (15:25-30), and childbirth (chap. 12), *so that the tabernacle of God may not be defiled* (Lev. 15:31). The most significant of the laws governing ritual purity (inasmuch as it would have affected the greatest number of persons) is that found in Num. 19 (n. v. 20) concerning the administration of the "water for cleansing" from the defilement incurred by touching a corpse.

concerned with the matter of ritual purity and table-fellowship as Dunn supposes.[129]

Dunn's failure to supply convincing answers should not, however, cause us to miss the cogency of the questions he is asking. The position he adopts reflects a genuine sensitivity to the complexity of the issues involved in the incident at Antioch. He seizes upon the notion of ritual purity and tithing as a good way to explain the fact that although there was a genuine rupture at Antioch, it was not of the cataclysmic proportions envisaged by some commentators. It is instructive to follow the way in which he sets up and then evaluates what he believes are the three alternative interpretations of the event.

1. The Jewish Christians at Antioch had "completely abandoned the laws governing table-fellowship," even those of clean and unclean foods. The group from James insisted on observance of the law, "perhaps no more than the laws explicitly set out in the Torah."[130]
2. Peter and the others had observed "the dietary laws, including even some of the *halakhic* elaborations concerning tithes and ritual purity. In this case the people from James were in effect insisting that these God-fearing Gentile believers go the whole way and become proselytes . . . and Peter and the other Jewish believers who followed him were giving their demand added force by their actions."[131]
3. Essential Torah observance was already a part of the mixed table-fellowship at Antioch, although considerable latitude was exercised in interpreting the regulations concerning ritual purity and tithing. The Jerusalem Christians maintained a higher standard in these matters, one that they subsequently required of their fellows in Antioch.

In favor of the first of these alternatives is the fact that it gives full weight to the two phrases "live like a Gentile" (ἐθνικῶς . . . ζῇς) and "Gentile sinners" (ἐθνῶν ἁμαρτωλοί, Gal. 2:14, 15). Against it, however, is the unlikelihood that these Jewish Christians had so quickly and unreservedly turned from the Torah. "So far as we know, such a complete abandoning of the law without protest from within the ranks of the local Jewish Christians themselves is without parallel. Both in Corinth and at Rome a substantial proportion of the Jewish believers clearly felt unable to go so far (Rom. 14:1-2; 1 Cor. 8)."[132]

Second, since we know that there were at Antioch substantial numbers of God-fearing Gentiles, and since it is likely that the first Gentile Christians came predominantly from their ranks, it is reasonable to suppose that among

---

[129] A thorough critique of Dunn's argument concerning each of these points is presented in E. P. Sanders: 'Purity," and "Jewish Association."
[130] Dunn, "Incident," p. 29.
[131] Ibid., p. 30.
[132] Ibid., p. 29.

the Gentile believers of Antioch a certain minimal standard of legal observance (e.g., the so-called Noahic Commandments of Gen. 9) was already customary practice. Third, "It must be doubted whether Paul would have reacted quite so sharply as he did to a requirement from the Jerusalem delegation merely that the Gentiles should observe the most basic laws of the Torah—the Noahic laws."[133]

The second alternative "would certainly fit with the background of considerable numbers of Gentiles at Antioch showing themselves willing to 'judaize.'"[134] It would also parallel the story of Izates, king of Adiabene, in which a Jew from Palestine, the Galilean Eleazar, proved more rigorous than his Diaspora counterparts with respect to the question of what was to be required of the Gentiles.[135] Likewise, it would make partial sense of the discrepancy between Galatians and Acts by equating the "certain people . . . from James" (Gal. 2:12) with the "certain individuals . . . from Judea" (Acts 15:1).

Dunn offers two objections to this view. First of all, it makes Paul's charge that Peter had been living like a Gentile almost meaningless. Second, if we are right in supposing that the Jerusalem Conference came first, the "pillars" would now be rescinding their earlier agreement—with the consent of the Antiochene Hellenists, no less.[136] The third alternative is Dunn's preference. It is well suited, we are told, to the language of Galatians 2:14-15:[137] "Paul's charge against Peter, then, is most likely that by his action he had raised the ritual barriers surrounding their table-fellowship, thereby excluding the Gentile believers unless they 'judaized,' that is, embraced a far more demanding discipline of ritual purity than hitherto." Similarly, "Paul's description of Peter as previously having lived 'like a Gentile and not as a Jew' could describe a practice of table-fellowship which fell within the limits of the Noahic laws, since already no doubt the view was current that the commandments given to Noah (Gen. 9) applied to all the nations (the

---

[133] Ibid., p. 30.
[134] Ibid.
[135] Josephus, *Ant.* 20.38-48 (cited by Dunn, "Incident," p. 24).
[136] Dunn's remark at this point is an interesting blend of old and new: "It is doubtful too that the . . . Hellenists . . . should succumb so completely to pressure of this sort *from the Jerusalem which had expelled them*" ("Incident," p. 31, emphasis added).
[137] Dunn offers a detailed analysis of the vocabulary of the passage (ibid., pp. 25-28). My general reaction is that Dunn takes his word studies a little too seriously; I doubt that Paul chose his terms because of their technical precision in describing the events at Antioch; instead, he used evocative language that suited his purposes in writing to the Galatians. Therefore, when Paul says that Peter is "compelling" the Gentiles by his example to "Judaize," I doubt very seriously that what he means is that Peter is making them take on a certain technical and rather more strict Judaized status. One could argue that this *is* what Paul meant by his words at Antioch and that in Galatians they have taken on a fuller meaning. But making Paul's argument more technical also makes it less forceful. Paul tended to see things in terms of polar opposites, and the force of the argument of Gal. 2:14 is that there is a clear-cut choice to be made between law and grace.

descendants of Noah) and not just the Jews (cf. Jub. 7:20)."[138] Furthermore, this interpretation fits in well with what we know of the sociopolitical background of the times. "The pressure would be on the good Jew to withdraw more and more into a stricter definition and practice of his national religion."[139] That such a strict definition could and did take on Christian coloring is proven by Matthew 5:19; 15:17-20 (vs. Mark 7:19); and 23:3.

I believe that Dunn is correct at two critical points. Many (and perhaps most) scholars have assumed that the mixed table-fellowship at Antioch was from the beginning based upon an abandonment of the law on the part of the Jewish Christian participants.[140] Dunn is right to question this view, especially since, as we have already seen, the issue of Jewish obedience did not arise at the council in Jerusalem. If mixed table-fellowship did begin in Antioch at an early date, it is most likely that it was of a form that was not considered inherently objectionable by the leaders of the church in Jerusalem. Dunn's instincts also led him to dismiss the notion that the Jerusalem Agreement was repudiated by James and Peter. That supposition is fraught with problems, and Dunn is on solid ground in rejecting it.

But Dunn is wrong in thinking that the three reconstructions he offers are the only alternatives available. By his reasoning, if the third choice (i.e., his own) is eliminated, we are left to believe either in an early and complete abandonment of the law on the part of the Jewish Christians of Antioch or else in their wholehearted observance of "the dietary laws, including even some of the *halakhic* elaborations concerning tithes and ritual purity."[141] I think that somewhere between these two poles a third point must be plotted. Because of our lack of knowledge of the early church, its precise location remains uncertain, but that it is there and that it provides us with a better answer than the alternatives on either side seems to me most reasonable.

Let us return for a moment to the story of the founding of the church in Antioch in Acts 11:19-20. We are told that the Jewish Christians who were scattered following the persecution in Jerusalem traveled as far as Phoenicia, Cyprus, and Antioch, "and they spoke the word to no one except Jews. But among them were some men of Cyprus and Cyrene who, on coming to Antioch, spoke to Greeks[142] also, proclaiming the Lord Jesus." There is a significance to these verses that has largely been missed, and the lack of controversy over it demonstrates what is, I think, a tacit agreement on the part of scholars that the Lukan account of the missionary activity of these

---

[138] Ibid., p. 32.
[139] Ibid.
[140] See, for example, Burton, *Galatians*, p. lix; Betz, *Galatians*, p. 112; and Lightfoot, *Saint Paul's Epistle to the Galatians*, p. 114.
[141] Dunn, "Incident," p. 30.
[142] Against the reading Ἑλληνιστάς, see Hengel, *Between*, p. 8 [164–65].

Jewish Christians has about it the ring of truth. Those who left Jerusalem were scattered—quite naturally, one would suppose, to their homes in the Diaspora.[143] "And they spoke the word *to no one except Jews*" (11:19). Why did they not preach to Gentiles? The obvious reason is that the mission to the Gentiles had not yet begun. The Christian message, whatever its content, was in the understanding of these first believers a message for Jews. Insofar as Gentiles were considered, it was probably thought, along the lines of conventional expectation,[144] that they would share at some future date in the blessings of a *redeemed* Israel. Therefore, Jewish Christians would naturally share their newfound perspective as Jews with Jews. It was only gradually, and (at least at first) to a minority (11:20), that the concurrent relevance of the gospel to a Gentile audience became apparent. This is all exactly as we should have expected.

We may further agree with Dunn's assessment and imagine that these first Gentile converts were among the God-fearers of one or more of the synagogues of Antioch.[145] These had already displayed a certain attention to the faith of Israel, and one can readily picture them taking an interest in the words of those returning from Jerusalem. The question would then arise as to their place in the order of things as it was now envisaged. Eventually, after how much time we do not know, someone took the revolutionary step of baptizing these first Gentile Christians. I am inclined to think that the rationale must have been the same one offered by Peter in Acts 10:45-47: the believing Gentiles had displayed "gifts of the Spirit," thus demonstrating their acceptance by God. The best evidence for this conclusion is the importance that Paul himself attaches to the argument in Galatians 3:2-5, the first and probably best-aimed salvo in his appeal to the sensibilities of the Galatians.

A number of things follow from this perspective. For one, we can see that the Gentile mission was not something that came "packaged whole" from the time of the earliest church in Jerusalem. It developed only gradually, and the problems it raised were even more gradually appreciated and, to one extent or another, solved by the early church. This strongly suggests what we might have expected in principle: reflection tended to follow experience, not vice versa. Once the door was opened to the Gentiles by the power of the Spirit, it became necessary to understand and to explain what had happened. Interpretations were bound to vary, and with variety would come conflict such as we find it in Galatians 2 and Acts 15.

A contemporary analogy comes to mind. Several years ago a handful

---

[143] It is reasonable to suppose that Christian Jews from the Diaspora who had made a home for themselves in Jerusalem (the Hellenist widows of Acts 6:1 are obvious candidates) continued to reside there.

[144] See Isa. 2:1-4; 42:1-9; 49; 55:4-5; 60:1-7; 66:18-23.

[145] Dunn, "Incident," p. 23, citing Josephus, *J.W.* 7.45-47.

of so-called Charismatic Christian groups were formed in my city that, naturally enough, emphasized personal experience of the Spirit. One of the most prominent features of these groups was their ecumenicity—although, to my knowledge, they never set out to be an ecumenical movement, much less organized around an ecumenical theory. Charismatic gatherings were not, in other words, dominated as one might have expected by members of Pentecostal or Neo-Pentecostal churches. Instead, a very broad denominational representation was consistently in evidence among both the leaders and the rank and file of the movement. What was particularly striking was the almost seamless integration of Catholics and Protestants. Apparently, so long as individuals spoke in tongues, whether Jesuit priests or Lutheran laity, they were accepted. But I do recall hearing of occasions when Lutherans attended mass with Charismatic Catholic friends, or Catholics went along to a Congregational service. It was at times like these that the more difficult questions of Christian unity did inevitably arise.

If the similar picture we are forming of the church at Antioch is accurate, it would in turn reinforce one of our earlier conclusions: that it is unlikely that the Hellenists in Jerusalem had already formulated (or acquired from pre-Christian days) a critical interpretation of the law. I consider it intrinsically more likely that law *criticism*[146] came as a function of the mission to the Gentiles and not the reverse.[147] As we have seen, it is not present in the sources we have examined, and where it is openly expressed, that is, in Galatians and Romans particularly, it has about it the look of an ex post facto justification of the law-free gospel to the Gentiles.[148] This phenomenon has been described by Sanders as backward reasoning, and it suits the evidence admirably.[149] We can thus see that the way in which the Gentile mission emerged is positive evidence for a case that has hitherto been argued primarily from the negative side: the Hellenists of Jerusalem were not an ideologically defined group typified by their radical criticism of the law and the temple. Such a representation of the Hellenists is almost certainly a projection back onto the "forward-thinking" members of the earliest Christian

---

[146] Criticism of the temple, as in Hebrews and, to a much greater degree, in the *Letter of Barnabas*, appears to have been a relatively late development. Otherwise it is present already in some form in the teaching of Jesus and was so widely received that it was not in itself the subject of controversy within the church. It is, in any case, much more difficult to trace than the issue of the law, which, in a sense, envelops it.

[147] Jacob Jervell has written both that "the mission among the Gentiles [was] . . . surely not the outcome of theological reflection . . . [but was instead] the result of ecstatic experiences," and that "one presupposition for the mission to the Gentiles lies in the fact that in Jerusalem there was a law-critical Christian group, namely the Hellenists" ("The Mighty Minority" [1980], p. 19; and "The Acts of the Apostles and the History of Early Christianity" [1983], p. 27).

[148] Such a view of the law also provides the possibility for freedom from the law for the Jew as well. See further the discussion of Paul and Jerusalem in the following chapter.

[149] E. P. Sanders, *Paul and Palestinian Judaism: A Comparison of Patterns of Religion*, p. 474.

community of positions developed only over time and then primarily as a result of the subsequent mission to the Gentiles.

What, then, are we to make of the incident at Antioch? A general picture of the events in question does indeed emerge from the present discussion, one that, in the terms of Dunn's argument, reveals a Antiochene practice (such as Dunn's third option) that lay between the extremes of position (1) (complete abandonment of food laws) and position (2) (the proselytism of Gentiles). While its portrayal here may be incorrect in terms of detail, its broad outline does inspire some confidence. I would therefore offer the reconstruction of the following few paragraphs as a better alternative than the other interpretations considered above.[150]

The first ongoing mission to the Gentiles was initiated by a group of Christians within the church of Antioch. It is likely that these first Gentile converts came from the ranks of the God-fearers already present in some numbers in the Antiochene synagogues. In time, Antioch became known for the mixed character of its church(es), a fact that, by one means or another, became known to some Jewish Christians of Judea. These challenged the Antiochene practice of admitting Gentiles apart from circumcision and in so doing created, in the words of Acts, "no small dissension" (15:2). In due course, it was decided that Barnabas and Paul should go up to Jerusalem to receive a ruling on the matter from the "pillar" apostles. These leaders of the church in Jerusalem, Peter and James among them, agreed that the Gentile believers at Antioch need not be circumcised.

If mixed table-fellowship was already practiced at this time in Antioch, it was not of a sort to arouse controversy in and of itself. This may be attributable to the fact that the Gentile Christians were to this point culled exclusively from the ranks of the God-fearers, who perhaps were already observing enough of the dietary laws to make possible table-fellowship with Jewish friends. Or maybe the earliest table-fellowship took place within the homes of Jewish believers, where the question of infringement of the law would not have been an issue. Similarly, it is possible that individual believers brought their own food to the common meal (see 1 Cor. 11:21). In any case, after the return of Paul and Barnabas, it appears that the practice among at least some of the Jewish Christians took on a more questionable appearance. Perhaps other Gentiles outside of the sphere of the synagogue were won, and perhaps invitations into the homes of Gentiles were now being accepted. It is fascinating to speculate about Paul's role in all of this, since it is he who in the end was in conflict with the rest of the Jewish Christians over the practice, and it is he about whom we know most concerning these very matters. Was it at Antioch that Paul first offered the advice, "Don't

---

[150] My perspective is probably closest to that of George S. Duncan (*Galatians*, pp. 55–63).

ask!" (1 Cor. 10:27)? Either way, it seems that there was a period in which greater freedom toward the Gentiles was exercised on the part of a significant number of the Jewish Christians of Antioch,[151] a freedom that may have contributed substantially to the growth of the church but that eventually led the Jewish Christians into conflict (particularly in the case of meat sacrificed to idols) with Jewish dietary scruples.

How these Jews justified their actions we do not know. It seems unlikely in light of subsequent events that they had thought the matter through carefully and formulated a code of practice based upon principle. At least, if they did, it was a principle that they would soon, with the exception of Paul, be willing to abandon.

Apparently word of this departure got back to James and others in the church of Jerusalem. We are not told how, but it is reasonable to suppose that there were dissenters among the Jewish members of the Antiochene congregation who appealed to James for a clarification of his position.

James's representatives then came to Antioch and upbraided the Jewish Christians, Peter and Barnabas among them, for their behavior. The effect of that behavior on the church in Judea may well have been a consideration, but it is safest to suppose that the matter had fundamentally to do with Jewish legal observance for its own sake. The "representatives of James" would therefore have said something to this effect: "You must know that this is not what we agreed to in Jerusalem. Just because Gentiles do not need to live like Jews does not mean that Jews are therefore free to live like Gentiles!" The Jewish Christians heeded these words, and they began to pull back (ὑπέστελλεν καὶ ἀφώριζεν, 2:12),[152] from what had been an increasingly indiscriminate practice of eating with Gentiles. In their actions, we witness the continued solidarity between the Hebrew Peter and the Hellenist Christians of Antioch. Upon his arrival, Peter chose to follow the practice of the

---

[151] How long, we do not know, but a reading of Gal. 2 along with considerations of Pauline chronology do not seem to favor anything but a relatively short span of time for what we might call the honeymoon period of the Gentile mission in Antioch. Jewett assumes at most a period of a few months (*Chronology*, chart).

[152] The terms are used in Gal. 2:12 with reference to Peter. The imperfect tense of the verbs is striking. That Peter did not make a single, clear-cut withdrawal from table-fellowship with Gentiles makes sense in light of the complexity of the issues at Antioch. Where were the Jewish Christians to draw the line? It can well be imagined how hard it would have been to reverse a policy of the sort the Antiochenes had pursued. Peter's gradual withdrawal fits well within this context.

Burton writes, "The imperfect is very expressive, indicating that Peter took this step not at once, immediately on the arrival of the men from James, but gradually, under the pressure ... of their criticism" (*Galatians*, p. 109). This interpretation, while similar to my own, seems somewhat artificial. The gradual aspect of Peter's withdrawal is better explained if it occurred as a matter of degrees rather than simply as the haphazard result of indecision. Peter knew he had to pull back, but it was not easy to know how far, especially since the Gentiles were by now accustomed to a freer fellowship and acceptance on the part of the Jewish Christians.

Hellenists; the situation being altered, the Hellenists chose to follow the example of Peter.

In the midst of this, Paul (having returned to Antioch from a brief absence),[153] seeing the Jewish retreat from the perspective of the Gentiles,[154] confronted Peter publicly concerning his actions. Peter now showed by his example that the old distinction between Jew and Gentile remained valid. But, as Luther (not an unbiased observer) remarked about this passage, "The establishing of the Law is the abolishing of the Gospel."[155] By recognizing barriers set up by the law, Peter invalidated the claim of Gentile Christians to equal standing before God apart from the law. "Ironically, therefore, by attempting to preserve the integrity of the Jewish Christians as Jews, Cephas destroys the integrity of the Gentile Christians as believers in Christ."[156]

This, from Paul's perspective, is the theological consequence of Peter's withdrawal. The immediate practical result would be a divided church in which the Gentiles would find themselves in some vaguely inferior position—a situation at least some of them would probably not have accepted. Yet unity in this case could be achieved only through Gentile recognition of the law of the Jews. Therefore, Peter by virtue of his practical example was, according to Paul, compelling (see v. 3) the Gentiles to live like Jews.

This behavior Paul labels as hypocrisy. Peter did not really believe that a Gentile needed to obey the law in order to be saved; his earlier conduct had proved this attitude. But now he was in effect forcing the Gentiles to do what he himself did not even believe to be necessary. Paul puts it another way in his commentary on the event in Galatians 2:15-21. This is to "build up again the very things I once tore down"; it is to "nullify the grace of God"; it is to say that "Christ died for nothing."

Whether one finds Paul's arguments convincing will depend on one's point of view. It seems probable, in any case, that Paul's fellow Jewish Christians at Antioch did not. To them it must have seemed quite the reverse. It was they, on reflection, who were in danger of being compromised. The issue, as was said before, was to them one of Gentilizing, not Judaizing. And it appears that their perspective became the dominant one at Antioch. Some clearer resolution of the conflict was needed, and it seems likely that we have a witness to it in the Apostolic Decree of Acts 15.

---

[153] See ibid., p. 110.

[154] One of the many things about which one would like to know more is the attitude of the Gentiles in this controversy. Perhaps they themselves were split on the matter, some (those with fewer previous attachments to Judaism?) being resistent to change, and others being quite willing to compromise for the sake of the unity of the church.

[155] Martin Luther, *A Commentary on St. Paul's Epistle to the Galatians*, p. 122.

[156] Betz, *Galatians*, p. 112.

THE APOSTOLIC DECREE

It is by no means a new suggestion that the prohibitions of Acts 15:20, 29 date from the period following the Antioch Incident and reflect an attempt on the part of the churches of Antioch and Jerusalem to come to terms with the phenomenon of mixed table-fellowship.[157] The development and widespread acceptance of this solution, from Weizsäcker (1866) to Kümmel (1953), is conveniently chronicled for us in Haenchen's commentary.[158] Haenchen's own views on the matter are particularly worthy of consideration, both because they are contrary to this traditional view and because of their undoubted influence in contemporary biblical studies.

Haenchen believes that the entire record of Acts 15 is unhistorical. He calls verses 4-18 "an integral essay on the part of Luke to depict and at the same time justify the ultimate acceptance of the Gentile mission without circumcision."[159] Peter's speech is a Lukan composition,[160] and the use of the Septuagint by James "at a point where it fundamentally departs from the Hebrew"[161] demonstrates its secondary nature. The section is, in other words, redactional, and hence, to Haenchen at least, fictitious.

Haenchen athetizes verses 19-35 in a similar though less convincing manner. The heart of the argument must concern the prohibitions mentioned in verses 20 and 29, since the majority of scholars whom Haenchen is opposing would in varying degrees show sympathy for the notion of Lukan composition of the rest of the account. Haenchen highlights the oft-noted correspondence between the decree and the laws governing the

---

[157] Paul J. Achtemeier, in his *Quest for Unity in the New Testament Church*, argues for the view that the Apostolic Decree was issued by James after the conference of Gal. 2 and was itself the cause of the Antioch Incident. Although the proposal is in some ways appealing, I do not find it convincing. Among my reasons are the following: (1) it fails to provide an adequate explanation (despite some attempts; see p. 54) for the creation of the decree; (2) it requires an improbable delaying of the Antioch Incident; (3) the heavy-handedness of James in abrogating the earlier agreement is not in keeping with his portrayal in Galatians (where it is Peter who is accused of hypocrisy) and in 1 Cor. 15; (4) it seems strange, in light of the tremendous significance attached to it, that Paul never mentions, much less opposes, the decree; (5) Paul's opponents, whose objections perhaps forced James to formulate the decree (p. 54), do not appear ever to have opposed him on any of its points (Achtemeier is left to suppose that "even after its promulgation, they [Judaizing opponents centered in Jerusalem] continued to proclaim that unless one were circumcised . . . one could not truly be a Christian [cf. Gal. 5:2-3, 11-12; 6:12 . . .]" [p. 55]); and (6) it proposes the existence of an open break between Paul and Jerusalem, which (as I argue in chap. 5 below) is not in keeping with the evidence of the Pauline epistles.

[158] Haenchen, *Acts*, p. 468 [410]. A good contemporary presentation of this view is provided by Alfons Weiser in his 1984 article "Das 'Apostelkonzil' (Apg 15,1-35): Ereignis, Überlieferung, lukanische Deutung" (see especially p. 152).

[159] Haenchen, *Acts*, p. 469 [411].

[160] Ibid., pp. 457-59, 469 [398-400, 410].

[161] Ibid., p. 459 [401]. See p. 448 [388-89] on Acts 15:16-18. The quotation in question is Amos 9:11-12.

conduct of resident aliens in Leviticus 17-18.[162] He then cites evidence to demonstrate that these prohibitions were still obeyed by many Gentile Christians of the second century.[163] Indeed, Luke's positive estimation of them ("it seemed good to the Holy Spirit and us," v. 28) shows that they "must have still been fully valid for the Gentile Christians of his own day."[164] This widespread acceptance, Haenchen infers, indicates that the prohibitions could have come to Luke from any number of possible sources. Moreover, since the Antioch Incident proves that James "regarded table fellowship of Jewish and Gentile Christians as inadmissible," the "prohibitions must have come into force in a strongly mixed community of the diaspora."[165] Therefore they have nothing to do with James and the Jerusalem church,[166] whom we must suppose would have repudiated them.

Haenchen's defense is indeed spirited, but in the end it rings hollow. A few pages earlier in his commentary, in reference to Galatians 2, Haenchen rightly observed that the "recognition of the Antiochian Gentile mission was something astounding, and does all honour to the men of Jerusalem. By admitting uncircumcised Gentiles to membership of the new people of God they in any case left Jewish thought behind them."[167] Yet only a few pages later we are told categorically that these open-minded Jerusalemites rejected as inadmissible any table-fellowship whatsoever with these very same Gentiles.

The problem is by now familiar. In posing the question as he has (for mixed table-fellowship or against it?), Haenchen has demanded an either-or answer to a question whose solution must surely have been more complex. The issue that was raised at Antioch, once again, concerned the conditions (on the Jewish side) governing such mixed fellowship. Since the crisis was precipitated by the arrival of James's representatives from Jerusalem, and considering the central place in the controversy of the apostle Peter, it does not seem at all fantastic to believe that the matter was subsequently taken up by the mother church of Jerusalem and a compromise effected along the lines

---

[162] Curiously, he takes πορνεία simply to be a reference to "marriage to near relatives" (Lev. 18:6-18; ibid., p. 469 [411]; cf. p. 449 [390]). But the reference to Gentile obedience in Lev. 18:26 has reference to the whole of the preceding list of prohibitions, which include, additionally, intercourse with a menstruating woman (v. 19), adultery (v. 20), homosexual intercourse (v. 22), and bestiality (v. 23).

[163] Haenchen (ibid., pp. 471-72 [413-14]) refers to Justin, *Dial. cum Tryph.* 34.8 (= *The Writings of Justin Martyr and Athenagoras*, p. 130); Minucius Felix 36.6 (= "The Octavius of Minucius Felix" [sec. 30 in the ANCL translation], p. 502); Eusebius, *Eccl. Hist.* 5.1.26 (= *Eusebius*, LCL, 1:418-19); and Tertullian, *Apology* 9.13 (= *The Writings of Quintus Sept. Flor. Tertullianus*, p. 72).

[164] Haenchen, *Acts*, p. 470 [412].

[165] Ibid., p. 471 [413].

[166] Haenchen states flatly, "Jerusalem does not come into consideration, and James cannot be the author" (ibid.).

[167] Ibid., pp. 467-68 [409]. This admission highlights again the significance of Gal. 2 as a check on unbridled speculation about the supposed conservatism of James.

of Acts 15. It should be noted that this is entirely consistent with the portrayal of James in Galatians, that is, as one who at first saw no need to impose the restrictions of the law upon Gentiles. Under the force of circumstances he had not foreseen, he proposed, or at least accepted, a compromise solution that would have allowed for continued obedience of the law on the part of Jewish Christians in the context of the mixed congregations of the Diaspora.

The apparently widespread acceptance and durability of these prohibitions also works against, rather than for, Haenchen's thesis. This phenomenon is surely better explained by reference to Jerusalem than to any other provenance. What "strongly mixed community of the diaspora" would have had the influence of the mother church? The church in Antioch? But that is nonsense. What is the point of their compromise if by it they had built a bridge neither to Paul nor to James? Why abandon their earlier freedom to receive nothing in return? And can we believe in a compromise influencing the wider church that was nevertheless against the wishes of the Jerusalem church whom the architects of that compromise had, at least in the first instance,[168] hoped to please?

Even Haenchen believes that the Apostolic Decree represents a compromise between Jewish Christians and Gentile Christians. This willingness to believe that various groups of apparently law-observant Jews could have agreed to the framework of Acts 15:20, 29 is telling. If these hypothetical Jews were willing to do so, why not also those to whom Luke actually credits the agreement? Their interest in the question seems assured, and their amenability to compromise has already been demonstrated. Therefore, I must conclude that a negative judgment on the Jerusalem setting of the decree of Acts 15 is based upon external and not internal considerations. The most plausible explanation for its existence and presence in Acts is that which has already been stated: it was formulated by (or at least with the participation of) the Jerusalem church as a compromise remedy to the difficulties raised by the incident at Antioch.[169]

That the Jerusalem Decree was a compromise needs to be emphasized. Jacob Jervell, for one, sees in the agreement (which he terms the "Jacobine decree") a significant hardening or tightening of the position of the Jerusalem church in comparison with that evidenced in Galatians 2:1-10. "This is a new situation. We have no signs that Jewish Christians demanded from Stephen, Antioch, Barnabas or Paul a law-obedient Gentile mission. The attitude of the council according to Luke is liberal only in the claim from the activists regarding circumcision and complete keeping of the law.... Acts 15 and

---

[168] I.e., in the incident at Antioch.

[169] One is not required to accept Luke's account of the events surrounding the decree, or even the words of the decree itself. But the general content of the prohibitions and their association with Jerusalem seem entirely plausible.

Gal 2 lead to the conclusion that the church of Jerusalem in connection with the council introduced a more conservative policy."[170]

These statements are misleading. While it might be reasonable to say, from the point of view of at least some of the Gentiles, that the Apostolic Decree represented a more conservative standard, the charge of conservatism is fair with respect to the Jewish Christians only if the same questions were at issue in both Galatians 2 and Acts 15. I have already argued that this was not the case. The position of the Jerusalem church had not hardened; indeed, faced with what was indeed a new situation, the Jewish Christians showed a considerable degree of flexibility. They did not close the door to Gentiles, nor did they determine that all mixed fellowship with Gentiles must cease. Instead, they sought a rapprochement, and it is understandable that, on this occasion, it was thought that the Gentiles would have the least to lose and the most to gain by compromising. It should also be said that there *never* existed a truly law-free mission to the Gentiles. Even Paul expected of his Gentile converts obedience to some (indeed many) Jewish laws.[171] Being "liberal only . . . regarding circumcision and complete keeping of the law" is, within this context, being only liberal. The Jerusalem Christians (and Antiochene Christians, for that matter) were not Paulinists, to be sure, but this alone hardly qualifies them as conservatives.[172]

CONCLUSION

Our understanding of the relationship between the Hellenists and the Hebrews, and more particularly the churches of Antioch and Jerusalem, is greatly enhanced by an examination of Galatians 2 and Acts 15. In the event to which they both testify, the council at Jerusalem, we see the leaders of the Aramaic-speaking Jewish Christians agreeing with their Greek-speaking fellow believers on the question of Gentile admission. Gentiles need not, as some had claimed, be circumcised. This position reflects what must have been a very significant concession on the part of the Hebrews.

In the second event, the incident at Antioch, we find the Hellenists compromising this time for the sake of the Hebrews. Their earlier willingness to experiment with a freer attitude to the law may distinguish them, but

---

[170] Jervell, "Mighty Minority," p. 20; see also "Acts," p. 26. Despite my criticisms, I consider that there is much to admire about Jervell's work. Of note especially is his attempt to do justice to the diversity and influence of Jewish Christianity after A.D. 70.

[171] See, for example, Paul's treatment of homosexuality in Rom. 1:24-28 and 1 Cor. 6:9-11.

[172] The apparent success of the decree is testimony, not simply to the power of the Jerusalem church (contra Jervell), but also to the persuasiveness of its position.

only by degrees.¹⁷³ When the matter of Jewish obedience was put to them plainly, they agreed as a body with the position of the Jerusalem church. In other words, on both occasions of which we have record of their meeting, there was compromise and accommodation between the churches of Jerusalem and Antioch. We find nothing that would incline us to think that there existed between the two some unbridgeable ideological chasm. Moreover, where controversy was known to exist, it tended to occur *within* the respective churches (Acts 15:1; Gal. 2:4, 11-12).

The later Jerusalem Decree also represents a compromise; it falls far short of compelling Gentiles to Judaize, at least in the sense in which Paul used the term. The authority and centrality of the Jerusalem church, however, and the mission to the Jews are reinforced. Controversy made it clear where the priority lay.

If, as most commentators assume, Paul did not prevail at Antioch, it is further evidence for one additional aspect of my hypothesis: that Paul was not representative of what was the more moderate position of the Antiochene Hellenists. Paul was in fact rebuffed in Antioch on the issue of the necessity of Jewish obedience, a fact that goes a long way toward explaining his subsequent difficulties with the Jewish Christian church of Jerusalem.

---

¹⁷³ And even then, we do not know to what extent they ignored (and thus, we assume, broke) the law, nor indeed what part of the Jewish Christians at Antioch engaged in such activities. Also, as I noted earlier, it was the Diaspora Jewish Christians who obviously were in the best position to associate with Gentiles.

Chapter Five
Further Evidence

> But there are also many other things that Jesus did; if every one of them were written down, I suppose that the world itself could not contain the books that would be written.[1]

Anyone who has attempted to write a book in the field of New Testament studies will, I suspect, give a smile of assent to this statement by the author of the Gospel of John. Like the life of Jesus, the New Testament itself is a topic of boundless proportions. Subject touches upon subject, and each new idea leads to a host of fresh associations. For this reason, one might liken a study such as this to a single page in a road atlas. For the sake of convenience and detail, each book charts only one part of a much larger landscape. The boundaries it sets around its subject are almost certain to be artificial, with incomplete routes leading off the page in every direction. In itself, the single map is of limited value; anyone wishing to travel widely must turn from it to other pages mapping the adjoining territories. The process is made simpler, of course, by the fact that the pages overlap one another, and so provide sufficient "common ground" to make their relationship understandable.

In the terms of this analogy, one might say that the present chapter is an attempt at "mapping" those areas at the borders of the present thesis. They cannot be treated with any completeness without, as it were, turning the page to whole other studies. But they can be represented to the extent that the links that exist between the subjects are clarified and thus traceable beyond the limits of this book.

What additional evidence may be cited in support of our interpretation of Acts 6:1–8:4? The link between the "Hellenists" of Jerusalem and the church of Antioch can take us no further than the judgments of the previous

---
[1] John 21:25 (NRSV).

chapter. We know almost nothing of the Antiochene church in the decades following the so-called Antioch Incident.[2]

Concerning the church in Jerusalem, however, the situation is more favorable.[3] We are fortunate to possess some further information about James, the leader of the Jerusalem church (and, by most accounts, the paragon of Hebrew conservatism). The other pertinent figure about whom we have supplementary data is the apostle Paul. Of relevance to our study is the character (and, indeed, the simple fact) of Paul's ongoing relationship to the mother church. We consider first what this relationship can tell us about the Jerusalem Christians themselves.[4]

PAUL AND THE CHURCH OF JERUSALEM

In the previous chapter, we examined two of the pivotal moments in the life of the primitive Church: the Jerusalem Council and the Incident at Antioch. We may now join Paul at the end of these events and consider his standing. He has, we might say, one plus and one minus. Positively, the circumcision-free gospel he preached to the Gentiles has been recognized by the leaders of the church in Jerusalem. He has not run, as he feared doing, "in vain" (Gal. 2:2). On the other hand, his perception of the relative value of the law, which may well have developed alongside his concern for the Gentiles,[5] has been rejected.

This rejection appears to have had two consequences. First, it led to a break (of disputed gravity) with the church of Antioch,[6] his former base, and

---

[2] The Gospel of Matthew is a potential source of insight, but its Antiochene provenance is by no means secure. Note however that Matthew's "conservative" interest in the law (e.g., 5:17-20; 23:3, 23) coexists with his "liberal" interest in the Gentile mission (12:18-21; 21:43; 28:19) in a way that is consistent with our depiction of the church at Antioch in the previous chapter.

[3] No thanks to Acts, of course, from which we learn relatively little about the Christian community in Jerusalem following the introduction of Paul. (The account of Paul's imprisonment in Jerusalem in Acts 21-23 is discussed below.)

[4] Additional evidence for first-century Jewish Christianity has not been included because its relationship (if any) to the Jerusalem church cannot be determined.

[5] The origin and (possible) development of Paul's understanding of the law is a topic worthy of book-length discussion. I am assuming here what seems to me most reasonable, namely, that Paul's interpretation of the law as it pertained to Jews (i.e., that laws that served to erect barriers between Jews and Gentiles—notably concerning circumcision, Sabbath, and food—were no longer considered binding for either group) grew out of his successful ministry to Gentiles. That it could have come earlier (at his conversion?) is not in principle denied. In either case, by the time of the Antioch Incident, it appears that Paul had formulated a position on the question of Jewish obedience that conflicted with that of James and the church in Jerusalem.

[6] That the break was not complete is evidenced by 1 Cor. 9:6 and Acts 18:22-23. It is evident, however, that while Paul may have returned temporarily to Antioch at a later date,

from that to a wider, more independent mission.⁷ Second, the conflict with Peter and the "representatives of James" made Paul's status and authority as an apostle more ambiguous. Although he had received his commission from the risen Christ himself, Paul was, after all, subject to others when it came to interpreting the significance of that commission for the church.

If I am correct in suggesting that the issue at stake in Antioch was that of Jewish obedience, then another, fundamental result must be considered. This is the likelihood that the issue separating Paul from his fellow Jewish-Christians, that of freedom from (at least portions of) the law *for Jews,* was never resolved. This possibility makes sense of several pieces of otherwise conflicting evidence. It means that there *was* genuine, sustained conflict between Paul and many other Jewish-Christians, most notably those of the church of Jerusalem. This conflict was of manifest significance; nevertheless, it did not obliterate the very considerable agreement that already existed between the parties on a variety of essential points. One does not have to believe, in other words, that James repudiated Paul and the Pauline mission (that is, that he rejected or perhaps never acceded to the agreement of Gal. 2:9) in order to account for the tension that appears to have existed between them. Furthermore, this view explains why Paul was more liable to persecution in Jerusalem than was James, but why neither party finally was exempted from it.

Supplementary evidence from the Pauline epistles themselves concerning the state of the apostle's relationship to Jerusalem is of two types. First, we have Paul's explicit references to the Jerusalem Christians. The greater part of these concern the Jerusalem apostles. In each of these verses the legitimacy of these leaders is either stated or assumed (1 Cor. 3:22; 9:5; 15:7, 9; Rom. 15:31).⁸ Additional references come in connection with the collection for the saints of Jerusalem (1 Cor. 16:1-4; 2 Cor. 8-9; Rom. 15:25-28). Together, these verses provide primary substantiation for the proposal advanced above, that Paul and the Jerusalem apostles continued to recognize one another as Christians, although they may have differed in significant respects.

Other evidence is secondary and more precarious. Most important are inferences made about the Jerusalem apostles based upon opposition to Paul as it is witnessed in Galatians, Philippians, and 2 Corinthians. The issue that concerns us in the case of Paul's adversaries is whether Judaizing opponents

---

the city was never again for him the home that it had been prior to the time of the second missionary journey. (The precise value of the Acts 18 reference is tied to the issue of Pauline chronology. If one believes, for example, that the incident at Antioch occurred *after* the second missionary journey [as does Jewett; *Chronology,* pp. 58, 83-84, 139], one might conclude that Paul never returned to Antioch.)

⁷ See Romans 15:20.
⁸ Problems concerning the interpretation of Rom. 15:31 are discussed in some detail below.

of Paul acted as legitimate representatives of the Jerusalem apostles.[9] The two modifiers "Judaizing" and "legitimate" are significant. To conflict with the view of the Jerusalem church advanced above, Paul's opponents would have to have been Judaizers—that is, would have to have opposed Paul's law-free gospel by requiring the proselytism of Gentiles—and would have to have done so on the authority of the Jerusalem apostles themselves. It is not enough to claim that Paul was opposed by representatives of the Jerusalem church. Such opposition was already evident both in Jerusalem and in Antioch and adds little to the discussion. What is vital is the reason for opposing Paul. Similarly, claims to represent the Jerusalem church, where they might perhaps be inferred, are not necessarily validated by such inference.

Additional secondary evidence regarding the relationship between Paul and the Jerusalem church is found in New Testament records concerning the collection and Paul's arrest in Jerusalem. These issues will be taken up following a discussion of the opponents of Paul as they are witnessed in Galatians, Philippians, and, especially, 2 Corinthians.

The Opponents of Paul

Galatians

There is widespread agreement that the Galatian Christians had heard an account of the events in Antioch, related to them by the Judaizers, which cast Paul in a very bad light.[10] Bligh characterizes what might have been their version: Peter "repented of having abandoned the law, so he withdrew from the Gentiles and lived as a Jew again." So did the others, including Paul's friend Barnabas. Paul alone refused to come over to the side of reason. Finally, "he made a shocking scene in which he virtually told Peter that he did not understand the Gospel!"[11]

Bligh's contention is an interesting one, since it gives this false report an essential place in the message of the Judaizers. It is not merely a convenient illustration; it is the centerpiece of their contention that the way of circumcision and Torah observance is the way of the apostles. Paul, on the defensive, does not correct their coverage of the story in some inconspicuous

---

[9] As has already been noted, by "Judaizing opponents" I do not mean Gentile opponents who had Judaized but rather opponents who required that Gentiles Judaize. The word "Judaizer" is used in the same sense, that is, to refer to one who would compel others to live like Jews.

[10] See, for example, Bring, *Galatians,* p. 78 [86]; Holmberg, *Paul and Power,* p. 28; and Bligh, *Galatians,* p. 175.

[11] Bligh, *Galatians,* p. 175.

"corner" of the epistle. Rather, "the whole of the autobiographical section has been leading up to this incident."[12]

This is an intriguing hypothesis. It makes sense of the central role of Peter in Galatians 1:12—2:14 (what Betz has called the letter's *Narratio*).[13] It also explains the abruptness with which the Antioch Incident is introduced into the narrative. Galatians 2:11-14 lacks the sense of progression and order of the preceding verses. It has the feel of a climax, the event for which the others have been set in preface. The Judaizers may well have stressed Paul's dependence on Jerusalem, whose (direct or indirect?) authority they then claimed for their own message. The fact that 2:15-21 (Betz's *Propositio*)[14] sounds so much like a commentary on this incident adds further weight to this proposal.

Thus, it seems reasonable that Paul has related the story of Peter's visit *defensively*. He wished to put the record straight. But he also used the story *offensively*, and for that use it is particularly suited. The incident at Antioch was, after all, something of a cameo of the present situation in Galatia. The Gentiles of Antioch, like the Gentiles of Galatia, had once enjoyed freedom in the gospel. Then interlopers, insincere and motivated by fear, came on the scene and threatened to destroy that freedom through spreading their bondage to the law. The situation grew worse and eventually had to be confronted by Paul. What was the outcome to be?

This is at least a partial explanation of Paul's use of the incident in Galatians. It was necessary for him to speak of Antioch, probably in the same way in which it was necessary for him to speak of Abraham: the matter had been raised by his opponents and needed answering.[15]

But who were these opponents? Does their apparent knowledge of the events at Antioch tell us anything about their identity? Specifically, can they be traced, as it is sometimes supposed, to the church of Jerusalem?[16]

What we may infer about their identity based upon their knowledge of the Antioch Incident is difficult to determine. In part, it depends upon whether or not we choose to believe Paul. If his emphatic tone (1:20) does not lead us to accept what he has to say about the events he is relating, then the field is wide open to speculation. But if he is to be believed, and if, as seems likely, he is composing this part of the letter in order to correct the erroneous account of the Judaizers concerning his relationship with Jerusalem, then it follows that his opponents either lied or else had only a sketchy

---

[12] Ibid., pp. 179-80.
[13] Betz, *Galatians*, pp. 57-60. Peter, it should be noted, is the only one mentioned by Paul in all three events related to the Jeruslaem church.
[14] Ibid., pp. 113-14.
[15] See Jewett, "Agitators," pp. 200-201; and Burton, *Galatians*, p. liv.
[16] See, for example, Lightfoot, *Galatians*, p. 29; Duncan, *Galatians*, pp. xxii-xxiv; Jewett, "Agitators," pp. 188-99, 204 (where the "Judean church" is specified); and Bruce, *Galatians*, pp. 31-32 (following Jewett).

knowledge of the events in question. The first of these options is not impossible but ought to be considered less likely; the initial working assumption should be that Paul's opponents genuinely believed that they were right.[17] But if they did not have an accurate understanding of the events Paul narrates, the closeness of their ties both with Jerusalem and Antioch must come into question.

Theories concerning the identity of Paul's Galatian opponents are legion, and I am therefore not willing, on the basis of such thin evidence as we possess, to lean heavily upon any one of them. It is possible that the opponents were either Jews[18] or Gentiles,[19] indigenous Galatians or foreigners. Nevertheless, it seems unlikely that they were authorized by James in Jerusalem or were themselves witnesses to the events in Antioch.

It is worth noting that Paul does not appear to recognize personally or even to know the origin of his opponents. His references to them are extraordinarily vague (e.g., τινές εἰσιν οἱ ταράσσοντες ὑμᾶς [some who are confusing you], 1:7; εἴ τις ὑμᾶς εὐαγγελίζεται παρ' ὃ παρελάβετε [if anyone proclaims to you a gospel contrary to the one you received], 1:9; τίς ὑμᾶς ἐβάσκανεν [who has bewitched you], 3:1; τίς ὑμᾶς ἐνέκοψεν [who prevented you], 5:7; ὅσοι θέλουσιν εὐπροσωπῆσαι ἐν σαρκί [those who want to make a good showing in the flesh], 6:12). It may be argued that this is purely a tactical move on Paul's part: by failing to name names he is lessening the stature of his opponents. But this is an unacceptable supposition in light of Paul's own narrative in Galatians. Elsewhere the apostle does not flinch from saying that he opposed Peter "to his face," from identifying the men from Jerusalem as coming "from James," and, most embarrassingly, from adding the name of Barnabas to the list of those with whom he disagreed.[20] Besides, it is difficult to see what Paul had to gain by such a strategy. The Galatians knew the identity of the Judaizers, and such uncharacteristic reluctance in confronting them directly (contrary to 2:11) could not have enhanced Paul's position.

Second, what was said in the previous chapter should be reiterated here: it makes no sense at all for Paul in Galatians—and then in subsequent epistles—to endorse the authority of his opponents. In writing to the Galatians, Paul accepts the theoretical possibility that the Jerusalem pillars might have chosen to invalidate his message. He reports that they did not. Does he continue to recognize their authority? If not, why cite it in support of his

---

[17] That is, allowing for exaggeration and distortion on their part as well as Paul's. If the parties in question are lying, then the scanty evidence we posses can tell us nothing. Again, this possibility cannot be ruled out, but it is not the proper place to begin such an investigation.

[18] This is the majority position. See, for example, Betz, *Galatians*, p. 7; Bruce, *Galatians*, p. 31; and Lüdemann, *Opposition*, p. 99 [146–47].

[19] See, for example, Munck, *Paul*, pp. 87–89 [79–81].

[20] Loisy makes much the same point in *L'Epître aux Galates*, p. 126.

argument with the Galatians? If it had been necessary for Paul to contest the authority of the Jerusalem apostles, surely he was capable of doing it. Paul's vilification of the "false apostles" in 2 Corinthians 11:13-15 shows this capacity at work where opponents match their authority against his own. Indeed, the calling down of curses upon potential enemies in Galatians 1:8-9 and the stigmatizing of others as "false believers" in 2:4 should provide adequate demonstration that Paul is not pulling his punches. Therefore, the apostle's continued link with Jerusalem, however strained, tells decisively against the identification of the Jerusalem leaders with the Galatian Judaizers.

This does not mean that the Judaizers could not have been Jewish-Christians[21] or indeed have come from Judea itself. All the evidence we possess supports the view that there was a segment of the church in Jerusalem that opposed, at least initially, the circumcision-free mission to the Gentiles.[22] This accords with the perspective I have advanced elsewhere: the churches of Jerusalem and Antioch were pluriform and cannot be stereotyped either as conservative or liberal. Hence, it is *possible* that the Galatian Judaizers had direct links with or were themselves Jerusalem Christians. It is also possible that they originated in one of a considerable number of other locations.[23] But the argument will not be settled here, and it is enough to leave it at this point.

Philippians

The question of the identity of Paul's opponents in Philippians is inseparably linked to the issue of the literary integrity of the letter. The problem is that apart from 3:2-21, the letter fails to suggest any opposition to Paul within the church at Philippi. The balance of the letter, both before and after chapter 3, is noticeably irenic in tone.

A variety of hypotheses have been advanced to account for this anomaly, perhaps the most popular being some form of partitioning theory.[24] Accordingly, it is said that the letter lacks congruence because it is,

---

[21] Although Gal. 6:13 might indicate otherwise. Munck used this verse (with effect, in my opinion) in support of his view that Paul's opponents were Gentiles (*Paul*, pp. 87-89 [79-81]). In contrast, Schlier thought that it pointed to Jewish-Christian representatives "of a proto-Gnosticism" (*Der Brief an die Galater*, pp. 20-21).

[22] Gal. 2:4-5 (depending upon the uncertain identity of these "false believers") and Acts 15:1, 5.

[23] Robert Jewett's "Zealot hypothesis" (in his article "Agitators") concerning the Judaizers' Judean origin is based largely upon the reference to persecution in Gal. 6:12. While he might be correct, our knowledge of the persecution of Christians is too limited to allow us to fix with confidence a locality based upon the threat of persecution. Paul refers in 5:11 to the persecution he himself has suffered, and it is not generally assumed that he has in mind events that occurred exclusively or primarily in Judea.

[24] Robert Jewett provides the reader with a helpful summary and review of partitioning theories in his article "The Epistolary Thanksgiving and the Integrity of Philippians," pp. 40-49.

in fact, not one but two or even three letters. Such, for example, is the claim of Helmut Koester, who advocates a tripartite division of Philippians, only the final letter of which (3:2–4:1) would have been written in response to the outbreak of heresy.[25] This solves rather neatly the problem of continuity between the various parts of the letter; however, its success is won at the expense of introducing new and more intractable difficulties into the discussion.

Behind the partitioning theories is the supposition that a new situation arose in Philippi to which Paul found it necessary to reply. Accepting this means believing that Paul was responding to specific opponents (as the definite articles in 3:2 might lead us to believe, Βλέπετε τοὺς κύνας, βλέπετε τοὺς κακοὺς ἐργάτας, βλέπετε τὴν κατατομήν [beware of *the* dogs, beware of *the* evil workers, beware of *those* who mutilate the flesh]), and so the verses of chapter 3 are combed for clues about their specific ideology. The resultant heresy is strange indeed, combining in some form all or most of the following elements: the nomism (3:2-9) of the Galatian Judaizers, the present eschatological perfectionism (3:10-16) of the Corinthian heretics, and the libertinism (3:17-21 – some would say, influenced by Gnosticism; see 3:8: τὸ ὑπερέχον τῆς γνώσεως Χριστοῦ Ἰησοῦ τοῦ κυρίου μου [literally, "the surpassing value of the knowledge of Christ Jesus my Lord"]) of other members of the Corinthian congregation.[26]

Responding to attempts by scholars to piece together such a heresy, E. P. Sanders writes:

> Rather than supposing that such a complicated heresy sprang up (or was introduced and started to take hold) and came to Paul's attention in such a short time [i.e., between the writing of the second and third letters to the Philippians, according to Koester's scheme], it seems better to suppose . . . that Paul has in mind the problems in Galatia and Corinth. On this understanding one would read Phil. 3:2-4:1 as beginning with a sharp attack on known opponents and then becoming increasingly general, although the language is influenced by previous polemic situations.[27]

The "known opponents," therefore, are not some persons in Philippi but those of Paul's earlier acquaintance in Galatia and Corinth. "He has in mind a specific problem but one that the Philippians have not yet experienced."[28] The chapter serves as a *warning* against *possible* heretical incursions. "The triple βλέπετε [beware] (v. 2), the very general εἴ τις δοκεῖ [if anyone

---

[25] Helmut Koester, "Philippians," pp. 665–66.

[26] See Jewett, "Epistolary Thanksgiving," pp. 44–49, for the view that libertinism and not nomism (contra Koester) is represented in 3:17-21.

[27] E. P. Sanders, "Paul on the Law, His Opponents, and the Jewish People in Philippians 3 and 2 Corinthians 11," pp. 81–82. Sanders cites Peter Richardson, *Israel in the Apostolic Church*, p. 113.

[28] Richardson, *Israel*, p. 113.

Further Evidence 157

has reason] (v. 4), and πολλοὶ γὰρ περιπατοῦσιν [for many walk] (v. 18) need indicate no more than an incipient incitement to abandon Christ."²⁹ This is an economical theory and makes better sense of the data of chapter 3 than does the postulation of a new, hybrid heresy at Philippi.

Additional support for this hypothesis comes from a quantity of evidence supporting the literary unity of Philippians. This is presented conveniently in Robert Jewett's *Novum Testamentum* article "The Epistolary Thanksgiving and the Integrity of Philippians" and need only be summarized here. Having concluded that an argument based on the psychological probability or improbability of Paul's shift of mood in 3:2 is meaningless,³⁰ Jewett considers what would constitute positive evidence for the unity of the epistle. He writes, "The decisive question is whether there is continuity of argument and vocabulary between the various parts of Philippians which would indicate it was written at one time."³¹ He finds this continuity displayed in the following themes: an "apocalyptic understanding of the suffering messianic apostle and community" (1:12ff., 27ff; 3:10; 4:14), an emphasis on joy (linking chaps. 1, 2, and 4), a stress placed on "correct mental attitude" (1:7; 2:2, 3, 5; 3:15, 19; 4:2, 10), the appearance of φρονέω a total of ten times in four short chapters (the word is found only eleven times in the remainder of Paul's letters),³² and the idea of humility and self-emptying (2:7-8; 3:4-11, 21; the only instance of ταπείνωσις [humiliation] in the Pauline epistles; note ταπεινόω [humble] in 2:8; 4:12). Examples of similarity of vocabulary include, in addition to χαίρω, φρονέω, and ταπεινόω (rejoice, think, humble), Paul's use of κέρδος (gain, 1:21 and 3:7 are the only occurrences in the New Testament), καρπός (fruit, 1:11, 22 and 4:17), πολίτευμα (citizenship) and πολιτεύομαι (conduct one's life, 3:20; 1:27—both hapax legomena in Paul), σχῆμα and μορφή (form, of Christ; 2:6-7) and μετασχηματίζω (transform) and συμμορφίζεσθαι/σύμμορφος (take on the same form/having the same form, of the believer; 3:21; 3:10, 21), and ἡγέομαι (regard, 2:3, 6; 3:7, 8 [twice]; appearing only three times elsewhere in Paul's letters).³³

To Jewett, the most significant indicator of the unity of Philippians is the manner in which the themes of the epistolary thanksgiving in 1:3-11 recur in succeeding sections of the letter. These themes include the close, material ties between the Philippians and Paul (1:3) and the ideas of joy (1:4), suffering (1:7), and mental attitude (1:7). "Despite the abrupt transitions, the entire letter as it now stands is the product of the author's intention set forth

---

²⁹ Ibid., p. 112.
³⁰ Like other arguments that rely upon contemporary perceptions of an author's internal state, it is unverifiable and has been used by scholars to support contradictory conclusions.
³¹ Jewett, "Epistolary Thanksgiving," p. 49.
³² Ibid., p. 51.
³³ Ibid., pp. 49–52.

in the epistolary thanksgiving. . . . In all probability Philippians was written within a short span of time and was sent in one piece to Philippi."³⁴

If this is correct, as seems likely, then it is clear that the letter to the Philippians can offer no direct evidence of the existence of Judaizing opponents of Paul acting under the aegis of the Jerusalem apostles. The most promising source of indirect evidence comes in Paul's defense in 3:3-6 against potential enemies, a passage strikingly similar to his apology in 2 Corinthians 11:22-29 and almost certainly written with his Corinthian experience in mind. What it may tell us about his opponents we thus consider in the context of the discussion of 2 Corinthians below.

Corinthians

There is no more interesting or problematic source for information on the opponents of Paul than the collection of materials commonly known as the Second Letter to the Corinthians.³⁵ Chapters 10–13 in particular are full

---

³⁴ Ibid., p. 53. Jewett gives favorable consideration to the suggestion of Victor Furnish (in "The Place and Purpose of Philippians iii," p. 88) that chap. 3 is an extended postscript "in which Paul deals with the delicate matter of circumcision which he had originally thought he would let his representatives Epaphroditus and Timothy handle orally" (Jewett, "Epistolary Thanksgiving," p. 53, n. 3).

³⁵ It is widely accepted that the opposition countered by Paul in 1 Corinthians was internal in nature, whereas 2 Corinthians evidences the presence of outside agitators. These latter opponents Paul attacks in a letter consisting of chaps. 10–13 (and possibly 2:14–7:4). Among other things, such a view helps to explain the shift between the two letters in the terms of the debate (e.g., away from γνῶσις and toward σημείοις . . . καὶ τέρασιν καὶ δυνάμεσιν, 12:12). See Barrett, *The Second Epistle to the Corinthians,* pp. 5–21 for a full statement of this position.

Gerd Lüdemann has challenged this conclusion. He contends that 1 Corinthians witnesses to the interference of *outside* opponents who seem to have had much in common with (although were not precisely equal to) Paul's adversaries at Galatia. The key passages are 1 Cor. 9:1-18 and 15:7-9, in which Paul defends the legitimacy of his apostleship to the Corinthians. Lüdemann finds four points of comparison between these passages and Galatians: (1) Paul is defending himself, (2) his apostleship is disputed, (3) he insists that he has seen Jesus, and (4) in each place he refers to the Jerusalem authorities. "These four points make the hypothesis compelling that Paul . . . is answering accusations of anti-Pauline Jerusalem opponents" ("Zum Antipaulinismus im frühen Christentum," pp. 451–52). The opponents of 1 Corinthians, identified as missionary preachers allied to Peter in Jerusalem, are then linked by Lüdemann to the controversies of 2 Corinthians, which were caused, we are told, by their further meddling in the affairs of the Corinthian church (e.g., *Opposition,* pp. 94–97 [141–43]).

Lüdemann's approach to the Corinthian opponents is fascinating, but I do not find it wholly persuasive. In particular, I am not convinced that the parallels between 1 Corinthians and Galatians, on the one hand, and 1 Corinthians and 2 Corinthians, on the other, are as straightforward as Lüdemann supposes. Paul was, by all accounts, the founder of the church at Corinth (1 Cor. 4:14-15; 9:2; Acts 18:1-18). If, as seems almost certain, he presented himself (as opposed, say, to Timothy; Acts 18:5; 1 Cor. 4:17; 16:10-11) to the Corinthians as an apostle of Christ, it is only natural that they should wonder what qualified him for such an office. Whatever else Paul might have said, he must have mentioned that he was commissioned by the resurrected Lord. (I take this experience to be bedrock for Paul's self-understanding as an apostle; Gal. 1:12, 16; 1 Cor. 9:1; 15:8-9. If we deny this, we are left with nowhere else to turn

of lively invective and exegetical promise. In reality, however, the evidence they yield is notoriously ambiguous, and a considerable number of very thorough reviews have failed to solve the problem to the satisfaction of the majority of scholars. Sanders writes: "The identity of the opponents in 2 Corinthians is as vexed a problem as one can find in Pauline studies. My last count, which I am sure was by no means complete, provided a list of fourteen different identifications."[36]

For this reason, I do not propose to create yet another reconstruction of the situation faced by Paul at Corinth. To recapitulate, our attention is focused on the issue of whether Judaizing opponents of Paul acted as legitimate representatives of the Jerusalem apostles. As we have seen, this issue actually comprises two questions: (1) Were the opponents Judaizers? and (2) Did they represent the views of the Jerusalem apostles? In the case of 2 Corinthians, the answer to the first of these questions is more critical and, I think, more straightforward than the second. Let us consider each of them in some detail.

Whether one believes that the Corinthian intruders were Judaizers depends very largely upon whether one is struck by the similarities or the differences between the arguments of Galatians and 2 Corinthians. Without doubt, the most striking similarities concern the uncompromising language with which Paul vilifies his opponents in both letters, as may be seen in figure 2.

The correspondence between these expressions has figured decisively in the conclusion drawn by many scholars that Paul's opponents at Corinth were, like those at Galatia, Judaizers.[37] Others, including myself, remain unconvinced.

---

for an explanation of Paul's self-concept [not to mention self-confidence].) In time, the Corinthians became exposed to other Christian preachers, the most obvious (and certain) example of which was Apollos (1 Cor. 1:12; 3:4-6, 22; 4:6; 16:12; Acts 18:24; 19:1). They would have learned more with each visitor, not only about the preachers themselves, but about the wider church from which they came. Comparisons would inevitably follow (as reported in 1 Cor. 1:11-16). None of this could be considered unexpected, especially in light of Paul's liabilities: his unimpressive presence (see below), his record as a persecutor of the church, and his late beginning as a follower of Christ.

Therefore, the challenges to his authority that Paul addresses directly in 1 Cor. 9, and perhaps indirectly in 15:9 (although I am not convinced of this), are understandable enough without necessitating the arrival on the scene of anti-Pauline opponents. There is no reference in this context (as there is in 2 Corinthians; e.g., 11:12-15) to persons outside the Corinthian congregation. Paul is addressing an internal issue, albeit one that has arisen after a period of what we might call ecumenical exposure. The overlap with Galatians and with 2 Corinthians is valid only insofar as each situation can be seen to have revealed Paul's weaknesses. However, we discover from the arguments of the letters themselves that the challenges that exposed and exploited these supposed deficiencies all differed. It is easy to join Lüdemann, though, in thinking that the tensions reflected in 1 Corinthians set the stage for the conflicts of 2 Corinthians.

[36] Sanders, "Paul on the Law," p. 84.
[37] E.g., C. K. Barrett, *The Second Epistle to the Corinthians,* p. 276 (see also pp. 29–30); "Paul's Opponents in II Corinthians," pp. 65, 78–82.

Figure 2. Paul's Opponents in Galatia and Corinth

Galatians	2 Corinthians
The opponents offer:	
ἕτερον εὐαγγέλιον (a different gospel, 1:6)	ἄλλον Ἰησοῦν . . . πνεῦμα ἕτερον. . . εὐαγγέλιον ἕτερον (another Jesus . . . a different spirit . . . a different gospel, 11:4)
Some opponents are called:	
ψευδάδελφοι (false believers, literally "false brothers," 2:4)	ψευδαπόστολοι (false apostles, 11:13)
Paul also refers to:	
οἱ δοκοῦντες στῦλοι (acknowledged pillars, 2:9, also v. 6)	ὑπερλίαν ἀπόστολοι (super-apostles, 11:5; 12:11)

That Paul could question the veracity, intentions, and very legitimacy of his opponents is, post Galatians, assumed. That anyone repudiated by him in this manner should of necessity have been a Judaizer is not. Paul may have been opposed on a number of fronts or to a variety of degrees, and it will not do to assume prima facie that opposition was uniform. "False believers" and "false apostles" do not necessarily agree for being false. In this point I return to a leitmotiv of this study: the observation that New Testament scholarship, in focusing resolutely on the theme of Gentile admission, has neglected the complexity of the issues that faced primitive Christian belief. This simplification has in turn encouraged a distortion of the early church's complex composition and history.

More difficult, yet similar, is the matter of the "different gospel" that these "false apostles" (and perhaps "super-apostles")[38] are said to have preached. Clearly, the notion of the "different" or "other" is one Paul favors. It presents the reader, as Paul's writing so often does, with a clear-cut, black-or-white choice of opposing alternatives. There is no middle ground between Paul and his opponents. This leads to a tendency to blur distinctions between opponents for the sake of rhetorical force, a device fully demonstrated in the account of the incident at Antioch, in which Peter is made to appear as a Judaizer and thus one with the "false believers," the "certain people . . . from James," and those currently troubling the Galatian congregation. In this sense, 2 Corinthians is indeed like Galatians: Paul wants a decision of absolute loyalty. But the ground does appear to have shifted. It is no longer simply a "different gospel" but also "another Jesus" and a "different spirit" that concern him. C. K. Barrett writes concerning this:

---

[38] The question of whether Paul is concerned with one or two groups of apostles is addressed below.

We learn from the additional words (Jesus, Spirit) what distinguishes the new gospel from Paul's.... In 4.5, Paul writes: "We preach not ourselves, but Christ Jesus as Lord, and ourselves as your slaves for Jesus" sake (διὰ 'Ιησοῦν)." *It is the humble behaviour of Paul that marks him out,* over against his adversaries, as a true witness to the lordship of Christ. Thus the interpretation of the earthly Jesus that Paul rejects at 11.4 is one that is bound up with the tradition used by his adversaries and with their own consciousness of spiritual authority.

The intruders proclaim another Jesus not so much (as far as we know) by heretical doctrine as by *the kind of behaviour* described in 2 Cor. 11:20 (where the recurrence of ἀνέχεσθαι [to endure] should be noted): ἀνέχεσθε [γὰρ] εἴ τις ὑμᾶς καταδουλοῖ, εἴ τις κατεσθίει, κτλ.[39]

In other words, the question of similarity and dissimilarity between Galatians and 2 Corinthians is again primary. We may find the fact of twin references to a "different gospel" significant, so much so that the "other Jesus" and "different spirit" of 2 Corinthians are reckoned to serve as embellishments complementing this fundamental similarity. In contrast, we can, like Barrett, pay particular heed to these additions and speculate on why it was that Paul modified his language for the sake of the situation at Corinth. In this case, the expansion of the idea of a different gospel may be explained as an attempt to accommodate Paul's preferred terminology to the differing situation in Corinth. Here the polarization between two types of ministry (weak and strong), which characterizes the whole of chapters 10–13, has perhaps been extended to include the notion of two models of Jesus (suffering and victorious) and two sorts of spirit (a seal of the life to come or a present empowering agent for charismatic manifestation). Whether or not this understanding is the correct one, it is important to note that similarity of expression does not require us to assume similarity of provenance.

The possibility that Paul himself realized that his language was inappropriately harsh might be evidenced by the conditional nature of 11:3-4 (φοβοῦμαι δὲ μή πῶς . . . φθαρῇ τὰ νοήματα ὑμῶν [but I fear lest somehow . . . your thoughts may be led astray]), in obvious contrast to the indicative mood of the verbs in Galatians 1:6. The obviously hyperbolic parallel in 2 Corinthians 11:20 leads to the same conclusion. Paul realized that the situation was not the same as the one he had encountered at Galatia, for which he had better justification to claim that his opponents preached a different gospel. Nevertheless, he wished to set the argument in these terms, although in 2 Corinthians he was more circumspect in doing so.

The most extraordinary dissimilarity between the two texts is the complete absence in 2 Corinthians of that which is at the very heart of Galatians: a defense of Paul's law-free gospel to the Gentiles. The question of Gentile circumcision, integral to the controversy at Galatia (and the issue for

---

[39] Barrett, "Paul's Opponents," pp. 68, 70, emphasis added.

which Paul himself claimed to have been persecuted: Gal. 5:11; cf. 6:12), is nowhere to be found.⁴⁰ Missing too is any discussion of justification by faith; remarkably, the words δίκαιος, δικαιόω, and νόμος (just, justify, and law), as well as περιτομή (circumcision), do not once show themselves in 2 Corinthians. Remove these same elements from Galatians, and only the shell of a letter remains; clearly, the same cannot be said of 2 Corinthians.

Where Paul does choose to defend himself, apparently in the terms of his opponents, the issue is not doctrine but: (1) Paul's eloquence and the extent of his knowledge (11:6), (2) the purity of his personal pedigree (11:22-23), (3) the impressiveness of his visionary experience (12:1-6), and (4) his capacity to perform "signs and wonders and mighty works" (12:12).

Significantly, the first and last of these passages occur in conjunction with Paul's two references to the super-apostles.⁴¹ On both occasions, Paul reckons that he is "not in the least inferior" to these super-apostles (11:5; 12:11). The equal ground on which he claims to stand has uniformly to do with the *practice* of ministry, namely, that it is exercised in knowledge (even if ἰδιώτης τῷ λόγῳ [untrained in speech], 11:6) and in works of power. Paul's account of his vision of Paradise (number [3] above) is a close parallel, since it originates from a discussion of the boasting of Paul's opponents (11:21b: ἐν ᾧ δ' ἄν τις τολμᾷ, ἐν ἀφροσύνῃ λέγω, τολμῶ κἀγώ [but whatever anyone dares to boast of—I am speaking as a fool—I also dare to boast of that]). Therefore, despite similarities between Galatians and 2 Corinthians, it seems most likely that Paul's opponents at Corinth were not Judaizers. Second Corinthians does overlap with Galatians in its defense of the apostolic authority of Paul; in this we may find an adequate explanation for the similarities between the epistles cited above. But nowhere does the issue of authority touch on the question of the legitimacy of a law-free mission to the Gentiles, the validity of which is assured throughout the whole of the Corinthian correspondence. Instead, Paul's apostolic claim is under attack from another quarter, one whose precise theology remains unknown to us,⁴² but whose emphasis clearly lay on the present realization of spiritual power.

---

⁴⁰ It appears in 1 Corinthians only in 7:18-19, a passage asserting indifference toward circumcision. Cf. Gal. 5:2-3.

⁴¹ The identity of the super-apostles is discussed below.

⁴² Probably the best-known attempt at reconstructing the theology of Paul's opponents is that of Dieter Georgi in his influential work *The Opponents of Paul in Second Corinthians*. It is Georgi's thesis that at the heart of the Christology of Paul's opponents lay a concept of the θεῖος ἀνήρ (pp. 155-59, 220-23 [192-200]). In their view, Christ was an archetype of the "divine man," other representatives of which could be found in the Jewish Scriptures (Moses being the most notable example) and among the present-day opponents themselves. Whether or not Georgi is correct in this identification, the emphasis it leads him to place on the charismatic authority of Paul's opponents is undoubtedly well founded. It is very different from the stuff of Gal. 1:11–2:14, where Paul's authority has been attacked on the basis of his supposed dependence upon the Jerusalem apostles. Galatians makes it clear that Paul can argue in those terms if they are indeed the terms of the debate.

It is interesting in this respect to note how Barrett, an authority on the Corinthian correspondence, deals with the issue of Judaizing at Corinth. More than once, Barrett states that the Corinthian opponents were "Judaizing Jews."[43] This claim, however, is deceptive. It is made possible only by virtue of a uncommonly broad definition of the term "Judaize." Barrett argues that "insistence upon circumcision is not an indispensable mark of Judaizing. There were Jewish missionaries who did not insist on circumcision."[44] "There were Judaizers, of whom Peter at Antioch (Gal. ii. II) is the most notable example, who maintained a legalist position without insisting upon these expressions of it [i.e., circumcision and Sabbath observance]."[45] Paul's opponents, therefore, did not require that the Corinthians receive circumcision, only that they in some unspecified way become more Jewish (i.e., in Barrett's terms, that they Judaize). Thus Barrett speaks, not of Judaizers, but of "legalistic Judaizers" or "downright Judaizers"[46] when referring to those who would compel Gentiles to become Jews. The final result of Barrett's argument is, therefore, very much the same as that outlined above. The Corinthian opponents did not demand the proselytism of Gentile believers. Hence, the issue was different from that at Galatia.

Let us now turn to the second point of our discussion. Did Paul's opponents come to Corinth as representatives of the church in Jerusalem? Fortunately, it is not critical for the purposes of the present study to settle this contentious issue; it is accepted that the Jerusalem apostles had their problems with Paul, and it should not astonish us to find these surfacing in a conflict of personalities, especially in a crossroads city like Corinth. Likewise, it must be restated that the church of Jerusalem did not always speak univocally; Paul in Corinth may have experienced what is recorded in both Acts 15:1-2 and (possibly) Galatians 2:4-5, that is, opposition from a *segment* of the Jerusalem church. That Paul's opponents do not appear to have required the Corinthian Gentiles to Judaize, therefore, is of greater significance than the opponents' specific origin. Nevertheless, a positive association of Paul's opponents with Jerusalem would be intriguing and could potentially shed light on the relationship between Paul and the "pillar" apostles.

C. K. Barrett, to whose work on the Corinthians epistles I have just referred, is one of many scholars who speak of a direct relationship between Paul's opponents in 2 Corinthians and the church of Jerusalem. In his view, the intruders at Corinth came as representatives of the Jerusalem church

---

[43] Barrett, "Paul's Opponents," p. 80; see also pp. 65, 78–82; *Second Corinthians,* pp. 29–30, 276.
[44] Barrett, "Paul's Opponents," p. 80.
[45] Barrett, *Second Corinthians,* p. 30.
[46] Barrett, "Paul's Opponents," pp. 78 and 86, respectively.

promulgating the terms of the decree (or something like it) of Acts 15.[47] They not only fulfilled their appointed task but, overstepping their bounds, called into question the apostleship of Paul.

This is an attractive proposal in many ways, providing a viable link to Jerusalem, a credible motive (to bring the Gentile churches into line with common practice), and a believable interpretation of the controversy between Paul and Jerusalem (i.e., that it does not have to do with the validity of the circumcision-free gospel but with its practical application).

Barrett might be right, but his thesis is not without problems. The weightiest of these is the silence of Paul on the law. It might be argued that only the requirement of circumcision—that is, a demand for full proselytism—would have been serious enough in itself to cause dissension, since Paul himself regarded favorably the obedience by Gentiles to some Jewish laws. I doubt, however, that this is an adequate explanation. All but one of the prohibitions of Acts 15:20, 29 are dietary restrictions, and it is abundantly clear from the Antioch Incident that the subject of food laws was important so far as Paul was concerned. Apparently the issue was one that concerned at least some of the Corinthians as well, since Paul devotes considerable space to the issue in 1 Corinthians (chap. 8; 10:19-33). It is a modern misperception to see in these verses an example of Paul the moderate, effecting a Solomonic compromise between legalists and libertines. From the point of view of contemporary Judaism (Jewish Christianity included), his perspective can only be characterized as radical (cf. 1 Cor. 9:20-23; 10:27), as indeed was his understanding of the law itself set forth in Galatians (and echoed, for example, in 1 Cor. 7:19). That Paul did not moderate these views is witnessed by Romans 14, a restatement of his position in 1 Corinthians that, if anything, exceeds it in boldness, since Paul explicitly states that no food is unclean (vv. 14, 20) and that special days may be disregarded (v. 5).

Hence, Paul was not essentially agreed with those who would have required of his Gentile converts obedience to the Apostolic Decree. Therefore, it seems certain that Paul would have mentioned the law had the objective of his opponents been the winning of obedience to certain Jewish prohibitions, food laws in particular. Had they promoted a decree issuing from Jerusalem, one might also have expected Paul to comment on his previous agreement with Jerusalem, as he seems constrained to do in Galatians. Furthermore, if the controversy concerned such stipulations, one might at least expect Paul to have mentioned them somewhere in his argument; instead, the debate is entirely personal.

Probably, then, the controversy did not concern the law at all, but something else. This conclusion would do nothing to rule out the possibility that the opponents originated in Jerusalem, although, for the purposes of this

---

[47] Barrett, *Second Corinthians*, pp. 6-7.

study, it would make their Corinthian adventures of lesser significance.

A connection with Jerusalem cannot be ruled out, but neither can it be proved. The evidence upon which such links are postulated is feebler than is usually acknowledged. This may be shown by referring briefly to the passages most often cited in defense of the Jerusalem origins of Paul's opponents at Corinth.

In 2 Corinthians 11:22 Paul boasts, "Are they Hebrews? So am I. Are they Israelites? So am I. Are they descendants of Abraham? So am I." As we have seen, this resembles Paul's self-description in Philippians 3:5: "circumcised on the eighth day, a member of the people of Israel, of the tribe of Benjamin, a Hebrew born of Hebrews." It cannot be disputed that Paul's real or imagined opponents were Jewish. But were they from Palestine? Of these appellations, the most evocative must certainly be "Hebrew." The term is often taken to mean one who spoke Aramaic or Hebrew, and it therefore had the geographic connotation of Judean origin.[48] But there are two complications. One is the fact that the term was also used in a general sense as a formal and impressive synonym for "Jew."[49] More significant, Paul's use of the term must necessarily dilute it, since he was not a native of Palestine, nor was he himself likely ever to have lived there.[50] Perhaps his family originated there and still spoke Aramaic. Whatever the designation may have meant precisely, it is clear that its use was by no means confined to those living in Judea. In Corinth itself, an inscription has been discovered identifying the "synagogue of the Hebrews."[51] Obviously, employment of the term by Paul's opponents, particularly in an address to a (predominately or exclusively?) Gentile audience, would not in itself lead us to conclude that they came from Palestine. Gerd Lüdemann has commented that "it is not possible to infer a Jerusalem or even a Palestinian origin for these anti-Paulinists on the basis of these three self-designations, because they were current also in extra-Palestinian Judaism—with a view to emphasizing the separateness of the elect people."[52]

The second argument in favor of a Jerusalem connection concerns the identity of the so-called super-apostles of 2 Corinthians 11:5 and 12:11. The similarity between this expression and Paul's description of the Jerusalem apostles in Galatians, noted above, has led a great many scholars to conclude that the references are indeed coterminous. Apart from this similarity, one

---

[48] Georgi, *Opponents*, p. 45 [58].
[49] According to Georgi: "the evidence shows that with the designation Ἑβραῖος the pagans already associated the idea of something special in the sense of mysterious.... When adversaries of Paul praised themselves before their audience as 'Hebrews,' they could count on attention" (ibid., pp. 44–45 [57–58]; the subject is covered on pp. 41–46, 69–72 [51–60]).
[50] This point is made in chap. 2 above.
[51] C. K. Barrett, *New Testament Background*, p. 53.
[52] Lüdemann, *Opposition*, p. 86 [132].

may grant that the Jerusalem apostles alone are conspicuous candidates for such a title.

The issue is complicated by three additional references to apostles in chapters 10–13 (11:13 [twice] and 12:12). One might naturally expect that the author had in mind that same group mentioned in 11:5 and 12:11, the super-apostles. Such correspondence, however, creates insoluble difficulties for the identification of the super-apostles with the "pillars" in Jerusalem. There are few who would be willing—in light of the ongoing collection for the church in Jerusalem, among other things—to believe that Paul would have denounced the "pillars" as "false apostles, deceitful workers, disguising themselves as apostles of Christ" (11:13) and "servants of Satan" (11:14-15). Furthermore, it seems clear that Paul was referring in 11:12-15 (as in 11:4, 20) to persons with whom the Corinthians had immediate contact.

Understandably, therefore, defenders of the Jerusalem proposal prefer a second option, the possibility that Paul had in mind two separate groups of apostles, those at Corinth and those in Jerusalem who stood behind them. This approach is thought to explain the difference in tone between Paul's appellations: "super-apostles" might be considered an example of mild irony, as Barrett terms it,[53] in contrast to Paul's scathing attack on the "false apostles/ servants of Satan" (compare the distinction between "those who were supposed to be acknowledged leaders" and the "false believers" of Gal. 2:6 and 2:4). Following along these lines, Käsemann has argued that it is impossible that those super-apostles to whom Paul is not inferior could also have been judged by him to be servants of Satan: "How can Paul tear open an unbridgeable gap between himself and the heretics—when he describes them in 11:3, 13ff. as carriers of Satanic deceit and in 11:4 accuses them of [offering] another Gospel, another Jesus, another Spirit—and then conclude that he is no less than they?"[54] Barrett agrees that "it is difficult to resist the force of Dr Käsemann's argument."[55]

Accepting for the moment the proposal that the false apostles/servants of Satan were not the same group as the super-apostles, we have still to determine the relationship between the two. Regarding this issue, the text is of little help: the opponents might have been sponsored by the super-apostles directly, or they might have made such a claim of sponsorship falsely, or they might simply have claimed to stand in the tradition of the super-apostles. None of these options is ruled out nor is any made likely by the vague references of Paul. On the whole, this has meant that scholars have been able to fit the Corinthian opponents to whatever scheme they prefer.

The vagueness of Paul's reference is usually taken as an example of

---

[53] Barrett, *Second Corinthians,* p. 31.
[54] Ernst Käsemann, "Die Legitimität des Apostels," p. 42.
[55] Barrett, *Second Corinthians,* p. 31.

ironic evasiveness. I think that it could just as well be interpreted to mean that he had no specific referent in mind. If so, he would be saying, "I have just as much right to be called an apostle as the very best of them." The justification for his claim is then supplied in the verses that follow. Paul need not, in this case, be assuming any relationship between the two groups, since the super-apostles do not themselves constitute an actual group. In support of this possibility, I would argue that it is a characteristic of Paul to favor sweeping and grandiose comparisons. Earlier, in his frustration with the Corinthians over the matter of spiritual gifts, he made the (surely unsubstantiated) claim that "I speak in tongues more than all of you" (1 Cor. 14:18). And, without meaning to depreciate the magnitude of Paul's sufferings, we might also note the same phenomenon occurring in 2 Corinthians 11:26, where Paul tells us that, in effect, he was in danger from everyone, everywhere.[56]

Another problem concerns the supposed parallels with Galatians, on which many scholars have leaned rather heavily. Barrett states the case as follows: "Galatians in fact reveals precisely the same attitudes as appear in 2 Corinthians: a vigorous attack upon false apostles (verse 13), or false brothers (Gal. ii. 4), and an ironical but unaggressive attitude to another group, clearly defined in Galatians as the 'pillars,' and named as James, Cephas, and John. There is some probability that, as the attitudes are the same, so too are the persons concerned."[57]

This approach, however, overlooks the fact that, despite similarity of terminology, the groups concerned are *not* parallel. In Galatians the "pillars" side with Paul against the "false believers"; in 2 Corinthians, we are told, the two groups are in some way united in opposing Paul. Paul speaks differently of the two groups in Galatians because they are indeed different groups holding different opinions. According to most interpreters, this is not the case in 2 Corinthians. Once again, similarity of rhetoric does not necessitate identity of situation.

Three other dissimilarities between the epistles might be mentioned: (1) there is no evidence that the Galatian Judaizers claimed to be apostles, whereas those at Corinth clearly did; (2) in Galatians, where Paul also uses irony, he refers to Jerusalem and to the Jerusalem apostles explicitly, but in 2 Corinthians 10–13 neither is mentioned; and (3) the debate in Galatians over apostolic authority is tied—from the side of the opponents—to the question of a historical relationship to the Jerusalem church, but the debate in 2 Corinthians concerns questions of immediate authority.

Looking at the matter from the other side, I think it quite reasonable to suppose that the super-apostles *were* the same persons as the false apostles/

---

[56] Note the "countless floggings" of 2 Cor. 11:23 (which Paul then counts in vv. 24–25).
[57] For example, see Barrett, *Second Corinthians,* p. 278.

servants of Satan. If we note the verses (11:13; 12:12) in which apostles, but not super-apostles, are mentioned, we see clearly a consistency of purpose. In 11:12-13, Paul denigrates as false apostles those who claim "to be . . . our equals in what they boast about." They are ἐργάται δόλιοι, μετασχηματιζόμενοι εἰς ἀποστόλους Χριστοῦ (deceitful *workers,* disguising themselves as apostles of Christ). Significantly, these apostles are identified, not by their names or by their origin (both of which figure prominently in Gal. 1:18– 2:14), but by their activity, a fact consonant with the theme of boasting and the emphasis on charismatic works that pervade this section. It seems clear that it is the work or mission of these apostles in Corinth to which Paul alludes. About this most scholars would be in agreement.

The final reference to super-apostles (12:12) concerns the "signs of a true apostle," which Paul claims to have demonstrated. Once again, the issue is that of apostolic activity, and there is no question that the site of this demonstration is Corinth itself.

Therefore, it is most probable that the Corinthian opponents considered themselves—and were considered by many of the Corinthians—to be apostles. Justification for this claim was found in the apostolic character of their activity. Apparently, they were eloquent and possessed knowledge (11:6), they accepted support from the Corinthians (11:7), they had visionary experiences (12:1, 11), and they performed "signs and wonders and mighty works" (12:12). Their only other warrant is the fact of their Jewish birth (11:22).

It is important to note how the references to the super-apostles fit within this scheme. In both instances, Paul is discussing, as he has been doing all along, the reputedly apostolic character of the activity of his opponents at Corinth.

Consider the context of 11:5. In 11:4, Paul is not concerned with the theoretical disposition of the Corinthians,[58] but with the willingness they have already demonstrated to receive those who oppose him. It is about these opponents that Paul immediately says, Λογίζομαι γὰρ μηδὲν ὑστερηκέναι τῶν ὑπερλίαν ἀποστόλων ("I think that I am not inferior to those super-apostles," 11:5). The relationship between verses 4 and 5 is confirmed by verses 6 and 7. In verse 6, the subject is a comparison between the eloquence of Paul and that of his opponents, surely a matter on which the Corinthians had passed judgment at first hand. Paul then enumerates a second difference between himself and these opponents: they accepted the Corinthians' support, but he did not.

In other words, the logic of verses 4-7 is as follows: some came whom you surprisingly accepted. But contrary to what these big shots say or you

---

[58] The subjunctive mood, however, probably indicates Paul's awareness that he is overstating his case. See my discussion of 11:3-4 on p. 161.)

might think, my ministry has no less an apostolic character than theirs, even though I am not eloquent in speech and refused to claim the maintenance that was rightfully mine.

Thus we may make two important observations about this section: (1) the reference to the super-apostles fits into Paul's single argument about the Corinthian opponents, a view more satisfying than that which imagines Paul jumping, without distinction, from Corinthian opponents to Jerusalem apostles back to Corinthian opponents in verses 4, 5, and 6 respectively; and (2) it is not necessary to think that Paul in verse 5 accepts the apostolic claim of the super-apostles; the point is simply that they are claiming nothing that he cannot also claim for himself.

The context of the second reference to super-apostles is much the same. Having spoken of his visionary experience, Paul upbraids the Corinthians for having forced him to commend himself, especially since they themselves ought to have commended him. What is worse, he has had to commend himself, as a fool, in the terms of his opponents. Paul remonstrates, "for I am not at all inferior to these super-apostles, even though I am nothing. The signs of a true apostle were performed among you . . . signs and wonders and mighty works" (12:11b-12). Once more, mention of the ὑπερλίαν ἀπόστολοι flows from and then back into a debate concerning the apostolic activity of the Corinthian opponents and of Paul. Hence, I see no compelling reason to conclude that the term "super-apostles" is anything but a sarcastic commentary on the lofty apostolic claims of the Corinthian opponents themselves.

Let us return to Käsemann's assertion that Paul could not have compared himself favorably with those whom he labeled false apostles/servants of Satan. The resolution of this difficulty is to be found in the recognition that the debate concerning apostolic legitimacy occurs on two levels.[59] At certain points (including both instances in which he mentions super-apostles), Paul compares himself with his opponents in their own terms; at others, he compares them with himself according to his own, better criteria. Thus the debate shifts back and forth between two sets of standards, producing two sets of results. So long as Paul is taking up the standards of his opponents, he compares himself favorably to them; even on the basis of what they consider to be important, he is not inferior. But when the standard in view is Paul's, he compares his opponents negatively to himself. This can be

---

[59] Clearly, the authority of Paul had long been an issue among the Corinthians. Neither his speech nor his presence was ever sufficiently impressive to suit some of them (2 Cor. 10:10). Throughout 1 Corinthians and most of 2 Corinthians, Paul has offered his readers a justification for his apostolic office based upon the criteria of obedience and suffering—or weakness, as he calls it (see, for example, 1 Cor. 2:1-5; 3:18-23; *4:8-13;* 2 Cor. 6:3-10). By the writing of 2 Corinthians 10-13, it has become clear that this strategy has failed. Paul must resort to being a "fool" and answer his critics in their own terms. Nevertheless, he retains his own standard—as he must, since it is this that distinguishes him from his opponents.

seen in the phrase that introduces the vituperation of 11:13-15: ἵνα ἐκκόψω τὴν ἀφορμὴν τῶν θελόντων ἀφορμήν, ἵνα ἐν ᾧ καυχῶνται εὑρεθῶσιν καθὼς καὶ ἡμεῖς (to deny an opportunity to those who want an opportunity to be recognized as our equals in what they boast about; 11:12, following a discussion in vv. 7-11 of Paul's ministry at Corinth). "They most certainly do not work on the same terms as we!" writes Paul. "In *our* (i.e., genuine) terms, they are no apostles at all."

The second place in which Paul asserts his own standard is in 11:23-33. Here he does not claim equality with his opponents, but superiority (v. 23). He does so by a return to the dichotomy between weakness and strength (a common coinage of the Corinthian letters: 1 Cor. 1:18—2:5; 3:18-23; *4:8-13;* 2 Cor. 6:3-10; 10:10): the true servant is the one whose obedience is shown in the endurance of suffering and hardship for Jesus' sake (cf. 12:7-10). Considering this correct test of an apostle, Paul says, ὑπὴρ ἐγώ (I am a better one, 11:23).

It is worth noting that Paul's comparison in 11:21b-23, like the one he makes between himself and the super-apostles, is phrased in such a way as to imply that he accepted their legitimacy (are they ministers of Christ? . . . I am a better one). But these over whom Paul claims superiority are the very ones lambasted as false apostles/servants of Satan, "fools" whom the Corinthians "gladly put up with" (11:19). So Käsemann's problem cannot be limited to the super-apostles; it must be equally intolerable from our perspective that Paul would call "ministers of Satan" the Corinthian opponents themselves, whose boast that they are "ministers of Christ" he appears to accept.

In summary, it seems most likely that Paul was concerned with only one group of opponents in 2 Corinthians 10-13. If there was a second group, there is no way of judging on the basis of the text what its relationship was to the first group—or even if the second group existed as an identifiable group at all. Whether there were two groups or one, we see that Paul's use of the term ὑπερλίαν ἀπόστολοι (super-apostles) is unconvincing evidence for the Jerusalem origin of the Corinthian opponents.

The other points made in favor of the Jerusalem sponsorship of Paul's opponents may be dealt with briefly. The first concerns the "commendatory letters"[60] mentioned in 2 Corinthians 3:1b: "surely we do not need, as some do, letters of recommendation to you or from you, do we?"

Two things might point to Jerusalem as the source of such letters. First, the church in Jerusalem is the obvious source for an authoritative commendation; second, it appears that the credentials of the opponents did make a favorable impression at Corinth. F. C. Baur wrote:

---

[60] On the use of commendatory letters in antiquity, including the Pauline epistles, see Barrett, *Second Corinthians,* p. 106.

Since they were Jewish opponents, these letters of recommendation could only have been brought from Jerusalem, because by the authority of the elder apostles alone could they [the opponents] so easily have found entry into the Pauline community. Admittedly, it is not said that they have been received by James or Peter, but who else could it have been, by whom they were sent out, directly or indirectly, other than by these pillars of the community, whose names alone were important enough to serve as a recommendation for others?[61]

The fact that a letter of recommendation from Jerusalem might carry considerable weight, however, is no proof that a weighty letter of recommendation must perforce have come from Jerusalem. Also, it is worth noting that Paul refers, not to a single letter or church, but to "letters," presumably from different churches. Last, it is assumed by Paul that such letters might just as well have come from the Corinthians themselves. Taken together, these observations lead me to believe that Paul's opponents were able to produce multiple letters of recommendation from churches at which they had previously ministered. It is even possible, in view of verses 2-3 and 12:11, that the opponents had asked the Corinthians to compose such a letter of commendation to add to those previously received. Therefore, the "letters of recommendation" of 2 Corinthians 3 add nothing to the debate concerning the origin of the opponents.

Last, it is sometimes said that Paul's statement that he no longer knows Jesus κατὰ σάρκα (5:16) is evidence for the belief that Paul's opponents *did* know Jesus "according to flesh," that is, that they had firsthand knowledge of Jesus.[62] The implication is that they came from Palestine, where they witnessed the ministry of the earthly Jesus. Thus Lietzmann says: "The Judaizers, supported by the disciples of Jesus, attack Paul 'because he had not known the Lord personally.'"[63] Accordingly, Paul is then forced to relativize the importance of such knowledge, claiming that, since "everything old has passed away" and "everything has become new," only his "new" knowledge of Jesus is of the sort that now matters.

The situation presented us by 5:16 is by now familiar. It is not impossible that the proposed link to Jerusalem is correct; there is no compelling reason, however, to believe that it is. The passage makes perfect sense in its own immediate context without the need to import Jerusalem adversaries into the discussion. As we have noted more than once above, a consistent theme of the Corinthian correspondence is the inversion of human values in the divine economy. Of his arrival at Corinth Paul acknowledged: "I come to you in weakness and fear and in much trembling. My speech and my

---

[61] Baur, "Beiträge zur Erklärung der Korintherbriefe," p. 165.
[62] Barrett presents a brief historical survey of opinion on this issue in *Second Corinthians*, pp. 170–72.
[63] Hans Lietzmann, *An die Korinther I, II*, p. 125.

proclamation were not with plausible words of wisdom" (1 Cor. 2:3-4). The content of his implausible message was the seemingly oxymoronic "Christ crucified" (v. 2). This reversal is at the heart of Paul's understanding of the cross ("a stumbling block" and "foolishness," 1 Cor. 1:22-25) and of his self-understanding as an apostle (e.g., 6:8-10). It was, apparently, a concept less endearing to the Corinthians than to Paul, and he has finally to supplement (though not quite abandon) it in his defense of his apostolic office in 2 Corinthians 10-13.[64]

Second Corinthians 5:16 comes at the end of one of Paul's long discussions of the paradoxical relationship between human and divine values. The gospel, which is the glory of God, is nevertheless veiled "to those who are perishing" (3:7—4:6). Similarly, the "treasure" of the gospel is now carried "in clay jars," that is, in weak and fallible human ministers, whose sole competence is that God has chosen them and given them the Spirit (4:7; 3:4-6; 1:21-22). Therefore, despite human suffering and failure, weakness and death, "we do not lose heart" because "we look not at what can be seen but at what cannot be seen" (4:16, 18; 5:1-15). So we must abandon judging others from a human perspective and judge instead as God judges, since we are now Christ's and not our own (5:14-15). "From now on, therefore, *we regard no one from a human point of view; even though we once knew Christ from a human point of view,* we know him no longer in this way. So if anyone is in Christ, there is a new creation; everything old has passed away, see, everything has become new!" (5:16-17). In other words, just as once we misjudged Christ, regarding him as weak and foolish, we ought now to be careful not to misjudge others but to regard them instead from the new perspective that informs our understanding of Christ, "the power of God and wisdom of God" (1 Cor. 1:24).

The assumption is that all who live "according to the flesh" regard Christ wrongly, and only now, with the veil being lifted by the Spirit, may those believing see him aright. Thus Paul's use of the first person plural: οἴδαμεν . . . ἐγνώκαμεν . . . γινώσκομεν (we regard . . . we knew . . . we know). Knowledge of Christ κατὰ σάρκα does not imply a knowledge of the historical Jesus, which neither Paul nor his readers possessed.[65] It has instead to do with a certain way of regarding Jesus apart from faith, with eyes veiled.[66]

---

[64] See Timothy H. Lim, "Not in Persuasive Words of Wisdom, but in the Demonstration of the Spirit and Power."

[65] If such knowledge were the issue, it is amazing that Paul did not make an appeal to the resurrection appearance of Jesus, on which he relies in similar arguments elsewhere (i.e., when contact with Jesus was an aspect of his defense; see, for example, 1 Cor. 9:1 and Gal. 1:11-17).

[66] The new perspective that Paul claimed is also to be found, for example, in 2 Corinthians 1:17, where he asks, "Do I make my plans according to ordinary human standards?"

One important implication (although by no means the only one) is that the Corinthians will also regard Paul rightly.[67] To this theme he turns explicitly in chapter 6, cataloguing what he considers to be the marks of an apostle, which highlight once again the paradoxical nature of his calling (6:9-10).

Thus, Paul's statement in 5:16 is of one piece with its surroundings — and with much of the argument of 1 Corinthians as well. As such it addresses the propensity of the Corinthians to misjudge others according to worldly values. The same temperament that requires Paul to point out that love is "a still more excellent way" than spiritual gifts (1 Cor. 12:31b) leads at least some Corinthians to undervalue the relatively unimpressive ministry of Paul, a point of view that makes them ripe for the incursion of the more outwardly imposing apostles whose claims he attacks in 2 Corinthians 10-13.[68] There is nothing in this that hints at an appeal to Jerusalem; only the Corinthians' inflated sense of the importance of human credentials and external appearances is required.

In summary, there does not seem to be any reason on the basis of the evidence of 2 Corinthians to suppose that Paul's opponents came to Corinth as Judaizing representatives of the Jerusalem church. The same conclusion has been reached in the case of opponents of Galatians, while the idea of an opposition to Paul at Philippi was rejected in toto.

Two other issues concerning the relationship between Paul and Jerusalem that may shed light on the thinking of the "pillar" apostles need still to be mentioned: the collection and Paul's arrival in Jerusalem and subsequent arrest.

The Collection

To my knowledge, there are only two instances in the whole of Baur's *Paul* in which the author refers to Paul's collection for "the saints in Jerusalem."[69] The collection simply does not fit into Baur's understanding of the relationship between Paul and the Jerusalem church. Instead it is, as Loisy noted, an unambiguous demonstration that Paul himself "did not regard the communities founded by him as enjoying an absolute autonomy. One would no more admit two apostolates than one would admit two Gospels."[70]

---

[67] See Rudolf Bultmann's discussion in *The Second Letter to the Corinthians*, pp. 153-55 [155-56].

[68] One reasonable possibility is that we are dealing in 2 Cor. 2:14—7:4 with the same opponents as in 10-13 but that Paul's knowledge of their activity in Corinth was incomplete and thus that he failed to realize the extent of their success or the precise nature of their claims.

[69] Baur, *Paul* 1:205, 378 [222, 402].

[70] Loisy, *L'Épître aux Galates*, p. 122; see p. 126, contra Achtemeier, who sees in the collection a desperate (and unsuccessful) attempt on the part of Paul to restore his broken relationship with the Jerusalem church (*Quest*, pp. 59-60).

In the first of Baur's references, the subject of the collection is dropped as quickly as it is raised. The second reference is more interesting. Here we find Baur "choking" on the kindly language of Romans 15:25-27; in fact, he is forced to use it as an argument against the legitimacy of Romans 15.

> How clearly is the Jewish Christian interest of the author of chap. xv. [i.e., the later redactor] expressed, when he recommends this contribution as only a labour of Christian love, and represents it as a token of thankfulness from the Gentile Christians....
>
> [But] On this subject the Apostle says nothing in those passages of his epistle in which this idea, if he had ever entertained it, must have been present in his mind ... there is not in any way the least hint, that he ever thought of the Church at Jerusalem as the Mother Church, as sustaining such a relation to the Gentile Christian churches.[71]

The reason for Baur's discomfort is that the Jerusalem collection materially demonstrated, at the very least, the ongoing recognition of the church in Jerusalem on the part of Paul and his churches. The significance of this fact should not be underestimated. Paul assumed that the Jerusalem Christians were Christians, that there was a unity and a consistency to the gospel both they and he preached (Rom. 15:27; Gal. 2:7-10).

It may be argued that Paul *had* to recognize the church of Jerusalem and therefore that such recognition is meaningless. I do not agree. Paul's recognition of Jerusalem was essentially an acknowledgment that there was one gospel and that this gospel originated in Jerusalem and still was, in a sense, a Jerusalem gospel. Thus he acknowledged (however grudgingly) in Galatians 2:2 that to be valid, his own preaching must be one with theirs. The point is simply that, in light of this conviction, Paul kept on preaching to Gentiles and kept on believing in a unity of purpose with the church in Jerusalem, a belief incarnated in the collection itself, which was a means of blessing those by whom the Gentiles themselves had been blessed (Rom. 15:27). As with Samuel Johnson's dancing dog, the wonder is not that Paul had a difficult relationship with Jerusalem but that he had a relationship at all.

Second, it is difficult to believe that the fact of the collection is consonant with the existence of a Jerusalem-sponsored, law-observant, anti-Pauline mission alongside—and intersecting—that of the apostle himself. Even if we imagine that Paul could have had the surreptitious motive of purchasing legitimacy for the Gentile mission,[72] it is unthinkable that his churches, by this time exposed to the authentic party line, would have bought the ruse. His argument in 1 Corinthians 16:1-4, 2 Corinthians 8—9,

---

[71] Baur, *Paul* 1:378 [402-3].

[72] According to Francis Watson: Paul was "trying by means of the collection to secure Jerusalem's recognition of their [the Pauline churches'] legitimacy" (*Paul,* p. 175).

and Romans 15:25-32 could not possibly have carried conviction if a fundamental Jerusalemic opposition to Paul had been exposed.[73] How hollow would Paul's references to "the saints"[74] have sounded in their ears![75] They must have believed in the collection as an act of charity and gratitude, even if Paul did not. And if the real purpose of the collection was to win recognition of the circumcision-free gospel, why did this objective, of evident concern to Paul's hearers, fail to surface, especially since it could not in any case have been hidden?

From the perspective of this study, the most interesting passage on the subject of the collection is Romans 15:30-31.[76]

Παρακαλῶ δὲ ὑμᾶς, ἀδελφοί, διὰ τοῦ κυρίου ἡμῶν Ἰησοῦ Χριστοῦ καὶ διὰ τῆς ἀγάπης τοῦ πνεύματος συναγωνίσασθαί μοι ἐν ταῖς προσευχαῖς ὑπὲρ ἐμοῦ πρὸς τὸν θεόν, ἵνα ῥυσθῶ ἀπὸ τῶν ἀπειθούντων ἐν τῇ Ἰουδαίᾳ καὶ ἡ διακονία μου ἡ εἰς Ἰερουσαλὴμ εὐπρόσδεκτος τοῖς ἁγίοις γένηται [I appeal to you, brothers and sisters, by our Lord Jesus Christ and by the love of the Spirit, to join me in earnest prayer to God on my behalf, that I may be rescued from the unbelievers in Judea, and that my ministry to Jerusalem may be acceptable to the saints.]

It is Paul's prayer that he might be delivered from the "unbelievers" — better, the "disobedient," that is, the non-Christian Jews, of Judea.[77] In light of subsequent events, this evidences a prudent — and, in retrospect, poignant — concern. But what are we to make of Paul's next statement: "and that my ministry to Jerusalem may be acceptable to the saints"? There are three principal possibilities:

---

[73] Romans 9-11 would also make a good deal less sense if written in such a situation. Paul is able to assume that there are two basic entities, the remnant of faithful Jews (11:4-5; i.e., Jewish Christians) together with Gentile believers (which is to say, the church) and unbelieving Israel. This argument presupposes on the part of both Paul and his Christian readers a common identity with the believers of Judea (as with Jewish Christians generally).

[74] Paul's references to the saints in Jerusalem are located in 1 Cor. 16:1; 2 Cor. 8:4; 9:12; and Rom. 15:25, 26, 31. Paul uses the term for Christians generally in 1 Cor. 1:2; 6:1-2, 14:33; 2 Cor. 1:1; 8:4; 13:12; Phil. 1:1; 4:22; 1 Thess. 3:13; 2 Thess. 1:10; Philem. 5, 7; and Rom. 1:7; 12:13. Notably, the Galatians are not addressed as saints.

[75] Or consider the statement of 2 Cor. 9:14: αὐτῶν [the saints in Jerusalem] δεήσει ὑπὲρ ὑμῶν ἐπιποθούντων ὑμᾶς.

[76] The collection is also discussed at length in 1 Cor. 16:1-4 and in 2 Cor. 8 and 9.

[77] This is certainly the correct interpretation of the phrase ῥυσθῶ ἀπὸ τῶν ἀπειθούντων ἐν τῇ Ἰουδαίᾳ. The best reason for accepting this conclusion is the parallel use of this terminology in Rom. 11:30-32. This view is supported by, among others, the commentaries of Barrett, *Second Corinthians*, p. 279 ("non-Christian Jews are meant"); Ulrich Wilckens, *Der Brief an die Römer* 3:128-29; William Sanday and Arthur C. Headlam, *A Critical and Exegetical Commentary on the Epistle to the Romans*, pp. 414-15; Emil Brunner, *The Letter to the Romans: A Commentary*, pp. 124-25 [113-14]; C. H. Dodd, *The Epistle of Paul to the Romans*, pp. 232-33; and C. E. B. Cranfield, *A Critical and Exegetical Commentary on the Epistle to the Romans* 2:778. The reader is also referred to Bauer's *Greek-English Lexicon*, p. 82, where we are told that the translation of ἀπειθέω as "disbelieve, be an unbeliever" "seems most probable in J 3: 36; Ac 14: 2; 19: 9; Ro 15: 31, and only slightly less prob. in Ro 2: 8; 1 Pt 2: 8; 3: 1, perh. also vs. 20; 4: 17."

1. Paul feared that the collection—and by implication, his ministry and gospel—would be rejected by the Jerusalem church.
2. Paul knew that there were unresolved tensions in his relationship with the Jerusalem church, and he hoped that these would not mar the occasion, which he hoped to be a joyous experience for the church (15:32).
3. Paul was not genuinely afraid that the Jerusalem church would refuse to accept the collection. His prayer should be taken as a formulaic expression typical of one making an offering or presenting a gift (just as Christian congregations today pray that their collection may be acceptable to God).

I am unwilling to accept the first of these options, at least in undiluted form, for reasons that have already been explained in detail. I do not think that the circumcision-free gospel of Paul was at stake, at least on the part of James and what appears to have been the mainstream of Jerusalem Christian opinion. One variable of which we cannot be certain, however, is the continued existence of a party within the Jerusalem church corresponding to the "false believers" of Galatians 2:4.[78] Perhaps Paul feared opposition from this group specifically. I do not consider this the most likely possibility, however, since acceptance by James would probably have been the significant indicator of the success of the collection to Paul (compare Gal. 2:4-6, in which it is the acceptance of the "pillars," James included, which was decisive).

James and his followers, however, perhaps viewed Paul's apostolic claims with a considerable degree of suspicion or even hostility for other reasons, most likely based upon a fundamental disagreement as to the implications of the gospel for Jewish legal observance. But these are personal details and do not necessarily impinge on the acceptance of the collection, which, after all, was initiated at the request of the Jerusalem church itself (Gal. 2:10).

These considerations incline me toward the second option, which sees urgency in Paul's request, but not desperation. Paul is taking with him to Jerusalem representatives of the Gentile churches. He has high hopes for the occasion, and he wishes that no scene such as that which occurred at Antioch may be allowed to tarnish it.

It may be, however, that both of these approaches miss the mark. A careful reading of Romans shows us just how high were Paul's expectations for the trip to Jerusalem. It seems that he had in his mind the hope that the offering of the Gentiles would play a role in the realization of the eschatological redemption of Israel. The mystery that he contemplates in 11:25 appears to be just such a divine reversal—the opposite of the customary expectation that the eschatological deliverance of Israel would result in the obedience and salvation of the Gentiles (see Isa. 2:1-4; 42:1-9; 49; 55:4-5;

---

[78] The point is discussed in the previous chapter.

60:1-7; 66:18-23). Paul perhaps was influenced here by Isaiah 2, in which it is said that "in days to come" the nations will journey to Mount Zion to be taught the ways of God. This would make sense of Paul's concept of "the full number of the Gentiles" in 11:25: their status is representational, signifying the obedience of the Gentiles won by the gospel (15:17-19). This leads to Paul's remarkable use of sacerdotal language in 15:16:

εἰς τὸ εἶναί με λειτουργὸν Χριστοῦ Ἰησοῦ εἰς τὰ ἔθνη, ἱερουργοῦντα τὸ εὐαγγέλιον τοῦ θεοῦ, ἵνα γένηται ἡ προσφορὰ τῶν ἐθνῶν εὐπρόσδεκτος, ἡγιασμένη ἐν πνεύματι ἁγίῳ. [to be a *minister* of Christ Jesus to the Gentiles in *the priestly service* of the gospel of God, so that *the offering* of the Gentiles may be *acceptable*, sanctified by the Holy Spirit.]

Paul saw himself as a priest offering up to God the gift of the Gentiles.[79] In light of 11:26, it would seem to be a reasonable hypothesis that Paul thought the pilgrimage of these Gentiles to "the mountain of the LORD" (Isa. 2:3) might precipitate the coming of "the Deliverer" to Zion (11:26, cf. Isa. 59:20-21).

Whether or not this interpretation is correct, it is clear that "acceptable" (εὐπρόσδεκτος) is here used in its common,[80] cultic sense. This use parallels that of the cognate adjective "acceptable" (δεκτός) in the Septuagint,[81] employed almost exclusively[82] in reference to the acceptability of offerings or persons to God.[83] Εὐπρόσδεκτος is used only five times in the New Testament; it is worth noting that three of these occurrences are in connection with the collection (Rom. 15:16, 31; 2 Cor. 8:12). The two other references are 2 Corinthians 6:2 (cf. Isa. 49:8) and 1 Peter 2:5. Paul uses δεκτός twice: in 2 Corinthians 6:2 (in parallel to εὐπρόσδεκτος) and in Philippians 4:18, a particularly interesting passage.

ἀπέχω δὲ πάντα καὶ περισσεύω· πεπλήρωμαι δεξάμενος παρὰ Ἐπαφροδίτου τὰ παρ' ὑμῶν, ὀσμὴν εὐωδίας, θυσίαν δεκτήν, εὐάρεστον τῷ θεῷ. [I have been paid in full and have more than enough; I am fully satisfied, now that I have received from Epaphroditus the gifts you sent, *a fragrant offering, a sacrifice acceptable and pleasing to God.*]

Paul assures the Philippians both of his own gratitude and of the fuller

---

[79] That "of the Gentiles" (τῶν ἐθνῶν) is appositional (i.e., the offering consists of the Gentiles themselves) seems most likely in light of vv. 15-16a ("grace . . . to be a minister . . . to the Gentiles") and v. 18 (the purpose of his ministry is "to win obedience from the Gentiles"). See C. K. Barrett, *A Commentary on the Epistle to the Romans*, p. 275.

[80] See Bauer, *Greek-English Lexicon*, p. 324.

[81] Εὐπρόσδεκτος does not occur in the LXX.

[82] Exceptions most frequently concern the acceptability of a person to the king, rather than to God (e.g., Prov. 14:35; 16:13; 22:11). Since the king is understood to be the servant of God, however, the difference is insignificant.

[83] See, for example, Exod. 28:38; Lev. 1:3, 4; 19:5; 22:19, 20; 23:11; Job 33:26; Prov. 11:1; 12:22; 14:9; 15:8, 28a; Isa. 56:7; 58:5; 60:7; Jer. 6:20; Mal. 2:13.

significance of their generosity: their gift to him has also been a sacrifice made to God. Thus we discover an instance in which the acceptance of support money is couched in unmistakably sacerdotal language.

Taken together, these considerations suggest that we should be wary of reading too much fear and trembling into Paul's statement concerning the acceptability of his service (διακονία) for the saints. His language is explicable in light of a very similar usage in Philippians and especially in view of its context in Romans, in which Paul has already reflected on the priestly significance of his "service." Hence, there may have been no real doubt in his mind that the collection would be received in Jerusalem—no more, for example, than was in the mind of the Philippians when they sent their support to Paul. Nevertheless, it must have seemed proper to make such offerings humbly and, along with this, to wish that they be of such value as to be greeted with thankfulness and joy.[84]

This view, of course, falls within the bounds of the third option presented above. In its favor, I would make one additional observation: it is highly improbable that Paul would have appealed for help against (at least the leaders of) the Jerusalem church from a church he had never visited. Paul does hope to win the support of the Roman Christians for a future mission to Spain (15:28-29); in such a context, he would hardly introduce the subject of his conflict with (what he himself admits to be) the mother church.

We are not able to venture far beyond the limits of these few comments regarding the meaning of Romans 15:31. There simply is not sufficient evidence to justify an assertion concerning *the* correct interpretation of the passage. Instead, I can only suggest what might constitute the reasonable range of interpretive possibilities. The verse could represent anything from a neutral and rather stereotypical intercession to a heartfelt entreaty for the vindication of the author's apostolic status. There is the additional (although perhaps more remote) possibility that Paul did fear rejection, but only from a conservative element within the Jerusalem church.

From the point of view of this study, however, the matter is more straightforward. The collection for the saints in Jerusalem presupposes and thus is evidence of an essential unity between Gentile and Jewish-Christian churches. Paul probably did have significant differences of opinion with the majority in Jerusalem, but the collection suggests strongly that beneath these lay, for both Paul and his followers, a genuine recognition of Gentile and Jewish solidarity in the gospel.

---

[84] According to Cranfield: "Those who still labour in the shadow of the Tübingen school's continuing influence are naturally prone to welcome these words [Rom. 15:30-31] as additional grist for their mill. . . . [but it would] be more likely to recognize in these words evidence of Paul's spiritual and human sensitivity and freedom from self-centred complacency than to draw from them any confident conclusions about the tensions between the Jerusalem church and Paul" (*Romans* 2:778).

Acts 21: Paul in Jerusalem

In Acts 21 we are told of Paul's final, tumultuous visit to Jerusalem. As Luke records the event, Paul and his companions traveled to Jerusalem, where they were received on the second day by James and the elders. These recognized Paul's ministry to the Gentiles (vv. 19-20) but worried about the reaction he might receive from others within (and, one assumes, without) the church, those "zealous for the law," who had heard that Paul taught Jews of the Diaspora to "forsake Moses." A compromise was effected that, it was hoped, would defuse the situation by demonstrating the piety of Paul (vv. 22-26). This plan failed when Paul was recognized in the temple on the seventh day by Jews from Asia (v. 27). These incited a crowd by claiming that Paul had spoken "everywhere against our people, our law, and this place" and, moreover, that he had brought a Gentile into the temple. An uproar ensued in which Paul was rescued from the mob and then taken prisoner by the Romans.

There are three critical points to this narrative: (1) Paul's ministry to the Gentiles was accepted by the leaders of the Jerusalem church; (2) there were other elements in the church thought likely to oppose Paul; and (3) such opposition was based on those aspects of Paul's teaching that were at least thought to impinge upon *Jewish* observance of the law. These same points figured prominently in our discussion of the Apostolic Council and the incident at Antioch. In Acts 21, therefore, we find continuity with these earlier events, witnessing similar degrees of unity and diversity, goodwill and bad feeling, both within the Jerusalem church and between the Jerusalem church and Paul. If it is judged historically credible, the account of Acts 21 could thus provide weighty confirmation of our earlier conclusions concerning the relationship between certain elements of the early church: the Hebrews, the Hellenists, and their successors.

Haenchen is among the many commentators who accept this account as historical, embracing even the great majority of its details. His own analysis of the passage is first-rate and clarifies certain points that might otherwise present the reader with difficulty.[85] Of particular interest is Haenchen's concern with the absence in the account of any mention of the collection. He proposes that James and the elders wished to receive the collection but that they could not do so until the situation created by the arrival of Paul, whose defamatory statements concerning the law had become known,[86] had first been ameliorated. "It was suggested to Paul that he

---

[85] Haenchen's consideration of the problems surrounding Paul's Nazarite vow is especially helpful (*Acts*, pp. 611-12 [541-43]).

[86] Perhaps they had seen a copy of the Letter to the Galatians. Perhaps, in addition, Paul had *not* circumcised Timothy, and this had become known to them (Haenchen, *Acts*, p. 609 [539-40]).

assume the relatively considerable cost of redeeming the four poor Nazirites. If he agreed to this—and he had already declared himself ready to support the poor saints—then the collection could be accepted, because such a redemption of Nazirites was considered as particularly pious by every Jew."[87]

Even if the plan had succeeded, Luke would have been left in an awkward position. The delicacy of Paul's situation within the Jerusalem church did not accord with the rosier account of Acts. The negotiations surrounding the acceptance of the collection would have presented his readers with unnecessary complications. "So he decided not to mention the collection at all. For the apparently easy way out, to report only its reception, was likewise precluded: how was he to make it comprehensible to the reader that the primitive community further required Paul to pay for the four Nazirites, when Paul had just handed over a considerable gift of love from his congregations?"[88]

In support of this proposal one may cite Acts 24:17, in which Paul mentions to Felix the occasion for his trip to Jerusalem: "Now after some years I come to bring alms to my nation and to offer sacrifices." One might presume that this demonstrates an awareness of the actual reason for Paul's journey.

It could be said, however, that Luke knew only vaguely about Paul's project to take money to the church in Jerusalem. His uncertain knowledge of details finds expression in the curious narrative of the so-called famine relief visit of 11:27-30.[89] Haenchen himself believes that this story owes its creation to a tradition concerning the Jerusalem collection,[90] although he makes no attempt to reconcile this opinion with his view of the redactional activity of Luke in omitting the collection in chapter 21. Perhaps Luke did not know that the collection was associated with this final visit; his statement in 24:17 would then be seen to correspond to, rather than to contradict, the other motive he assigns to Paul in making the pilgrimage to Jerusalem: that of celebrating Pentecost in Jerusalem (20:16; 24:11).[91] This would not, in any case, be an argument against Haenchen's historical reconstruction, since we know of the collection independently. Therefore we cannot discount the possibility that the collection played a part in the events recounted by Luke.

It would be difficult to select any segment of Acts about whose historicity there is a scholarly consensus. The narrative of Acts 21:17-36 is no

---

[87] Ibid., p. 614 [544]. Achetemeier contends, on the basis of the silence of Acts, that "the collection was not accepted" (*Quest*, p. 60). I do not find this assertion convincing.
[88] Haenchen, *Acts*, p. 614 [545].
[89] See Alfred Loisy, *L'Épître aux Galates*, p. 102.
[90] Haenchen, *Acts*, pp. 378-79 [322].
[91] Because "pilgrims from the Diaspora . . . brought [to the temple] free-will offerings of gold and silver" (Safrai and Stern, *The Jewish People* 1:203), it is not unreasonable to suppose that Luke would have imagined Paul as having done the same. Such a detail is well suited to the defense of Paul's Jewish piety in chap. 24.

exception. Not surprisingly, one dissenting voice is that of F. C. Baur. Though there is much here to displease him, his criticism focuses on two points. He contends that the account of Acts is fraudulent, since (1) it does not account for the fact that the enmity of the Jews was directed solely against Paul, and (2) the portrayal of Paul in this chapter is a fantasy of Luke's apologetic imagination.

On the first of these points Baur argues:

> And how shall we explain the great collision into which the Apostle came with his brethren in the faith, and the irreconcilable hate with which he was persecuted by them? The faith in Jesus as the Messiah cannot have been the origin of this hatred, or it would have been shown in the same manner against the Jewish Christians who lived together with the Jews of Jerusalem. . . . why should the hatred of the Jews be directed exclusively towards him, and not equally towards the elder Apostles, who were completely in accord with him on the subject of circumcision? But if, as we may assume from the epistle to the Galatians, the elder Apostles did not agree with him on this point . . . then we must naturally suppose that the Apostle was held as an enemy on account of his doctrine of freedom from the law, not only by the Jews, but by the Jewish Christians also.[92]

Baur's argument makes one serious mistake and one serious omission. The mistake is in failing to distinguish between the issues of circumcision and of law criticism—or put somewhat differently, between Gentile and Jewish obedience to the law. This is a matter on which I have already commented in detail. The omission is just as critical. Baur asks why the other apostles were not persecuted but then fails to recognize that they were.

We thus require a perspective that explains why Paul would have been persecuted earlier than, although not finally instead of, James. Such a perspective is, of course, that which was advanced in the previous chapter: Paul was a more controversial figure than James, being more radical in his understanding of the law (and hence of the necessity of Jewish obedience); nevertheless, they had enough in common that was objectionable to strict Judaism (including the willingness to receive uncircumcised Gentiles into the covenant community) to have run afoul of the Jewish authorities. Also, if Luke is correct in identifying Paul's opponents as "Jews from Asia" (21:27), it might be that Paul would have avoided arrest had not these Hellenists interfered. It is even possible that Paul's arrest paved the way for the eventual martyrdom of James—the leader of the Jerusalem sect having failed to repudiate the criminal Paul.[93]

---

[92] Baur, *Paul* 1:206–7 [222–23].
[93] According to Josephus (*Ant.* 20.200–203), James's martyrdom occurred in A.D. 62, probably a short time before Paul's own death in Rome.

Baur's second objection is more substantial. In summary, his case is this: Luke erroneously portrays Paul throughout Acts as a law-abiding Jew; Acts 21 is simply an extension of this program. The accusations against Paul were patently true, Luke notwithstanding. Finally, it is utterly unthinkable that Paul would have resorted to the subterfuge suggested in 21:23-25. Paul was emphatically not a law-abiding Jew and would not have made a pretense of being one. Luke's apologetic motive is the only sufficient explanation for the report of Paul's behavior in this chapter.[94]

I agree that Acts is untrustworthy on the subject of the piety of Paul. I would also agree with Baur in attributing this phenomenon to the redactional activity of Luke, although I would disagree in limiting its scope to Paul.[95] Nevertheless, I cannot conclude that every act of obedience to the law on the part of Paul in Acts must be a tendentious invention. This makes a nonsense of Paul's own statement in 1 Corinthians 9:20 that "to the Jews I became a Jew, in order to win Jews. To those under the law I became as one under the law (though I myself am not under the law) so that I might win those under the law."

Like it or not, the expedient of 21:23-25 is consistent with this principle, and the principle itself could nowhere have been more appropriately applied than in Jerusalem. I do not doubt that there is an implicit inconsistency to Paul's actions. But if Paul is a hypocrite, it is because the principle he espouses in 1 Corinthians is itself duplicitous. What Paul actually says about his willingness to live "under the law" for the sake of his mission fits perfectly with the description of his actions in Acts 21.[96] It fails only to accommodate itself to Baur's interpretation of Paul.

I also disagree with Baur in his claim that the accusations against Paul in 21:21 were unambiguously true. Paul did not "teach all the Jews living among the Gentiles to forsake Moses . . . [instructing] them not to circumcise their children or observe the customs." Paul did not believe in the *necessity* of obedience to (at least some parts of) the law,[97] but neither did he

---

[94] Baur, *Paul* 1:207-11 [223-27].

[95] It is telling that a great number of scholars who reject outright Luke's portrayal of Paul on these grounds accept unquestioningly the description in Acts of the irreproachable piety of the Jerusalem church, although Jerusalem Christians also faced opposition from their contemporaries in Judaism.

[96] This does not mean that the assertion of the previous chapter concerning the unacceptability of the terms of the Jerusalem Decree must be rescinded. The point in that case was that Paul would not have accepted additional *requirements* for his Gentile converts. (That he did not accept any such requirements is proved by 1 Cor. 8; 10:19-33 and Rom. 14.) That Paul himself would have obeyed laws he otherwise ignored on certain occasions is demonstrated by 1 Cor. 9:19-21 and, if accepted as historical, Acts 16:3.

[97] I.e., the parts that distinguished and separated Jews from Gentiles: food laws, days, and circumcision.

believe, at least in principle,[98] that it was necessary for Jews to *forsake* the law (a question addressed explicitly in 1 Cor. 7:17-24 and Rom. 14). Therefore, while there was a basis for the charges of 21:21, they did not accurately reflect the position of Paul.[99] The distinction is more than one of splitting hairs; it was undoubtedly the margin within which the Jerusalem apostles were able to accept their difficult brother, Paul. That the distinction did not impress other Jews or even all Jewish Christians is not surprising.

These arguments do not mean that we have established the historicity of Acts 21:17ff. I accept that this is not possible, given the absence of corroborating evidence. Haenchen, however, is willing to attribute the story to a credible source.[100] If he is correct (and I can see no legitimate reason for supposing that he is not), then we have valuable evidence in favor of the present thesis. If Luke's account cannot be trusted, as Baur contends, then it can contribute nothing, positive or negative, to the discussion. While I do not find Baur's objections convincing—and I see good reason for accepting the account on the basis of its internal coherence and external correspondence to the evidence of the Pauline epistles—I am well aware of the problems of Acts and of the danger of circular reasoning in the use of unconfirmed evidence. The account, then, is consistent with our previous findings and, I think, historically probable, if not provable.

JAMES, THE BROTHER OF JESUS

We turn now from Paul to the other leader of the early church prominent in our discussion: James, the brother of Jesus. James is by now a familiar figure to the reader of this book. Already we have considered evidence for the beliefs of James taken both from the Pauline epistles and from Acts. We concluded that James was not an archconservative archenemy of Paul, as has sometimes been claimed. In particular, there is no evidence that James ever repudiated the circumcision-free mission to the Gentiles. That he was more conservative than Paul seems assured; that this made him a conservative does not. Within the Jerusalem church, in particular, it appears that James exercised a moderating influence. In fact, at every place in which James has appeared on these pages—in connection with the Jerusalem Conference, the Antioch Incident and subsequent Jerusalem Decree, and the arrival of Paul

---

[98] That this was not an absolute principle is demonstrated by the incident at Antioch. When forced to choose, the principle of Gentile inclusion took precedence for Paul.

[99] Not even this much can be said in favor of the accusations in 21:28. There is no evidence to suggest that Paul had taught against the temple, much less that he had brought Greeks into its restricted precincts. Otherwise unsubstantiated accusations against the temple, like those made against Stephen in 6:11-14, are best explained as reflections of the accusations made against Jesus himself.

[100] Haenchen, *Acts,* p. 612 [542-43].

in Jerusalem—we have seen him filling the roles of pragmatist and mediator. He had to contend with Paul, to be sure, but also with those opposed to Paul.

Why does this matter? The claim has been made that the church from its earliest days was split into liberal and conservative wings, between those who criticized the law and those who championed it, between those who supported a circumcision-free mission to the Gentiles and those who opposed it—between, in other words, Hellenists and Hebrews. Beyond the alleged evidence of Acts 6 and 7, advocates of this view point to subsequent tensions between Jerusalem and Antioch and between Jerusalem and Paul to justify the essentially two-toned picture they have painted of the earliest church. At the summit of their allegations stands James, who, as leader of the Hebrews (or their heirs), behaved and believed, we are told, in a way antithetical to Paul, opposing him at Antioch and instigating a countermission in competition and conflict with the circumcision-free mission of Paul.

We have seen that this reconstruction is faulty at every point. There is no valid evidence to support the notion of a neat theological split between the Hellenists and the Hebrews of Jerusalem. Likewise, subsequent events in Antioch and Jerusalem attest to the complex view of events advanced in the Introduction. The churches of Antioch and Jerusalem, and the Hellenists and Hebrews with them, were not uniform ideological entities.

In the course of examining these subsequent events, our attention came to focus on the relationship between Paul and Jerusalem as evidenced by opposition to Paul at Galatia and Corinth and as witnessed by the collection for the saints. We concluded our discussion of Paul by considering briefly his arrival in Jerusalem and his arrest. Similarly, our consideration of James concludes with a discussion of his martyrdom.[101]

One of the few incontrovertible facts we possess concerning James is the occasion of his death: he was tried and martyred at the instigation of the

---

[101] It is tempting to introduce into the argument evidence gleaned from the New Testament Epistle of James. The fact that it is written in good Greek, the manner in which it treats the law (e.g., "the law of liberty," in 1:25 and 2:12), and the moderate approach it takes to the controversy with Paul (2:14-26) would present us with a James very unlike the hidebound legalist so often encountered in the pages of New Testament criticism.

The majority of scholars believe the epistle to be the product of a second- or third-generation Jewish Christian author writing under the cloak of pseudonymity. While I would wish to challenge some of the assumptions used in passing this judgment (particularly, employment of the supposedly narrow legalism of James as a rule by which to measure what he could or could not have written), I do accept the conclusion as ineluctable. It seems clear that the author of the epistle is writing about the law from a perspective that is once removed from the original controversy. The problems of circumcision and food laws, for example, are passed over with a generalizing ease reminiscent of the treatment of the law in Acts. A detailed treatment of the question of authorship is provided by most critical commentaries. See, for example, Martin Dibelius (with revisions by Heinrich Greeven), *James: A Commentary on the Epistle of James*, pp. 11–21 [23–35]; Sophie Laws, *A Commentary on the Epistle of James*, pp. 2–6, 38–42; and James Hardy Ropes, *A Critical and Exegetical Commentary on the Epistle of St. James*, pp. 6–18, 43–52.

high priest Ananus the Younger, probably in the year 62. Unlike other details of his life already considered, the report of his death comes to us from extrabiblical sources. We find the account in two distinct forms: that of Josephus in *Antiquities* 20.200 and that of Hegesippus in Eusebius's *Ecclesiastical History* 2.23 (with which we may classify other reports, such as the one in *The Second Apocalypse of James,* that are dependent on Hegesippus or on some common source).[102]

Of these two, Hegesippus's version is by far the more problematic. It was written more than a century after the account of Josephus and was "plainly composed in order to do honour to James as an ascetic and martyr."[103] The details of the encomium are quite fantastic. We are told that (1) James alone was "permitted to enter the Holy Place"; (2) some leaders of the Jews urged James, the Christian, to dissuade the people from believing in Jesus, "for we all listen to thee"; (3) surprised (!) and dismayed by the Christian testimony of James, they cried out, "Even the Just One has gone astray!"; (4) they cast James from the pinnacle of the temple and then stoned him, whereupon he prayed for his executors; and, (5) following (and, it is implied, because of) this, Vespasian immediately began the siege of Jerusalem.

Even the oft-repeated title "the Just" is suspect: it appears to come from Isaiah 3:10, which the author quotes in connection with the stoning of James. The "prayer of the righteous" of James 5:16 might also have contributed to the author's characterization. Other motifs are borrowed from the life of Jesus (dying intercession, pinnacle of the temple, witness to the Son of man) and from stereotypical portrayals of the lives of saints. Attributed to James are "practices of the Nazirite, which the author has intensified (and at the same time distorted) by means of other characteristics of cultural nonconformity: abstinence from eating flesh, from anointing with oil, and from bathing."[104]

In short, the account is late and legendary, and there is nothing to commend it as a credible historical source. Dibelius writes, "This legend from Hegesippus cannot be considered a serious rival to the short, clear, and prosaic statement of Josephus," with which "it does not agree at all."[105] Ropes calls the narrative "a legend, betraying no close contact with the events." For this reason, "nothing can be drawn from it to add to the picture of James' character and position derived from the N.T. In the bare tradition of a violent death Hegesippus agrees with the account found in Josephus, but

---

[102] Gerd Lüdemann has provided a useful chart displaying the relationships between these and subsequent accounts (*Opposition*, p. 177 [237]).
[103] Ropes, *James*, p. 66.
[104] Dibelius, *James*, p. 16 [30].
[105] Ibid., pp. 17, 15 [30, 28].

nearly all the details of the two accounts vary."[106] Therefore it is necessary to reject Hegesippus as a source for information about James. Instead, we turn to the account of Josephus, commended to us already by both Dibelius and Ropes.

Most scholars accept that Josephus himself is the author of the whole account of *Antiquities* 20.197-203.[107] The only argument against this attestation is based on the presence of Christian interpolations elsewhere in the text (especially at *Ant.* 18.3). However, this should not lead us to doubt the authenticity of the passage, since it has a different stamp from those generally acknowledged to be Christian interpolations.[109] It is not apologetic; in fact, as we shall see, it is probably silent as to the question of James's guilt or innocence. Apart from this, the story is not intrusive; it serves a clear purpose in Josephus's narrative. Thus it seems probable that Josephus's report of the death of James is genuine. The account is as follows:

> The younger Ananus, who, as we have said, had been appointed to the high priesthood, was rash in his temper and unusually daring. He followed the school of the Sadducees, who are indeed more heartless than any other of the Jews, as I have already explained, when they sit in judgement. Possessed of such a character, Ananus thought that he had a favorable opportunity because Festus was dead and Albinus was still on the way. And so he convened the judges of the Sanhedrin and brought before them a man named James, the brother of Jesus who was called the Christ, and certain others. He accused them of having transgressed the law and delivered them up to be stoned. Those of the inhabitants of the city who were considered the most fair-minded and who were strict in observance of the law were offended at this. They therefore secretly sent to King Agrippa urging him, for Ananus had not even been correct in his first step, to order him to desist from any further such actions. Certain of them even went to meet Albinus, who was on his way from Alexandria, and informed him that Ananus had no authority to convene the Sanhedrin without consent. Convinced by these words, Albinus angrily wrote to Ananus threatening to take vengeance upon him. King Agrippa, because of Ananus' action, deposed him from the high priesthood which he had held for three months and replaced him with Jesus the son of Damnaeus.[110]

Josephus's account leaves the reader with two contradictory impressions. On the one hand, we hear that "the most fair-minded," who "were

---

[106] Ropes, *James*, p. 66. See also the discussion in Munck, *Paul*, pp. 113-18 [105-10].

[107] "Unlike the passage on Jesus (*Ant.* xviii.63-64), few had doubted the genuineness of this passage on James. . . . If it had been a Christian interpolation it would, in all probability, have been more laudatory of James" (*Ant.*, LCL 10:108, note a).

[108] One nonextant interpolation maintained that the killing of James occasioned the destruction of Jerusalem (Eusebius, *Eccl. Hist.* 2.23.20 [*Eusebius*, LCL 1:176-77]; Origen, *Contra Celsum* 1.47 and 2.13 [*The Writings of Origen* 1:447 and 2:20]).

[109] See Emil Schürer (revised and edited by Geza Vermes and Fergus Millar), *The History of the Jewish People in the Age of Jesus Christ (175 B.C.-A.D. 135)* 1:430-32.

[110] Josephus, *Ant.*, LCL 10:107, 109.

strict in observance of the law," protested so vociferously at the death of James that they were able to secure the removal of Ananus, the high priest. This creates the impression that these upright and fair-minded citizens supported James because they believed in his innocence. To have gone to such lengths on his behalf, one must imagine that they knew James well. One might even conclude that James had been a legalist of the first order to have won the enthusiastic support of so conservative a body of defenders. Needless to say, this is the interpretative twist put on the story by those who see in James the center of conservative opposition to the apostle Paul.[111]

On the other hand, however, we find the high priest Ananus eager to execute James (and others with him). This gives the impression that James (and perhaps others of his ilk) had somehow inspired the enmity of at least a segment of official Judaism.

The explanation for this anomaly is straightforward. Josephus is not concerned with the issue of James's innocence, about which he says nothing. Instead, his purpose is to give a brief account of the deposing of Ananus, son of Ananus.[112] The son Ananus is introduced with a reference to his character: he was "rash ... and unusually daring." The only other detail thought worthy of mention is the fact that he was a Sadducee, which means specifically that he was "heartless" when he sat in judgment. This is a matter on which Josephus claims to have spoken already. The reference is probably to *Antiquities* 13.294, in which Hyrcanus enquired of the Pharisees, whom he had deserted for the Sadducees, what penalty Eleazar deserved for slandering the king. They responded that Eleazer deserved only stripes and chains. Josephus comments, "for they [the Pharisees] do not think it right to sentence a man to death for calumny, and anyway the Pharisees are naturally lenient in the matter of punishments."[113]

Having set the stage, Josephus immediately introduces the subject of the trial and death of James "and certain others," at which the most fair-minded were offended. What precisely was the offense? From the context in which the discussion occurs, it seems certain that it was the irregularity of the trial (reflecting the rashness and daring of Ananus, for which we have just been prepared) and the harshness (and probably illegality)[114] of the punishment (about which, also, we were warned) that troubled them. This is confirmed in the lines that follow: because "Ananus had not even been correct in his first step [i.e., 'convening the Sanhedrin without Albinus's

---

[111] E.g., Bo Reicke, "Der geschichtliche Hintergrund des Apostelkonzils und der Antiochia-Episode, Gal. 2, 1-14," p. 186.

[112] The narrative of Ananus's three-month priesthood begins immediately with the subject of his fall from power.

[113] Josephus, *Ant.,* LCL 7:375.

[114] See Josephus, *J.W.* 6.126, and the necessity of drawing Pilate into the trial of Jesus in Matt. 27, Mark 15, Luke 23, and John 18-19.

consent'],"[115] King Agrippa ordered him "to desist from any further such actions" (20.201). The implication is that in the trial itself and in the punishment to which it led, Ananus had exceeded his authority. The "further such actions" from which he was to desist were not the trials of innocents before a sanhedrin but *any* trials before a sanhedrin. Likewise, those who went to Albinus complained that "Ananus had no authority to convene the Sanhedrin without his consent" (20.202). Over this usurpation of power the anger of Albinus burned, and on the basis of such a presumption Agrippa deposed Ananus.[116]

Therefore, so far as the text is concerned, the issue in question was the legality of Ananus's actions and not the innocence of James. This is not to say that the charges against James were just; I do not imagine for a moment that James was guilty of breaking the law in the sense of violating an objective proscription (but I would say the same of Jesus). The point is that, according to Josephus, opposition to Ananus arose on grounds that had nothing to do with the convicted individuals (of whom James was only the most prominent member) per se.[117]

Similarly, this does not mean that some might not have been spurred to action because of offense taken at injustice as well as what we might call rough justice. This is a conjecture, however, that Josephus himself does nothing to confirm. (Cf. the very different account of the death of John the Baptist in *Ant.* 18.116-19, in which the question of injustice is primary and obvious.) In light of the circumstances surrounding the event, however, so selfless a motive seems highly unlikely. It is worth pausing a moment to recall this historical context.

The decade leading up to the revolt in 66 was characterized by an intense struggle for power between several factions of the Judean ruling class.[118] One of these was led by the sons of Ananus, another by the former high priest Ananias, and still others by Ananias's son Eleazer and by the Herodians Costbar and Saul. In the early 60s, the rivalry between the

---

[115] Josephus, Ant., LCL 10:108, note *c*.

[116] The action of Herod in deposing Ananus is not so extreme as might be imagined. In fact, between the years 37 B.C. and A.D. 66, no fewer than twenty-seven high priests were deposed, one after holding office for only a single day (Goodman, *Ruling Class,* pp. 41, 141). Depositions occur just prior to the story of Ananus, in 20.197, and just after, in 20.213.

[117] One is reminded of the controversy surrounding the trial of Winston Silcott on a charge of murder. To the surprise of many, Silcott, already a convicted murderer, won a significant measure of public support, demonstrated most conspicuously by his election on 27 April 1989 as honorary president of the students' union of the London School of Economics. The controversy had nothing to do with the guilt or innocence of Silcott, but with the character of the trial itself, described by Lord Gifford QC as "a terrible miscarriage of justice" (*London Daily Telegraph,* 29 April 1989, front and back pages).

[118] See Martin Goodman's excellent analysis of the social and political factors that lay behind the Jewish Revolt of A.D. 66: *The Ruling Class of Judaea: The Origins of the Jewish Revolt against Rome A.D. 66-70.*

families of Ananias and Ananus was especially bitter. "Certainly by A.D. 62 Ananias was in firm opposition to Jonathan's brother Ananus b. Ananus."[119] It might even be that Jonathan was murdered at the behest of Ananias.[120] The deposition of Ananus in 62 led to a brief period in which the influence of Ananias reached its zenith (20.205). Later Ananias's son Eleazar betrayed his father; his companions ransacked Ananias's home and, discovering Ananias the next day, murdered him (*J.W.* 2.441). Ananus allied himself with Eleazar and, for a period during the revolt (between the autumn of 66 and the spring of 68), Ananus became the leading figure in Jerusalem, propped up by an uneasy coalition of competing factions.[121] Ironically, during this time Ananus himself deposed one high priest, Eleazar b. Simon. Eventually his alliance crumbled, and Idumaean allies of the wronged Eleazar b. Simon killed Ananus (*J.W.* 2.652-53). Internecine strife continued all the way up to the arrival of Titus in 70. "As Tacitus (*Hist.* 5.12.3-4) remarked, there were three generals and three armies, and between these three there was constant fighting, treachery and arson."[122]

It takes little imagination to see how the deposition of Ananus fits into this amazing story. He was one of "at least six High Priests [who] were deposed by Agrippa II in the turbulent ten years before the revolt."[123] In his case, Ananus lost the priesthood when opponents (of whom Ananias was the most prominent of many) complained that Ananus had blatantly exceeded his authority, taking advantage of the absence of the procurator in order to eliminate some enemies, albeit under a pretext of legality.[124] The appeal to Albinus and Herod by a number of influential Jews foreshadows the one made only a few years later by a deputation dispatched to Florus by opponents of Eleazer (*J.W.* 2.418-19).

Although their complaint was just in itself, it is most improbable, from all that we know of the intrigues surrounding the office of high priest, that the motives of Ananus's opponents were as pure as Josephus makes them out to be. Those who would have had the clout to make and to win such an appeal probably would themselves have had something to gain by it. Nevertheless, the tone of the account is understandable, especially if we take Josephus's own apologetic interests into account.[125] It should be clear, therefore, that Josephus's favorable description of the opposition to Ananus was meant to emphasize, not the justness of James (which issue, again, he neglects

---

[119] Ibid., pp. 145-46.
[120] Ibid., p. 145.
[121] Ibid., p. 183.
[122] Ibid., p. 177.
[123] Ibid., p. 112.
[124] This is the verdict of Martin Goodman (ibid., pp. 144-46, 212).
[125] Josephus wrote in part to "exculpate his own class from blame for the revolt." For this reason, the culpability of their motives and actions is frequently obscured (ibid., p. 20; see also pp. 198-206).

entirely), but the legitimacy of the complaint against Ananus, whose deposition he is describing.

One interesting observation related to our reading of Josephus is that membership in a particular religious sect appears to have been irrelevant to factional allegiances. "In matters of public policy there was no reason for members of these sects to differ.... Thus Ananus b. Ananus was a Sadducee ([*Ant.*] 20.199), but his coalition after Cestius Gallus' defeat included a number of Pharisees."[126] Apparently, Pharisees also numbered in the opponents of Ananus, since it appears that some of those who petitioned Albinus for the removal of Ananus came from their ranks.[127] It is unlikely, however, that the opposition to Ananus came only from Pharisees or that all Pharisees were united in opposing him. Instead, as Goodman's statement suggests, the incident described in *Antiquities* 20.200-203 was very likely part and parcel of the ongoing and complex jostling for power that typified the political scene in Jerusalem in the years leading up to the Jewish Revolt. Such a consideration makes all the more unlikely the common opinion that it was the strict, law-abiding Pharisees en bloc who supported James against the (equally uniform party of the) Sadducees, led by Ananus. While such a view may be used to advance the notion of the archconservatism of James, it does not accurately reflect the complex political realities of the A.D. 60s. Again, it is not unlikely that some Jews, Pharisees among them, were genuinely offended at the injustice done to James. If so, however, their concern is not addressed by Josephus, whose interest is in the severity and illegality of the actions of Ananus.

Two further observations should be made concerning priestly opposition to the early church. First, it is significant that Caiaphas, who, probably more than anyone else, was responsible for the death of Jesus, was the brother-in-law of Ananus (John 18:13), responsible for the death of James (and, according to Acts 4:6, for the punishment of Peter and John). Recognition of this fact might perhaps help to explain the animosity of Ananus toward James. The connections, however, go deeper still. Caiaphas's high priesthood spanned the years A.D. 18-36.[128] Therefore, if Stephen was tried before a sanhedrin, it would almost certainly have been Caiaphas himself who, as high priest (Acts 7:1), presided. Moreover, Caiaphas would then have been the one (assuming for the moment the historicity of the account)

---

[126] Ibid., p. 209.

[127] This is the most likely interpretation of περὶ τοὺς νόμους ἀκριβεῖς in 20.201. See Baumgarten, "The Name of the Pharisees," pp. 413-14. Baumgarten does note exceptions to this usage on p. 413, nn. 6 and 8. Morton Smith has argued that Josephus deliberately exaggerated the significance of the Pharisees in composing *Antiquities*. By this time, Smith believes, the Pharisees were gaining the ascendancy within Judaism, and Josephus sought by accentuating their importance to help them to win political recognition from the Romans ("Palestinian Judaism," p. 76). Such a view, if true, could shed light on the passage in question.

[128] Goodman, *Ruling Class*, p. 143.

who authorized the persecution of Christians reported in Acts 8:1 and 9:1-2. Thus, it is well within the range of possibility that the men responsible for the deaths of Stephen and James—that is, the reputed champions of the Hellenists and of the Hebrews—were members of the same family. It should be obvious what this would do for theories concerning the selective persecution of the Hellenists.

Second, it is interesting to note that opposition to Christianity (if I may include Jesus under this umbrella) was not restricted to the priestly family of Ananus. According to Acts 23:2 and 24:1, it was Ananias, the great rival of Ananus b. Ananus, who was the chief prosecutor of the apostle Paul following his arrest in Jerusalem.[129] Therefore, there is no reason to suppose that opposition to the leaders of the Jerusalem church was merely a matter of personal animosity, although in the case of the death of James this factor cannot be ruled out.

On what issue(s) opposition to Jewish Christians was centered is a matter of vital interest. A thorough treatment would need to attempt first to understand the antipathy that led to the death of Jesus, a topic unfortunately beyond the scope of this book, although it will arise again briefly in the Conclusion.

In summary, Josephus's report of the death of James meshes well with what we know of opposition to the Jerusalem church generally, and with what we know of the political situation in Jerusalem specifically. So the fact of James's martyrdom will not go away. Nor can its significance, though often ignored, be explained away. It is also highly likely that James died for much the same reason(s) as did Stephen, James (the brother of John), Paul—and Jesus himself. Thus we see the ultimate solidarity of James and Paul confirmed in the extreme test. Against this, conjectures and inferences as to their intrinsic opposition do not stand. They had enough in common to share a common fate.

CONCLUSION

In this and previous chapters, we have considered events that spanned the first three decades of the church. In these we discovered a consistent witness to the perspective advanced in these chapters: the church of Jerusalem was not divided into ideological groups corresponding to the designations "Hellenist" and "Hebrew." Evidence for such an early division does not exist, nor do subsequent effects testify to such a cause. In particular, the little we

---

[129] See ibid., p. 146. The story of the oath of the forty Jews and their vow to kill Paul is reminiscent of what we learn of the methods of Ananias elsewhere (*Ant.* 20.206; see also 20.213-14).

know of Paul's opponents does not support the view that they were Judaizing countermissionaries acting under the authority of the Jerusalem church. The collection, and the martyrdom of James, on the other hand, bear witness to a complicated situation in which the Jerusalem church was neither in direct opposition to nor in complete agreement with the apostle to the Gentiles. Such a result is entirely in keeping with the complex beginnings of the church postulated in this study.

Conclusion:
Of People and Pigeonholes

As we have seen, it is a commonplace of contemporary New Testament scholarship that the Hellenists were the liberal, progressive party of the early church, over against the conservative, legalistic Hebrews. Dunn's view is typical.

> [The] persecution following Stephen's death simply pushed *further apart* the two sides of the schism which Stephen's views had already brought about. Here then is *a considerable element of diversity within Christianity almost at the very beginning of its existence,* in fact *a schism within the first Christian community.* In effect we have uncovered in part at least the first division between two types of Christian—conservative and liberal (to use broad and recognizable categories)— the one holding fast to tradition, the other sitting loose to it in the light of changing circumstances.[1]

In the preceding chapters, however, I have presented a picture of the Hellenists as not so liberal and the Hebrews as not so conservative as has typically been imagined. Neither did the Hellenists maintain a uniformly liberal body of opinion that contrasted with an equally uniform but conservative outlook of the Hebrews.

Looking at those Hellenists about whom we have the most knowledge—the church at Antioch—we have seen that, despite their very real distinctiveness (especially in relation to the Gentile mission), they do not provide us with a bridge to the liberal, if not radical, theology of Paul. Paul's differences with the Hebrews in Jerusalem have been noted often enough, but we should not forget that he differed with the Antiochene Hellenists as

---

[1] Dunn, *Unity and Diversity,* p. 275.

well. Likewise, we have seen that the evidence we possess points to an ongoing diversity of opinion within the church of Jerusalem.

The Hellenists have suffered no want of attention in recent years. Assertions of their prominence have dotted the literature in a way that other, lesser luminaries (e.g., the Twelve) might envy. By contrast, it is curious to note a general lack of interest in Palestinian Jewish Christianity. One might almost be justified in observing that New Testament scholarship has taken up the program of the Acts of the Apostles, wherein the mother church in Jerusalem is considered only as it serves as preparation or foil to the cause that truly matters: the Pauline mission to the Gentiles. This bias has led to an unfair stereotyping of non-Pauline Jewish Christianity as backward, severe, and legalistic. The mostly unspoken judgment is that the closer we come to Paul, the nearer we are to the truth of the gospel. Hence the favorable treatment of the Hellenists, the supposed bridge to Paul.[2] Paulinism is thus taken to be the normative center, and everything to its right—that is, virtually the whole of Jewish Christianity[3]—is stigmatized as conservative.

Such an assessment is both inaccurate and unfair. For one thing, it is an unrealistic appraisal of what the category "conservative" might designate with respect to Judaism and Jewish Christianity of the first century. The term is used, in other words, more by way of defamation than as a genuine description. A citizen of Palestine would not have been conservative because he or she obeyed the law; he or she would simply have been Jewish. I take it as axiomatic that being a Jew meant being obedient to the law, even if the exact nature of that obedience was subject to debate. Consequently, Paul is being very radical indeed when he suggests that he is able as a Jew to live ἄνομος (outside the law, 1 Cor. 9:21). To claim that anyone not as liberal as Paul is therefore conservative is ridiculous.

We may see how strained the categories "conservative" and "liberal" become when used to describe the church in Jerusalem. When we use a term like "conservative," we need to ask, Conservative in relation to what? Thinking about Jewish Christianity as a subset of Judaism makes me wonder whether it is not misleading even to speak of a "conservative" Jewish *Christian*. Scholars who have written of the conservatism of the Jerusalem church have fallen into the trap that has caught some modern expositors of the life of Jesus. In the latter's case, Jesus has been depicted as such a good Jew that no one would have wanted to kill him. Likewise, if the Jerusalem church were half so conservative as has been claimed, the opposition it managed to arouse would be without explanation.

---

[2] See, for example, Gerhard Schneider, "Stephanus, die Hellenisten, und Samaria," p. 240; and Schmidt, *Der Bericht,* p. 23.

[3] See Gal. 2:13: καὶ Βαρναβᾶς συναπήχθη.

Even the question of Jewish legal observance was a matter of secondary importance in defining the identity of the emergent Christian community. Christian Jews differed in their treatment of the law because they differed in their understanding of what had now changed as a result of the ministry of Jesus. But they were Christians together because they believed that something had actually changed. After all, a conservative Jewish Christian is not the same thing as a conservative Jew.

Is there not something inherently offensive to Judaism about Christian faith? Surely, the greater the function assigned to Jesus as the Christ, the greater the gap in Judaism he must be assumed to have filled.[4] And we should remember that we are speaking of the role of a crucified man. Paul spoke of the cross as a stumbling block to Jews (1 Cor. 1:23), and I have no doubt that he was correct in this assessment.[5]

In short, while I can agree that obedience to the law would afford a Christian Jew some protection against charges of disloyalty, I think that by making such behavior (along with questions concerning the Gentiles) the test of conservatism (and Christian heterodoxy!), we have missed the mark. Was Jesus put to death because of relationships with Gentiles or denunciations of the law? His attitude to sinners and (perhaps) his conflicts over the Sabbath would have set some against him, but these can hardly account for the virulence of the opposition. Jesus did not have to be an extreme liberal in terms of these issues to be crucified. The best guess is that his offensiveness can be traced ultimately to his self-claim. He believed that he had a unique and central role in the final realization of God's purposes for Israel, a belief that was the wellspring of his other attitudes—including his attitude to the temple—and this more than anything else accounts for his death.

Classifications of Jewish Christians as liberal and conservative are, therefore, inherently misleading. A Jewish Christian's attitude toward the law or toward the Gentiles was a function of a larger attempt to understand what faith in Christ meant within the context of Judaism. That was the central question, and it is only because we live at such a distance from it that its importance is missed. Above all, this question impinged upon the believing Jew's understanding of the identity and election of Israel. What would Christian baptism have meant to such a Jew? How would a community of Jews have understood their identity while celebrating the Lord's Supper? We know that these Christians carried out a mission to their fellow Israelites. What was their message, and how would Jews consider their status to have changed for having believed? What was the status of those Jews who had not believed? Were they in or out, or had the "gospel for the circumcised" (Gal.

---

[4] One need look no further than Gal. 2:21 to see this principle at work.
[5] If, for no other reason, because of the apparent lack of success of the Jewish mission.

2:7) to do with something else entirely? These are very difficult questions (as a look at Rom. 9–11 will demonstrate), well beyond the scope of the present study. But they point to the fact that there was much more at stake than has ordinarily been recognized. To label Jewish Christians "conservative" simply because they obeyed the law demonstrates an altogether inadequate appreciation of the complexity of their position.

We thus cannot fairly characterize the leaders of the Jerusalem church as conservative, either in terms of their context in Judaism or in terms of the more narrow field of Jewish Christianity. It is probably fairer to generalize about the liberalism of the Antiochene church, although, as we have seen, this is a liberalism not far removed from the moderating position of a Christian such as James, the brother of Jesus, and the leader of the church in Jerusalem.

In this book I hope to have demonstrated with reference to Jewish Christianity that "God made the spectrum; man made the pigeonholes."[6] We are not justified in assigning the membership of the early Jerusalem church to Hellenist and Hebrew ideological pigeonholes. Nor does the subsequent development of the church in the first century sanction such generalizations. The situation was undoubtedly much more complex.

This simple conclusion has important ramifications. Most significantly, it lends support to the view that Christian theology did not develop along straightforward or readily accessible lines. As we have seen, we cannot appeal to the Hellenists of Antioch as the obvious and definitive source for the theology of Paul; neither can we assume that opposition to Paul must have found its source in the Hebrews of Jerusalem. Theories that delineate similar stages of christological (or other theological) development (e.g., Palestinian Jewish, Jewish Hellenistic, Hellenistic Gentile) likewise must be questioned.[7] Such scholarly constructions are a convenience, but they just as readily obscure as explain. Easy answers may be worse than no answers to questions as difficult as these.

This study raises intriguing questions about Jewish Christianity. I have contended that the traditional denigration of Judaism by New Testament scholarship has manifested itself in a pejorative stereotyping of Jewish Christianity. If we are freed from both prejudice and the predominance of our own concerns, what will we find?

Together with the traditionally negative portrayal of non-Pauline Jewish Christianity has come the customary tendency to minimize (if not to vilify) the role of the Jerusalem church in early Christianity. In light of the

---

[6] This aphorism of A. G. N. Flew is quoted by Marshall in "Palestinian and Hellenistic Christianity," p. 287.

[7] See Marshall's discussion of Heitmüller, Bousset, Bultmann, Dibelius, and Hahn in "Palestinian and Hellenistic Christianity."

significance of the Jerusalem church for Paul himself, if for no other reason, this must surely be considered an unfair appraisal. There is ample scope for a reassessment of Jerusalem's place at all levels in the development and life of the primitive church.

It is well worth noting, in conclusion, that Luke did not return to the opposition of "Hellenists" and "Hebrews" beyond its resolution in Acts 6:5. We would do well to follow his example.

Bibliography

TEXTS

The Apocryphal Old Testament. Ed. H. F. D. Sparks. Oxford: Oxford University Press, 1987.
Saint Chrysostom: Homilies on the Acts of the Apostles and the Epistle to the Romans. Ed. Philip Schaff. Trans. J. Walker et al. Rev. George B. Stevens. LNPNF 11. Grand Rapids: Eerdmans, 1956.
Saint Chrysostom: Homilies on Galatians, Ephesians, Philippians, Colossians, Thessalonians, Timothy, Titus, and Philemon. Ed. Philip Schaff. "Oxford translation" rev. Gross Alexander. LNPNF 13. Grand Rapids: Eerdmans, 1956.
Eusebius: The Ecclesiastical History. 2 vols. Trans. Kirsopp Lake (vol. 1) and J. E. L. Oulton (vol. 2). LCL. London: William Heinemann; Cambridge: Harvard University Press, 1926–32.
The Writings of Irenaeus. Ed. Alexander Roberts and James Donaldson. Trans. Alexander Roberts and W. H. Rambaut. ANCL 5. Edinburgh: T. and T. Clark, 1868.
Josephus. 10 vols. Trans. and ed. H. St. J. Thackeray (vols. 1–5), Ralph Marcus (vols. 5–8), and Louis Feldman (vols. 9–10). LCL. London: William Heinemann; Cambridge: Harvard University Press, 1926–65.
The Writings of Justin Martyr and Athenagoras. Ed. Alexander Roberts and James Donaldson. Trans. Marcus Dods et al. ANCL 2. Edinburgh: T. and T. Clark, 1867.
Minucius Felix. "The Octavius of Minucius Felix." In *The Writings of Cyprian, Bishop of Carthage,* ed. Alexander Roberts and James Donaldson, trans. Robert Ernest Wallis, 2:451–517. ANCL 13. Edinburgh: T. and T. Clark, 1869.
The Nag Hammadi Library in English. Trans. members of the Coptic Gnostic Library Project of the Institute for Antiquity and Christianity, James M. Robinson, director. San Francisco: Harper and Row, 1978.
The New Oxford Annotated Bible with the Apocryphal/Deuterocanonical Books: New Revised Standard Version. Ed. Roland E. Murphy and Bruce M. Metzer. New York: Oxford University Press, 1991.

Novum Testamentum Graece. 26th ed. Ed. Kurt Aland et al. Stuttgart: Deutsche Bibelgesellschaft, 1979.
The Old Testament Pseudepigrapha. Ed. James H. Charlesworth. 2 vols. London: Darton Longman and Todd, 1983-85.
The Writings of Origen. Ed. Alexander Roberts and James Donaldson. Trans. Frederick Crombie. 2 vols. ANCL 10 and 23. Edinburgh: T. and T. Clark, 1869-72.
Philo. 10 vols. Ed. and trans. F. H. Colson (vols. 1-10) and G. H. Whitaker (vols. 1-5). LCL. London: William Heinemann; Cambridge: Harvard University Press, 1929-43.
Septuaginta. Ed. Alfred Rahlfs. Stuttgart: Deutsche Bibelgesellschaft, 1979.
The Writings of Quintus Sept. Flor. Tertullianus. Ed. Alexander Roberts and James Donaldson. Trans. S. Thelwall and Peter Holmes. ANCL 11. Edinburgh: T. and T. Clark, 1869.
Thucydides. 4 vols. Trans. Charles Forster Smith. LCL. London: William Heinemann; Cambridge: Harvard University Press, 1919-22.

REFERENCE WORKS

Bauer, Walter. *A Greek-English Lexicon of the New Testament and Other Early Christian Literature.* 2d ed. Rev., trans., and augmented by F. Wilbur Gingrich and Frederick W. Danker. Chicago: University of Chicago Press, 1979. From *Griechisch-Deutsches Wörterbuch zu den Schriften des Neuen Testaments und der übrigen urchristlichen Literatur.* 5th ed. Berlin: Alfred Töpelmann, 1958.
Eerdmans' Handbook to the History of Christianity. Ed. Tim Dowley et al. Grand Rapids: Eerdmans, 1977.(= *The Lion Handbook to the History of Christianity.* Berkhamsted: Lion, 1977.)
The Interpreter's Dictionary of the Bible. 5 vols. Ed. Keith Crim et al. Nashville: Abingdon, 1962 (vols. 1-4) and 1976 (suppl. vol.).
Mattill, A. J., Jr., and Mary Bedford Mattill. *A Classified Bibliography of Literature on the Acts of the Apostles.* NTTS 7. Leiden: E. J. Brill, 1966.
Mayer, L. A. *Bibliography of the Samaritans.* Ed. Donald Broadribb. Leiden: E. J. Brill, 1964.
Metzger, Bruce M. *Index of Articles on the New Testament and the Early Church Published in* Festschriften. *JBL* Monograph Series 5. Philadelphia: SBL, 1951.
———. *Index to Periodical Literature on Christ and the Gospels.* NTTS 6. Leiden: E. J. Brill, 1966.
———. *Index to Periodical Literature on the Apostle Paul.* NTTS 1. Leiden: E. J. Brill, 1960.
———. *A Textual Commentary on the Greek New Testament.* London: United Bible Societies, 1971.
Mills, Watson E. *A Bibliography of the Periodical Literature on the Acts of the Apostles, 1962-1984.* Supplements to *NovT* 58. Leiden: E. J. Brill, 1986.
The NIV Study Bible. New International Version with Study Notes and References, Concordance and Maps. Ed. Kenneth Barker. London: Hodder and Stoughton; Grand Rapids: Zondervan, 1987.
Theological Dictionary of the New Testament. Ed. and trans. Geoffrey W. Bromily. 10 vols. (Index, vol. 10, comp. Ronald E. Pitkin). Grand Rapids: Eerdmanns,

1964–78. From *Theologisches Wörterbuch zum Neuen Testament.* 10 vols. Ed. Gerhard Kittel (vols. 1–4) and Gerhard Friedrich (5–10). Stuttgart: W. Kohlhammer, 1932–78.

GENERAL

Achtemeier, Paul J. *The Quest for Unity in the New Testament Church: A Study in Paul and Acts.* Philadelphia: Fortress, 1987.
Alon, Gedalyahu. "The Levitical Uncleanness of Gentiles." In the author's *Jews, Judaism, and the Classical World: Studies in Jewish History in the Times of the Second Temple and Talmud,* trans. Israel Abrahams, pp. 146–89. Jerusalem: Magnes, 1977.
Aquinas, St. Thomas. *Commentary on Saint Paul's Epistle to the Galatians.* Trans. F. R. Larcher. Albany: Magi Books, 1966.
Arichea, Daniel Castillo, Jr. "A Critical Analysis of the Stephen Speech in the Acts of the Apostles." Ph.D. diss., Duke University, 1965.
Aune, David E. "Orthodoxy in First Century Judaism? A Response to N. J. McEleney." *JSJ* 7 (1976): 1–10.
Bacon, Benjamin Wisner. "Stephen's Speech: Its Argument and Doctrinal Relationship." In *Biblical and Semitic Studies: Critical and Historical Essays by the Members of the Semitic and Biblical Faculty of Yale University,* pp. 211–76. London: Edward Arnold; New York: Charles Scribner's Sons, 1901.
Barnard, L. W. "Saint Stephen and Early Alexandrian Christianity." *NTS* 7 (1960): 31–45.
Barr, James. *The Semantics of Biblical Language.* Oxford: Oxford University Press, 1961.
Barrett, C. K. "Acts and Christian Consensus." In *Context: Essays in Honour of Peder Borgen,* ed. Peter Wilhelm Bockman and Roald E. Kristiansen, pp. 19–33. Relieff 24. Trondheim: Tapir, 1987.
———. *A Commentary on the Epistle to the Romans.* Black's New Testament Commentaries. London: Adam and Charles Black, 1957.
———. *Essays on Paul.* London: SPCK, 1982.
———. *The First Epistle to the Corinthians.* 2d ed. London: Adam and Charles Black, 1973.
———. *Freedom and Obligation: A Study of the Epistle to the Galatians.* London: SPCK, 1985.
———. *The New Testament Background: Selected Documents.* Rev. ed. London: SPCK, 1987.
———. *New Testament Essays.* London: SPCK, 1972.
———. "Old Testament History according to Stephen and Paul." In *Studien zum Text und zur Ethik des Neuen Testaments: Festschrift zum 80. Geburtstag von Heinrich Greeven,* ed. W. Schrage, pp. 57–69. BZNW 47. Berlin: de Gruyter, 1986.
———. "Paul's Opponents in II Corinthians." *NTS* 17 (1971): 233–54.
———. *The Second Epistle to the Corinthians.* Black's New Testament Commentaries. London: A. and C. Black, 1986.

———. "Stephen and the Son of Man." In *Apophoreta: Festschrift für Ernst Haenchen zu seinem siebzigsten Geburtstag am 10. Dezember 1964*, pp. 32–38. BZNW 30. Berlin: Alfred Töpelmann, 1964.

Bauernfeind, Otto. *Die Apostelgeschichte*. THKNT 5. Leipzig: A. Deichertsche, 1939.

———. "Die Begegnung zwischen Paulus und Kephas Gal 1 18-20." *ZNW* 47 (1956): 269–70.

Baumgarten, A. I. "The Name of the Pharisees." *JBL* 102 (1983): 411–28.

Baumgarten, Michael. *The Acts of the Apostles; or, The History of the Church in the Apostolic Age*. 3 vols. Clark's Foreign Theological Library, n.s., 2. Edinburgh: T. and T. Clark, 1854. Trans. A. J. W. Morrison (vols. 1–2) and Theodore Meyer (vol. 3) from *Die Apostelgeschichte oder der Entwickelungsgang der Kirche von Jerusalem bis Rom*. 3 vols. Halle: C. U. Schwetschke und Sohn, 1852.

Baur, Ferdinand Christian. "Beiträge zur Erklärung der Korinthierbriefe." 1. "Die Reisen des Apostels Paulus nach Korinth"; 2. "Die Gegner des Apostels"; 3. "Die Beisteuer für die Christen in Jerusalem"; 4. "Die Ekstasen des Apostels." *TJ* 9 (1850): 139–85.

———. "Die Christuspartei in der korinthischen Gemeinde, der Gegensatz des petrinischen und paulinischen Christenthums in der ältesten Kirche, der Apostel Petrus in Rom." *TZT* 4 (1831): 61–206.

———. "Einige weitere Bemerkungen über die Christuspartei in Corinth." *TZT* 4 (1836): 1–32.

———. *History of the Church in the First Three Centuries*. 3d ed. 2 vols. London: Williams and Norgate, 1878–79. Trans. Allan Menzies from *Das Christenthum und die christliche Kirche der drei ersten Jahrhunderte*. 2d ed. Tübingen: Fues, 1860.

———. *Paul, the Apostle of Jesus Christ, His Life and Works, His Epistles and Teachings: A Contribution to a Critical History of Primitive Christianity*. 2 vols. Theological Translation Fund Library. London: Williams and Norgate, 1873–75. Trans. A. P. Menzies (vol. 1) and A. Menzies (vol. 2) from *Paulus, der Apostel Jesu Christi: Sein Leben und Wirken, seine Briefe und seine Lehre*. 2d ed. (issued after the author's death by E. Zeller). 2 vols. Leipzig: Fues (L. W. Reisland), 1866–67.

Beare, Francis Wright. *The Gospel according to Matthew: A Commentary*. Oxford: Basil Blackwell, 1981.

———. "The Sequence of Events in Acts 9–15 and the Career of Peter." *JBL* 62 (1943): 295–306.

Beker, J. Christiaan. *Paul the Apostle: The Triumph of God in Life and Thought*. Edinburgh: T. and T. Clark; Philadelphia: Fortress, 1980.

Betz, Hans Dieter. *Galatians: A Commentary on Paul's Letter to the Churches in Galatia*. Hermeneia. Philadelphia: Fortress, 1979.

———. Review of *Stephen: A Singular Saint*, by Martin H. Scharlemann. *Interp* 23 (1969): 252.

Bickerman, Elias J. *The Jews in the Greek Age*. Cambridge: Harvard University Press, 1988.

Bihler, Johannes. "Der Stephanusbericht (Apg 6,8-15 und 7,54 – 8,2)." *BZ* 3 (1959): 252–70.

———. *Der Stephanusgeschichte im Zusammenhang der Apostelgeschichte*. Münchener Theologische Studien 16. Munich: Max Hueber, 1963.

Blackman, E. C. "The Hellenists of Acts vi. 1." *ExpTim* 48 (1937): 524–25.

Bligh, John. *Galatians: A Discussion of St. Paul's Epistle.* Householder Commentaries 1. London: St. Paul Publications, 1969.
———. *Galatians in Greek.* Detroit: University of Detroit Press, 1966.
Blunt, A. W. F. *The Acts of the Apostles in the Revised Version, with Introduction and Commentary.* Clarendon Bible. Oxford: Clarendon, 1946.
———. *The Epistle of Paul to the Galatians.* Clarendon Bible. Oxford: Clarendon, 1942.
Boismard, M.-É. "Le martyre d'Étienne: Actes 6,8–8,2." *RSR* 69 (1981): 181-94.
Boman, Thorlief. *Hebrew Thought Compared with Greek.* Library of History and Doctrine. London: SCM; Philadelphia: Westminster, 1960. Trans. Jules L. Moreau from *Das hebräische Denken im Vergleich mit dem Griechischen.* 2d ed. Göttingen: Vandenhoeck und Ruprecht, 1954 (and including the author's revisions to 1960).
Bonnard, Pierre. *L'Épitre de Saint Paul aux Galates.* 2d ed. Commentaire du Nouveau Testament 9. Paris: Delachaux et Niestlé, 1972.
Borgen, Peder. *Paul Preaches Circumcision and Pleases Men, and Other Essays on Christian Origins.* Trondheim: Tapir, 1983.
Bornkamm, Günther. *Paul.* London: Hodder and Stoughton, 1985. Trans. M. G. Stalker from *Paulus.* Urban Bücher 119. Stuttgart: W. Kohlhammer, 1969.
Boussett, Wilhelm. *Kyrios Christos: A History of the Belief in Christ from the Beginnings of Christianity to Irenaeus.* Nashville: Abingdon, 1970. Trans. John E. Steely from *Kyrios Christos: Geschichte des Christusglaubens von den Anfängen des Christentums bis Irenaeus.* 5th ed. FRLANT 21, n.s., 4. Göttingen: Vandenhoeck und Ruprecht, 1964.
Brandon, S. G. F. *The Fall of Jerusalem and the Christian Church.* London: SPCK, 1951.
Brawley, Robert L. *Luke-Acts and the Jews: Conflict, Apology, and Conciliation.* SBL Monograph Series 33. Atlanta: Scholars, 1987.
Bring, Ragnar. *Commentary on Galatians.* Philadelphia: Muhlenberg, 1961. Trans. Eric Wahlstrom from *Pauli Brev till Galaterna.* Stockholm: Svenska Kyrkans Diakonistyrelses Bokförlag, 1958.
Brodie, Thomas Louis. "The Accusing and Stoning of Naboth (1 Kgs 21:8-13) as One Component of the Stephen Text (Acts 6:9-14; 7:58a)." *CBQ* 45 (1983): 417-32.
Brown, Raymond E., and John P. Meier. *Antioch and Rome: New Testament Cradles of Catholic Christianity.* London: Cassell, 1983.
Brown, Raymond E. "Not Jewish Christianity and Gentile Christianity but Types of Jewish/Gentile Christianity." *CBQ* 45 (1983): 74-79.
Brown, Raymond E., Karl P. Donfried, and John Reumann, eds. *Peter in the New Testament: A Collaborative Assessment by Protestants and Roman Catholic Scholars.* Minneapolis: Augsburg; New York: Paulist Press, 1973.
Brown, Scott Kent. "James: A Religio-historical Study of the Relations between Jewish, Gnostic, and Catholic Christianity in the Early Period through an Investigation of the Traditions about James the Lord's Brother." Ph.D. diss., University of California at Berkeley, 1967.
Bruce, F. F. "The Acts of the Apostles." In *The New Bible Commentary: Revised,* ed. D. Guthrie and J. A. Motyer, pp. 968-1011. 3d ed. London: Inter-Varsity; Grand Rapids: Eerdmans, 1976.
———. *The Acts of the Apostles: The Greek Text, with Introduction and Commentary.* 2d ed. London: Tyndale, 1956.

———. "The Church of Jerusalem in the Acts of the Apostles." *BJRL* 67 (1985): 641–61.
———. *Commentary on the Book of Acts: The English Text, with Introduction, Exposition, and Notes.* New London Commentary on the New Testament. London: Marshall, Morgan and Scott, 1954.
———. *The Epistle of Paul to the Galatians: A Commentary on the Greek Text.* Exeter: Paternoster, 1982.
———. *I and II Corinthians.* New Century Bible Commentary. London: Marshall, Morgan and Scott; Grand Rapids: Eerdmans, 1971.
———. *New Testament History.* 4th ed. Basingstoke: Pickering and Inglis, 1982.
———. *Peter, Stephen, James, and John: Studies in Early Non-Pauline Christianity.* Grand Rapids: Eerdmans, 1980.
———. *The Speeches in the Acts of the Apostles.* Tyndale New Testament Lecture, 1942. London: Tyndale, 1943.
———. "The Speeches in Acts—Thirty Years After." In *Reconciliation and Hope: New Testament Essays on Atonement and Eschatology Presented to L. L. Morris on His 60th Birthday*, ed. Robert Banks, pp. 53–68. Grand Rapids: Eerdmans; Exeter: Paternoster, 1974.
Brunner, Emil. *The Letter to the Romans: A Commentary.* London: Lutterworth, 1959. Trans. H. A. Kennedy from *Der Römerbrief.* Bibelhilfe für die Gemeinde 6, 3d ed. Kassel: J. G. Oncken, 1956.
Bultmann, Rudolf. *Primitive Christianity in Its Contemporary Setting.* Meridian Books. Cleveland: World, 1970. Trans. R. H. Fuller from *Das Urchristentum im Rahmen der antiken Religionen.* Zürich: Artemis, 1949.
———. *The Second Letter to the Corinthians.* Minneapolis: Augsburg, 1985. Trans. Roy A. Harrisville from *Die zweite Brief an die Korinther.* Ed. Erich Dinkler. KEKNT. Göttingen: Vandenhoeck und Ruprecht, 1976.
———. *Theology of the New Testament.* 2 vols. London: SCM, 1952–55. Trans. Kendrick Grobel from *Theologie des Neuen Testament.* 3 vols. Neue Theologische Grundrisse. Tübingen: J. C. B. Mohr (Paul Siebeck), 1948–53.
———. "Zur Frage nach den Quellen der Apostelgeschichte." In *New Testament Essays: Studies in Memory of Thomas Walter Manson, 1893–1958*, ed. A. J. B. Higgins, pp. 68–80. Manchester: Manchester University Press, 1959.
Burton, Ernest De Witt. *The Epistle to the Galatians.* ICC. Edinburgh: T. and T. Clark, 1980.
Cadbury, Henry J., and Kirsopp Lake. *The Beginnings of Christianity.* Vol. 5, *English Translation and Commentary.* London: Macmillan, 1933.
Cadbury, Henry J. *The Book of Acts in History.* London: Adam and Charles Black, 1955.
———. "Four Features of Lucan Style." In *Studies in Luke-Acts: Studies Presented in Honor of Paul Schubert, Buckingham Professor of New Testament Criticism and Interpretation at Yale University*, ed. Leander E. Keck and J. Louis Martyn, pp. 87–102. London: SPCK, 1978.
———. *The Making of Luke-Acts.* New York: Macmillan, 1927.
———. *The Style and Literary Method of Luke.* Vol. 1, *The Diction of Luke and Acts;* Vol. 2, *The Treatment of Sources in the Gospel.* HTS 6. Cambridge: Harvard University Press; London: Oxford University Press, 1919–20.
Caird, George B. *The Apostolic Age.* London: Gerald Duckworth, 1955.

Chadwick, Henry. *The Early Church.* Pelican History of the Church. Ed. Owen Chadwick. Harmondsworth: Penguin, 1978.
Coggins, R. J. "The Samaritans and Acts." *NTS* 28 (1982): 423-34.
———. *Samaritans and Jews: The Origins of Samaritanism Reconsidered.* Oxford: Basil Blackwell, 1975.
Cohen, Shaye J. D. "The Political and Social History of the Jews in Greco-Roman Antiquity: The State of the Question." In *Early Judaism and Its Modern Interpreters,* ed. R. A. Kraft and G. W. E. Nickelsburg, pp. 33-56. The Bible and Its Modern Interpreters 2. Philadelphia: Fortress; Atlanta: Scholars, 1986.
Collins, Raymond F. *Studies on the First Letter to the Thessalonians.* BETL 66. Louvain: Louvain University Press, 1984.
Conzelmann, Hans. *Acts of the Apostles: A Commentary on the Acts of the Apostles.* Ed. Eldon Jay Epp with Christopher R. Matthews. Hermeneia. Philadelphia: Fortress, 1987. Trans. James Limburg, A. Thomas Kraabel, and Donald H. Juel from *Die Apostelgeschichte.* 2d ed. Handbuch zum Neuen Testament 7. Tübingen: J. C. B. Mohr (Paul Siebeck), 1972.
———. *History of Primitive Christianity.* London: Darton, Longman and Todd, 1973. Trans. John E. Steely from *Geschichte des Urchristentums.* Grundrisse zum Neuen Testament, Das Neue Testament Deutsch, Ergänzungsreihe 5. Göttingen: Vandenhoeck und Ruprecht, 1969.
———. *The Theology of St. Luke.* New York: Harper and Row, 1961. Trans. Geoffery Buswell from *Die Mitte der Zeit.* 2d ed. Tübingen: J. C. B. Mohr (Paul Siebeck), 1957.
Cousar, Charles B. *Galatians.* Atlanta: John Knox, 1982.
Cousins, Peter. "Stephen and Paul." *EvQ* 33 (1961): 157-62.
Cragg, Kenneth. *Paul and Peter: Meeting in Jerusalem.* London: Bible Reading Fellowship, 1980.
Cranfield, C. E. B. *A Critical and Exegetical Commentary on the Epistle to the Romans.* 2 vols. ICC. Edinburgh: T. and T. Clark, 1979.
Cross, Frank Moore, Jr. "Aspects of Samaritan and Jewish History in Late Persian and Hellenistic Times." *HTR* 59 (1966): 201-11.
Cullmann, Oscar. "The Significance of the Qumran Texts for Research into the Beginnings of Christianity." *JBL* 74 (1955): 213-26.
Daube, David. *The New Testament and Rabbinic Judaism.* Jordan Lectures, 1952. London: University of London, Athlone Press, 1956.
———. "A Reform in Acts and Its Models." In *Jews, Greeks, and Christians: Festschrift für W. D. Davies,* pp. 151-63. Leiden: E. J. Brill, 1976.
Davies, W. D. *Jewish and Pauline Studies.* Philadelphia: Fortress, 1984.
———. *Paul and Rabbinic Judaism: Some Rabbinic Elements in Pauline Theology.* London: SPCK, 1948.
Dehandschutter, B. "La persécution des chrétiens dans les Actes des Apôtres." In *Les Actes des Apôtres: Traditions, rédaction, théologie,* pp. 541-46. BETL 48. Leuven: Leuven University Press; Gembloux: J. Duculot, 1979.
Dexinger, Ferdinand. "Limits of Tolerance in Judaism: The Samaritan Example." In *Jewish and Christian Self-Definition,* ed. E. P. Sanders et al., 2:88-114, 327-38. 3 vols. London: SCM, 1980-82.

Dibelius, Martin. *From Tradition to Gospel*. London: Ivor Nicholson and Watson, 1934. Trans. Betram Lee Woolf from *Die Formgeschichte des Evangeliums*. 2d ed. Tübingen: J. C. B. Mohr (Paul Siebeck), 1933.

———. *James*. Ed. Helmut Koester. Hermeneia. Philadelphia: Fortress, 1976. Trans. Michael A. Williams from *Der Brief des Jakobus*. Rev. Heinrich Greevan. 11th ed. KEKNT 15. Göttingen: Vandenhoeck und Ruprecht, 1964.

———. *Studies in the Acts of the Apostles*. Ed. Heinrich Greeven. London: SCM, 1956. Trans. Marz Ling and Paul Schubert from *Aufsätze zur Apostelgeschichte*. Ed. Heinrich Greeven. FRLANT, n.s., 42. Göttingen: Vandenhoeck und Ruprecht, 1951.

Dillon, Richard J., and Joseph A. Fitzmyer. "Acts of the Apostles." In *Jerome Biblical Commentary*, ed. Raymond E. Brown et al., 2:165–214. 2 vols. Englewood Cliffs, N.J.: Prentice-Hall, 1968.

Dixon, W. S. *Analysis of the "Acts of the Apostles," with Appendices and Notes, for Undergraduates and Schools*. Oxford: James Thornton; London: Simpkin, Marshall, Hamilton, Kent, 1899.

Doble, P. "The Son of Man Saying in Stephen's Witnessing: Acts 6.8 – 8.2." *NTS* 31 (1985): 68–84.

Dodd, C. H. *The Epistle of Paul to the Romans*. Moffatt New Testament Commentary. London: Hodder and Stoughton, 1947.

Donfried, Karl Paul, ed. *The Romans Debate*. Minneapolis: Augsburg, 1977.

Dudley, Merle Bland. "The Speeches in Acts." *EvQ* 50 (1978): 147–55.

Duncan, George S. *The Epistle of Paul to the Galatians*. Moffatt New Testament Commentary. London: Hodder and Stoughton, 1934.

Dunn, James D. G. "The Incident at Antioch (Gal. 2:11-18)." *JSNT* 18 (1983): 3–57.

———. "Mark 2.1 – 3.6: A Bridge between Jesus and Paul on the Question of the Law." *NTS* 30 (1984): 395–415.

———. "The Relationship between Paul and Jerusalem according to Galatians 1 and 2." *NTS* 28 (1982): 461–78.

———. *Unity and Diversity in the New Testament: An Inquiry into the Character of Earliest Christianity*. Philadelphia: Westminster; London: SCM, 1977.

Dupont, Jacques. *Les Actes des Apôtres*. Including an introduction to Acts by L. Cerfaux. La Sainte Bible. Paris: Les Éditions du Cerf, 1953.

———. "Pierre et Paul à Antioche et à Jerusalem." *RSR* 45 (1957): 42–60, 225–39.

———. *The Salvation of the Gentiles: Essays on the Acts of the Apostles*. New York: Ramsey; Toronto: Paulist, 1979. Trans. J. R. Keating from *Études sur les Actes des Apôtres*. Lectio Divina 45. Paris: Les Éditions du Cerf, 1967.

———. *The Sources of Acts: The Present Position*. London: Darton, Longman and Todd, 1964. Trans. Kathleen Pond from *Les sources du Livre des Actes: État de la question*. Brugge: Desclée De Brouwer, 1960.

Easton, Burton Scott. "Jewish Christianity." In *The Interpreter's Bible* 12, ed. George Arthur Buttrick, pp. 6–9. New York: Abingdon, 1957.

Ehrhardt, Arnold. *The Acts of the Apostles: Ten Lectures*. Manchester: Manchester University Press, 1970.

Ellis, E. Earle. "The Circumcision Party and the Early Christian Mission." In the author's *Prophecy and Hermeneutic in Early Christianity*, pp. 116–28. WUNT 18. Tübingen: J. C. B. Mohr (Paul Siebeck), 1978.

Esler, Philip F. *Community and Gospel in Luke-Acts: The Social and Political Motivations of Lucan Theology.* SNTSMS 57. Cambridge: Cambridge University Press, 1987.
Evans, Ernest. *The Epistles of Paul to the Corinthians.* Clarendon Bible. Oxford: Clarendon, 1930.
Feldman, Louis H. "Hengel's *Judaism and Hellenism* in Retrospect." *JBL* 96 (1977): 371–82.
Ferguson, Everett. "The Hellenists in the Book of Acts." *RestQ* 12 (1969): 159–80.
Ferguson, John. "Athens and Jerusalem." *RelS* 8 (1972): 1–13.
Filson, Floyd V. *A New Testament History: The Story of the Emerging Church.* New Testament Library. London: SCM, 1965; Westminster Aids to the Study of the Scriptures. Philadelphia: Westminster, 1964.
———. *Three Crucial Decades: Studies in the Book of Acts.* London: Epworth, 1964.
Fitzmyer, Joseph A. "Jewish Christianity in Acts in the Light of the Qumran Scrolls." In the author's *Essays on the Semitic Background of the New Testament,* pp. 271–303. London: Geoffrey Chapman, 1971.
Foakes Jackson, F. J. *The Acts of the Apostles.* London: Hodder and Stoughton, 1938.
Foakes Jackson, F. J., and Kirsopp Lake, eds. *The Beginnings of Christianity.* Part 1, *The Acts of the Apostles.* 5 vols. London: Macmillan, 1920–33.
Foakes Jackson, F. J. *The Rise of Gentile Christianity.* London: Hodder and Stoughton, 1927.
———. "Stephen's Speech in Acts." *JBL* 49 (1930): 283–86.
Fotheringham, D. R. "Acts xi. 20." *ExpTim* 45 (1933–34): 430.
Furneaux, William Mordaunt. *The Acts of the Apostles.* Oxford: Clarendon, 1912.
Furnish, Victor. "The Place and Purpose of Philippians iii." *NTS* 10 (1963–64): 80–88.
Gaechter, Paul. "Geschichtliches zum Apostelkonzil." *ZKT* 85 (1963): 339–54.
———. "Petrus in Antiochia (Gal. 2:11-14)." *ZKT* 72 (1950): 177–212.
Gager, John G. *The Origins of Anti-Semitism: Attitudes toward Judaism in Pagan and Christian Antiquity.* New York: Oxford University Press, 1983.
Gasque, W. Ward. *A History of the Criticism of the Acts of the Apostles.* 2d ed. Peabody, Mass.: Hendrickson, 1989. First published as BGBE 17. Tübingen: J. C. B. Mohr (Paul Siebeck), 1975.
Gaston, Lloyd. "Anti-Judaism and the Passion Narrative in Luke and Acts." In *Anti-Judaism in Early Christianity.* Vol. 1, *Paul and the Gospels,* ed. Peter Richardson with David Granskou, pp. 127–53. Studies in Christianity and Judaism 2. Waterloo, Ontario: Wilfrid Laurier University Press, 1986.
———. *No Stone on Another: Studies in the Significance of the Fall of Jerusalem in the Synoptic Gospels.* Supplements to *NovT* 23. Leiden: E. J. Brill, 1970.
———. "Paul and Jerusalem." In *From Jesus to Paul: Studies in Honour of F. W. Beare,* ed. Peter Richardson and John C. Hurd, pp. 61–72. Waterloo, Ontario: Wilfrid Laurier University Press, 1984.
Georgi, Dieter. *The Opponents of Paul in Second Corinthians.* Studies of the New Testament and Its World. Edinburgh: T. and T. Clark, 1987. Trans. by the author from *Die Gegner des Paulus im 2. Korintherbrief: Studien zur religiösen Propaganda in der Spätantike.* WMANT 11. Neukirchen-Vluyn: Neukirchener, 1964.
Glasson, T. Francis. "The Speeches in Acts and Thucydides." *ExpTim* 76 (1965): 165.

Glombitza, Otto. "Zur Charakterisierung des Stephanus in Act 6 und 7." *ZNW* 53 (1962): 238-44.
Goguel, Maurice. *The Birth of Christianity.* London: George Allen and Unwin, 1953. Trans. H. C. Snape from *La naissance du Christianisme.* Paris: Payot, 1946.
———. *The Primitive Church.* London: George Allen and Unwin, 1953. Trans. H. C. Snape from *L'église primitive.* Payot: Paris, 1947.
Goodman, Martin. *The Ruling Class of Judaea: The Origins of the Jewish Revolt against Rome, A.D. 66-70.* Cambridge: Cambridge University Press, 1987.
———. *State and Society in Roman Galilee, A.D. 132-212.* Towanda, N.J.: Rowman and Allanheld, 1983.
Goppelt, Leonhard. *Theologie des Neuen Testaments.* Ed. Jürgen Roloff. Göttingen: Vandenhoeck und Ruprecht, 1976.
Grabbe, Lester L. "Orthodoxy in First Century Judaism: What Are the Issues?" *JSJ* 8 (1977): 149-53.
Groh, Dennis E., and Robert Jewett, eds. *The Living Text: Essays in Honor of Ernest W. Saunders.* Lanham, Md.: University Press of America, 1985.
Grundmann, Walter. "Das Problem des hellenistischen Christentums innerhalb der Jerusalemer Urgemeinde." *ZNW* 38 (1939): 45-73.
Gundry, Robert A. *Matthew: A Commentary on His Literary and Theological Art.* Grand Rapids: Eerdmans, 1982.
Gutbrod, Walter. Notes on Ἑβραῖος (in the study of Ἰσραήλ). *TDNT* 3: 388-91.
Guthrie, Donald. *Galatians.* Rev. ed. New Century Bible. London: Oliphants (Marshall, Morgan and Scott), 1974.
Haenchen, Ernst. *The Acts of the Apostles: A Commentary.* Philadelphia: Westminster, 1971. Trans. Bernard Noble and Gerald Shinn, rev. R. M. Wilson, from *Die Apostelgeschichte.* 14th ed. KEKNT. Göttingen: Vandenhoeck und Ruprecht, 1965.
———. "Petrus-Probleme." *NTS* 7 (1960-61): 187-97.
———. "Quellenanalyse und Kompositionsanalyse in Act 15." In *Judentum, Urchristentum, Kirche: Festschrift für Joachim Jeremias,* pp. 153-64. BZNW 26. Berlin: Verlag Alfred Töpelmann, 1960.
Hahn, Ferdinand. *Titles of Jesus in Christology.* London: Butterworth, 1969. Trans. Harold Knight and George Ogg from *Christologische Hoheitstitel: Ihre Geschichte im frühen Christentum.* FRLANT 83. Göttingen: Vandenhoeck und Ruprecht, 1963.
Hanson, John S., and Richard A. Horsley. *Bandits, Prophets, and Messiahs: Popular Movements in the Time of Jesus.* Minneapolis: Winston, 1985.
Hanson, Paul D. *The Acts in the Revised Standard Version, with Introduction and Notes.* Oxford: Clarendon, 1967.
———. "Prolegomena to the Study of Jewish Apocalyptic." In *Magnalia Dei. The Mighty Acts of God: Essays on the Bible and Archaeology in Memory of G. Ernest Wright,* ed. F. M. Cross et al., pp. 389-413. Garden City, N.Y.: Doubleday, 1976.
Hanson, R. P. C. "Ye Stiffnecked and Uncircumcised in Heart and Ears." *Th* 50 (1947): 142-45.
Harnack, Adolf von. *The Mission and Expansion of Christianity in the First Three Centuries.* Introduction and bibliography by Jaroslav Pelikan. New York:

Harper and Brothers, 1961. Ed. and trans. James Moffatt from *Die Mission und Ausbereitung des Christentums in den ersten drei Jahrhunderten*. 2d ed. 2 vols. Leipzig: J. C. Hinrichs'sche, 1906.

———. *New Testament Studies*. Vol 3, *The Acts of the Apostles*. Crown Theological Library 27. London: Williams and Norgate; New York: G. P. Putnam's Sons, 1909. Trans. J. R. Wilkinson from *Beiträge zur Einleitung in das Neue Testament*. Vol. 3, *Die Apostelgeschichte*. Leipzig: J. C. Hinrichs, 1908.

Hemer, Colin J. *The Book of Acts in the Setting of Hellenistic History*. Ed. Conrad H. Gempf. WUNT 49. Tübingen: J. C. B. Mohr (Paul Siebeck), 1989.

Hengel, Martin. "Acts and the History of Earliest Christianity." In the author's *Earliest Christianity*. Philadelphia: Fortress, 1979. Trans. John Bowden from *Zur urchristlichen Geschichtsschreibung*. Stuttgart: Calwer, 1979.

———. *Between Jesus and Paul: Studies in the Earliest History of Christianity*. London: SCM, 1983. Articles trans. John Bowden as follows:

1. "Between Jesus and Paul" (pp. 1–29, 133–56) = "Zwischen Jesus und Paulus: Die 'Hellenisten,' die 'Sieben,' und Stephanus (Apg 6,1-15; 7,54–8,3)." *ZTK* 72 (1975): 151–206.
2. "Christology and New Testament Chronology" (pp. 30–47, 156–66) = "Christologie und neutestamentliche Chronologie: Zu einer Aporie in der Geschichte des Urchristentums." In *Neues Testament und Geschichte: Historisches Geschehen und Deutung im Neuen Testament. Oscar Cullman zum 70. Geburtstag,* ed. Heinrich Baltensweiler and Bo Reicke, pp. 43–67. Zurich: Theologischer Verlag; Tübingen: J. C. B. Mohr (Paul Siebeck), 1972.
3. "The Origins of the Christian Mission" (pp. 48–64, 166–79) = "Die Ursprünge der christlichen Mission." *NTS* 18 (1971): 15–38.
4. "'Christos' in Paul" (pp. 65–77, 179–88) = "Erwägungen zum Sprachgebrauch von Χριστός bei Paulus und in der 'vorpaulinischen' Überlieferung." In *Paul and Paulinism: Essays in Honour of C. K. Barrett,* ed. M. D. Hooker and S. G. Wilson, pp. 135–59. London: SPCK, 1982.
5. "Hymns and Christology" (pp. 78–96, 188–90) = "Hymnus und Christologie." In *Wort in der Zeit: Festgabe für Karl Heinrich Rengstorf zum 75. Geburtstag,* ed. Wilfred Haubeck and Michael Bachmann, pp. 1–23. Leiden: E. J. Brill, 1980.
6. "Luke the Historian and the Geography of Palestine in the Acts of the Apostles" (pp. 97–128, 190–210) = "Der Historiker Lukas und die Geographie Palästinas in der Apostelgeschichte." *ZDPV* 99 (1983): 147–83.

———. *Jews, Greeks, and Barbarians: Aspects of the Hellenization of Judaism in the Pre-Christian Period*. Philadelphia: Fortress; London: SCM, 1980. Trans. John Bowden from *Juden, Griechen, und Barbaren: Aspekte der Hellenisierung des Judentums in vorchristlicher Zeit*. Stuttgarter Bibelstudien 76. Stuttgart: Katholisches Bibelwerk, 1976.

———. *Judaism and Hellenism: Studies in Their Encounter in Palestine during the Early Hellenistic Period*. 2d ed. 2 vols. London: SCM, 1981. Trans. John Bowden from *Judentum und Hellenismus: Studien zu ihrer Begegnung unter besonderer Berücksichtigung Palästinas bis zur Mitte des 2 Jh.s v. Chr.* Ed. Joachim Jeremias and Otto Michael. 2d ed. 2 vols. WUNT 10. Tübingen: J. C. B. Mohr (Paul Siebeck), 1973.

———. *The Zealots: Investigations into the Jewish Freedom Movement in the Period from Herod I until 70 A.D.* Edinburgh: T. and T. Clark, 1989. Trans. David Smith from *Die Zeloten: Untersuchungen zur Jüdischen Freiheitsbewegung in der Zeit von Herodes I. bis 70 n. Chr.* 2d ed. Leiden: E. J. Brill, 1976.

Hodge, Charles. *Commentary on the Epistle to the Romans.* Grand Rapids: Eerdmans, 1974.

Holmberg, Bengt. *Paul and Power: The Structure of Authority in the Primitive Church As Reflected in the Pauline Epistles.* Lund: Studentlitteratur AB, 1978.

Holtz, Traugott. "Die Bedeutung des Apostelkonzils für Paulus." *NovT* 16 (1974): 110–48.

———. *Untersuchungen über die alttestamentlichen Zitate bei Lukas.* TU 104. Berlin: Akademie, 1968.

Holtzmann, H. J. *Die Apostelgeschichte.* 3d ed. Hand-Commentar zum Neuen Testament 1.2. Tübingen: J. C. B. Mohr (Paul Siebeck), 1901.

Hornblower, Simon. *Thucydides.* London: Gerald Duckworth, 1987.

Horsley, Richard. *Jesus and the Spiral of Violence: Popular Jewish Resistance in Roman Palestine.* San Francisco: Harper and Row, 1987.

Howard, George. *Crisis in Galatia: A Study in Early Christian Theology.* SNTSMS 35. Cambridge: Cambridge University Press, 1979.

Hyldahl, Niels. *Die paulinische Chronologie.* Acta Theologica Danica 19. Leiden: E. J. Brill, 1986.

Jacquier, E. *Les Actes des Apôtres.* 2d ed. Paris: Librairie Victor Lecoffre, 1926.

Jaeger, Werner. *Early Christianity and Greek Paideia.* London: Oxford University Press, 1961.

Jeremias, Joachim. "Untersuchungen zum Quellenproblem der Apostelgeschichte." *ZNW* 36 (1937): 205–21.

Jervell, Jacob. "The Acts of the Apostles and the History of Early Christianity." *ST* 37 (1983): 17–32.

———. *Luke and the People of God: A New Look at Luke-Acts.* Minneapolis: Augsburg, 1972.

———. "The Mighty Minority." *ST* 34 (1980): 13–38.

———. "Paul in the Acts of the Apostles: Tradition, History, Theology." In *Les Actes des Apôtres: Traditions, rédaction, théologie.* BETL 48, pp. 297-306. Leuven: Leuven University Press; Gembloux: J. Duculot, 1979.

———. "The Unknown Paul." In the author's *The Unknown Paul: Essays on Luke-Acts and Early Christian History.* Minneapolis: Augsburg, 1984. Trans. by the author from "Der unbekannte Paulus." In *Die Paulinische Literature und Theologie,* ed. Sigfred Pederson, pp. 29–49. Skandinavische Beiträge. Aarhus: Forlaget Aros; Göttingen: Vandenhoeck und Ruprecht, 1980.

Jewett, Robert. "The Agitators and the Galatian Congregation." *NTS* 17 (1970–71): 198–212.

———. *A Chronology of Paul's Life.* Philadelphia: Fortress, 1979.

———. "The Epistolary Thanksgiving and the Integrity of Philippians." *NovT* 12 (1970): 40–53.

———. *The Thessalonian Correspondence: Pauline Rhetoric and Millenarian Piety.* Foundations and Facets: New Testament. Philadelphia: Fortress, 1986.

Johnson, Luke T. *The Writings of the New Testament: An Interpretation.* Philadelphia: Fortress; London: SCM, 1986.

Jones, Alan H. *Independence and Exegesis: The Study of Early Christianity in the Work of Alfred Loisy (1857–1940), Charles Guignebert (1857–1939), and Maurice Goguel (1880–1955)*. BGBE 26. Tübingen: J. C. B. Mohr (Paul Siebeck), 1983.
Jones, Maurice. "The Significance of St. Stephen in the History of the Primitive Christian Church." *Exp*, ser. 8, 13 (1917): 161–78.
Käsemann, Ernst. "Die Legitimät des Apostels: Eine Untersuchung zu II Korinther 10–13." *ZNW* 41 (1942): 33–71.
Keck, Leander E., and J. Louis Martyn, eds. *Studies in Luke-Acts: Studies Presented in Honor of Paul Schubert, Buckingham Professor of New Testament Criticism and Interpretation at Yale University*. London: SPCK, 1978.
Kilgallen, John. *A Brief Commentary on the Acts of the Apostles*. New York: Paulist Press, 1988.
———. *The Stephen Speech: A Literary and Redactional Study of Acts 7,2–53*. Analecta Biblica 67. Rome: Biblical Institute, 1976.
Kilpatrick, George D. "Acts vii.56: Son of Man?" *TZ* 21 (1965): 209.
———. "Again Acts vii.56: Son of Man?" *TZ* 34 (1978): 232.
———. "Galatians I:18 ΙΣΤΟΡΗΣΑΙ ΚΗΦΑΝ." In *New Testament Essays: Studies in Memory of Thomas Walter Manson, 1893–1958*, ed. A. J. B. Higgins, pp. 144–49. Manchester: Manchester University Press, 1959.
———. "Some Quotations in Acts." In *Les Actes des Apôtres: Traditions, rédaction, théologie*. BETL 48, pp. 81–97. Leuven: Leuven University Press; Gembloux: J. Duculot, 1979.
Klijn, A. F. J. "Stephen's Speech – Acts VII. 2–53." *NTS* 4 (1957): 25–31.
Knox, John. *Chapters in the Life of Paul*. Nashville: Abingdon, 1950.
Knox, Wilfred L. *The Acts of the Apostles*. Cambridge: Cambridge University Press, 1948.
———. *St. Paul*. London: Thomas Nelson and Son, 1938.
———. *St. Paul and the Church of Jerusalem*. Cambridge: Cambridge University Press, 1925.
———. *St. Paul and the Church of the Gentiles*. Cambridge: Cambridge University Press, 1961.
Koester, Helmut. *Introduction to the New Testament: History, Culture, and Religion of the Hellenistic Age*. 2 vols. Philadelphia: Fortress, 1982. Trans. by the author from *Einführung in das Neue Testament im Rahmen der Religionsgeschichte und Kulturgeschichte der hellenistichen und römischen Zeit*. Berlin: De Gruyter, 1980.
———. "Philippians (Letter to the)." *IDB*, suppl. vol. pp. 665–66.
Kraabel, A. Thomas. "The Roman Diaspora: Six Questionable Assumptions." *JJS* 33 (1982): 445–64.
———. "Traditional Christian Evidence for Diaspora Judaism: The Book of Acts." In *Society of Biblical Literature 1986 Seminar Papers*, ed. Kent Harold Richards, pp. 644–51. SBL Seminar Papers 25. Atlanta: Scholars, 1985.
Kraft, Robert A. "The Multiform Jewish Heritage of Early Christianity." In *Christianity, Judaism, and Other Greco-Roman Cults: Studies for Morton Smith at Sixty*. Part 3, *Judaism before 70*, ed. J. Neusner, pp. 174–99. Studies in Judaism in Late Antiquity 12. Leiden: E. J. Brill, 1975.
Krodel, Gerhard. *Acts*. Augsburg Commentary on the New Testament. Minneapolis: Augsburg, 1986.

Kümmel, Werner Georg. *Introduction to the New Testament.* Rev. ed. Nashville: Abingdon, 1975. Trans. Howard Clark Kee from *Einleitung in das Neue Testament.* 17th ed. Heidelberg: Quelle und Meyer, 1973.

———. *The New Testament: The History of the Investigation of Its Problems.* New Testament Library. London: SCM, 1973. Trans. S. McLean Gilmour and Howard C. Kee from *Das Neue Testament: Geschichte der Erforschung seiner Probleme.* 2d ed. Stuttgart: Karl Alber, 1970.

Lake, Kirsopp. *The Earlier Epistles of St. Paul.* London: Rivingtons, 1911.

Larsson, Edvin. "Die Hellenisten und die Urgemeinde." *NTS* 33 (1987): 205–25.

Laws, Sophie. *A Commentary on the Epistle of James.* Black's New Testament Commentaries. London: Adam and Charles Black, 1980.

Lechler, Gotthard Victor. *The Apostolic and Post-Apostolic Times: Their Diversity and Unity in Life and Doctrine.* 3d ed. 2 vols. Edinburgh: T. and T. Clark, 1886. Trans. A. J. K. Davidson from *Das apostolische und das nachapostolische Zeitalter: Mit Rücksicht auf Unterschied und Einheit in Leben und Lehre.* 3d ed. Karlsruhe: H. Reuther, 1885.

Lechler, Gotthard Victor, and K. Gerok. *Theological and Homiletical Commentary on the Acts of the Apostles, Specially Designed and Adapted for the Use of Ministers and Students.* 2 vols. Clark's Foreign Theological Library, 4th ser., 21 and 24. Edinburgh: T. and T. Clark, 1864. Trans. Paton J. Gloag from *Der Apostel Geschichten. Theologisch-homiletisches Bibelwerk. Des Neuen Testaments 5.* Bielefeld: Velhagen und Klasing, 1860.

Lienhard, Joseph T. "Acts 6:1-6: A Redactional View." *CBQ* 37 (1975): 228–36.

Lietzmann, Hans. *An die Korinther I, II.* Handbuch zum Neuen Testament 9. 5th ed., including supplements by W. G. Kümmel. Tübingen: J. C. B. Mohr (Paul Siebeck), 1969.

———. *The Beginnings of the Christian Church.* International Library of Christian Knowledge. London: Ivor Nicholson and Watson, 1937. Trans. Bertram Lee Woolf from *Geschichte der Alten Kirche.* Vol. 1, *Die Anfänge.* Berlin: Walter de Gruyter, 1932.

Lightfoot, J. B. *Essays on the Work Entitled Supernatural Religion: Reprinted from The Contemporary Review.* London: Macmillan, 1889.

———. *Saint Paul's Epistle to the Galatians: A Revised Text with Introduction, Notes, and Dissertations.* 10th ed. London:: Macmillan, 1900.

Lim, Timothy H. "Not in Persuasive Words of Wisdom, but in the Demonstration of the Spirit and Power." *NovT* 29 (1987): 137–49.

Loisy, Alfred. *Les Actes des Apôtres.* Paris: Émile Nourry, 1920.

———. *The Birth of the Christian Religion.* London: George Allen and Unwin, 1948. Trans. L. P. Jacks from *La naissance du Christianisme.* Paris: Émile Nourry, 1933.

———. *L'Épitre aux Galates.* Paris: Émile Nourry, 1916.

Longenecker, Richard N. "The Acts of the Apostles." In *John-Acts,* ed. Frank E. Gaebelein, pp. 205–573. Expositor's Bible Commentary 9. Grand Rapids: Zondervan, 1981.

Luce, H. Kenneth. *The Acts of the Apostles (Revised Version): Edited with Introduction and Notes for the Use of Schools.* London: A. and C. Black, 1947.

Lüdemann, Gerd. *Early Christianity according to the Traditions in Acts: A Commentary.* London: SCM, 1989. Trans. John Bowden from *Das frühe Christentum nach den*

Traditionen der Apostelgeschichte: Ein Kommentar. Göttingen: Vandenhoeck und Ruprecht, 1987.

———. *Opposition to Paul in Jewish Christianity*. Minneapolis: Fortress, 1989. Trans. M. Eugene Boring from *Paulus, der Heidenapostel*. Vol. 2, *Antipaulinismus im frühen Christentum*. FRLANT 130. Göttingen: Vandenhoeck und Ruprecht, 1983.

———. *Paul, Apostle to the Gentiles: Studies in Chronology*. London: SCM; Philadelphia: Fortress, 1984. Trans. F. Stanley Jones from *Paulus, der Heidenapostel*. Vol. 1, *Studien zur Chronologie*. FRLANT 123. Göttingen: Vandenhoeck und Ruprecht, 1980.

———. "Zum Antipaulinismus im frühen Christentum." *EvT* 40 (1980): 437–55.

Luther, Martin. *A Commentary on St. Paul's Epistle to the Galatians*. Ed. and Trans. Philip S. Watson. London: James Clarke, 1961.

McCaughey, J. D. "The Intention of the Author: Some Questions about the Exegesis of Acts 6:1-6." *AusBR* 7 (1959): 27–36.

McClelland, Scott E. "Super-Apostles, Servants of Christ, Servants of Satan: A Response." *JSNT* 14 (1982): 82–87.

Macdonald, John. *The Theology of the Samaritans*. London: SCM, 1964.

McEleney, Neil J. "Orthodoxy in Judaism of the First Christian Century." *JSJ* 4 (1973): 19–42.

———. "Orthodoxy in Judaism of the the First Christian Century: Replies to David E. Aune and Lester L. Grabbe." *JSJ* 9 (1978): 83–88.

Maddox, Robert. *The Purpose of Luke-Acts*. Studies in the New Testament and Its World. Edinburgh: T. and T. Clark, 1985. First published as FRLANT 126. Göttingen: Vandenhoek und Ruprecht, 1982.

Malina, B. J. "Jewish Christianity: A Select Bibliography." *AusJBA* 2 (1973): 60–65.

Mann, C. S. "'Hellenists' and 'Hebrews' in Acts VI 1." In *The Acts of the Apostles*, by Johannes Munck, rev. William F. Albright and C. S. Mann, pp. 301–4 (Appendix 6). Anchor Bible 31. Garden City, N.Y.: Doubleday, 1967.

Manson, T. W. "St. Paul's Letter to the Romans—and Others." *BJRL* 21 (1948): 224–40.

———. "Stephen and the World-Mission of Christianity." In the author's *The Epistle to the Hebrews: An Historical and Theological Reconsideration*, pp. 25–46. The Baird Lecture, 1949. London: Hodder and Stoughton, 1961.

Mare, W. Harold. "Acts 7: Jewish or Samaritan in Character?" *WTJ* 34 (1971): 1–21.

Marshall, I. Howard. *The Acts of the Apostles: An Introduction and Commentary*. Ed. Leon Morris. Leicester: Inter-Varsity, 1980.

———. *1 and 2 Thessalonians*. New Century Bible Commentary. London: Marshall Morgan and Scott; Grand Rapids: Eerdmans, 1983.

———. "Palestinian and Hellenistic Christianity: Some Critical Comments." *NTS* 19 (1972–73): 271–87.

Martyn, J. Louis. "A Law-Observant Mission to Gentiles: The Background of Galatians." *SJT* 38 (1985): 307–24.

Meeks, Wayne A., and Robert L. Wilken. *Jews and Christians in Antioch in the First Four Centuries of the Common Era*. SBL Sources for Biblical Study 13. Missoula, Mont.: Scholars, 1978.

Meyer, Ben F. *The Early Christians: Their World Mission and Self-Discovery.* Good News Studies 16. Wilmington, Del.: Michael Glazier, 1986.
Meyer, Eduard. *Ursprung und Anfänge des Christentums.* 3 vols. Vol. 3, *Die Apostelgeschichte und die Anfänge des Christentums.* Stuttgart: J. G. Cotta'sche Buchhandlung Nachfolger, 1923.
Meyer, Heinrich August Wilhelm. *Critical and Exegetical Handbook to the Acts of the Apostles.* Ed. William P. Dickson. 2 vols. Critical and Exegetical Commentary on the New Testament 4. Edinburgh: T. and T. Clark, 1877. Trans. Paton J. Gloag from *Kritisch exegetisches Handbuch über die Apostelgeschichte.* 4th ed. KEKNT 3. Göttingen: Vandenhoeck und Ruprecht, 1870.
Meyers, Eric M. "Ancient Synagogues in Galilee: Their Religious and Cultural Setting." *BA* 43 (1980): 97–108.
Moessner, David P. "Paul and the Pattern of the Prophet like Moses in Acts." In *Society of Biblical Literature 1983 Seminar Papers,* ed. Kent Harold Richards, pp. 203–12. SBL Seminar Papers 22. Chico, Calif.: Scholars Press, 1983.
Morgan, Robert. "Biblical Classics II. F. C. Baur: Paul." *ExpTim* 90 (1978): 4–10.
Moule, C. F. D. *The Birth of the New Testament.* Black's New Testament Commentaries. 3d ed. London: Adam and Charles Black, 1981.
———. "Once More, Who Were the Hellenists?" *ExpTim* 70 (1958–59): 100–102.
Moxnes, Halvor. *Theology in Conflict: Studies in Paul's Understanding of God in Romans.* Supplements to *NovT* 53. Leiden: E. J. Brill, 1980.
Munck, Johannes. *The Acts of the Apostles.* Rev. William F. Albright and C. S. Mann. Anchor Bible 31. Garden City, N.Y.: Doubleday, 1967.
———. *Paul and the Salvation of Mankind.* London: SCM, 1959. Reprint. Atlanta: John Knox, 1977. Trans. Frank Clarke from *Paulus und die Heilsgeschichte.* Acta Jutlandica. Publications of the University of Aarhus 26.1. Copenhagen: Ejnar Munksgaard; Aarhus: Universitetsforlaget, 1954.
———. "Sanctuary and Sacrifice in the Church of the New Testament." *JTS,* n.s., 1 (1950): 29–41.
Mundle, Wilhelm. "Die Stephanusrede Apg. 7: Eine Märtyrerapologie." *ZNW* 20 (1921): 133–47.
Mussner, Franz. *Apostelgeschichte.* Echter-Verlag Kommentar zum Neuen Testament mit der Einheitsübersetzung 5. Würzburg: Echter, 1984.
Neander, Augustus. *History of the Planting and Training of the Christian Church by the Apostles.* 2 vols. Biblical Cabinet; or, Hermeneutical, Exegetical, and Philological Library 35–36. Edinburgh: Thomas Clark, 1842. Trans. J. E. Ryland from *Geschichte der Pflanzung und Leitung der christlichen Kirche durch die Apostel, als selbständiger Nachtrag zu der allgemeinen Geschichte der christlichen Religion und Kirche.* 3d ed. 2 vols. Hamburg: Friedrich Perthes, 1841.
Neil, William. *The Acts of the Apostles.* New Century Bible. London: Oliphants (Marshall, Morgan and Scott), 1973.
Neill, Stephen, and Tom Wright. *The Interpretation of the New Testament, 1861–1961.* Firth Lectures, 1962. New ed. Oxford: Oxford University Press, 1988.
———. *Paul to the Galatians.* New York: Association Press, 1958.
Nestle, Eberhard. "Acts 7:55–56." *ExpTim* 11 (1899–1900): 94.
———. "Sirs, Ye Are Brethren." *ExpTim* 23 (1911–12): 528.
———. "The Vision of Stephen." *ExpTim* 22 (1910–11): 423.

Neudorfer, Heinz-Werner. *Der Stephanuskreis in der Forschungsgeschichte seit F. C. Baur.* Monographien und Studienbücher 309. Giessen: Brunnen, 1983.
Neusner, Jacob. *From Politics to Piety: The Emergence of Pharisaic Judaism.* Englewood Cliffs, N.J.: Prentice-Hall, 1973.
Nickelsburg, George W. E., with Robert A. Kraft. "Introduction: The Modern Study of Early Judaism." In *Early Judaism and Its Modern Interpreters,* ed. R. A. Kraft and G. W. E. Nickelsburg, pp. 1–30. Bible and Its Modern Interpreters 2. Philadelphia: Fortress; Atlanta: Scholars, 1986.
Niven, W. D. *The Conflicts of the Early Church.* London: Hodder and Stoughton, 1930.
O'Neill, John C. *The Theology of Acts in its Historical Setting.* London: SPCK, 1961.
Overbeck, Franz. "Introduction to the Acts." In *The Contents and Origin of the Acts of the Apostles Critically Investigated,* by Eduard Zeller, 1:31–64. 2 vols. Theological Translation Fund. Edinburgh: Williams and Norgate, 1875–76.
Owen, H. P. "Steven's Vision in Acts VII. 55-6." *NTS* 1 (1954–55): 224–26.
Page, Thomas Ethelbert. *The Acts of the Apostles, Being the Greek Text As Revised by Drs Wescott and Hort, with Explanatory Notes.* London: Macmillan, 1895.
Pahncke, Karl H. "Der Stephanismus der Apostelgeschichte." *TSK* 85 (1912): 1–38.
Pesch, Rudolf. *Die Apostelgeschichte.* 2 vols. EKKNT 5.1-2. Neukirchen-Vluyn: Neukirchener; Zurich: Benzinger, 1986.
Pesch, Rudolf, E. Gerhart, and F. Schilling. "'Hellenisten' und 'Hebräer': Zu Apg 9, 29 und 6, 1." *BZ,* n.s., 23 (1979): 87–92.
Polhill, John B. "The Hellenist Breakthrough: Acts 6–12." *RevExp* 71 (1974): 475–86.
Porton, Gary G. "Diversity in Postbiblical Judaism." In *Early Judaism and Its Modern Interpreters,* ed. R. A. Kraft and G. W. E. Nickelsburg, pp. 57–80. Bible and Its Modern Interpreters 2. Philadelphia: Fortress; Atlanta: Scholars, 1986.
Preuschen, Erwin. *Die Apostelgeschichte.* Handbuch zum Neuen Testament 4.1. Tübingen: J. C. B. Mohr (Paul Siebeck), 1912.
Pummer, Reinhard. "The Samaritan Pentateuch and the New Testament." *NTS* 22 (1975–76): 441–43.
Purvis, James D. "The Fourth Gospel and the Samaritans." *NovT* 17 (1975): 161–98.
Rackham, Richard Belward. *The Acts of the Apostles: An Exposition.* Oxford Commentaries. London: Methuen, 1901.
Räisänen, Heikki. *Paul and the Law.* Tübingen: Mohr, 1983.
———. *The Torah and Christ: Essays in German and English on the Problem of the Law in Early Christianity.* Publications of the Finnish Exegetical Society 45. Helsinki: Kirjapaino Raamattutalo, 1986.
Ramsay, William M. *The Church in the Roman Empire before* A.D. *170.* Mansfield College Lectures, 1892. London: Hodder and Stoughton, 1883.
———. *A Historical Commentary on St. Paul's Epistle to the Galatians.* London: Hodder and Stoughton, 1899.
———. *St. Paul the Traveller and Roman Citizen.* Morgan Lectures, 1894, and Mansfield College Lectures, 1895. London: Hodder and Stoughton, 1895.
Reicke, Bo. "Der geschichtliche Hintergrund des Apostelkonzils und der Antiochia-Episode, Gal. 2, 1–14." In *Studia Paulina in honorem J. de Zwaan septuagenarii,* ed. J. N. Sevenster and W. C. van Unnik, pp. 172–87. Haarlem: De Erven F. Bohn N. V., 1953.

———. *The New Testament Era: The World of the Bible from 500 B.C. to A.D. 100.* London: Adam and Charles Black, 1978. Trans. David E. Green from *Neutestamentliche Zeitgeschichte: Die biblische Welt von 500 v. chr. bis 100 n. chr.* Sammlung Töpelmann 2.2. Berlin: Alfred Töpelmann, 1965.

Rénan, Ernest. *The Apostles.* London: N. Trübner, 1869. Trans. from *Histoire des origines du christianisme.* Vol. 2, *Les apôtres.* Paris: Michel Lévy Frères, 1866.

Rhoads, David M. *Israel in Revolution: 6–74 C.E. A Political History Based on the Writings of Josephus.* Philadelphia: Fortress, 1979.

Richard, Earl. *Acts 6:1–8:4: The Author's Method of Composition.* SBL Dissertation Series 41. Missoula, Mont.: Scholars, 1978.

———. "Acts 7: An Investigation of the Samaritan Evidence." *CBQ* 39 (1977): 190–208.

———. "The Creative Use of Amos by the Author of Acts." *NovT* 24 (1982): 37–53.

———. "The Old Testament in Acts: Wilcox's Semitisms in Retrospect." *CBQ* 42 (1980): 330–41.

———. "The Polemical Character of the Joseph Episode in Acts 7." *JBL* 98 (1979): 255–67.

Richardson, Peter, and John C. Hurd, eds. *From Jesus to Paul: Studies in Honour of F. W. Beare.* Waterloo, Ontario: Wilfrid Laurier University Press, 1984.

Richardson, Peter. *Israel in the Apostolic Church.* SNTSMS 10. Cambridge: Cambridge University Press, 1969.

———. "Pauline Inconsistency: I Corinthians 9:19-23 and Galatians 2:11-14." *NTS* 26 (1980): 347–62.

———. *Paul's Ethic of Freedom.* Philadelphia: Westminster, 1979.

Ridderbos, Herman Nicolas. *The Epistle of Paul to the Churches of Galatia.* Trans. from the Dutch by H. Zystra. 2d ed. London: Marshall, Morgan and Scott, 1954.

———. *Paul: An Outline of His Theology.* Grand Rapids: Eerdmans, 1975. Trans. John Richard De Witt from *Paulus: Ontwerp van zijn theologie.* Kampen: Uitgeversmaatschappij J. H. Kok N. V., 1966.

———. *Paul and Jesus: Origin and General Character of Paul's Preaching of Christ.* Trans. from the Dutch by David H. Freeman. Philadelphia: Presbyterian and Reformed, 1958.

Rieu, C. H. *The Acts of the Apostles by Saint Luke.* Penguin Classics. Harmondsworth: Penguin, 1957.

Ritschl, Albrecht. *Die Entstehung der altkatholischen Kirche.* 2d ed. Bonn: Adolph Marcus, 1857.

Robinson, James M., and Helmut Koester. *Trajectories through Early Christianity.* Philadelphia: Fortress, 1971.

Roloff, Jürgen. *Die Apostelgeschichte.* 17th ed. Neues Testament Deutsch. Neues Göttinger Bibelwerk 5. Göttingen: Vandenhoeck und Ruprecht, 1981.

Ropes, James Hardy. *A Critical and Exegetical Commentary on the Epistle of St. James.* ICC. Edinburgh: T. and T. Clark, 1978.

Rowland, Christopher. *Christian Origins: An Account of the Setting and Character of the most Important Messianic Sect of Judaism.* London: SPCK, 1987.

Sabbe, M. "The Son of Man Saying in Acts 7, 56." In *Les Actes des Apôtres: Traditions, rédaction, théologie.* BETL 48, pp. 241–79. Leuven: Leuven University Press; Gembloux: J. Duculot, 1979.

Safrai, S., and M. Stern (with D. Flusser and W. C. van Unnik), eds. *The Jewish People in the First Century: Historical Geography, Political History, Social, Cultural, and Religious Life and Institutions.* 2 vols. Compendia Rerum Iudaicarum ad Novum Testamentum. Assen: Van Gorcum, 1974.
Sanday, William, and Arthur C. Headlam. *A Critical and Exegetical Commentary on the Epistle to the Romans.* 5th ed. ICC. Edinburgh: T. and T. Clark, 1980.
Sanders, E. P. *Jesus and Judaism.* London: SCM, 1985.
———. "Jewish Association with Gentiles and Gal. 2.11-14." In *The Conversation Continues: Studies in John and Paul In Honor of J. Louis Martyn,* ed. Robert T. Fortna and Beverly R. Gaventa, 170-188. Nashville: Abingdon, 1990.
———. *Jewish Law from Jesus to the Mishnah: Five Studies.* Philadelphia: Trinity; London: SCM, 1990.
———. *Paul and Palestinian Judaism: A Comparison of Patterns of Religion.* Philadelphia: Fortress; London: SCM, 1977.
———. "Paul on the Law, His Opponents, and the Jewish People in Philippians 3 and 2 Corinthians 11." In *Anti-Judaism in Early Christianity,* ed. Peter Richardson with David Granskou (vol. 1) and Stephen G. Wilson (vol. 2), 2:75-90. 2 vols. Waterloo, Ontario: Wilfrid Laurier University Press, 1986.
———. *Paul, the Law, and the Jewish People.* Philadelphia: Fortress, 1983.
———. "Purity, Food, and Offerings in the Greek-Speaking Diaspora." In the author's *The Jewish Law from Jesus to the Mishnah.* Philadelphia: Trinity; London: SCM, 1990.
———. Review of *Between Jesus and Paul: Studies in the Earliest History of Christianity,* by Martin Hengel. *JTS* 37 (1986): 167-72.
Sanders, Jack T. "The Jewish People in Luke-Acts." In *Society of Biblical Literature 1986 Seminar Papers,* ed. Kent Harold Richards, pp. 110-29. SBL Seminar Papers 25. Atlanta: Scholars, 1985.
———. *The Jews in Luke-Acts.* London: SCM, 1987.
———. "The Salvation of the Jews in Luke-Acts." In *Society of Biblical Literature 1982 Seminar Papers,* ed. Kent Harold Richards, pp. 467-83. SBL Seminar Papers 21. Chico, Calif.: Scholars, 1982.
Sandmel, Samuel. "Palestinian and Hellenistic Judaism and Christianity: The Question of the Comfortable Theory." *Hebrew Union College Annual* 50 (1979): 137-48.
Scharlemann, Martin H. *Stephen: A Singular Saint.* Analecta Biblica 34. Rome: Pontifical Biblical Institute, 1968.
Schille, Gottfried. *Die Apostelgeschichte des Lukas.* THKNT 5. Berlin: Evangelische Verlagsanstalt, 1983.
Schlatter, Adolf. *Die Apostelgeschichte.* Schlatters Erläuterungen zum Neuen Testament 4. Stuttgart: Calwer Verlag, 1948.
———. *Die Briefe an die Galater, Epheser, Kolosser und Philemon.* Schlatters Erläuterungen zum Neuen Testament 7. Stuttgart: Calwer Verlag, 1949.
Schlier, Heinrich. *Der Brief an die Galater.* 5th ed. KEKNT 7. Göttingen: Vandenhoeck und Ruprecht, 1971.
Schmidt, Woldemar Gottlob. *Der Bericht der Apostelgeschichte über Stephanus.* Leipzig: Alexander Edelmann, 1882.

Schmithals, Walt[h]er. *Die Apostelgeschichte des Lukas.* Zürcher Bibelkommentare NT 3.2. Zurich: Theologischer Verlag, 1982.
———. *Paul and James.* Studies in Biblical Theology 46. London: SCM, 1965. Trans. Dorothea M. Barton from *Paulus und Jakobus.* FRLANT 85. Göttingen: Vandenhoeck und Ruprecht, 1963.
Schneider, Gerhard. *Die Apostelgeschichte.* 2 vols. Herders Theologischer Kommentar zum Neuen Testament 5. Freiburg: Herder, 1980-82.
———. *The Epistle to the Galatians.* New Testament for Spiritual Reading. London: Burns and Oates, 1969. Trans. Kevin Smyth from *Der Brief an die Galater.* Geistliche Schriftlesung. Ed. Wolfgang Trilling with Karl Hermann Schelkle and Heinz Schürmann. Düsseldorf: Patmos-Verlag, 1964.
———. "Stephanus, die Hellenisten und Samaria." In *Les Actes des Apôtres: Traditions, rédaction, théologie.* BETL 48, 215-40. Leuven: Leuven University Press; Gembloux: J. Duculot, 1979.
Schürer, Emil. *The History of the Jewish People in the Age of Jesus Christ (175 B.C.-A.D. 135).* 2d ed. 3 vols. Organizing ed. Matthew Black. Rev., trans., and ed. Geza Vermes, Fergus Millar, and Martin Goodman (vol. 3). Adapted from Schürer's *Geschichte des jüdischen Volkes im Zeitalter Jesu Christi.* Edinburgh: T. and T. Clark, 1973-87.
Schweizer, Eduard. "Concerning the Speeches in Acts." In *Studies in Luke-Acts: Studies Presented in Honor of Paul Schubert, Buckingham Professor of New Testament Criticism and Interpretation at Yale University,* ed. Leander E. Keck and J. Louis Martyn, pp. 208-16. London: SPCK, 1978.
———. "The Son of Man." *JBL* 79 (1960): 119-29.
Scobie, Charles H. H. "The Origins and Development of Samaritan Christianity." *NTS* 19 (1972-73): 390-414.
———. "The Use of Source Material in the Speeches of Acts III and VII." *NTS* 25 (1979): 399-421.
Scott, James Julius, Jr. "The Church of Jerusalem, A.D. 30-100: An Investigation of the Growth of Internal Factions and the Extension of Its Influence in the Larger Church." Ph.D. diss., University of Manchester, 1969.
———. "Parties in the Church of Jerusalem As Seen in the Book of Acts." *JETS* 18 (1975): 217-27.
———. "Stephen's Defense and the World Mission of the People of God." *JETS* 21 (1978): 131-41.
———. "Stephen's Speech: A Possible Model for Luke's Historical Method?" *JETS* 17 (1974): 91-97.
Scroggs, Robin. "The Earliest Hellenistic Christianity." In *Religions in Antiquity: Essays in Memory of Erwin Ramsdell Goodenough,* ed. Jacob Neusner, SHR 14, pp. 176-206. Leiden: E. J. Brill, 1968.
Seccombe, David. "Was There Organized Charity in Jerusalem before the Christians?" *JTS,* n.s., 29 (1978): 140-43.
Selwyn, E. G. "St. Stephen's Place in Christian Origins." *Th* 5 (1922): 306-16.
Simon, Marcel. *St. Stephen and the Hellenists.* Haskell Lectures, 1956. London: Longmans, Green, and Company, 1958.

———. "St. Stephen and the Jerusalem Temple." *JEH* 2 (1951): 127-42.
Smith, Dennis E. "Social Obligations in the Context of Communal Meals: A Study of the Christian Meal in 1 Corinthians in Comparison with Graeco-Roman Communal Meals." Th.D. diss., Harvard Divinity School, 1980.
Smith, Morton. "Palestinian Judaism in the First Century." In *Israel: Its Role in Civilization,* ed. Moshe Davis, pp. 67-81. New York: Seminary Israel Institute of the Jewish Theological Seminary of America, 1956.
———. "Zealots and Sicarii, Their Origins and Relation." *HTR* 64 (1971): 1-19.
Soltau, Wilhelm. "Die Herkunft der Reden in der Apostelgeschichte." *ZNW* 4 (1903): 128-54.
Spiro, Abram. "Stephen's Samaritan Background." In *The Acts of the Apostles,* by J. Munck, pp. 285-300. Anchor Bible 31. New York: Doubleday, 1967.
Stählin, Gustav. *Die Apostelgeschichte.* 11th ed. Neues Testament Deutsch. Neues Göttinger Bibelwerk 5. Göttingen: Vandenhoek und Ruprecht, 1966.
Stanton, Graham. "Stephen in Lucan Perspective." In *Studia Biblica, 1978.* Vol. 3, *Papers on Paul and Other New Testament Authors,* ed. E. A. Livingston, pp. 345-60. From the Sixth International Congress on Biblical Studies. *JSNT* suppl. ser. 3. Sheffield: JSOT Press, 1980.
Stern, Menahem. *Greek and Latin Authors on Jews and Judaism.* 3 vols. Jerusalem: Israel Academy of Sciences and Humanities, 1976-1984.
Strange, James F. "Diversity in Early Palestinian Christianity: Some Archaeological Evidences." *ATR* 65 (1983): 14-24.
Sylva, Dennis D. "The Meaning and Function of Acts 7:46-50." *JBL* 106 (1987): 261-75.
Synge, F. C. "Studies in Texts: Acts 7:46." *Th* 55 (1952): 25-26.
Tannehill, Robert C. *The Narrative Unity of Luke-Acts: A Literary Interpretation.* Vol. 1, *The Gospel according to Luke.* Philadelphia: Fortress, 1986.
———. *The Narrative Unity of Luke-Acts: A Literary Interpretation.* Vol. 2, *The Acts of the Apostles.* Minneapolis: Fortress, 1990.
———. "Rejection by Jews and Turning to Gentiles: The Pattern of Paul's Mission in Acts." In *Society of Biblical Literature 1986 Seminar Papers,* ed. Kent Harold Richards, pp. 130-41. SBL Seminar Papers 25. Atlanta: Scholars, 1985.
Thornton, T. C. G. "Stephen's Use of Isaiah LXVI. 1." *JTS,* n.s., 25 (1974): 432-34.
Thrall, Margaret E. "Super-Apostles, Servants of Christ, and Servants of Satan." *JSNT* 6 (1980): 42-57.
Tiede, David L. "'Glory to Thy People Israel!': Luke-Acts and the Jews." In *Society of Biblical Literature 1986 Seminar Papers,* ed. Kent Harold Richards. pp. 142-51. SBL Seminar Papers 25. Atlanta: Scholars, 1985.
Torrey, Charles Cutler. *The Composition and Date of Acts.* HTS 1. Cambridge: Harvard University Press; London: Oxford University Press, 1916.
———. "James the Just, and His Name 'Oblias.'" *JBL* 63 (1944): 93-98.
Trocmé, Étienne. *Le "Livre des Actes" et l'histoire.* Études d'Histoire et de Philosophie Religieuses 45. Paris: Presses Universitaires de France, 1957.
Trudinger, Paul. "Stephen and the Life of the Primitive Church." *BTB* 14 (1984): 18-22.

Tyson, Joseph B. "The Emerging Church and the Problem of Authority in Acts." *Interp* 42 (1988): 132–45.

———. "The Problem of Food in Acts: A Study of Literary Patterns with Particular Reference to Acts 6: 1-7." In *Society of Biblical Literature 1979 Seminar Papers*, ed. Paul J. Achtemeier, 1:69–85. 2 vols. SBL Seminar Papers 16. Missoula, Mont.: Scholars, 1979.

Veltman, Fred. "The Defense Speeches of Paul in Acts." In *Perspectives on Luke-Acts*, ed. Charles H. Talbert, pp. 243–56. Special Studies Series 5. Danville, Va: Association of Baptist Professors of Religion; Edinburgh: T. and T. Clark, 1978.

Via, E. Jane. "An Interpretation of Acts 7:35-37 from the Perspective of Major Themes in Luke-Acts." In *Society of Biblical Literature 1978 Seminar Papers*, ed. Paul J. Achtemeier, 2:209–22. 2 vols. SBL Seminar Papers 14. Missoula: Scholars Press, 1978.

Vielhauer, Philipp. "On the 'Paulinism' of Acts." In *Studies in Luke-Acts: Studies Presented in Honor of Paul Schubert, Buckingham Professor of New Testament Criticism and Interpretation at Yale University*, ed. Leander E. Keck and J. Louis Martyn, pp. 33–50. London: SPCK, 1978.

Waal, C. van der. "The Temple in the Gospel according to Luke." In *Essays on the Gospel of Luke and Acts*, pp. 49–59. *Neotestamentica* 7 (1973).

Walter, Nikolaus. "Apostelgeschichte 6.1 und die Anfänge der Urgemeinde in Jerusalem." *NTS* 29 (1983): 370–93.

Watson, Francis. *Paul, Judaism, and the Gentiles: A Sociological Approach.* SNTSMS 56. Cambridge: Cambridge University Press, 1986.

Webber, Martin I. "Iakobos Ho Dikaios: Origins, Literary Expression, and Development of Traditions about the Brother of the Lord in Early Christianity." Ph.D. diss., Fuller Theological Seminary, 1985.

Weiser, Alfons. *Die Apostelgeschichte.* 2 vols. Ökumenischer Taschenbuch-kommentar zum Neuen Testament 5.1-2. Gütersloh: Gütersloher Verlagshaus Mohn, 1981-85.

———. "Das 'Apostelkonzil' (Apg 15,1-35): Ereignis, Überlieferung, lukanische Deutung." *BZ*, n.s., 2 [=28] (1984): 145–67.

Weiser, Artur. *The Psalms: A Commentary.* London: SCM, 1962. Trans. H. Hartwell from *Die Psalmen.* 5th ed. 2 vols. *Das Alte Testament Deutsch 14 and 15.* Göttingen: Vandenhoeck und Ruprecht, 1959.

Weiss, Bernhard. *Die Apostelgeschichte: Textkritische Untersuchungen und Textherstellung.* TU 9. Leipzig: J. C. Hinrichs'sche, 1893.

Weiss, Johannes. *Earliest Christianity: A History of the Period* A.D. *30–150.* 2 vols. Harper Torchbooks. New York: Harper and Brothers, 1959. First published as *The History of Primitive Christianity.* Ed. Frederick C. Grant. New York: Wilson-Erickson, 1937. Trans. "four friends" from *Das Urchristentum.* Completed after the author's death by Rudolf Knopf. Göttingen: Vandenhoeck und Ruprecht, 1917.

———. "Das Judenchristentum in der Apostelgeschichte und das sogenannte Apostelkonzil." *TSK* (1893): 480–540.

Wellhausen, Julius. "Kritische Analyse der Apostelgeschichte." *Abhandlungen der königlichen Gesellschaft der Wissenschaften zu Göttingen, philologisch-historische Klasse,* n.s., 15.2 (1914): 1–56.
Wendt, Hans Hinrich. *Kritisch exegetisches Handbuch über die Apostelgeschichte.* 5th ed. KEKNT 3. Göttingen: Vandenhoeck und Ruprecht, 1880.
Wette, Wilhelm Martin Leberecht de. *Kurze Erklärung der Apostelgeschichte.* 2d ed. Kurzgefasstes exegetisches Handbuch zum Neuen Testament 1.4. Leipzig: Weidmann'sche, 1841.
Wilckens, Ulrich. *Der Brief an die Römer.* 3 vols. EKKNT 6.1–3. Neukirchen-Vluyn: Neukirchener; Zurich: Benziger, 1978–82.
———. *Die Missionsreden der Apostelgeschichte: Form- und traditionsgeschichtliche Untersuchungen.* 2d ed. WUNT 5. Neukirchen-Vluyn: Neukirchener, 1963.
Wilcox, Max. "A Foreword to the Study of the Speeches in Acts." In *Christianity, Judaism, and Other Greco-Roman Cults: Studies for Morton Smith at Sixty.* Part 1, *New Testament,* ed. Jacob Neusner, pp. 206–25. Studies in Judaism in Late Antiquity 12. Leiden: E. J. Brill, 1975.
———. *The Semitisms of Acts.* Oxford: Clarendon, 1965.
Wild, Robert A. "The Encounter between Pharisaic and Christian Judaism: Some Early Gospel Evidence." *NovT* 27 (1985): 105–24.
Williams, C. S. C. *A Commentary on the Acts of the Apostles.* 2d ed. Black's New Testament Commentaries. London: Adam and Charles Black, 1978.
Willink, M. D. R. "The Exodus in the New Testament." *Th* 30 (1935): 105–9.
Willis, Wendell Lee. *Idol Meat in Corinth: The Pauline Argument in I Corinthians 8 and 10.* SBL Dissertation Series 68. Chico, Calif.: Scholars, 1985.
Wilson, Jack H. "Luke's Role as a Theologian and Historian in Acts 6:1–8:3." Ph.D. diss., Emory University, 1962.
Wilson, Stephen G. "From Jesus to Paul: The Contours and Consequences of a Debate." In *From Jesus to Paul: Studies in Honour of F. W. Beare,* ed. Peter Richardson and John C. Hurd, pp. 1–21. Waterloo, Ontario: Wilfrid Laurier University Press, 1984.
———. *The Gentiles and the Gentile Mission in Luke-Acts.* SNTSMS 23. Cambridge: Cambridge University Press, 1973.
———. "The Jews and the Death of Jesus in Acts." In *Anti-Judaism in Early Christianity.* Vol. 1, *Paul and the Gospels,* ed. Peter Richardson with David Granskou, pp. 155–64. Studies in Christianity and Judaism 2. Waterloo, Ontario: Wilfrid Laurier University Press, 1986.
———. "Law and Judaism in Acts." In *Society of Biblical Literature 1980 Seminar Papers,* ed. Paul J. Achtemeier, pp. 251–65. SBL Seminar Papers 19. Chico, Calif.: Scholars, 1980.
———. *Luke and the Law.* SNTSMS 50. Cambridge: Cambridge University Press, 1983.
Windisch, Hans. Study of Ἕλλην. *TDNT* 2:504–16.
Wolff, L. "Der Bericht der Apostelgeschichte über Stephanus vertheidigt gegen die Angriffe Baur's." *ZLTK* 8 (1847): 86–97.
Zahn, Theodor. *Die Apostelgeschichte des Lucas.* 2 vols. Kommentar zum Neuen Testament 5.1–2. Leipzig: A. Deichert (Werner Scholl), 1919–21.

Zeller, Eduard. *The Contents and Origin of the Acts of the Apostles Critically Investigated.* Introduction by Franz Overbeck. 2 vols. Theological Translation Fund. Edinburgh: Williams and Norgate, 1875-76. Trans. Joseph Dare from *Die Apostelgeschichte nach ihrem Inhalt und Ursprung kritisch untersucht.* Stuttgart: Carl Mäcken, 1854.

Zeitlin, Solomon. "Zealots and Sicarii." *JBL* 81 (1962): 395-98.

Ziesler, John A. "Luke and the Pharisees." *NTS* 25 (1979): 146-57.

Topical Bibliography

A number of notes in the book contain or refer to sources of bibliographical information. Twenty of the most important of these are listed by topic below:

>Ancient historiography and the speeches of Acts, 51 *n. 43*
>Antiochene source, 55 *n. 64,* 93 *n. 279*
>Baur and the Tübingen school, 8 *n. 21*
>Cornelius, the conversion of, 122 *n. 77*
>Gal. 2:1-10 = Acts 11:27-30 (famine relief visit), 111 *n. 29,* 112 *nn. 31-32*
>Hellenists and Hebrews, history of the question, 5 *n. 1*
>Identification of the "Hellenists," 22-23 *n. 12*
>James, authorship of the Epistle of, 184 *n. 101*
>Jewish law referred to as "customs," 63 *n. 108*
>Jewish Revolt, pace of events, 130 *n. 107*
>Judaism and Hellenism, 1-2 *nn. 1-4*
>Opponents of Paul, 158 *n. 35,* 171 *n. 62*
>Opponents of Stephen, 28 *n. 34*
>Samaritan source, 95 *n. 291*
>Sources of Acts, 6:1—8:4, 50 *n. 39,* 55 *n. 64,* 93 *n. 279,* 95 *n. 291*
>Stephen in church tradition, 41 *n. 2*
>Stephen research, 41 *n. 3*
>Temple-criticism in Stephen's speech, 70 *n. 146*
>1 Thess. 2:14-16, the authenticity of, 36-37 *n. 69*
>Zealots, 130 *n. 106*

The most useful topical bibliography on subjects related to this book is Mattill and Mattill's *A Classified Bibliography of Literature on the Acts of the Apostles.* The commentaries of Ernst Haenchen and Gerhard Schneider on Acts also provide detailed bibliographies organized by subject and passage.

Index of Ancient Sources*

OLD TESTAMENT

Genesis
9	136
12	99
12:6-7	97
12:10	85
15	99
15:1-21	97
15:14	97
17:8	99
17:10-11	99
23:16	99
33:19	99
41:40	84-85
41:43	84-85
43:32	120
46:6	85
48:4	97
50:13	99

Exodus
1:9-22	86
2:13	88
2:24	85
3:5	85
3:6	85
3:7	85, 88
3:8	86
3:10	86
3:12	62, 97
6:26	86
6:26-27	85
7:3	85
18:13-27	25-26
28:38	177
32:1	85, 86
32:23	86
33:3	74
33:5	74
34:9	74

Leviticus
1:3-4	177
11:1-23	133
11:1-38	125
11:41-47	125
12	134
15:13-15	134
15:25-30	134
15:31	134
17-18	144
18:6-18	144
18:19-23	144
18:26	144
19:5	177
22:19-20	177
23:11	177
26:41	74
27:30	134

Numbers
11	25-26
19:20	134

Deuteronomy
1:9-18	25-16
2:5	76, 97
6:20-24	100
9:6	74
9:13	74
10:16	74
14:3-21	133
17:3	85
18:15	85, 87, 98
18:18	85, 87
26:5-9	100
34:11	85

Joshua
24:2-13	100
24:32	99

1 Samuel
13:14	87

2 Samuel
6	72-73
7:13	71-72
24:18	97

1 Kings
5:3	71, 73
5:5	73
6:2	71, 73
6:14	73
8:16-17	71
8:17-18	73
8:27	74, 77
8:37	9
21:1-16	65-66
28:24	97
28:38	97

1 Chronicles
21:18-26	97
28:19	97

2 Chronicles
1:4	72

*Principal passages are indicated by italics.

Index of Ancient Texts

2 Chronicles (*cont.*)		**Daniel**		15:34	59
3:1	97	1:3-17	119	15:37	59
6:41f.	72	7:25	64		
7:1	97			**Luke**	
		Amos		1:11-20	69
Nehemiah		5:25-27	79	1:26-38	69
9:6-31	100	5:26	85	2:9-15	69
				2:21	69
Job		**Malachi**		5:21	65
33:26	177	2:13	177	6:16	75
				6:22	60
Psalms		NEW TESTAMENT		6:27	37
31:5	60			9:31	98
78	100	**Matthew**		10:33	99
78:68-69	97	5:11-12	37	11:47-51	75
89:20	87	5:12	75	11:49-51	37
105	100	5:17-20	150	11:50	75
106	100	5:19	137	12:14	28
132	70-73	5:44	37	13:14	19
132:5	87	10:23	37	13:34	19, 75
135	100	12:18-21	150	13:34-35a	77-78
136	100	15:17	134	13:35	78, 81, 98
		15:17-20	137	17:16	99
Proverbs		15:20	134	19:41-44	19
11:1	177	21:33-41	69, 78, 81	20:9-18	78, 98
12:22	177	21:42-44	69	20:9-19	81
14:9	177	21:43	150	21:20-24	19
14:35	177	22:7	75	21:24b	78
15:8	177	23:3	137, 150	22	77
15:28a	177	23:23	150	22:4	63
16:13	177	23:30-35	75	22:21	63
22:11	177	23:31	75	22:48	63
		23:34-36	37	22:65	65
Isaiah		23:35	75	22:67	59
2:1-4	138, 176-77	23:37	75	22:69	59, 60
2:3	177	23:38	78, 81	23	30, 187
3:10	185	26:60-61	59	23:9-10	54
41:20	85	26:61	59, 62	23:24	60
42:1-9	138, 176	26:63	59	23:31	78
42:49	138, 176	27	30, 187	23:34	54, *59-61*
49:8	177	27:46	59	23:39	65
55:4-5	138, 176	27:50	59	23:46	*59-60*
56:7	177	28:19	150	24	124
58:5	177				
59:20-21	177	**Mark**		**John**	
60:1-7	138, 177	3:29	65	2:19	62
60:7	177	7:19	134, 137	2:21	62
63:10	74	12:1-12	78, 81	18:13	69, 190
66:1-2	85, 97	13:9	33	18-19	30, 187
66:18-23	138, 177	14:53	59	21:25	149
		14:55-56	61		
Jeremiah		14:56-57	59, 65	**Acts**	
4:4	74	14:58	59, 62, 64, 78	1:6	57
6:10	74	14:61	59	1:8	38-39
6:20	177	14:62	59	2	124
9:26	74	14:64	59	2:5	24
		15	30, 187	2:9-11	24
Ezekiel		15:5	54	2:17	25
44:7	74				

Acts (*cont.*)		6:13-14	56, *59-64*, 66	7:46	85		
2:22-24	57	6:14	56, 57, 59, 62-64,	7:46a	87		
2:23	60		77, 85, 97	7:46b	*70-71*		
2:29	57	6:15	56, 60, 86	7:46-50	*70-79*		
2:39	57	7:1	33, 59, *190*	7:47	70, 71, *73-74*		
2:44-45	26	7:1-54	54	7:47-50	98		
2:45	27	7:2	85, 87	7:48	59, 62, 74		
2:46	57	7:2-8	99	7:48-50	9, *76-77*, 80,		
3:1	57	7:2-53	53, 54, 68		97, 98		
3:13	63	7:4	85, 96	7:48-53	84, 100		
3:14	75	7:5	73, 76, 85, 96,	7:49	97		
3:17	78		97, 98	7:49-50	85		
3:17-19	78	7:6	85, 88	7:50	62		
3:17-26	60	7:7	62, 85, *97-98*	7:51	75, 76		
3:22-23	*87*, 98	7:8	73, 85	7:51-53	*74-75*, 80		
4:1f.	31	7:9	85	7:52	75		
4:1-22	36, 123	7:9-10	85	7:53	17, 58, 65, 68-69		
4:5	35	7:10	73, 85	7:54	87		
4:6	190	7:10c	84-85	7:54-60	29, 32		
4:19	124	7:11	75	7:54—8:4	86		
4:23	36	7:12	86	7:55	60, 74, 75, 86		
4:34-35	26	7:13	85, 88	7:55-56	*59-61*		
4:36	24, 94	7:15	85	7:56	59, 60		
4:36-37	26, 105	7:15-16	85	7:58b	29		
4:37	27	7:16	85, *99*	7:59	59, 60		
5:1-10	26	7:17	85, 88	7:60	59		
5:12-13	57	7:17-43	75	8:1	24, 93, 191		
5:17f.	31	7:18	88	8:1b	7, 9, 17, 20, 21, 43		
5:17-40	123	7:19	85, 86, 88	8:1-3	104, 113		
5:17-41	36	7:20-21	86	8:1-4	*32-40*		
5:19-20	69	7:24	86	8:4-5	39		
5:34ff.	57	7:25	85	8:5-40	20		
5:34-39	35	7:26	85, 88	8:14	28		
5:34-40	78	7:29	85, 86, 88	8:26	69		
5:38b-39	124	7:30	69, 85	8:26-40	28		
6:1	16, 19, *22-24*, 46	7:31	85, 86	8:30	42		
6:1-4	94	7:31-33	85	8:40	94		
6:1-7	*24-28*, 86, 94	7:32	85, 88, 96	8-9	38		
6:1-7:2a	94	7:33	97	9:1-2	33, 35, 191		
6:3	74, 75, 85	7:34	85, 86, 88	9:3-22	38		
6:2	20, 49	7:34-35	85	9:23-25	104		
6:5	49, 74, 75, 94, 197	7:35	69, 84, 85, 100	9:27	105		
6:7	49, 78, 88	7:35-41	85	9:28-30	30		
6:8-11	20	7:36	85, 86	9:29	23, 24, 47-48		
6:8-12	32	7:37	84, 85, 87, 96,	9:30	39		
6:8—7:2a	86		98, 100	9:31	103		
6:8—7:60	*41-101*	7:38	68, 69, 85, 86	9:42	88		
6:9	27, 28, *46-47*	7:38-39	69	10	38, *122-25*		
6:10	74	7:39	86, 87, 88	10:3-7	69, 122		
6:11	*55-56*, 59, 64-67	7:39-43	*79-80*, 84, 100	10:4	88		
6:11-14	*53-67*, 68, 183	7:40	73, 85, 86	10:10	88		
6:12	*29-31*, 33, 34-35,	7:41	62, 85	10:10-16	122		
	56, 59	7:42	78, 85	10:11-16	125		
6:12b-15	56	7:42-43	76, 85, 86	10:15	57		
6:12f.	31	7:43	62, 73	10:22	69		
6:12—7:1	32	7:44	62, 72, 85	10:25-26	57		
6:13	56, *57-58*,	7:45	85	10:28	125		
	59, *68-69*, 85, 97	7:45b-47	7	10:34-35	125		

Index of Ancient Texts 227

Acts (cont.)
10:44-46	122
10:45-47	138
11	111-113, *122-25*
11:1-18	28
11:3	125
11:5-10	125
11:13	69
11:17	124
11:18	*122-23*
11:19	39
11:20	105
11:19-20	24, 39, *105, 137-38*
11:19-21	38, 46, *93-94*
11:19-30	93
11:22	105
11:22-26	28, 105
11:25-26	38
11:27-30	180
11:30	*111-13*
12:1-3	80
12:1-11	36
12:2	43, 58
12:3-5	123
12:7-11	69
12:17	123
12:23	69, 88
12:24	88
12:25	111
12:25 – 15:35	93
13:1	94, 105
13:22	87
13:39	57
13:45	65
15	104, 106, *107-15*, 123, 132, *143-46*, 162
15:1	114, 117, 136, 147, 155
15:1-2	111, 112, 116, 163
15:2	105, 109, 140
15:4-18	143
15:6	109
15:10	57
15:12	109
15:16-18	143
15:19-35	143
15:20/29	*108-109*, 112, 113, 116, 121, 131, *143-46*, 164
15:22	109
15:22-29	28
15:24	114, 128
15:28	108, 112, 144
15:29/20	*108-109*, 112, 113, 116, 121, 131, *143-46*, 164
15:29-31	104
15:36-41	116
16	63
16:3	182
16:4	63
16:11	88
16:19f.	31
16:27	88
16:29	88
16:34	125
17:5	37
17:5f.	31
17:24	77
18:6	65
18:12f.	31
18:13	58
18:22-23	150-51
18:24	159
19:1	159
19:17	88
19:24f.	31
20:15	88
20:16	180
21	*179-183*
21:8	94
21:18	88, 123
21:18f.	31
21:19-20	179
21:20	57, 115
21:21	58, 115, 182, 183
21:22-26	179
21:23-25	182
21:24	58
21:25	109
21:27	24, 48, 179, 181
21:27-28	47
21:27-32	30
21:28	58, 59, 61, 63, 77, 98, 183
22:1	87
22:3	58, 113
22:4	63
22:5	33
22:12	5y
22:17	58
22:20	87
22:22	87
22:30 – 23:10	31
23:2	191
23:5	58
23:6	58
23:6-10	35
23:9	58, 69
23:10	31
23:11	88
24:1	191
24:11	180
24:11-13	53
24:14-16	58
24:17	180
25:7-8	53
25:8	58
26:4	113
26:10	33
26:11	65
26:19	124
27:1	63
27:23-24	69
27:33	88
28:4	75
28:28	78, 81

Romans
1:7	175
1:16	133
1:23	63
1:24-28	146
2:17-24	69
2:22	76
7:7-11	55
7:13-17	55
7:19-20	55
9-11	175, 196
10:4	63
11:25	177
11:25-27	78
11:30-32	175
12:13	175
14	108, 110, 112, 182, 183
14:1ff.	108
14:1-2	135
14:1 – 15:2	108
14:5	164
14:14	164
14:20	164
15:16	177
15:17-19	177
15:20	126, 151
15:25	175
15:25-27	*174*
15:25-28	151
15:25-32	175
15:26	175, 177
15:27	174
15:28-29	178
15:30-31	*175-78*
15:31	133, 151, 175, 177
15:32	176

1 Corinthians
1:2	175
1:11-16	159
1:12	123, 159
1:12-13	133
1:18 – 2:5	170
1:22-25	172
1:23	195

1 Corinthians (*cont.*)

Reference	Pages
1:24	172
2:1-5	169
2:3-4	172
3:4-6	159
3:18-23	169, 170
3:22	133, 151, 159
4:6	159
4:8-13	169, 170
4:17	158
6:1-2	175
7:17-24	183
7:18-19	162
7:19	108, 164
8	108, 110, 112, 135, 164, 182
8:1ff.	108
8:8	108, 112
9:1	158, 172
9:1-18	158
9:5	38, 123, 133, 151
9:6	150
9:19-21	182
9:20	*182*
9:20-23	164
9:21	*194*
10	108, 112
10:14-33	110
10:19-33	164, 182
10:26-28	110
10:27	140-41, 164
10:28-30	108
11:21	121, 140
12:31b	173
14:18	167
14:33	175
15	143
15:7	133, 151
15:7-9	158
15:8-9	158
15:9	133, 151
15:11	133
15:51	63
15:52	63
15:56	55
16:1	175
16:1-4	151, 174, 175
16:10-11	158
16:12	159

2 Corinthians

Reference	Pages
1:1	175
1:17	172
1:21-22	172
2:14—7:4	158, 173
3:1	8, *170-71*
3:2-3	171
3:4-6	172
3:7	55
3:7—4:6	172
4:5	161
4:7	172
4:16	172
4:18	172
5:1-15	172
5:16	*171-73*
5:16-17	172
6:2	177
6:3-10	169, 170
6:9-10	173
8-9	151, 174, 175
8:1-15	26
8:4	175
8:12	177
9:12	175
9:14	175
10-13	*158-70*
10:10	169, 170
11:3	166
11:3-4	161
11:4	160, 161, 166, 168-69
11:5	160, 161, *165-70*
11:6	162, 168-69
11:7	168
11:7-11	170
11:12-13	168
11:12-15	159, 166
11:13	160, 166, 168
11:13-15	155, 170
11:14-15	166
11:19	170
11:20	161
11:21b	162
11:21b-23	170
11:22	16, *47*, *165*, 168
11:22-23	162
11:22-29	158
11:23	167, 170
11:23-33	170
11:24	33
11:24-25	167
11:26	167
11:32-33	104
12:1	168
12:1-6	162
12:7-10	170
12:11	160, 162, *165-70*, 171
12:11b-12	169
12:12	158, 162, 166, 168
13:13	175

Galatians

Reference	Pages
1:6	160, 161
1:7	154
1:8-9	133, 155
1:9	154
1:11-17	172
1:11—2:14	162
1:12	158
1:12—2:14	153
1:18—2:14	168
1:19	104, 123
1:20	109, 153
1:22	29, 35, 104, 113
1:23	109
2	104, 132, 144
2:1	103, 105, 106, 109
2:1-10	8, 106, *107-15*, 123, 132, 145-46
2:2	114, 132, 133, 150, 163, 174
2:3	142
2:3-5	114
2:4	115, 117, 147, 155, 160, 166, 167, 176
2:4-5	155, 163
2:4-6	176
2:6	115, 160, 166
2:7	195-96
2:7-8	*124*
2:7-9	133
2:7-10	174
2:9	114, 133, 151, 160
2:10	26, 27, 176
2:11	108, 116, 154
2:11-12	147
2:11-14	109, *126-42*, *152-54*
2:12	116, 128, 136, *141*
2:12-13	105
2:13	105, 110, 131, 194
2:13f.	132
2:14	*110, 127, 132*, 135, 136
2:14-15	135, 136
2:15-21	142, 153
2:21	195
3:1	154
3:2-5	138
3:10	55
3:17	55
3:19	55, 69
3:20	55
3:24-26	55
4:1-5	55
4:20	63
5:2-3	143, 162
5:4	133
5:6	108
5:7	154
5:11	155, 162
5:11-12	143

Index of Ancient Texts 229

Galatians (cont.)	
5:12	133
6:12	129, 143, 154, 155, 162
6:13	155
6:15	108

Philippians

1:1	175
1:3-11	*157-58*
1:7	157
1:11	157
1:12ff.	157
1:21	157
1:22	157
1:27	157
1:27ff.	157
2:2	157
2:3	157
2:5	157
2:6	157
2:6-7	157
2:7-8	157
3:2	37, 133, 156, 156, 157
3:2-9	156
3:2-21	155
3:2 – 4:1	*156*
3:4	156-57
3:4-11	157
3:5	16, *47*, 165
3:7	157
3:8	156, 157
3:10	157
3:10-16	156
3:15	157
3:17-21	156
3:18	157
3:19	157
3:20	157
3:21	157
4:2	157
4:10	157
4:12	157
4:14	157
4:17	157
4:18	177-78
4:22	175

1 Thessalonians

2:13-14	133
2:14-16	*36-37*
3:13	175

2 Thessalonians

1:10	175

2 Timothy

3:4	75

Philemon

5	175
7	175

Hebrews

1:12	63
2:2	69
11	100
11:39-40	75

James

1:25	184
2:12	184
2:14-26	
5:16	185

1 Peter

2:5	177

2 Peter

2:11	64

GREEK AND LATIN REFERENCES

Diodorus Siculus
Bibliotheca Historica

63.1	118, 119

Philostratus
Life of Apollonius of Tyana

5.33	119

Tacitus
Historiae

5	119, 189

Thucydides
History of the Peloponnesian War

1.22.1	51

OTHER EARLY JEWISH SOURCES

Letter of Aristeas

181	120

4 Esdras

3:4-36	100
4:29-31	100

Esther (apocryphal book of)

14:17	119-20

Joseph and Asenath

7:1	119-20

Josephus
Antiquities

3.86f.	100
4.43-45	100
4.287	26
6.126	187
7.45-47	138
13.294	187
14.213	63
14.216	63
14.223	63
15.127ff.	52
15.268	63
18.116-19	188
20.38-48	136
20.197	188
20.197-203	69, *185-91*
20.200-203	30, 43, 181
20.205	189
20.206	191
20.213	188
20.213-14	191

Jewish War

1.373ff.	52
2.418	189
2.441	189
2.568-71	26
2.652-53	189
5.379-419	100
6.124-26	30

Jubilees

7:20	137
22:16b	120

Judith

5:6-18	100
10:5	120
12:2	120
12:17-19	120

1 Maccabees

1:49	64
2:52-60	100

3 Maccabees

2:2-20	100

Qumran CD

2.14 – 6.11	100

Tobit

1:11	119-20

OTHER EARLY
CHRISTIAN SOURCES

Epistle of Barnabas   49-50,
                       92, 139

Chrysostom
Homilies 14 and 21
on Acts   23
Homily 2 on Galatians   129

Pseudo-Clementines   8

Eusebius
The Ecclesiastical History
2.23.19-25   185-86

5.1.26   144

Irenaeus
Contr. Haer.
III, 12, 10   41
IV, 15, 1   41

*Second Apocalypse
of James*   185

Justin Martyr
Dial. cum Tryph.
34.8   144

Minucius Felix
The Octavius of Minucius Felix
36.6   144

Origen
Letter to Africanus   30
Contra Celsum
1.47   186
2.13   186

Tertullian
Apologia
9.13   144

Index of Modern Authors

Achtemeier, P. J., 143, 173, 180
Albright, W. F., 44
Alon, G., 125
Aquinas, St. Thomas, 129
Arichea, D. C., Jr., 76
Aune, D. E., 1

Bacon, B. W., 79, 92
Barnard, L. W., 92
Barr, J., 2
Barrett, C. K., 16, 59, 70, 91, 159, 160-61, 163-64, 165, 166, 167, 170, 171, 175, 177
Bauer, W., 110, 175, 177
Baumgarten, A. I., 190
Baumgarten, M., 10, 17
Baur, F. C., 5-9, 19, 29, 36, 37, 53, 56, 71, 107, 108, 113, 115, 170-71, 173-74, 181-83
Beare, F. W., 37
Beker, J. C., 13-14
Betz, H. D., 19-20, 107, 119, 123, 128, 137, 142, 153, 154
Bickerman, E. J., 1
Bihler, J., 22, 70, 76, 81-82, 89
Bligh, J., 116, 117, 128, 152-53
Bonnard, P., 126
Bornkamm, G., 14
Brawley, R. L., 58, 75, 78
Bring, R., 126, 128, 129, 152
Brodie, T. L., 53, 65-66
Bruce, F. F., 12-13, 14, 30, 31, 51, 70, 78, 79, 107, 108, 130, 153, 154
Brunner, E., 175
Bultmann, R., 13, 56, 93, 173
Burton, E. D. W., 110, 137, 141-42, 153

Cadbury, H. J., 22-23, 51-52, 54, 60, 62, 71, 99

Coggins, R. J., 95
Cohen, S. J. D., 1
Collins, R. F., 37
Conzelmann, H., 14, 70-71
Cranfield, C. E. B., 175, 178
Cullmann, O., 22, 91, 92, 93

Daube, D., 25-26
Davies, W. D., 1, 2
Dehandschutter, B., 80
Dibelius, M., 41, 51-52, 53, 54, 68, 83, 122-23, 184, 185
Doble, P., 59
Dodd, C. H., 175
Droyson, J. G., 1
Dudley, M. B., 51
Duncan, G. S., 109, 128, 129, 140, 153
Dunn, J. D. G., 23, 33, 34, 114, 127, 130, 133-38, 193
Dupont, J., 14, 50, 51, 55, 79, 92, 93, 107, 116

Esler, P. F., 105, 118-22, 125, 131, 132

Ferguson, E., 23
Ferguson, J., 1
Findlay, J. A., 93
Fitzmyer, J. A., 93
Flew, A. G. N., 196
Foakes Jackson, F. J., 30, 39, 42, 53, 54, 100
Furnish, V., 158

Gager, J. G., 118
Gasque, W. W., 8, 9, 10, 51, 112
Gaston, L., 75
Georgi, D., 1-2, 162, 165
Gerok, K., 10
Glasson, T. F., 46

Goodman, M., 27, 35, 130, 188-91
Grabbe, L. L., 1
Greeven, H., 184, 185 (Dibelius)
Gundry, R. A., 37

Haenchen, E., 5, 14-15, 19, 21, 22, 26, 27, 28, 29, 30-31, 41, 43, 50, 53, 55, 60, 68, 71, 74-75, 84, 89, 91, 92, 93, 94, 100-101, 104, 121, 122, 123, 125, 143, 144, 179-80, 183
Hahn, F., 70
Hanson, J. S., 130
Hanson, P. D., 1
Harnack, A. von, 55, 69, 93
Headlam, A. C., 175
Hemer, C. J., 111, 112
Hengel, M., 1, 2, 5, 15, 17, 19, 20, 22, 24, 28, 29, 30-31, 33, 34, 35, 41, 54, 55, 56, 62, 63, 93, 95, 103, 113, 130, 137
Hill, C. C., 51
Holmberg, B., 113, 114, 124, 152
Holtz, T., 100
Holtzmann, H. J., 11
Horsley, R. A., 130
Hyldahl, N., 130

Jacquier, E., 13, 27
Jeremias, J., 93, 94
Jervell, J., 37, 139, 146
Jewett, R., 111, 127, 130, 141, 151, 153, 155, 156-58
Johnson, L. T., 13
Jones, M., 45, 92

Käsemann, E., 166, 169-70
Kilgallen, J., 53, 88-89
Kilpatrick, G. D., 59
Klijn, A. F. J., 92
Knox, J., 113
Knox, W. L., 43, 49-50, 57, 60, 69
Koester, H., 13, 54-55, 156
Kraabel, A. T., 1
Kraft, R. A., 1
Krodel, G., 14, 70
Kümmel, W. G., 8, 19, 108, 143

Lake, K., 22, 53, 54, 60, 71, 99, 130
Larsson, E., 17
Laws, S., 184
Lechler, G. V., 10
Lienhard, J. T., 89
Lietzmann, H., 171
Lightfoot, J. B., 8, 153
Lim, T. H., 172
Loisy, A., 13, 53, 70, 109, 111, 114, 115, 117, 122, 123, 126, 154, 173, 180
Longenecker, R. N., 14
Lüdemann, G., 13, 154, 158-59, 165, 185

Luther, M., 142

Macdonald, J., 97
Maddox, R., 41, 46, 70, 75
Mann, C. S., 44
Mare, W. H., 95
Marshall, I. H., 14, 16, 19, 26, 28, 30, 31, 37, 47, 108, 111, 196
Mattill, A. J. and M. B., 5, 50, 51, 112
McCaughey, J. D., 25
McEleney, N. J., 1
Meeks, W. A., 14
Metzger, B., 54, 70
Meyer, E., 11, 70, 74
Meyers, E. M., 1
Miller, F., 186
Moessner, D. P., 80
Moule, C. F. D., 23, 76
Munck, J., 44, 50, 68, 154, 155, 186
Mundle, W., 11

Neander, A., 6
Neill, S., 112
Nestle, E., 59
Neudorfer, H.-W., 5, 41, 42
Neusner, J., 35
Nickelsburg, G. W. E., 1

O'Neill, J. C., 43
Overbeck, F., 10
Owen, H. P., 59

Pahncke, K. H., 11
Porton, G. G., 1
Pummer, R., 96
Purvis, J. D., 95

Räisänen, H., 21, 57, 58, 60, 61, 64, 65, 76, 77, 78, 89, 94, 95, 105
Ramsay, W. M., 112
Reicke, B., 12, 187
Rhoads, D. M., 130
Richard, E., 5, 25, 28, 31, 47, 48, 53, 59, 61, 62, 64, 70, 71, 73, 74, 75, 79, 83-88, 89, 95, 96, 97, 98, 100
Richardson, P., 129, 156
Ridderbos, H. N., 117
Robinson, J. M., 13
Ropes, J. H., 184, 185, 186
Rowland, C., 12

Sabbe, M., 59, 60
Safrai, S., 2, 180
Sanday, W., 175
Sanders, E. P., 15, 33, 35, 63, 69, 119, 125, 135, 139, 156-57, 159
Sanders, J. T., 75

Scharlemann, M. H., 5, 41, 42, 44, 46, 47, 57, 62, 92, 93, 95, 97, 99
Schlatter, A., 115
Schlier, H., 110, 155
Schmidt, W. G., 11, 34, 41, 194
Schmithals, W., 55, 57, 64, 67, 68
Schneider, G., 5, 14, 112, 194
Schürer, E., 186
Schweizer, E., 51, 52, 59
Scobie, C. H. H., 43, 44-45, 80, 95-99
Scott, J. J., Jr., 13, 45, 61
Scroggs, R., 20, 44, 95, 96
Seccombe, D., 27
Simon, M., 42, 45, 53, 61, 68, 69-70, 71, 72, 79, 90
Smith, M., 1, 2, 27, 35, 130, 190
Soltau, W., 11, 92
Sparks, H. F. D., 120
Spiro, A., 44, 95, 96, 97
Stanton, G., 42
Stern, M., 2, 118-119, 180
Sylva, D. D., 70, 74, 75

Tannehill, R. C., 50, 75
Tiede, D. L., 75
Torrey, C. C., 92

Trocmé, E., 31, 47

Vermes, G., 186
Vielhauer, P., 89

Watson, F., 131, 132, 174
Weiser, Alfons, 143
Weiser, Artur, 72
Weiss, J., 30, 38, 76, 93
Weizäcker, K. H. von, 143
Wellhausen, J., 11, 70
Wendt, H. H., 93
Wette, W. M. L. de, 38, 70
Wilckens, U., 51, 175
Wilcox, M., 51, 82, 83, 88, 92, 98
Wild, R. A., 35
Wilken, R. L., 14
Williams, C. S. C., 14
Wilson, J. H., 70
Wilson, S. G., 57-58, 63, 75, 77
Wolff, L., 9, 10, 17, 30
Wright, N. T., 112

Zeitlin, S., 130
Zeller, E., 10, 34, 57, 113
Ziesler, J. A., 35

Index of Subjects

Acts of the Apostles (*see* Luke-Acts)
Alexandrian source, 82, 92-93
Antioch, the church of:
    diversity within, 104, 135, 141, 146-47
    founded by Hellenists?, 44, 45, 46 n. 27, 93, 94, 105-106, 137-38
    relationship to Paul, 104, 110, 114, 116-17, 126-27, 133, 139-42, 140-41, 143, 147, 150-51, 152-53
    in tension with Jerusalem church?, 4, 7-8, 34 n. 57, 103-104, 147
    (*see also* Conservatism/liberalism, Antioch Incident)
Antioch Incident,
    cause of, 109-11, 116-17, 126, 127-42, 152
    chronology, 111-14, 115-17
    historical reconstruction, 106-107, 126-42
    significance of, 4 n. 8, 34 n. 57, 104, 126-27, 142-43, 146-47, 150-51, 152-53
Antiochene source, 54 n. 7, 55-56, 66 n. 131, 75 n. 175, 76-77, 82, 89 n. 269, 91, 92, 93-95
Apostolic decree (Acts 15:20/29):
    Jerusalem its source, 121-22, 144-45
    Paul not a party to, 107-109, 111, 112-13, 164, 182 n. 96
    reason for, 111-14, 121-22, 126, 131, 143-46
Aramaic source, 92-93

Baur, F. C. (*see also* Baur, F. C., in Index of Modern Authors):
    critics of, 8-11, 16-17
    prevalence of Baur's views, 8-16, 20
    views on the subject of:
        Acts 6:1-8:4, 5-9, 19-20, 29 n. 38, 53, 56 n. 72, 71 n. 149

        the collection for the saints, 173-74
        the journeys of Paul in Acts, 107 n. 13
        the commendatory letters of 2 Cor. 3:1, 170-71
        Paul's arrest in Jerusalem, 181-83
        the persecution of the apostles, 36 n. 65
Barnabas, 19-20 n. 4, 24 n. 19, 94, 105-106, 109, 110, 114, 116, 117, 124 n. 85, 126, 128, 129, 132, 133, 140, 141, 145, 152, 154, 194 n. 3

Chronology, 107, 111, 112, 115-17, 125, 130 n. 108, 141 n. 151, 150-51 n. 6
Collection for the saints, 116 n. 46, 133 n. 118, 151, 166, 173-78, 179-80, 184, 192
Conservatism/liberalism of Hebrews/ Hellenists, 3, 6, 7, 8 n. 19, 12, 13-14, 15 n. 68, 20, 23-24, 43 ("radical"; *see also* 49, 68, 72, 74), 126, 145-46, 155, 183-84, 187, 193-96
Corinthians:
    Paul's opponents, 158-73
        Jerusalem sponsored?, 165-73
        knowledge of Christ "according to the flesh," 171-73
        letters of recommendation, 170-71
        nature of controversy, 159-63, 168-70, 171-73
        relationship to Galatian Judaizers, 158-62, 167
        super-apostles, 160, 162, 165-70
Cornelius, Conversion of, 122-25

Daily distribution (Acts 6:1):
    in conflict with synagogue distribution?, 27

Index of Subjects 235

Daily distribution *(cont.)*
    historicity, 20, 24-28, 47-48, 65 *n. 124,* '86, 89, 94
    masks true conflict?, 6, 13, 19-20
    (see also The Seven)
Diversity:
    of first-century Judaism, 1-3
    of first-century Jewish-Christianity, 2-4
    of the church of Antioch, 104, 135-36, 141, 146-47
    of the church of Jerusalem, 106 *n. 12,* 114-16, 146-47, 163, 176, 179

Essene source, 80-81, 82, 91, 92-93

Galatians:
    Paul's opponents, 152-55
        Jerusalem sponsored? 153-55
        relationship to Corinthian opponents, 158-62, 167
        Use of Antioch Incident, 152-53

Hebrews:
    identification, 3 *n. 7,* 16, 19-24, 47-48, 165
    portrayed as an ideological faction, 3, 5-16, 19-21, 23 *n. 17,* etc.
    (see also Conservatism/liberalism of Hebrews/Hellenists)
Hegesippus, credibility of, 185-86
Hellenists:
    identification, 3 *n. 7,* 16, 19-24, 47-48, 105-106
    portrayed as an ideological faction, 3, 5-16, 19-21, 23 *n. 17,* etc.
    (see also Conservatism/liberalism of Hebrews/Hellenists)
High priest(s), 29, 33, 34-35, 36, 40, 59, 69 *n. 145,* 77 *n. 191,* 78 *n. 193,* 134, 185-91
    (see also Pharisees, Sanhedrin)
Historicity:
    and the problem of circular reasoning, 43, 93, 183
    relationship of author's literary/redactional activity to, 19 *n. 3,* 35 *n. 62,* 36 *n. 65,* 38-39, 44, 50 *n. 39,* 77-78, 80-81, 83-89, 122-24, 132 *n. 114,* 143-44, 179-83
    relationship of literary modelling to, 25-26, 27-28 *n. 32,* 58-67
    relationship of sources to, 25-26, 44 *n. 17,* 46, 50-53, 55, 61, 65, 67-68, 80, 89-91, 144, 183
Historiography and Stephen speech, 51-52, 67
History of the question, 5-17

James, the brother of Jesus:
    and the Antioch Incident, 105 *n. 7,* 109, 110, 113, 121 *n. 73,* 126, 128-33, 135-37, 141, 154, 160
    and the Apostolic Decree, 143-46
    and the collection/arrest of Paul (Acts 21), 176, 179-81
    and the Jerusalem Conference, 140, 146-47
    portrayed as a conservative, 3, 4, 6, 8 *n. 19,* 13, 15 *n. 68,* 16 *n. 73,* 121 *n. 73,* 132 *n. 112,* 143 *n. 157,* 144, 145-46, 167, 171, 187
    "conservatism" challenged, 121 *n. 74,* 140, 145, 146-47, 151, 154, 183-84, 190-91, 196
    martyrdom, 36, 43 *n. 11,* 69 *n. 145,* 80, 151, 184-91
James, the brother of John, 36, 43 *n. 11,* 58, 80, 191
James, the Epistle of, 184 *n. 101*
Jerusalem, the church of:
    authority/centrality of, 27, 28, 114, 124-25, 132, 144-45, 147, 150-51, 154-55, 167, 196-97
    diversity within, 106 *n. 12,* 114-16, 146-47, 163, 176, 179
    relationship to Paul, 5-6, 8-9, 16 *n. 73,* 28, 103-104, 107-110, 112, 114-15, 117, 131, 133, 139-42, 150-73, 173-8, 179-83, 191-92
    in tension with Antioch church?, 4, 7-8, 34 *n. 57,* 103-104, 147
    (see also Conservatism/liberalism, Antioch Incident, Apostolic Decree)
Jerusalem Conference/Council:
    chronology, 111-14, 115-17
    historical reconstruction, 106-15, 140
    reason for, 114, 116, 137, 140
    significance of, 4 *n. 8,* 34 *n. 57,* 104, 146-47, 150-51
Jerusalem Decree *(see* Apostolic Decree)
Jews and Judaism *(see* Luke-Acts: Jews and Judaism in)
Josephus, credibility of, 186 *(see also* Index of Ancient Texts)

Law *(see* Luke-Acts: Jews and Judaism in; Stephen: a critic of the law?)
Liberalism *(see* Conservatism/liberalism of Hebrews/Hellenists)
Lord's Supper, 121, 195
Luke-Acts:
    Jews and Judaism in, 19 *n. 3,* 38-39, 54, 57-58, 60, 63, 65, 68-69, 74-79, 80-81, 98
    provenance, 19 *n. 3*
    literary/thematic unity of, 83-89
    (see also Historicity; Sources)
    use of the Old Testament, 25-26, 60, 64, 65-67, 70-74, 79-80, 84-88
    (see also Index of Ancient Texts)

Moses and Moses christology, 25-26, 54, 68, 75-76, 78, 80-81, 87, 98

Naboth story (1 Kings 21:1 - 16), 65-67 (*see also* Historicity: relationship of literary modelling to)
Neutral source, 77 *n. 191,* 83, 91, 99-101

Old Testament (*see* Luke-Acts: use of the Old Testament; and Index of Ancient Texts)

Passion of Jesus:
　borrowing from Stephen account?, 60-61
　compared with Stephen's martyrdom, 69, 80, 190-91
　model for Stephen account, 41, 54, 59-66, 68 *n. 135,* 76, 77 *n. 191,* 78 *n. 194,* 183 *n. 99*
Paul:
　arrest in Jerusalem, 179-83
　and the church of Antioch, 104, 110, 114, 116-17, 126-27, 133, 139-42, 140-41, 143, 147, 150-51, 152-53
　and the church of Jerusalem, 5-6, 8-9, 16 *n. 73,* 28, 103-104, 107-110, 112, 114-15, 117, 131, 133, 139-42, 150-73, 173-8, 179-83, 191-92
　a resident of Jerusalem?, 29, 35 *n. 62,* 39, 50 *n. 40*
　opponents, 150-73 (*see above* Paul: and the church of Jerusalem)
　(*see also* Corinthians; Galatians; Philippians; Collection; Antioch Incident; Apostolic Decree)
Persecution:
　also of Hebrews, 24, 36-37, 40, 43 *n. 11,* 69 *n. 145,* 80, 151, 184-92
　selective persecution of Hellenists? 7, 9-17, 19-40, 43, 48-49, 104, 190-91
Peter:
　and the Incident at Antioch, 106, 108-10, 117, 126-27, 128-30, 133, 135, 136-37, 141-42, 143 *n. 157,* 144, 151, 160, 163
　movements of, 15 *n. 68,* 123-24 *n. 85*
　the object of persecution, 36, 123-24 *n. 85,* 190
　portrayed as a conservative, 6, 13, 121 *nn. 73-74,* 132 *nn.* 112 115, 135, 152-53, 154, 163, 171
　not portrayed as a conservative, 123, 140
Pharisees, 23 *n. 13,* 31, 34-35, 57 *n. 73,* 58 *n. 80,* 78 *n. 193,* 81, 134-35, 187, 190
　(*see also* High priest(s), Sanhedrin)
Philippians:
　Paul's opponents, 155-58
　epistolary thanksgiving, 157-58
　the integrity of Philippians, 155-58
　the collection for the saints, 177-78
Purity, 109, 125 *n. 87,* 119-21, 133-37, 164

Qumran (*see* Essene source)

Samaritan source, 44-45, 50 *n. 40,* 62 *n. 98,* 80 *n. 201,* 83, 91-92, 95-99
Sanhedrin, 6, 23, 29-30, 31, 33 *n. 56,* 34-35, 56 *n. 70,* 59, 124, 186-88, 190
　(*see also* High priest(s), Pharisees)
The Seven:
　duties, 12-13, 20, 24-28
　historicity, 20, 24-28, 47-48, 65 *n. 124,* 86, 89, 94
　identity, 20, 46-48, 105
　relationship of account to OT models, 25-26
　(*see also* Daily distribution)
Sources:
　problems associated with, 50-52, 58, 66-67, 68, 76-77, 80-81, 82-83, 84, 88, 89-92, 120, 185
　relationship to historicity, 25-26, 44 *n. 17,* 46, 50-53, 55, 61, 65, 67-68, 80, 89-91, 144, 183
　(*see also* Stephen: source(s) of account; Historicity:)
Stephen:
　accusations as the locus of tradition, 53-67
　a critic of the law?, 6-7, 10-17, 20-21, 23, 34, 37 *n. 71,* 45, 46 *n. 27,* 55, 56-58, 61, 62-65, 67-70, 75, 76, 77, 79-81, 91, 101, 103-104, 139
　a critic of the temple?, 6-7, 9-17, 20-21, 23, 34, 37 *n. 71,* 44 *n. 17,* 46 *nn. 26-27,* 55, 56-58, 59, 61-62, 64, 68, 69-81, 92-93, 95, 96-98, 101, 103, 106, 139, 183 *n. 99*
　(*see also* Temple)
　identity, 43-50
　identification of opponents, 28-31
　relationship between accusations and speech, 53-56, 67-69
　a representative Hellenist?, 49-50
　Son of man saying (7:56), 59, 60
　source(s) of account:
　　Alexandrian, 82, 92-93
　　Antiochene, 54 *n. 7,* 55-56, 66 *n. 131,* 75 *n. 175,* 76-77, 82, 89 *n. 269,* 91, 92, 93-95
　　Aramaic, 92-93
　　Essene, 80-81, 82, 91, 92-93
　　Neutral, 77 *n. 191,* 83, 91, 99-101
　　Samaritan, 44-45, 50 *n. 40,* 62 *n. 98,* 80 *n. 201,* 83, 91-92, 95-99
　　(*see also* Sources:)

Stephen (*cont.*)
  speech (Acts 7):
    and ancient historiography, 51-52, 67
    literary-critical analysis of, 50 *n. 39*, 82-90
    redaction-critical analysis of, 38-39, 57-58, 63-65, 68-69, 74-79, 80-81, 89-90, 98
    as the locus of tradition, 67-81
    (*see also* Luke-Acts: Jews and Judaism in; Sources; Historicity)
  trial, 29-31, 32, 34-35, 54, 59, 61 *n. 94*, 68 *n. 135*, 77 *n. 191-92*
    (*see also* High priest(s), Sanhedrin)

Table-fellowship, mixed, 109-11, 117-22, 123, 125 *n. 87*, 126-27, 131, 133-42, 143-44

Temple (miscellaneous references to), 19 *n. 3*, 30 *n. 43*, 62, 69 *n. 145*, 76 *n. 182*, 85 *n. 233*, 134, 179, 180 *n. 91*, 185, 195
  (*see also* Stephen: a critic of the temple?)